Giants:

Sons of the Gods

Giants:

Sons of the Gods

Douglas Van Dorn

Waters of Creation Publishing
1614 Westin Drive, Erie, Colorado 80516

Unless otherwise noted, references are from the *English Standard Version* (ESV) of the Bible.

Cover Design by Stephen Van Dorn

ISBN-13:978-0615815374

Acknowledgements

No book worth its salt is the product of a single person. Therefore, I want to thank the following people. First and foremost, thank you to my loving and supportive wife Janelle. You are my strength and my joy. You always support me in anything I attempt, be it climbing a crazy mountain or writing on such a strange topic as this. Thank you to Annie, Tim, Janelle, Tony, Marsha, Justin, Jonathan, Monte, Jeff, Rob, Scott and Meg and others who proofread part or all of this book and/or offered ideas and suggestions. It isn't perfect, but it is immensely closer thanks to you. Thanks to my bro Steve for the sweet cover design. I can only dream of having your talents. Thanks to my mom and dad for being the best parents ever. There is no repaying all that you have done for me, especially being so willing to learn from your son. Thank you to my Bible Study guys who were tolerant enough to let me take you through this material (and its predecessor on the fathers of these giants: the Sons of God, a book that will probably never see the light of day). Thanks to the church family who listens patiently. Thanks to my girls—just for being you: Alesha, Breanna, Annika, and Elianna. I love you dearly. One day, you'll read this. I hope you enjoy it! Thanks to Tom who called me out of the blue after hearing Tony and I discuss this topic on the radio show. I have a friend-for-life because of it. I treasure our conversations. And special thanks to Dr. Michael Heiser. Because I "accidently" stumbled onto your article on Deuteronomy 32 in preparation for a sermon on Exodus, my life has never been the same. Thank you for sharing so much of this information with others. I've often told my wife that now, because of you, I know I'm able to actually understand the people of the Old Testament.

Endorsements

"This intriguing book will shed tremendous light on an often neglected but important biblical subject. By examining ancient records and comparing them with the biblical record, Doug Van Dorn has put together one of the most detailed studies on the subject of giants. Even though I have studied and written at length on the subject, I still found a wealth of new data to mull over."

-- Tim Chaffey, MDiv., ThM., apologist, and author of *The Sons of God and the Nephilim*

"What do Buffalo Bill Cody and Katy Perry/Kanye West have in common? They talk and sing about "giants" and "aliens." Maybe they referenced these subjects in ignorance, but now Doug Van Dorn has revealed the light of Biblical Truth on these matters in his book GIANTS: Sons of the Gods. About three years ago my studies caused me to become a Berean on the subject of "sons of god" in Genesis chapter six. I discovered some very helpful works done by extremely capable researchers and scholars, but Doug's work has taken me to another level on what scripture has to say on this matter. In addition, on a practical matter, the Apostle Paul's writing on spiritual warfare as become more than just words. Without a doubt if you've ever wondered if Goliath was only biblical folklore read this book and you will greatly benefit from a scholarly effort and an obvious labor of love from Doug."

-- Tom Graham, NFL Linebacker (1972-78), Denver Broncos (1972-74)

"When I first read this book, I was skeptical. Nearly every theological giant (pun intended) in history has denied the spiritual view of Genesis 6 and the many implications that follow. Augustine, Calvin, and Luther each dismissed it, and nearly every professor and pastor I have ever known has denied this view, or at least minimized it.

What Doug demonstrated in this book, using Scripture and a wealth of research from both Jewish and early Christian sources, is that the spiritual view of Genesis 6 is the only view that is consistent with Scripture and what most interpreters believed for most of history.

As I have slowly assimilated and adopted this world-view, so many Scriptures that I previously considered difficult or even odd are now beginning to make sense. Above all, Doug's book is no mere book of facts about Sons of God and the giants. It is first and foremost about the Unique Son of God who has triumphed over all other gods and has been given a name above every other name, the Lord, Jesus Christ."

-- Tony Jackson, M.Div.

"Do you have the courage to look at Scripture objectively and explore what is actually there with an openness to have truth revealed rather than seeing only what you have always been taught? Doug Van Dorn does. He is deeply committed to the historic Christian faith, and at the same time willing to jettison preconceived notions and let the Scriptures speak for themselves. Read "Giants: Sons of the Gods"-- You will be entertained, fascinated, informed and challenged by Van Dorn's careful and passionate discussion of this largely ignored topic of the Bible. Warning: It could radically change the way you see the world."

-- Monte J. King, Th.M., M.A., author of *The Simple Math Diet*

Table of Contents

Preface xiii

Introduction.. 1

Chapter 1: Pre-Flood Giants 49

Chapter 2: The Giant of Babel..69

Chapter 3: Abram and the Giant Wars 95

Chapter 4: Patriarchal Giants..109

Chapter 5: Moses Meets Amalek 115

Chapter 6: Spying Out the Land 123

Chapter 7: The "Law" of Canaan 129

Chapter 8: On the Way to Canaan..135

Chapter 9: Giant Wars, the Sequel..149

Chapter 10: Goliath and His Brothers 157

Chapter 11: Agag the Amalekite 169

Chapter 12: Demons and the Giants...175

Chapter 13: Chimeras...183

Chapter 14: Jesus vs. the Demons 201

Chapter 15: Victory 213

Appendix: Extra-Biblical Literature...233

Appendix: 2 Peter 2:4 and Jude 6..237

Appendix: The Stories of the Greeks...243

Appendix: Giants in the Americas...251

Appendix: Giants of Monument & Myth 267

Glossary..289

Bibliographies (Written and Images)..293

Endnotes 310

Abbreviations

AD	Anno Domini (Year of our Lord)
BC	Before Christ
BBE	Bible in Basic English
CTA	*Corpus tablettes alphabetiques*
ca.	circa
cf.	consult, compare
DDD	*Dictionary of Deities and Demons in the Bible*
DULAT	*A Dictionary of the Ugaritic Language in the Alphabetic Tradition*
ESV	English Standard Version
etc.	et cetera
JPS	Jewish Publication Society (Old Testament)
KJV	King James Version
KTU	*Keilalphabetische Texte aus Ugarit*
LA	Last Accessed (image references)
LXX	Septuagint
NAS	New American Standard
NIV	New International Version
NLT	New Living Translation
NT	New Testament
OT	Old Testament
RSV	Revised Standard Version
TNK	JPS Tanakh

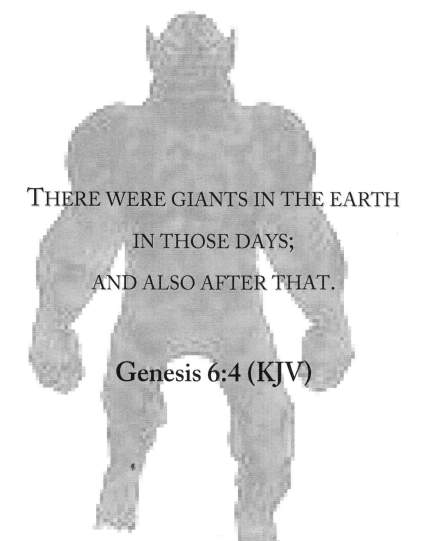

THERE WERE GIANTS IN THE EARTH

IN THOSE DAYS;

AND ALSO AFTER THAT.

Genesis 6:4 (KJV)

Preface

The sons of men, being insensitive to [God, spirits, heavenly armies, Holy Ones, archangels, angels, thrones, and authorities], keep sinning and provoking the anger of the Most High.

Testament of Levi (3:10)

I'll be honest.[1] My initial interest in this topic grew out of a life-long curiosity of our very mysterious human past and a gut-level feeling that people need to begin to understand it better. As a youngster, one of my favorite shows was *In Search Of...*, starring Leonard Nimoy. The show presented conspiracy theories, unorthodox views of history, mysteries of the paranormal, speculations into the origins of ancient stone monuments, and so on. Since the 1970's, these kinds of shows have flourished.

Yet, even though a part of me enjoys the speculation about our past and, to some degree about our future, there is a rational and, frankly, biblical part of me that is very concerned with books that come out on this topic, using this subject especially to promote end-times speculations. Though there is always some truth in these books, these speculations are neither safe nor good. They create anxiety caused by worrying about the future. They can distract the reader from what has taken place in Christ's first coming, and put the focus on what has not yet come to pass, often times on things that even Jesus said he did not know in the flesh, such as the day and hour of his return. They delve into mysteries that no human being could possibly know all the answers to, but they claim a kind of authority that some people take as virtually equal to the Bible itself.

With that in mind, I am writing this book for the following reasons. First, I am convinced that the biblical topic of giants is little understood. Few dare to tread upon the things about them that we can know; and those who do dare are far too quick to jump into things that cannot be known. Because of "guilt by association" with the latter, it would seem that most everyone else stays away from this topic.

This is bizarre and disconcerting, because the subject of giants is quite important to understanding the spiritual battle about which the Bible has so much to say. For example, the basic idea of this battle is outlined by the Apostle in Ephesians, "We do not wrestle against flesh and blood, but against the rulers, against the authorities, against the cosmic powers over this present darkness, against the spiritual forces of evil in the heavenly places" (Eph 6:12). The giants are not these rulers, authorities, powers, and forces *per se*. But, they were (and in their present form are) related to them in ways that you have probably never dreamed was possible. Their influence continues to be felt in our world today.

Second, the topic of giants ranges through much more landscape of biblical history than most people are aware, just as the giants themselves do in the land of Canaan and beyond. If for no other reason, the sheer volume alone makes this an important topic. Therefore, it deserves serious attention.

Third, there is a dearth of serious work out there on the subject of giants in the Bible. I have grown weary of books on this subject which cannot be taken seriously because they are poorly sourced, poorly written and poorly edited, making it difficult to check if what people are saying is true, and harder to accept by people already predisposed to disbelieving it. To give an example of the way this subject is often thought of for these reasons and others, a few years back one of my favorite pastors and authors—a man who received his Ph.D. from Fuller Theological Seminary on the subject of eschatology—took a jab at this whole subject as he aimed his words at the popular book *The Nephilim and the Pyramid of the Apocalypse*[2] in a section of his blog titled, "Just Plain Nutty." He wrote, "So let's see, the Nephilim are the product of human and angelic procreation . . . How would that work? This is theology at the level of the National Enquirer or the Star—but then that explains why it is a best seller."[3] Part of me resonates with this sarcasm, because I have a similar knee-jerk reaction to the same kind of Christian upbringing that this pastor had. This particular book sometimes indulges in bizarre numerology, views Bible codes positively (which is a serious error)[4], and engages in the very speculation I find improper for teachers of the Bible.

But not *everything* in the foresaid book is fit for tabloid magazines, and this goes for other authors who are adding to the corpus of books on giants[5]—books which bring some important contributions to this subject even if they contain some "wacky" things. You can't just click your theological heels three times and make it all just go away. This isn't Oz or Wonderland. Throwing the giant baby out with the nutty eschatological bathwater doesn't help anything.

The giants were real. Their origin, steeped in an almost unimaginable conception, is chilling. Their impact upon our present world continues to be profound ... and dangerous. Pretending that they were not (or are not) here is like ignoring the warning of your neurologist that he found a malignant tumor in your brain. Knowledge of this kind is power. I want to give you well-researched power that you can verify in your own studies.

Finally and candidly, like so many others who write on this subject, I'm writing this because I find it utterly fascinating and fun. Who doesn't like to figure out a deep mystery or unsolved puzzle, especially one as crazy and interesting as this one? I hope you will share my enthusiasm.

Introduction

It is the glory of God to conceal things,
but the glory of kings is to search things out.

Proverbs 25:2 (RSV)

> ### *** A PLEA FROM THE AUTHOR ***
>
> Please read at least the first three pages of this Introduction

Genesis 6:1-4

This is not a book about "slaying the giants in your life." If you want a self-help book, you should probably look elsewhere. This is a book about the slaying of literal historical physical giants: strange beings that line the pages of Scripture like Terracotta warriors lining the tomb of the first Emperor of a unified China: Qin Shi Huang (259 BC – 210 BC).[1]

FIG. I.1 TERRACOTTA ARMY

TERRACOTTA ARMY PIT 1, (XI'AN, CHINA)

The analogy is fitting in a way. Like the Terracotta, the giants were mighty warriors of prehistory. But unlike them, our warriors are huge and preternatural, having their origin in a story so fantastic, conservatives feel the need to reinterpret it to something tamer and less absurd, while liberals say it proves that the whole Bible must be make-believe. This makes for strange bed-fellows indeed.

This story is told succinctly in Genesis 6:1-4, one of the most enigmatic and misinterpreted passages in the Bible. Here is how it reads in the oldest surviving copy—the Bible that Jesus, the Disciples, and the Church Fathers often quoted—the Greek *Septuagint*[2] (LXX),

> [1] And it came to pass when men began to be numerous upon the earth, and daughters were born to them, [2] that the sons of God having seen the daughters of men that they were beautiful, took to

themselves wives of all whom they chose. [3] And the Lord God said, My Spirit shall certainly not remain among these men for ever, because they are flesh, but their days shall be an hundred and twenty years. [4] Now the giants were upon the earth in those days; and after that when the sons of God were wont to go in to the daughters of men, they bore children to them, those were the giants of old, the men of renown.[3]

Beginning in Chapter 1, we will proceed upon the premise that this passage tells of a time in the remote past when heavenly beings entered the abode of humans, and through our women were able to spawn a race of half-breed children, giants that *all cultures* throughout the world remember as powerful and often wicked, ruthless *demigods*.

It is important to establish at the very beginning that this passage tells the *true* story of bizarre and unthinkable proceedings. It is important to say this because the giants' tale does not stop at the Flood. It does not stop with the Old Testament. In fact, to this day, they have a very real, frightening, and powerful impact upon the world, and that is quite apart from the speculation of some writers on this subject that the giants of the past will return in the flesh in the future.

Were these merely tall people, I would simply invite you to an NBA game where we could share a hotdog and a beer together, I could tell you stories about ancient giants, you could roll your eyes at me, we could get a few autographs of the "real" giants after the game, and then go our separate ways. But this is something altogether different. To paraphrase Gandalf the Grey, "Be on your guard. There are older and fouler things than giants in the deep places of the world." The Bible speaks of dark entities, shades who roam aimlessly, demons that haunt deserts and seek to indwell unsuspecting or uninviting hosts. These and other mysteries cannot be separated from the truth about giants.

Moses tells us, "They sacrificed to demons, not God, to gods they had never known, new gods *that had come along recently* whom your fathers never dreaded" (Ex 32:17). What does this mean: they came along recently? From where did these demons originate? Apparently, they were not here in elder days; but they were here when Moses traveled through their long journey towards the Promised Land. How did they get there? Why weren't they there before this? Are they make-believe, figments of the fertile imaginations of the Jews? Such are the fascinating questions that will occupy our minds as we travel through this ancient land of the giants together.

To arrive at our destination, this Introduction will *exegete* how and why I make the assumption about Genesis 6:1-4 that I do. It will bear the burden of demonstrating why this interpretation is not only a reasonable interpretation, but the only exegetically compelling one. This is a strong claim to say that this is the "only exegetically compelling interpretation." Therefore, let me move through this Introduction like a scientist seeking to validate a hypothesis.

If you do not feel the need to have this view proven to you, then feel free to skip the rest of this semi-technical Introduction, though I do believe you will find this Introduction quite fascinating. If you are a skeptic or hold strongly to one of the other interpretations of this passage, I invite you to sit down, grab a warm cup of coffee, perhaps a velvet jacket and pipe if it suits your fancy, and prepare for a little critical thinking and a lot of eye opening, but very old, ideas.

Preliminary Questions

The first thing to do is ask some basic questions of this text. Who are the different groups of people in Genesis 6:1-4 (i.e. "men," "sons of God," "daughters of men," "giants," "giants of old," and "men of renown")? What was going on between these people and what was the outcome of their interaction? What do these four verses add to our understanding of why God destroyed the world with the Flood?

History of Interpretation

The answer to these questions has fallen into two basic categories: the natural and the supernatural. That is, there are two main lines of interpretation proposed for dealing with the characters of this story, its plot, and the outcome of the plot beginning with the Flood, continuing through the conquest of Canaan (the Promised Land), and reaching right into the pages of the New Testament. There are also two major subsets of each view. Over time, each view has seen its fair share of advocates. Take a moment to familiarize yourself with them:

Table 1		
THEORY OF GEN 6:1-4	**ABB.**	**EXPLANATION OF THE THEORY**
Natural Theory 1: Divine Kingship Theory	**(NT1)**	The "sons of God" are dynastic rulers who married multiple women (polygamy) and their offspring were powerful, albeit human tyrants of old.
Supernatural Theory 1: Angelic Procreation Theory	**(ST1)**	Heavenly beings came down from heaven and bred with human women producing hybrid offspring called *nephilim*.
Natural Theory 2: Sethite Antithesis Theory	**(NT2)**	The "sons of God" are the sons of Seth (Adam's replacement son for Abel) and the "daughters of men" are the daughters of Cain. The two groups intermarried, produced gigantic offspring, and consequently God destroyed the world in a flood.
Supernatural Theory 2: Demonic Infestation Theory	**(ST2)**	Heavenly beings came down from heaven and genetically manipulated human DNA to create clones or hybrids through human women.

Supernatural Angelic View

The earliest view (ST1) is the Angelic Procreation Theory. Now, just because it is the oldest view, this does not necessarily make it correct. However, it does make it something to be carefully examined. This was no fringe or heretical Johnny-come-lately to the scene of biblical interpretation. It has never been condemned by any official church council, only ridiculed and mocked. Yet, please understand something. From at least a couple centuries prior to Christ until well after the close of the New Testament (NT) canon and the destruction of the second temple in Jerusalem in 70 AD, this is the only attested Jewish view. Jesus and his disciples would have been quite familiar with it. In the Church, this was the only known view until the middle of the third century, and was virtually the only view for 150 years after that. We will return to this view (our view) momentarily.

Naturalistic Dynastic View of the Rabbis

The first non-supernatural view to gain a foothold was NT1. Please understand something about this view as well. It originated in *Jewish circles*—among *those who deliberately rejected Christ* as the Messiah—long after ST1 had been established as the standard view among Jews. The history of this view goes something like this. Rabbis, beginning with the *Targums* (Aramaic paraphrases of the Hebrew OT, sort of like The Message Bible or The Living Bible), began to stomp out the supernatural interpretation, due in no small measure to the rapid rise of Christianity and their claims of a God-man come down out of heaven in the flesh, something similar—and yet not so similar— to the angelic procreation view of Genesis 6:1-4. As a Christian, I cannot think of a more profoundly disturbing motivation for eliminating a long cherished belief than this.[4]

How did this work itself out in the text? The de-supernaturalization begins with the crucial phrase: "sons of God." Who are these persons? *Targum* Neofiti (1st – 4th cent.AD), Targum Onkelos (2nd cent.) and the Greek Symmachus (late 2nd cent.)—all Jewish works—refer to them as natural beings, ordinary humans: "judges," "mighty ones," and "powerful ones" respectively. By the time the *Mishnah* was written (3rd c. AD), it became a matter of importance to condemn the supernatural view in the strongest possible terms.

Earlier, Trypho (believed by some to be Rabbi Tarfon, ca. 135 AD), who was the opponent of Justin Martyr in Justin's defense of Christianity, called the view—Justin's view—"contrivances" and "blasphemies" (Justin Martyr, *Dialogue* 79). Even worse, Rabbi Simeon ben Yohai (c.a. 130 – 160 AD) was said to have "cursed all who called them the sons of God."[5] Never mind that "sons of God" is the language the Hebrew and LXX use. This Rabbinical condemnation of the original words in favor of theological interpretations that smooth out the unthinkable implications that the sons of God are supernatural beings can easily be seen as a reaction against Christ. Jesus is called The *only begotten* Son of God. This refers to his *heavenly* origin (this is the favorite title demons had for him. "Son of man" was his more earthly, human title). But most Jewish leaders rejected Jesus as the Messiah. If he is a son of God, and there are other heavenly sons of God (though of a very different quality, i.e. they were created by the uncreated Christ; Col 1:16), what implication could this have for this rejection? Sons of God as heavenly beings would be a pillar he could use to support his own claim to deity. Thus, they suppressed the older view.[6]

Naturalistic Sethite View of Christians

In the church, things did not change nearly as fast, but once it did, personal anathematizing of the older view hit the church with the same fury as it did in the Jewish community, though (thankfully) not for the same damnable reasons. From the extant literature, the Church Fathers did not deviate from ST1 until sometime into the third century, and a non-supernatural view did not gain a true foothold until the fifth century. The first inkling that Christians no longer bought into the idea that the sons of God were heavenly beings is put forth by Julius Africanus (160 – 240 AD), an early Christian traveler and historian who deeply influenced Eusebius' *Histories* book some 50 years later. Africanus writes the following comments on Genesis 6:1-4,

> When men multiplied on earth, the angels of heaven came together with the daughters of men. In some copies I found 'sons of God.' What is meant by the Spirit in my opinion, is that the descendants of Seth are called the sons of God on account of the righteous men and patriarchs who have sprung from him, even down to the Saviour Himself; but that the descendants of Cain are named the seed of man, as having nothing divine in them.
>
> (Julius Africanus, *History of the World* [Fragment])[7]

Here, Julius puts forward a novel view with no known precedent in *church* history, a view which some have labeled the Sethite Antithesis theory. This theory came to dominate Christianity after Augustine, and again after some of the Reformers revived his view put forward in the *City of God* (more on that below). Before we get to that, let us take note of the context in which this citation is found. These "copies" of the Scripture that Africanus refers to are probably the Aramaic Jewish texts discussed above, mostly paraphrases of the Bible, but not actual copies of the Bible. Julius was indigenous to eastern Africa and was a well acquainted traveler to Israel, which by this time was a "Christian-free" zone, thanks to the Rabbis. It is significant to note, however, that Julias immediately goes on to say,

But if it is thought that these refer to angels, we must take them to be those who deal with magic and jugglery, who taught the women the motions of the stars and the knowledge of things celestial, by whose power they conceived the giants as their children, by whom wickedness came to its height on the earth, until God decreed that the whole race of the living should perish in their impiety by the deluge.

In other words, Julius is not writing a polemical or dogmatic work, but Christian history. While he comments on his personal agreement with these Jewish *targumim* concerning their interpretation of the sons of God, he recognizes that others understand them to refer to angels. (Perhaps Julius was not aware of the virtual unanimity on the ancient understanding of angels, but that is speculation).

The first known dogmatic Christian adherent to the Sethite View will not come along for over 100 years after this, in one Ephrem the Syrian who wrote around 325 AD. Let that sink in. From the birth of Christ, this is almost seventy-five years longer than the entire history of our own beloved United States of America. He stated,

[Moses] called the sons of Seth "sons of God," those who, like the sons of Seth, had been called "the righteous people of God." The beautiful daughters of men whom they saw were the daughters of Cain who adorned themselves and became a snare to the eyes of the sons of Seth. Then Moses said "they took to wife such of them as they chose," because when "they took" them, they acted very haughtily over those whom they chose. A poor one would exalt himself over the wife of a rich man, and an old man would sin with one who was young. The ugliest of all would act arrogantly over the most beautiful.[8]

After Ephrem, only John Chrysostom (349 – 407 AD) in his *Homily on Genesis* 22:6-8 holds this view in the church until Augustine who writes the *City of God* sometime after 410 AD. This means that virtually no known Christian *until the fifth century* held any other view than the supernatural angelic view.[9]

Again, let that sink in, because it is really a pretty staggering thought, especially in light of the popularity of the Sethite view ever since. This view was perpetuated by the following four "giants" of the faith (whom I personally admire and adore): Chrysostom, Augustine, Martin Luther, and John Calvin. Listen carefully to what they say.

Augustine writes on his denial of the older angelic view saying that because angels are ministering "spirits" (Psalm 104:4), "I could by no means believe that God's holy angels could at that time have so fallen" (Augustine, *City of God 15:23*).[10] *I could by no means believe?* Luther similarly says, "That anything could be born from [the union of a devil and a human being], this I do not believe" and then refers to this as "the silly ideas of the Jews" (Martin Luther, *Genesis 6:2*).[11] *I do not believe?* Calvin is utterly mocking in his tone when he says, "That ancient figment, concerning the intercourse of angels with women, is abundantly refuted by its own absurdity; and it is surprising that learned men should formerly have been fascinated by ravings so gross and prodigious" (John Calvin, *Genesis 6:1*).[12] *That ancient figment?*

To put it in a nutshell, these heroes of mine on so many other doctrines, dismiss with a flick of the wrist and the upturn of the nose, the views of Justin Martyr;[13] Irenaeus;[14] Athenagoras;[15] Pseudo Clement;[16] Clement of Alexandria;[17] Tertullian;[18] Lactantius;[19] Eusebius;[20] Commodian;[21] Ambrose;[22] Jerome;[23] Sulpicius Severus,[24] and others—not to mention a host of Jewish traditions—on the grounds that it is absurd and because they could not believe it. This is the worst possible form of *exegesis* (it is actually called *eisogesis*) for it understands only what the reader wants the text to say on already biased, presupposed terms. Historically, the Sethite view stands firmly planted in emotional nausea rather than rational logic or exegetical refutation.[25]

Ad Hominem dominates both early and later rejection of the angelic view.[26] This does not mean decent arguments have not been offered by adherents to the Sethite view (see below), only that its conception and roots are planted on the sandy soil of emotional irritation.

Angelic View Revisited

Until recently, the Sethite view dominated the Protestant church.[27] (A few Christians have adopted the old Rabbinical view with modifications, but it has never really caught on like it did in Judaism. We might call it the Divine Kingship Theory. This theory is not necessarily incompatible with a supernatural view, though most of its recent adherents believe these kings were quite human).[28] Then came the (re)discoveries and a newly acquired interest in early Jewish writings which were circulating at the time of Christ. Books like 1 Enoch (which had been lost for a thousand years to the western church), Jubilees, Judith, Sibylline Oracles, Baruch, The Testament of the Twelve Patriarchs, Sirach, Wisdom of Solomon, and the Genesis Apocryphon from the Dead Sea Scrolls could have all been read by the Apostles. In fact, some of them are quoted in the New Testament (cf. 1 Enoch 1:9 in Jude 14-15). Each has a supernatural take on Genesis 6:1-4.

In light of this, most scholars today[29] (including conservative Evangelicals) argue that the supernatural view must have been the view of Peter and Jude, who both comment on this passage. The passages are: "For if God did not spare angels when they sinned, but cast them into hell and committed them to chains of gloomy darkness to be kept until the judgment; if he did not spare the ancient world, but preserved Noah ..." (2 Pet 2:4-5); and "And the angels who did not stay within their own position of authority, but left their proper dwelling, he has kept in eternal chains under gloomy darkness until the judgment of the great day ..." (Jude 1:6). For an exegetical explanation of these verses, see "Appendix: 2 Peter 2:4 and Jude 6."

If our analysis in the Appendix is correct, then critically, this must be *the inspired infallible view* and thus, for anyone who believes in the infallibility of Scripture, a supernatural interpretation is *necessarily* correct. If this is in fact what Jesus' half-brother and the great Apostle Peter are talking about, it is the last nail in the coffin for any non-supernatural view, unless a person wants to say that Jude and Peter were "mad fools." The very conservative John Murray, who does not agree with the angelic view admits as much saying, "Without question, if [Peter] refers to angelic beings, whether exclusively or partially so as to include also the disembodied souls of men, this interpretation would necessarily turn the scales in favour of the view that the sons of God in Genesis 6:1–3 were angelic beings."[30]

Supernatural Genetic Modification View

With the resurfacing of the supernatural view and the rise of modern science (especially the human genome project), a fourth view has become popular in our own day. This view (ST2) is a modification of ST1 and says that the Nephilim were the result of genetic tamper-ing by beings that have existed since God created the heavens and the earth. If we, in just a matter of a few decades, now have the ability to map the entire human genome, create living *chimeras*, and feel the need to pass laws outlawing hybridization, these heavenly beings would probably have the intelligence to do the same thing if they so chose (we will talk about some of these things as we make our way through this book). After all, they have been here a *lot* longer than we have.

To me, the historical question really comes back to the two main views (natural vs. supernatural). Variations within each view are not the main point, and it does not particularly matter for our purposes here which view a person holds within these two broader ideas. It is the reason *why* someone would want to reject the original supernatural view in favor of a naturalistic explanation that interests me most. As I have demonstrated, some of the most influential Christians from my own (Protestant) tradition dismissed and made fun of it for emotional reasons. Also, because of even earlier stalwarts, almost the entire church (Eastern, Roman, and Protestant) has come to reject the ancient theory with very little reason other than it seems strange and silly. Yet, today the claim is made that the Sethite Antithesis view is more exegetically sound than the angelic view. Therefore, let us test this hypothesis by looking at the text and asking some questions.

Sethite Antithesis Argument Explained

Let's see how the Sethite argument proceeds from the text. First, it is noted correctly that Genesis 6:1-4 falls immediately after Genesis 4-5 which traces the genealogies of Cain and Seth, the two named sons of Noah after Abel is murdered. The genealogy of Cain the murderer ends in the seventh generation from Adam with Lamech. This wicked man becomes a polygamist and murderer *par excellence* (Gen 4:19, 23-24). Since Genesis 6:1-4 deals with marriage (perhaps even polygamy in some views), and since Genesis 6:5 and 13 explicitly refer to the terrible violence on the earth, the dots are connected back to Lamech from the line of Cain. This seems a clear hint that the same sin is going on throughout the story, and there is no need to make up ridiculous stories of fallen angels having sex with women.

Meanwhile, as soon as the Cainite line reaches its tragic, wicked apex in Lamech, the Sethite line is immediately picked up and carried for a while. We read that Seth has a descendent named Enosh who "began to call upon the name of the LORD" (Gen 4:26). The seventh descendant on Seth's side is named Enoch who was said to have walked with God and been taken to heaven without dying (Gen 5:22-24). Lamech is the seventh descendant from Adam on Cain's side and Enoch is the seventh on Seth's side. This shows the antithesis between the line of Cain and the line of Seth. The former is wicked. The later is godly.

When we come to Genesis 6:1-4, it is thus quite natural to read "the sons of God" as being godly Sethites and the "daughters of men" as being ungodly Cainites. Who else could they be in the context? Again, we are told that we have no reason to hold any other view. It fits in perfectly with the genealogies, and acts as a nice transition to God's anger with men. In my own tradition, this is seen as good biblical covenant theology. It is the plain meaning of the text.

When we come to the passage itself, we are shown how it explicitly states that God is angry with "men" (Gen 6:3), not "angelic beings." In fact, the passage refers to man *('adam)* no less than 10 times in the first seven verses, and many more if you add the pronouns. This theory is neat, tidy, and best of all entirely natural. There is no need to see it as mythology or as talking about supernatural beings doing impossible things with human women.

Case closed. Right? Not so fast. There are actually many problems with this *exegesis*.

Sethite Antithesis Argument Deconstructed

Were all Cainites Evil and All Sethites Godly?

First, let's look at the broader context. While it is true that Lamech and Enoch are set apart as opposites, there is no incontrovertible evidence that everyone in the line of Cain was wicked, nor that everyone in the line of Seth was godly. Yet, this is the lynchpin of the entire theory. In fact, it is plausible the text shows us that—almost immediately—*all men* began to become wicked, including many in the line of Seth (think about the kings of Israel in the line of Christ, they were not all godly). Let us look a little more closely at Genesis 4:26.

The verse concerns the grandson of Adam (if the passage is read without genealogical gaps). Most translations render it something like, "At that time people <u>began</u> to call upon the name of the LORD." This is said about the days of Seth's first named descendant: Enosh. The word "began" implies that either 1. Prior to this time no one called upon God in a worshipful way or 2. No one knew the personal name of God (Yahweh, i.e. the LORD) until this time. Neither implication is supportable.

Early in Genesis 4, both Cain and Abel went to offer sacrifices (that is "worship") "to the LORD" (Gen 4:3-4). Apparently, people from both lines *were* worshiping Yahweh prior to the birth of Enosh. That removes option #1. But maybe they did not know God's name until the days of Enosh? This is clearly not the case either. When Cain was born Eve exclaimed, "I have gotten a man with the help of the LORD (*Yahweh*)" (Gen 4:1). She uses the personal, covenantal name of God. Obviously, God's name was known long before Enosh was born. How then can we make sense of this text?

For these reasons, the Jewish *Targums* (which are not all bad) read the verb *chalal* ("began") as something like "pollute" (a possible meaning). Pseudo-Jonathan paraphrases the idea, "And to Seth also was born a son, and he called his name Enosh. That was the generation in whose days they began to err, and to make themselves idols, and surnamed their idols by the name of the Word (*memra*) of the Lord." The Onkelos Targum is similar, "To Seth also was born a son, and he called his name Enosh. Then in his days the sons of men desisted (or forbore) from praying in the name of the Lord." The grammar for this idea is not very compelling. Nevertheless, it is obvious that the meaning has been disputed in history, and this ought to give us pause.

No English translation renders the passage like the *targums*. All take it as an act of godly worship. Let's assume that this is correct. What is important to note now is that none of the Hebrew-to-English translations say that *only Sethites* were calling upon God's name.[31] They all use the more generic term "men" or "people."[32] This is important. "Seth" is not equivalent to "man." His name does not mean "man." "Man" is a broader term than "Seth" in this verse. This will have implications later on in Genesis 6:1-4. For now, this means that *the text* gives no indication that only Sethites were godly. That is nothing but speculation. To conclude, even though Lamech and Enoch are obvious spiritual opposites, the verse in question here does not support the idea that everyone in each line followed rank. To import this idea into Genesis 6:1-4 is to go against the very clear teaching of Genesis 4:26. One might be able to argue against this view systematically or using biblical theology, but the text simply can't support the weight of the theology *at this point*.

There is something more subtle going on with this argument of an antithesis between Seth's lineage and Cain's in the Sethite view of Genesis 6. What often goes unnoticed in the view itself is a switch in the "godliness" of the line of Seth. First, we are told that all of the named descendants of Seth are godly. This is the bait, and we are expected to eat it hook, line, and sinker. This point cannot be proven either way from the genealogy,[33] yet this "fact" creates the justification for reading the passage this way.

Here's the switch. After this has been established, we are then supposed to just accept that in Noah's day, all of this godly line has abandoned true religion for unbridled lust. Huh? *No one* in the line prior to this rebelled. *Everyone* in the line in Noah's day did. This is why it is called the "Sethite" view. We are not just talking about the 10 names mentioned in the genealogy, but everyone who is descended from Seth, presumably millions and millions of men (and I do mean "men"). The entire Sethite interpretation of Genesis 6 hangs on this.

What is strange is that when you stop to think about it, from this point of view it is the godly line—the Sethites—who are committing the wickedness in this passage. *They* are the ones taking ungodly women as their wives. In fact, it is possible to understand the "taking" of wives in Gen 6:2 to be a violent taking against the will of the women (see chapter 4 n. 3 and context). In the passage, what then are the daughters of Cain even doing wrong? This only compounds the problem. All the good men are suddenly acting wickedly, while all the wicked women are acting innocently. Say what?

Equivocation

The second point, and it is a major one that you should take seriously, has to do with equivocation. *Equivocation* is a logical fallacy. It is the misleading use of a term with more than one meaning or sense. The equivocation occurs with the term "man" (*'adam*) and the term "God" (*'elohim*) in the Sethite view.

"Adam" was the name of the first man. In fact, his name means "man" (just like Enosh can mean "man," see above). These two names are equivalent to "man" in Hebrew. "Cain" is not. Cain does not mean "man." The first equivocation occurs in Genesis 6:1-2. "It came to pass when <u>men</u> (*ha'adam*, literally "the men") began to be numerous upon the earth, and daughters were born to them, that the sons of God having seen the daughters of <u>men</u> (*ha'adam*) that they were beautiful." In the Sethite view, in the first instance, "men" means "mankind." Very few dispute this. I certainly don't. In the second instance, however, "men" supposedly means "daughters of <u>Cain</u>."[34] What justification *in these two verses* is there for such a change in meaning? No where are the names "Seth" or "Cain" used in this chapter. They haven't been mentioned for many scores of verses.

In fact, the parallel phrase to the "daughters of *'adam*" would be "sons of *'adam.*" "Sons of Adam" occurs later on at the Tower of Babel, *after the flood* (Gen 11:5). If the phrase refers to Cainites in Genesis 6, and all Cainites were wiped out in the flood, then how would we account for their reappearance at the Tower of Babel? Now, we will have to change the meaning of *'adam* once more to be something like "sons of Ham" or "sons of Cush." Or I suppose we could just spiritualize the term. If we do this, it needs to be recognized that even in the spiritualization that we are talking about biological family trees, because supposedly God did not choose anyone from these family trees to be saved.

There is another problem. Up to this point, Cain has never been called the son of Adam. It is obviously true that Cain *is* Adam's son (Gen 4:1 explicitly tells us that Adam lay with Eve who gave birth to Cain), but he is never *called* Adam's son, only Eve's son. Why then would "daughters of *'adam*" in Genesis 6:2 suddenly mean "daughters of Cain" when we have no grammatical precedent for it? This is not an insurmountable problem, but it is certainly curious that if we are going to argue so stringently for the meaning of a phrase that it would have no actual precedent in the Bible.

Furthermore, Seth *is* referred to as Adam's son (Gen 5:3) as are many sons that he had after Seth (Gen 5:4). If we want to let the text speak, then of the two boys, it is *Sethites* whom we should rightly call the daughters of *'adam*, not Cainites. Thus, while it is true that the genealogies point out some kind of antithesis between the two lineages (in a general sense, Augustine is correct, there is a "city of man" and a "city of God"), there are many more issues to consider than just the genealogies when determining the meaning of "daughters of men." At the end of the day, "men" appears to be a serious equivocation.

The second equivocation is with the word *'elohim*. This word means "God" or "gods", depending upon the context. This equivocation occurs in Genesis 6:2-3. "The sons of <u>God</u> having seen the daughters of men that they were beautiful, took to themselves wives of all whom they chose. And the Lord <u>God</u> said ..." In the first instance, we are told that "God" really means "Sethites" (see "Spiritualization" below). But in the second instance it clearly refers to God himself. Again we must ask, what justifies this switching of definitions? Theological systems must have exegetical justification to back them up.

Curiously, as we saw with Cain, so now we see with Seth. Nowhere in the Bible is Seth called the "son of God," just as nowhere was Cain ever called the "son of Adam." But, as we pointed out already, *Seth* is called the "son of man" (*'Adam*) in both the OT and the NT (Luke 3:38).

Spiritualization

The third point has to do with spiritualizing the text. I'm actually not against this, when it is consistently practiced and justified by the context. In this case, I do not think either one is true. The spiritualization occurs when we take the term "sons of God" to mean "godly" Sethites, while "daughters of men" means "wicked" Cainites. Something very tricky is going on here.

Very simply, this is a strange mixture of spiritualizing and physicalizing the text inconsistently, as it suits the interpreter's purposes.

While it is theologically conceivable that sons of "God" might refer to "godly" people, it is very difficult to see how daughters of "men" has to refer to "wicked" people. "Godly," I suppose could correspond to "God," but why does "wicked" correspond to "men," or better, "women" (and isn't that inherently sexist)? Are not Sethites also men and their daughters also women? Since all the people involved are human beings, the second case of spiritualizing seems arbitrary and inconsistent with the first.

Only if we presuppose that these daughters of men are Cainites (which as we have seen is logically precarious), *and also* that God did not save *any* Cainites would this even be plausible. But given what we know about God and election, this would be most unlike what he does elsewhere in the Scripture. Throughout the rest of the Bible, he often saves very "unsavable" Gentiles such as Rahab or Ruth (I'm assuming a Reformed view of election here since many or most of the Sethite adherents have been Reformed). Not only does this go against what we know of God's later choice in election, but now we have moved back into the physical realm to justify our spiritualizing. God now chooses all the people he wants saved because of ancestral heritage.

To get out of this problem, we might assume that the "sons of God" and "daughters of men" simply mean "believers" vs. "unbelievers" without any reference to biology (something I'm not aware that anyone does). This would defeat the whole point of the Seth-Cain antithesis. If some (many?) of the daughters of men are actually from the line of Seth, and some (many?) of the sons of God are actually from the line of Cain, what's the point? Spiritualizing these names consistently defeats the whole argument of an antithesis of the family trees.

The inconsistent spiritualization I am claiming is going on in Genesis 6:1-4 is the same problem that regularly occurs in interpretations of Genesis 3:15. The verse reads, "I will put enmity between you

(Satan) and the woman, and between your seed and her seed" (NAS). Where is the double standard? Most people will say that the first seed is a *spiritual* seed (i.e. wicked people, those whose spiritual father is the devil; cf. John 8:44), while the second seed is a *biological* seed—Jesus Christ. What justification is there for splicing up the meaning of the two seeds in this way?

I do not have a problem saying that both seeds are spiritual or even that both seeds are at the same time physical. I have a big problem interpreting one seed as spiritual and the other as biological. This is not consistent. In fact, this verse is one of the primary exegetical reasons to understand that Genesis 6:1-4 is in fact talking about heavenly beings. It predicts that Satan will have a "seed." This seed will be of the same kind that the woman is. It will be physical, able to wage war, etc. Without discussing it in full here, I'm sure you can already see a little of why this verse has bearing upon our passage.

Let's return again to Genesis 6:1-4. The inconsistency of spiritualizing the sons of Seth has a very glaring textual problem. The passage tells us that *all mankind* was violent and wicked. In fact, the most "in your face" declaration of total depravity in the Bible occurs in *this* passage, and it does not refer merely to Cainites. "The LORD saw that the wickedness of man was great in the earth, and that every intention of the thoughts of his heart was only evil continually. (Gen 6:5). Biology is in view here. "Man" is not "Cainites." Group A sees that Group B is "beautiful." They get "married." They have offspring. All of this occurs because *mankind* was "multiplying." It would seem then, that if there is a way to understand "sons of God" and "daughters of men" biologically, this would be better than the spiritualizing.

Laws about Marriage

A fourth objection is that to assume that Sethites were not allowed to marry Cainites is anachronistic. *Anachronism* is an inconsistency in a chronological arrangement. For example, today it would
be anachronistic to use a typewriter or to wear a top-hat or to write
with a quill. Instead we write with computers, wear baseball caps, and
write with pens. Logical arguments work the same way. What do I
mean with this objection?

First, we have no indication anywhere in Genesis 1-6 that it was
wrong for Sethites to marry Cainites. This idea comes from the laws
of Israel who were not allowed to marry foreigners (Ex 34:16; Ezra
10:3; Mal 2:11; 2 Cor 6:14). This is a reading back into the text what
is not there; hence *anachronism*. I would argue that the *principle* of
not being yoked with unbelievers or the world is sound and eternal.
The problem is, we have no concrete proof that all Cainites were unbelievers, nor that all Sethites were believers. It just isn't in the text.

Other Sons and Daughters

A fifth objection arises from the fact that we are told that Adam
had other sons and daughters (see above). If this is true, then why are
we only picking out Sethites and Cainites? Let's say, since we do not
know their names, that Adam also had sons named Bilbo, Frodo,
Samwise, Peregrin, Meriadoc, Gandalf, Aragorn, Boromir, Legolas, and
Gimli.[35] Where he got these names, I have no idea. Here's the point.
None of these other sons or their descendants would be in either the
Sethite or Cainite lines. They are directly descended from Adam, not
from Seth or Cain.

Now let's say that Adam's eight other sons all had the same
number of sons as Abel and Cain. This would mean that 80% of the

people on earth had nothing whatsoever to do with the events of Genesis 6, according to a strict Sethite interpretation. So why were they wiped out in the flood? One could respond that these people were also wicked for other reasons, even if they were not involved in the sins of Genesis 6:1-4. The problem with this reply is that Genesis 6:1-4 explains why there was such violence on the earth. It was a direct result of these marriages and almost certainly, their offspring. The violence and wickedness of *mankind* was so intimately tied to these marriages and children, that Moses thought it was critical to put Genesis 6:1-4 at the beginning of his story of the Flood.

How Do Giants Come from Men?

What I want to introduce now is the offspring of these marriages to whomever it was that got married. This final objection to the Sethite view will focus on Genesis 6:4 and the beings referred to in the LXX as "giants." These "giants" are really the focus of the book, but it has been necessary to talk about their fathers until this point, though honestly, their fathers deserve an entire book themselves. The Greek word for giants is *gigantes*. Here is what the *Dictionary of Deities and Demons in the Bible* (*DDD*) says about them,

> In the strict sense the Gigantes in Greek mythology were the serpent-footed giants who were born from the blood-drops of the castration of Uranus (→Heaven) that had fallen on →Earth (Hesiod *Theogony* 183–186). The term *gigantes* occurs about 40 times in the LXX [Greek *Septuagint*] and refers there respectively to: a) the giant offspring of 'the sons of God' and 'the daughters of mankind' (Gen 6:1–4; Bar 3:26–28; Sir 16:7); b) strong and mighty men, like →Nimrod (Gen 10:8–9); c) several pre-Israelite peoples of tall stature in Canaan and Transjordania. The etymology of the name, which may be pre-Greek, is unknown, but was in Antiquity thought to be *gēgenēs*, or 'born from earth'.[36]

A perusal of ancient Greek art gives a striking visual of these *gigantes*:

FIG. I.2 SERPENTINE GIANTS OF GREEK MYTHOLOGY

VILLA DEL CASALE, (ROMAN MOSAIC 3ʳᵈ C. A.D.)   *GIGANTOMACHIA*, ISTANBUL ARCHAEOLOGICAL MUSEUM, TURKEY

Notice how these giants are depicted with human torsos and serpentine legs. In fact, it is not only the Greeks who portray them this way.

FIG. I.3 SERPENTINE GODS OF WORLD MYTHOLOGY

SERAPIS
(EGYPT)   *FUXI AND NÜWA*
(CHINA)   *Kukulcan*
(Central & South America)   *Kaliya Daman*
(India)

The significance of the whole world—the *whole world* mind you(!), which supposedly had no interaction with one another until recently—depicting the same creatures (everyone pictured above is considered a god or a giant) the same way must not be ignored. For such a thing to occur by chance is statistically ridiculous. To come to that conclusion would be completely irrational, a faith based in nothing verifiable, nothing objective, nothing but wishful thinking.

Moderns classify the above pictures as *mythology*. While most people relegate myth to the realm of fantasy and fiction (which is why it is the unforgivable sin in many circles to suggest that anything in Scripture is "mythological"), it is increasingly understood by many that these ancient stories, while shrouded in mystery and certain embellishment, nevertheless recollect some token of true events of world history. In fact, speaking of our very text (Genesis 6:1-4), the late Christian apologist Francis Schaeffer wrote,

> More and more we are finding that mythology in general, though greatly contorted, very often has some historic base. And the interesting thing is that one myth that one finds over and over again in many parts of the world is that somewhere a long time ago supernatural beings had sexual intercourse with natural women and produced a special breed of people.[37]

J.R.R. Tolkien and C.S. Lewis were of the same opinion as Schaeffer about mythology.[38] In other words, there is nothing inherently evil about mythology, *if* it is a vehicle used to transmit historical information. As Lewis said, the Bible just so happens to be the "True Myth" (that is, it is 100% historically accurate).

Moving on, the Greek word *gigantes* translates the Hebrew word *nephilim*. Nephilim is the word that appears in Genesis 6:4. The ESV leaves it untranslated. It is commonly thought that *nephilim* is related to the Hebrew word *naphal* meaning "to fall." Hebrew was originally written without vowels, and viewed in this light the two words are almost identical (*nphlm* and *nphl*). Theologically, "to fall" may fit with either the angelic view (children of those who fell to earth) or a Sethite view (those who fell into sin).[39] If the word means "to fall," there is an interesting relationship with *nephilim* and *gigantes* or those born from the blood "fallen on earth" from the castrated Uranus (*gigantes* means "born of the earth," and in this context it is easy to see why). Keep in mind that Uranus is a Greek word meaning "heaven," but he was also a god. In other words, perhaps more than any other god of the Greek pantheon, his name shows that he is a *heavenly being*.

A better possibility is that *nephilim* is related to the Aramaic word *naphil*.[40] Aramaic is a sister tongue of Hebrew. It was also the language of the exiled Jews who returned from Babylon. If this relationship is genuine, then we have to consider the transmission of the ancient text to those in the captivity. The Hebrew text was being recopied for each generation as the older copies degraded. Because the course of human events included wars, captivity, the changing of languages etc., sometimes it was necessary to help "modern" people understand what they were reading. An Aramaic speaker might need a special note in a copied manuscript in order to understand the meaning of a particularly important, but now obscure, word. We see this in the NT when a Hebrew or Aramaic word is translated into Greek (cf. John 5:2; 19:13, 19:17; 20:16; Rev 9:11) for the sake of the audience reading the original text. We probably also see it in Numbers 13:33, the only other time *nephilim* definitely occurs in the Scripture. In this verse, *nephilim* occurs twice, but it is spelled differently. This is tremendously significant.

VERSE	HEBREW
Numbers 13:33a	*ne-phy-l-m*
Numbers 13:33b	*ne-ph-l-m*

The first spelling cannot be easily accounted for by the Hebrew verb "to fall." But it is accounted for in the Aramaic word. This word *naphil* means "giant," and makes perfect sense if these people in Canaan were "of great height" (Num 13:32). This is identical to the LXX version of *gigantes*. Importantly, this Aramaic word appears in the Dead Sea Scrolls on several occasions in conjunction with giants.[41] For example, the *Targum* of Job 38:31 uses this word to translate the constellation Orion, which was regarded by Homer (*Odyssey* 5.121) as a gigantic hunter and *demigod*—that is half god and half human.

This leads to the final word study in the group. We have looked at *gigantes* and *nephilim*. Now we want to look at the Hebrew word *gibborim*. Reading the LXX, you would not even know that there was another word in the Hebrew, for the LXX translates both *nephilim* and *gibborim* as *gigantes*. "Now the giants (*nephilim/gigantes*) were upon the earth in those days; and after that when the sons of God were wont to go in to the daughters of men, they bore *children* to them, those were the giants (*gibborim/gigantes*) of old, the men of renown." This speaks volumes about the how Jews before Christ interpreted this passage.

In Hebrew to English translations, *gibborim* is usually translated as something like "mighty men," though in the Dead Sea Scrolls its Aramaic equivalent is, as with the Greek, regularly translated as "giants."[42] In Genesis 6:4 it is apparently parallel to *nephilim* and certainly parallel to "men of renown" or more literally "men of the name (*shem*)."[43] The word is next used in the Bible of Nimrod who "was the first on earth [after the Flood] to become a *gibborim*" (Gen 10:8). He was the builder of the Tower of Babel (see Note #43), and as we will see in the first chapter, Nimrod, like Orion, was a hunter (Gen 10:9). In the stories of the ancient near east, he is also identified as a giant.

This also parallels the idea set forth by Hesiod that there were half-god heroes from of old.[44] Thus, the *gibborim* in Genesis 6:4 are said to have been "from of old." This distinguishes them from very human *gibborim* in David's (2 Sam 23:8-39) or Joshua's (cf. Josh 8:3) armies. Instead, the identification "from of old" clearly places them in the "primeval period and not in the recent historical past."[45] Clearly this is the case, since they were destroyed in the Flood. Thus, we can finally see this last objection to the Sethite view. If *nephilim* means "giant," as it so clearly does in Numbers 13:33, and in the LXX of Genesis 6:4, then the obvious question becomes, how would marriages of Sethites and Cainites result in gigantic offspring? There has never been a satisfactory answer to this question by anyone.

The Heavenly Interpretation of the "Sons of God."

As you can now see, there are plenty of reasons to be suspicious of the Sethite view. There is no consistent way to understand all Sethites as godly, nor do we have any compelling exegetical reason for interpreting "sons of God" or "daughters of men" as Sethites and Cainites. It seems better, given a choice, not to equivocate on the terms "men" and "God." These words should be interpreted consistently in this passage, unless we have some compelling exegetical reason for not doing so. There is no consistent way to spiritualize these phrases, nor is it contextually necessary to do so. Objections about intermarriages between believers and non-believers are both anachronistic and unsubstantiated. Adam had other sons and daughters that are not taken into account. Finally, giants are being born of these unions with no rational explanation for how, if these are just human intermarriages.

There is only one view of this passage that can answer all of these objections satisfactorily. This is the supernatural, heavenly, or angelic view that the sons of God came down out of heaven and somehow produced gigantic offspring with human women. Whether they did it through semen, genetic manipulation, or if they later became tyrant kings of the earth, it doesn't really matter. The idea is simple, if not also bizarre. But "bizarre," in itself, is not a good enough justification for jettisoning it. The Trinity, the Virgin Birth, and the Two Natures of Christ are all incredibly difficult ideas to wrap one's mind around, and to unbelievers, they are just as bizarre sounding as this. Christians ought to keep that in mind before mocking the supernatural view of Genesis 6. Do we really want to engage in the same arguments that those who hate our most deeply held convictions engage in against us?

Usage of the "Sons of God"

Thus far, I've tried to show why the arguments against the angelic view are not solid. But what are the exegetical reasons for taking a supernatural view? The most important has to do with the term "sons of God" as it is used in the Bible. Chrysostom boldly dares, "Let them demonstrate firstly where angels are called sons of God; they would not, however, be able to show this anywhere. While human beings are called sons of God, angels are nowhere so called."[46] I accept the challenge. This isn't difficult. Not even slightly.

It is undoubtedly the case that Israel is called God's "son" (Ex 4:22-23; Deut 14:1) or his "children" (Ps 73:15; Deut 32:5) in the Bible.[47] But never are they called this using the phrase "*beney ha'elohim*," the Hebrew phrase used in Genesis 6:2 and 4. In fact, Chrysostom could not have been more wrong. In the Bible, this phrase is a technical term for heavenly beings. Let me explain.

Giants of the Bible

First, let's understand the Hebrew. "*Ben*" is a son, as in Benjamin: Son of My Right Hand. "*Beney*" is the plural form of *ben*.[48] *Ha* is the definite article ("the"). Finally, *'elohim* is the generic word for God or gods.[49] So the phrase is literally then, "sons of the God," meaning that it is God and not gods in mind here.

Note that the oldest versions of the LXX read, "the angels of God,"[50] where "sons" become "angels." Of course, this is more properly called a translation/interpretation; so it proves nothing more than that our earliest records indicate the angelic view was understood to be the correct view. However, it should be kept in mind, that the LXX was the Bible most often read and cited by the NT evangelists. With that in mind, let us now turn to how this phrase is used in other places.

As noted above, the phrase "sons of God" is a technical term. It is used sparingly in the OT. Below are all of the occurrences:

"Sons of God" Passage	Hebrew Phrase
Genesis 6:2	*beney ha-'elohim*
Genesis 6:4	
Job 1:6	
Job 2:1	
Job 38:7	
Psalm 29:1	*beney 'elim*
Psalm 89:6	
Psalm 82:6	*beney 'elyon*
Deut 32:8	*aggelōn theou**
Deut 32:43	*uioi theou**
* signifies only found in LXX[51]	

If we were to study these passages out, we would find that some of them have differing opinions as to who the "sons of God" are. While disagreements will never go away, two things are certain. Each and every instance of the phrase *can be* explained as referring to super-

natural referents. In fact, I would argue that this is the best explanation for each, given their contexts. What is equally certain is that some
of these references can *only* refer to heavenly beings.

For example, Job 38 is God's great rhetorical question to Job. He
asks, "Where were you when I laid the foundation of the earth"? (vs.
4). The next verses explain that what is in mind is the creation week
prior to day six when Adam was created. However, there were others
there watching God do his work. These were "the sons of God" who
are also called "morning stars." These beings "sang together" and
"shouted for joy" (Job 38:7). It is impossible for this to refer to human
beings. Chrysostom is simply mistaken, unless he wants to say that
human beings were there watching God create Adam and Eve. Earlier
in the book, the sons of God go with Satan into the heavenly throne
room of God to present themselves before him (Job 1:6, 2:1). If
someone wants to argue that these are human beings, they have to explain why Satan is coming with them and how that would look in real
life.

Importantly—and also never mentioned by those who want to
interpret the sons of God as referring to human beings—the phrase is
also used in cousin languages of the surrounding nations, particularly
Ugaritic. *Ugarit* was an ancient Canaanite city-state located about
45 miles southwest of Antioch in Syria by the coast, in the shadow of
Mt. Zaphon or Saphon (5,607 ft.). It became a vassal state of Egypt
during the time of the Exodus, and so Moses, the writer of Genesis,
trained in the best schools in Egypt, would have been quite familiar
with it.[52] Their language and Hebrew are probably akin to comparing
the Queen's English to that of "Spanglish," so dubbed by those who
border the United States and Mexico because it is a hybrid of the
Spanish and English.

Two of the more obviously identifiable phrases in the Ugaritic tablets are *phr bn 'ilm* – "the assembly of the sons of El/the gods," and *mphrt bn 'il* – "the assembly of the gods."[53]　Comparing these phrases with ours is instructive:

UGARIT	HEBREW
bn 'il	*beney ha-'elohim*
bn 'ilm	*beney 'elim*

In these ancient tablets, all scholars agree that the terms refer to heavenly beings. They make up the seventy sons of El and Asherah, his female consort.[54] El is a name used of Israel's God in the OT.[55] "Seventy" is a number that finds parallels in biblical texts and ancient Jewish and Christian interpretations of sons of God passages.[56] These seventy sons are the pantheon of gods of the Canaanite religion, beings that have real existence in the Scripture,[57] but are created by Yahweh[58] (and hence, perhaps to eliminate confusion, are translated as "angels" rather than "gods" by the LXX).[59]

Curiously, one of the phrases in the chart on "sons of God," refers to God as *'elim.* "*Elim*" is the plural form of *El,* a proper name for God in the OT, and the name just mentioned for the high god *at *Ugarit*.[60] What the findings of Ugarit have done is brought forth compelling evidence that the phrase "sons of God" in the biblical context refers to heavenly or angelic beings.[61] This evidence was not available prior to their discovery (in 1928), for this information was buried in the desert sands for over 3,000 years. What near-eastern comparisons like this do is show us how others understood the identical phrase in the context of the same name for God. If someone is going to argue against this "sons of God" being angelic, they must also show why Israel's view would differ from their neighbors to the north, especially when so many elements, including the name of God and the number of the sons of God ("70") overlap. Sethite proponents never deal with Ugarit.

After Their Kind

A second exegetical reason to think these marriages refer to a mixing of species has to do with the oft repeated phrase in Genesis 1-7: "according to its kind" (Gen 1:11, 12 [2x], 21 [2x], 24 [2x], 25 [3x]; 6:20 [3x], and 7:14 [4x]). When reading the Genesis 1 creation story out loud, it is immediately obvious that God is concerned with getting across the point that he made all living things "according to their kinds." If Moses merely wanted you to know this as a piece of trivia, a single mention at the end of the creation would have sufficed. The sheer volume and repetition of the phrase in this chapter (ten of the sixteen occurrences in the Bible) demonstrates that he wants you to notice *and remember it*.

Why is this such a concern to Moses? The most curious thing about this phrase is that it never occurs again anywhere *in the entire Bible* after Genesis 7. This is a clue that whatever the phrase refers to, its main purpose was to point out something important in the world prior to the Flood. When reading the Flood story and the repetition of this same phrase found only in creation, the mind naturally goes back to the *creation* of life on earth.

We are told in Genesis 6:12 that "God saw the earth, and behold, it was corrupt, for all flesh had <u>corrupted</u> their <u>way</u> on the earth." The word "corrupt" (*shachath*) has many meanings. One meaning, found in the very next verse is "to destroy" (Gen 6:13, 17). Thus, it seems that they destroyed themselves, therefore God will destroy them. But how might they have destroyed themselves?

It is interesting that this word is used in conjunction with "the way" (*derek*) in other places. For example, the LORD said to Moses, "Go down, for your people, whom you brought up out of the land of Egypt, have corrupted themselves. They have turned aside quickly out of the way." And what way was that? "They have made for themselves a golden calf and have worshiped it and sacrificed to it and said, 'These are your gods'" (Exodus 32:7-8; cf. Deut 9:12; Jdg 2:17-19).

Sometimes this is referred to as "whoring after the gods" (e.g. Jdg 2:17) where the idolatrous worship is exactly parallel with sexual fornication. In the Old Testament, people "play the whore" with "goat demons" (Lev 17:7), "Molech" (Lev 20:5), and other "foreign gods" (Deut 31:16). They can commit "adultery" with "stone and tree" (Jer 3:9). While we (rightly) spiritualize these kinds of things (people are not literally exchanging bodily fluids with non-physical gods and demons), it must be recognized that we frankly don't have any idea what takes place in the spiritual realm when people commit idolatry, not to mention the temple prostitution that regularly took place here. What is clear is that God uses the idea of sexual immorality, the intimate coming together of two different people, to explain what occurs. Clearly, the mixing of different "kinds" is here at least spiritual in these passages, even if no offspring result from the unions.

The word *shachath* can also mean "to spoil" (cf. Jer 13:7). It can mean "to ravage" (cf. 2 Sam 11:1). Both can have similar sexual connotations. Given these word meanings and usage in other places, it is not inconceivable that the people prior to the flood have been "destroyed" through cross-breeding or genetic manipulation, which came about through spiritual beings that transgressed the proper abode.

Let me bring three more points from the Scripture to bear upon this idea of mixing kinds. The first is the language used of Noah in Genesis 6:9. It tells us, "These are the generations of Noah: Noah was a just man and perfect in his generations, and Noah walked with God" (KVJ). The opening phrase, "These are the generations" is repeated 10 times in Genesis. It is used the way we use chapter titles to introduce the ten main sections of Genesis. As Meredith Kline notices, "What follows the formula is always an account of the descendants of the person named."[62] The word (*toledoth*) is always concerned, then, with genealogy and *physicality*.

Curiously, a similar word (*dor*) occurs later in the same verse. It is often translated as "generation,"[63] as the KJV puts it, Noah was "perfect in his generations." Most English translations understand this phrase as a reference to Noah's *spiritual* estate (notice how much spiritualizing is going on in this passage from conservative scholars). That is, they see this as a continuation of the previous and following phrases about Noah's "righteousness," which is a spiritual thing. A good example is the New Jerusalem Bible, "Noah was a *good* man, an upright man among his contemporaries (*dor*), and he *walked* with God." The idea is that "good," "upright," and "walked with God" all refer to Noah's *character*. The main problem with this translation is that "generations" has just referred to descendants in the line of Noah ("These are the generations of Noah"). Now it is supposed to refer to contemporaries of a completely different family tree. Though not the identical word, this is perhaps yet another discovery of *equivocation*.

The ESV tries a different translation. "Noah was a righteous man, blameless in his generation. Noah walked with God." The idea is similar, but "contemporaries" has been changed to "generation." The main problem with this kind of translation is that "generation" in the Hebrew is plural, not singular. The NJB at least saw this (with the

plural "contemporaries"). Thus, the KJV has "perfect in his generations." This is a more faithful translation, but what might this mean?

According to Perfectionists like Betty Champion it means we
can be morally perfect on earth and Noah is the proof. In her book *Yes
We Can Be Perfect In Our Generation* she writes, "If nobody is perfect
why does scripture say Noah was a perfect man? See Genesis 6:9."[64]
Never mind that almost as soon as Noah gets off the Ark after his miraculous deliverance, he plants a vineyard, gets drunk, and lets his son
sleep with his wife.[65] Some sinless perfectionist Noah was.

To understand what Moses might mean by, "perfect in his generations," it will help to see how else the word "perfect" (*tamim*) is used
by him (in Genesis – Deuteronomy). Sometimes it is associated with
"walking before God," as it is here with Noah and again with Abraham
(Gen 17:1). According to a detailed study of this phrase done by a
noted scholar, it most properly does not mean "keeping the law," but
rather "serve as an emissary" for God.[66] Moses' regular use of this
phrase is certainly not a help to the perfectionist point of view.

Other times the word is used in reference to spotless animals. In
fact, of the approximately 50 times that Moses uses this word, this is
the context over 80% of the time. What is in mind in these passages is
that the worshiper must take a *physically* unblemished spotless animal
and offer it to the LORD. This has nothing to do with spiritual perfection, but everything to do with physical purity. Thus, if the uses of
the words are any indication, it is more than plausible—it is highly
probable—that for Noah to be "perfect in his generations" means that
he was physically pure, that is, unpolluted, undefiled, and perhaps genetically untainted. "In his generations" (plural) would mean that all of
his direct forefathers (that is his lineage including his father Lamech,
his grandfather Methuselah and so on) were also physically pure. This

is viewed by Moses as an aberration of the way things were in the world in Noah's day. This is a main purpose of Noah's genealogy.[67]

The next point about the significance of "different kinds" regards the practices of the inhabitants of the land of Canaan. This gets us a little ahead of ourselves, so I'll say only what needs to be said here. God was bringing Israel into Canaan. When the 12 spies came back from the land, they carried with them a cluster of grapes so large that Jewish tradition says eight of the 12 spies carried the cluster, one carried a pomegranate, one carried a fig, and Joshua and Caleb carried nothing, because they did not share the plan to discourage the Israelites from attacking Canaan (Num 13:23).[68]

At any rate, it is important to notice a couple of the particular laws that God put in place for Israel, specifically saying that they were not to follow after the practices of these people. The first kind of law refers to bestiality. One says, "You shall not have intercourse with any animal to be defiled with it. . . for by all these the nations which I am casting out before you have become defiled" (Lev 18:23-24 NAS; cf. Lev 20:15-16 and 23). This is the precursor to mixing kinds, whether any offspring can come from such unions is not the point.

The other kind of law involves something we today may find strange and unimportant. "You shall keep my statutes. You shall not let your cattle breed with a different kind. You shall not sow your field with two kinds of seed, nor shall you wear a garment of cloth made of two kinds of material" (Lev 19:19).[69] The other day I walked into a discussion on tattoos. The argument was that tattoos are wrong because of a law against them in the Old Testament. When they asked me what I thought, I went over to one of them, lifted up the tag on the back of their shirt, and pointed out that they were wearing a garment made of cotton and wool. This law comes in the middle of the previous set of laws, and thus has in mind the same context of not doing what the inhabitants of Canaan were doing. This conclusion is quite possible: They were trying to engineer hybrid plants and animals. This isn't even rocket science, for we even see Jacob practicing an early stage of genetic modification when he worked with Laban (Gen 30:31-40).

With this in mind, enter into a speculative thought experiment with me. There are many Christians, and even a few non-Christians, who believe that dinosaurs may not have been as ancient as the theory of evolution teaches. Let's assume that there were dinosaurs on the earth prior to the flood, living side by side with Noah. Why is there little to no concrete proof that there have been land-dwelling dinosaurs after the flood? There is an interesting theory that because dinosaurs are believed to have had both avian (bird) and reptilian (lizard) characteristics, they could have been *chimeras* (hybrids). If this is the case, then they could not rightly have been said to be "after their kind." Thus, they were an abomination to God and Noah would not have taken them on the ark.[70] It's an interesting idea at any rate.

The point is, before Genesis 6, right in the middle of Genesis 6, and after Genesis 6 a good deal of time is taken up discussing mixing kinds. Therefore, we have good reason to believe that the origin of this problem occurred sometime prior to the Flood. It made God extremely angry, for he made all things "according to their own kind."[71]

All flesh has corrupted itself

A third argument for the supernatural view of Genesis 6 is that the passage says "all flesh" had corrupted itself (Gen 6:12), therefore God destroyed "all flesh" that was on the earth (Gen 6:13, 17, 7:21, 9:11-17). It is sometimes argued against the supernatural view that God was only angry at *mankind*. These verses obviously fly in the face of that idea.

Clearly, God was angry at birds, reptiles, and crawling things as well as men and women. Did all of the critters on the earth "sin"? Can you even apply "sin" to spiders or earthworms, which clearly are included in "all flesh" (6:7, 20)? In my mind, it is a certainty that many animals misbehave on purpose. I owned a dog, which is better behaved than a cat. It is a difficult question to know whether or not we should call their misbehavior "sin." The farther down the food chain we go, the more difficult this question becomes. But "sin," as I said before, is the usual way that "corruption" is taken in this passage. When we start stretching this to animals, it becomes a thorny theological pursuit.

But what if "all flesh" were corrupt because of the mixing of kinds? What if this refers to physicality rather than spirituality? If this is the case, then the only objection would be one of science: How could they have done it? Most people do not think genetic engineering back then was possible, and yet scientists in our own day are eagerly pursuing the Nazi dream of creating a super race, genetically altered to live forever. We are making such strides in this area that several states have now passed laws making human hybridization a crime.[72] You would not pass a law if it were impossible to do. If we can to it today, what makes us so sure they couldn't do it back then? Is it the theory of evolution that makes us think our ancestors were stupid apes? These people lived a lot longer than we do. And what about beings that are more ancient, powerful, and intelligent than us?

Nephilims are Giants

Previously I pointed out that the offspring of the unions of the sons of God and daughters of man were giants. Some people deny this to be the case, however. They read the passage as saying something like this: "The Nephilim were on the earth in those days. And after that [that is after the Nephilim were on the earth], the sons of God came into the daughters of man and bore them children. These were the mighty men, the men of renown." I consulted over 30 different English translations and the only one that definitely reads this way is the Bible in Basic English, which is hardly a literal translation.[73]

Though it is possible from the grammar to argue that the Nephilim do not refer to the union in question, it is extremely difficult to find anyone today who will give it a try, because it makes the point about Nephilim superfluous. If the Nephilim were already on the earth, and if the children born to the sons of God and daughters of men are not Nephilim but Gibborim (totally different people), why mention the *nephilim* at all? But even if this were the case, we still have to deal with who these Nephilim were in the other place they are mentioned in the Bible. In this instance, it is irrefutable that they are literal giants. How so?

The spies told Moses, "... The land, through which we have gone to spy it out, is a land that devours its inhabitants, and all the people that we saw in it are of great height. And there we saw the Nephilim (the sons of Anak, who come from the Nephilim), and we seemed to ourselves like grasshoppers, and so we seemed to them." (Num 13:32-33). We learn from other places that the sons of Anak were extremely tall men (Deut 9:1-2). Therefore, the *nephilim* sons of Anak in Num 13:33 are not some smaller group of people compared with those of "great height" in vs. 32. No. The Anakim are part of a group of giant clans listed in vv. 28-29. If we take "land" here as personification of these tall giants, we learn that the "devouring" going on may very well be a reference to the unthinkable practice of cannibalism (that's how some ancient Jews took it), or if it is not technically correct to call it cannibalism, because the giants were not eating themselves, then to the eating and consumption of human flesh.

On every continent on the planet, the indigenous people tell stories of gods coming down to earth, copulating with human women, who produced very tall offspring that were violent ruthless cannibals. There is nothing inconsistent here with a supernatural interpretation of Genesis 6:1-4 if "gods" merely means supernatural heavenly created beings. The fact that the Nephilim are here in Genesis 6:4 tells us that they were part of the reason for the Flood. They were in fact giants. These giants are not rare genetic abnormalities, but the normal product of the union in the verse. How can this be if both groups are perfectly human? The Sethite view has no answer for that question.

Angels Before Genesis 6:1-4

Another objection sometimes raised against the supernatural view is that, if the sons of God are angels (or heavenly beings), this would be the first instance of such creatures in the Bible. The idea is that such an introduction here, in the middle of Genesis, is unprecedented and therefore false (as if God can't introduce a character into his storyline anytime he feels like it). The use of the cryptic "sons of God" as angels would make absolutely no sense, since we have no previous referent in the text to angels.

There are two problems with this theory. The first is that the story of Job with its three angelic references to the sons of God (see above), predates the writing of Genesis. Even if the book were not written with ink on paper until later, the story would have been well known not only to Moses, but to all of the children of Israel, including the references to the sons of God.

The second problem is that the objection is patently false. There are in fact two very glaring references to heavenly beings prior to Genesis 6. Genesis 3 tells the story of the fall due to the temptation of *Satan*, a heavenly being. Elsewhere Satan is called "an angel of light"

(2 Cor 11:14). He is given the royal title of a prince (Matt 12:24; Mark 3:22; Luke 11:15; John 12:31; 16:11; Eph 2:2). Princes are sons of the king. Who is the king? God is the king. Therefore, Satan is in some sense a son of God, even though that sense is qualitatively different from the only begotten son of God, the Lord Jesus; for Satan is a created son, and Jesus—who created Satan—is not. The second instance occurs after God drives our first parents out of Eden. Outside of the gate of Eden he places two cherubim to guard the way to the tree of life (Gen 3:24). These instances prove the assertion false. The angelic idea of the sons of God does not just arrive out of the blue.

Serpent Seed

As mentioned previously, Satan was in the garden with Adam and Eve. After he tempted our parents to sin, he was cursed by God. Part of this curse involves a war that Satan will ultimately lose, "I will put enmity between you and the woman, and between your offspring and her offspring; he shall bruise your head, and you shall bruise his heel" (Gen 3:15). Clearly, the woman will have offspring and the serpent will have offspring. I have already dealt with the inconsistency of seeing one line as biological and the other only as spiritual.

There are some who hold the supernatural view of Genesis 6:1-4 who believe the first son of Satan was Cain; that Satan lay with Eve, and Cain is the first demi-god. This "serpent seed" doctrine blatantly contradicts Genesis 4:1, which teaches that Adam is Cain's biological father. This doctrine is heresy. Nevertheless, the point I'm making here is that there is compelling exegetical reason from this verse to see that sometime in the future, there would be physical offspring from fallen heavenly beings that would wage war against mankind and try to wipe out the coming seed of the woman. In fact, this is "The Storyline" of the giants in the Bible (see Chapter 1).

Here then we have several textual reasons for thinking that the sons of God are angels and that the giants are their half-breed offspring. Whenever the actual phrase "sons of God" occurs in the OT, it can *always* be read as a reference to heavenly beings. Because of the book/story of Job, the Israelites would have been quite familiar with this as a reference to heavenly beings. The insistence that Noah take with him only animals "after their kind" makes sense if there were lots of mixed animals on the earth. Noah's own physical perfection can easily be read that he is a full blooded son of Adam with no biological pollution from heavenly beings, but it makes little sense if it refers to something spiritual in Noah's character. God was angry, not just at mankind, but with all flesh on the earth. Nephilim means giant, and it is difficult to see how ordinary marriages of believers to non-believers could regularly and normally produce gigantic offspring. Finally, there are heavenly beings present in the Bible well before Genesis 6 begins. The main figure, Satan, is told that his offspring will make war on Eve's offspring, but that her seed will prevail.

Supernatural Theories Deconstructed?

There have been several charges leveled against the supernatural theories. One resource I found gave no less than 15 arguments against it.[74] I have already dealt with some of these objections, but here they are with brief explanations of why these objections are weightless.

1. The "sons of God" would be the first mention of angels in the Bible. Answer: No, Satan and two cherubim are mentioned in Genesis 3 and the sons of God story of Job was well known to Moses and Israel.
2. The Bible says that God creates life after its kind. If a hybrid view is correct, then the Nephilim are not after any kind. Answer: This is exactly why God became so angry and destroyed the world in the flood.

3. The Flood was a judgment on mankind, not angels. Answer: God destroyed "all flesh," not just mankind. All flesh had become corrupt.

4. "And also after that" means that the Nephilim were originally not the children of the sons of God. They were born before that union. This objection goes back at least as far as Augustine (*City of God* 15.23). Answer: We have seen the implausibility of this interpretation of Genesis 6:4. It does not explain why the Nephilim would be mentioned, nor does it deal with how the Nephilim were still here at some point. What were they?

5. Angels are not physical beings, but spiritual beings as it says, "Who maketh his angels spirits; his ministers a flaming fire" (Ps 104:4 KJV; Heb 1:7). Answer: This objection also has roots in the same section of Augustine's *City of God*. No one doubts that angels are spiritual beings. But in answer to the objection it can be said that the Psalmist could be talking about human messengers like prophets just as easily as heavenly messengers, for humans also have spirits. This is probably not the case, so the second point is that angels very often take on physicality in the Bible. They can eat, drink, speak, wrestle, grab, and apparently as the men of Sodom thought ... have sex. I make no claim to know how they do it, but I do claim to believe the Bible which says that they do. Besides, the Bible explicitly teaches that angels have bodies (1 Cor 15:40-41), but not all flesh is of the same glory.

6. Angels do not have DNA. Answer: How could anyone possibly know that? There is good reason to believe that they knew about DNA a very long time ago. You can Google this idea and up will come thousands of websites. We'll deal with this later in the book.

7. Angels only *appeared* as men in the Bible. Answer: The Bible says that they ARE men (Gen 18:2; 19:10; 32:24; Dan 3:25; Luke 24:4 and many others). Undoubtedly, they are a different "kind" of man, but Scripture uses the term "man" to describe angels dozens of times.

8. We have no examples in the Bible of fallen angels appearing as a man. Answer: "Angel" means "messenger." Angel is a designation of function not of being. Angels are sent by God to relay messages. Why would God trust fallen angels to send messages to men? We shouldn't

expect any fallen angels to come to men. Furthermore, the Bible seems to indicate that the particular beings who sinned at this time in the flood were locked up so that they could not do it again (see 2 Peter 2:4; Jude 6).[75]

9. How can spiritual beings produce physical offspring? Only the Holy Spirit can do this through the virgin, and it was the miraculous birth of the God-man. Answer: First of all, comparing Jesus to a Nephilim is heretical. Jesus is not a *demigod*, but very God of very God and fully in every way man. Angels were not able to duplicate this. Nephilim are half heavenly and half human. Angels are not the same species of man as us. Second, if angels can in *some sense* be called men and can manifest themselves physically, then our lack of knowledge about the sexual abilities of heavenly beings is no proof against the supernatural view. Even if it was impossible biologically speaking, genetic manipulation of DNA is theoretically plausible.

10. Christ says angels do not marry. This objection is one of the most common. Answer: Christ says angels "in heaven" do not marry. This may seem like a trivial answer, but it isn't. These heavenly beings clearly came down to earth. This was their sin. They were no longer *in heaven*. Marriage seems to be a temporary reality here on earth. In heaven even we will not marry (Luke 20:34-35), though we will be married to Christ as the church. Because we will not marry each other in heaven, it does not follow that we do not marry here. These creatures were fallen out of heaven, willfully rebellious against God, and thus it is entirely feasible that if they could materialize here, they could also marry. If an angel can wrestle with Jacob (by the way, this angel is called "a man;" Gen 32:24), why couldn't they also marry?

11. If Nephilim means "giant," we have Nephilim today. Just watch a pro basketball game. Answer: The point of the text is that *whenever* the sons of God had children with the daughters of man, a Nephilim was born. Giants in our day are rare, but this seems to have been an ordinary occurrence.

12. These people are called mighty "men" not angels. If they were angels, why didn't it just say so? Answer: It did. It called them Nephilim and

Gibborim, words that are both associated with the supernatural. Their fathers are the sons of God, which are also supernatural. Finally, "men" is a term often used to describe supernatural beings.

13. The Nephilim in Numbers 13 are not the children of the sons of God, but of Anak. Therefore, they are not hybrids. Anak was a man not an angel. Answer: Anak was himself a giant Nephilim, as were his three sons and his ancestor Arba. Hence, the comparison between Anakim and Nephilim in the passage. The whole point of Genesis 6:4 mentioning that there were Nephilim on the earth after the flood is to point forward to Numbers 13. It directly implies that these later Nephilim are also children of fallen sons of God, even if it is a different group than those who originally descended prior to the flood.

14. Christ offered proof of his resurrection when questioned saying, "Spirits do not have flesh and bone." Answer: This question fails to distinguish between angels and spirits. As we will see, spirits are most definitely *not* fallen angels. They are disembodied entities, meaning that at one time they had bodies, which is why they seek to inhabit bodies now. Jesus' point is that he kept his resurrected body, not that he became a demon or ghost or spirit. But just in case an angel decided to pretend that he was Jesus, he tells them to look at the execution marks on his body. Apparently, this cannot be duplicated by an angel ... because they have bodies.

15. If a new race of beings existed, could they be saved? Jesus came to save men not angels. If a Nephilim is a man, he could be saved, but if he is also an angel he could not be saved. This problem is posed not as irrefutable proof against the view, but as a theological danger of the view. Answer: A Nephilim is neither an angel nor a man. It is a Nephilim. Nephilim are half-breeds and therefore this tricky dilemma should not be applied to them anymore than to the animal kingdom. Whether or not there will be animals (or Nephilim) in heaven is a question that must be pursued apart from whether they trust that Christ died for them.

As you can see, *every* objection brought against the supernatural view can be answered. The same cannot be said for purely naturalistic views. I believe this is a critical point to come to grips with. All that remains is our individual incredulity and personal offense about the idea. But if we have a preconceived bias against any such ideas from the start, no amount of logic or biblical proof will convince. If this is still your view, I ask you to remember one thing. At the end of the day, Chrysostom, Augustine, Luther, and Calvin did the only thing they could do to attack the older belief. *They made fun of it.* I certainly won't condemn anyone who wants to stick with the Sethite view, but I want to offer a warning about mocking the older view.

Demythologization is a word coined by the late Liberal theologian Rudolf Bultmann (1884-1976). Strictly speaking, demythologization is reinterpreting the message of the New Testament for a time in which people no longer think in the mythological terms of the ancients.[76] The same thing can easily be applied to the OT. The idea is not that we should pursue truth rather than fable (i.e. mythology), but that we no longer need to think about the Bible as an historical document with real people and events. We just need to take the "spiritual" lessons from it. We will still have the core of the faith in doing so. This is the heart and soul, the warp and woof, of liberalism.

In all honesty, while the term may be recent, the idea most certainly is not. When Jesus rose from the dead, the chief priests of Israel practiced *demythologization* by telling the soldiers to spread the news that "his disciples came by night and stole him away while we were asleep" (Matt 28:13). They couldn't deal with the resurrection. Arius practiced *demythologization* by claiming that Jesus was not a divine person, not The Son of God. Thomas Jefferson practiced demythologization by literally taking a pair of scissors and cutting out every instance of a miracle that he could find in his Bible.

I am not the first person to suggest that more recent interpretations of Genesis 6:1-4 are essentially the same thing. It is a "reinterpretation" for "modern" people (even if they lived 1,600 years ago) that the supernatural events of this passage did not—indeed *could* not—occur. Rather, it was a spiritual thing that happened. Godly men sinned with ungodly women, and that's the end of the story. Period.

To put it bluntly, there is no reason to throw out the oldest view known on this passage, other than our own personal disgust for it. But if we do so, we need to remember that atheists refuse to believe in the virgin birth, the deity of Christ, and the resurrection of the dead *for the exact same reasons*. They are silly and absurd to them.

I've given solid exegetical reasons for holding to the ancient view of this passage. The ramifications of this interpretation are literally to be seen in almost every book of the Bible. This is not a time for vain speculation, inferences, and clever theories. The Ancient Ones believed what they believed for good reasons. The evidence is very strong that the sons of God, the Nephilim, Gibborim, and the correlative Greek translations all point towards the identification of the giants as demi-gods, half-breed children of heavenly beings and human women. It really does not matter if this sounds like the *National Enquirer*, because frankly, it is what the text says. Our choice is to "believe it or not," though I personally think that God is much more reputable than Robert Ripley.

Chapter 1: Pre-Flood Giants

*The Nephilim were on the earth in those days (and
also after this) when the sons of God were having
sexual relations with the daughters of humankind,
who gave birth to their children. They were the
mighty heroes of old, the famous men.*

Genesis 6:4 (NET)

The Story of the Bible

When I tell people about the giants, inevitably one question
comes up time and again. It is not a question about whether they
really existed or how tall they might have been. The question is prag-
matic: How does learning about the giants matter to my life? It is a
fair question, though I sometimes get frustrated by it. Learning about
the giants does matter to your life; but as I explain how, I want you to
be thinking about something else.

Imagine yourself living seventy years ago. You have just come
out of the top grossing film of all time. Suddenly a reporter comes up
to you with one of those silly hats, a pencil, and paper. He asks, "I'm
sure *Gone with the Wind* was a nice movie, but how did that matter to
your life?" Wouldn't you think this to be a pretty strange question? I
know I would. At the very least, you would probably not think it
would be the first question someone would ask you.

We do not ordinarily go to movies because we want to learn some tip for living, though I suppose you might be moved as a by-product of good character development to emulate (or not) a character you liked or hated. In the Bible, Peter and Jude (see Appendix – 2 Peter 2:4 and Jude 6 for *exegesis* of these passages) use the story of the fall of the sons of God in Genesis 6. This includes the abandonment of their preternatural domain, their sexual immorality, and the punishment God inflicted upon them. Peter and Jude use this as part of the overall ethical warning in their letters. Clearly, when we see what they did (not to mention their sons; see Chapter 7: The "Law" of Canaan), we must not copy their ways. As Jude puts it, do not be like the "wandering stars" (Jude 13). I opened the Preface with a little passage I discovered in an ancient Jewish writing, one that I think really gets at this in a thought provoking way, "The sons of men, being insensitive to [God, spirits, heavenly armies, Holy Ones, archangels, angels, thrones, and authorities], keep sinning and provoking the anger of the most High." That passage comes in the middle of an ancient Jewish testament concerned with teaching people to act rightly in God's world. This is a chief lesson of the story of the giants.

But the point about being moved by a character in a movie is, to me, more profound, because it works on a deeper level of the human psyche than overt moral instruction. It is able to foster the obedience without a command. I think most of us go to movies because we love *to be swept up* in the story. Oh, that people would long to be swept away by God's story once more. If, by the end of this book, I have caused you to be swept up in the invisible story of the Bible, I have accomplished one thing I set out to do.

We love stories. Stories are actually practical, though not in the sense a pragmatist would appreciate. Stories move us at the core of our being. Stories change us as people (including ethically). They help us to imagine, to create, to love, to ponder, to wonder. Everyone is looking for a story that they can relate to, a story that will move them emotionally, a story that will thrill them, or a story that will scare them, a story they can in some way fantasize and live out as the main or supporting character. God made us this way, because human beings take center stage in his drama of creation. Not even angels have this role in the story; actually, that's one of the reasons Satan took out his revenge on us. Imagine now a story that read like fantasy, but was actually true.

It is odd the way the Bible is used today. Some read it as a cookbook, a coaching manual, to gain leadership tips, or to prove scientific theories. This is wrong headed, but also boring. Few people read it as it is supposed to be read—a story. Perhaps they are afraid that if they did that, it would be like saying it is no different than *Gone With the Wind* (just fiction). More likely, they just don't think that would be ... "practical."

If I were to ask you, "What is the story of the Bible," would you have an answer? What would it be? My answer begins with what many believe is the thesis of the Word of God: Genesis 3:15. "And I will put enmity Between you and the woman, And between your seed and her Seed; He shall bruise your head, And you shall bruise His heel" (NKJV). The reason we have the Bible is so that God might tell you about *this* story and that in the hearing of the story, you might believe in Christ. Often the Bible takes the form of story-telling, especially in the narrative sections. However, even the Psalms, Proverbs, and general Epistles (letters) tell this story in their own unique way.

The whole Bible works out the fulfillment of this promise to Eve and curse to Satan. The New King James demonstrates good theology by capitalizing Eve's Seed, for ultimately Jesus Christ is that Seed.

Theologians point out that this verse is the "first gospel" (*proto-evangelium*). It is a *promise* that from the body of the first woman, one will eventually come who will crush the head of the serpent. Yet, some of the same scholars will say that if we view Genesis 6:1-4 as some kind of supernatural angelic intervention in history, then this somehow destroys biblical theology (particularly the thread of the *two kingdoms* first set forth by Augustine in *The City of God*).[1] Nothing could be further from the truth.

This verse contains a prophecy of a war and the ultimate victory of Christ over evil. Good biblical theology is not only about God's people vs. those who are not. It is about good vs. evil and God's absolute sovereignty in both the physical and *spiritual* realms. In the war's final manifestation, Jesus conquers *Satan,* and ushers in his own kingdom, which intrudes upon the kingdoms of the world today through the church and the gospel. But before Jesus arrives on the scene in the flesh, we have wars and stories that foreshadow and precede The Great War and Heavenly Kingdom.[2] War drums of hatred, disdain, and violence thumping steadily in the ears of the people of God; beginning with Cain they resound through the valleys of time, echoing even into the days of Esther.

What many people fail to notice in all this is how a main earthly antagonist throughout this OT war are the giants, or people in some way related to them, either through marriage or cultural assimilation (like victims of the Borg in Star Trek). Most are wholly unaware of how many giants there are in the Bible, and why God bothers to tell us about them. Read the "first gospel" again. Eve will have a Seed, *and Satan will have a seed.* As I pointed out in the Introduction, the consistent way to read this is that both seeds are spiritual and/or both seeds are physical. The inconsistent way is that one is physical (Jesus is born literally from a woman), but that the other is spiritual (those who have Satan as their father only have him so in a spiritual sense). There is simply no justification in the text to read it that way. That's an *equivocation*. The verse begs that we interpret the seeds consistently.

Spiritual Giants

If we want to say that both seeds are spiritual, then the first seed of the woman is Abel, while the first seed of the serpent is Cain. Here, we are not viewing either son biologically, but through the prism of faith and faithlessness. This is more than permissible. Other Scripture mandates that we do this. The Bible comments on the spiritual condition of both boys. 1 John 3:12 tells us, "We should not be like Cain, who was of the evil one and murdered his brother."[3] Meanwhile it is said of Abel, "By faith Abel offered to God a more acceptable sacrifice than Cain, through which he was commended as righteous" (Heb 11:4). This spiritual interpretation can consistently be carried out with anyone in the Bible who trusts and obeys God vs. those who do not. This is why believers are called sons of God and unbelievers are called children of the devil. Though I disagree with his interpretation of Genesis 6:1-4, Augustine had this basic theological idea correct.

At its core, this is the doctrine of election. When comparing Israel to the nations, election is corporate. God chose one nation over all the others to be the vessel through which his grace would come to the world. With regard to salvation, however, God chooses individuals who do not deserve to be saved. These people are not good. They are not looking for God. They are not smart or wise by the world's standards. He does it because it pleases him to do so, and because if he didn't, no one would be saved. In both instances, it is the weak, the small, and the foolish in the eyes of the world who are the spiritual giants of the Bible. If, however, we want to read the seed physically, which is also necessary since Christ came *in the flesh*, then who would be the physical seed of the serpent?[4] The answer is: The giants.

Physical Giants

Half Breeds

It would be nice to learn something about these giants before we begin our tour of Scripture. What can we learn about their makeup and character? Genesis 6:1-4 tells us that the giants were born of a union between heavenly beings and earthly women (see Introduction). This makes the giants half-breeds or *demigods*. We do not know how this occurred exactly. Certainly there were conjugal unions or marriages in those days; Jesus affirms as much (Matt 24:38). Angels often take physical form in the Bible, so nothing biblical prevents this as a possibility. Most translations say that the sons of God "took wives."[5] These marriages could have been consensual or not, and the women involved could have been full of passion for them,[6] or not.

However, the term "wife" (*ishshah*) could just mean "women." As such, at least some of these unions could refer to a kind of rape. This is doubtful, because the taking of wives is often a good thing. Believe it or not, the Jews, Greeks, and other ancients believed the sons of God could shape-shift (see note #7), and offered this as a reason for pregnancies.[7] Others suggest some kind of genetic manipulation or other unlawful taking.[8] Though marriages occurred, further details are sketchy. We do know that offspring were brought forth somehow. It really did happen.

Violent Warriors and Heroes of Old

In the Bible you find various tribes of humans fighting against the giants (cf. Gen 14; Deut 2). This is because the giants were fierce, violent warriors. We learn the following things in regard to this. First, Genesis 6:4 calls them *gibborim*. The Greek *Septuagint* (LXX) translated the Hebrew *gibborim* as "giant" (*gigantes*). This word comes straight out of Greek mythology. The Gigantes were the children of heaven (Uranus) and earth (Gaia), just as they are in this verse. Strictly speaking, the Gigantes were serpent-footed giants born after Cronus, the youngest son of Uranus, castrated his father (see Appendix: The Stories of the Greeks). This is how the Jewish translators of the Old Testament, 200 years before Jesus was born, understood the Nephilim.

Gibborim is sometimes used to describe the brave, though very human, heroes. For example, David had his thirty *gibborim* ("mighty men," cf. 2 Sam 23:17-18). You find the same thing in Joshua's army. They are called *chayil gibborim* ("valiant warriors;" cf. Josh 10:7). Curiously, both accounts come in the context of these brave warriors fighting and defeating real giants. This makes the use of the term for Israelite warriors ironic; who are the real giants of the story, the literal giants or the much smaller warriors of God?

The last phrase of Genesis 6:4 refers to these giants as "men of renown" (lit. "men of the name"), for they sought to make a name for themselves. Thus, some translations offer "these were the heroes and warriors of old." The mind cannot help but be drawn to the stories and legends known around the world, stories of *demigods* like Hercules or Orion, Thor or Gilgamesh, Garuda, and many more. But the Bible does not want you to fixate on them here. Instead, it just glances at them, for it wants you to see what their actions brought the LORD to do to the earth.

A Major Reason for the Flood

The LORD was sorry that he made man on earth and was grieved over what we had become (Gen 6:6). For the LORD saw the wickedness of man (6:5), how all flesh had corrupted its way (6:12) and had become full of violence (6:11). Notice how the violence was not just contained with man, but extended to "all flesh." It is interesting that you can actually see the progression of what took place on the earth in the names of the descendants of Cain and, especially Seth. A person's name is very often an important clue into events or facts contained in the Bible.

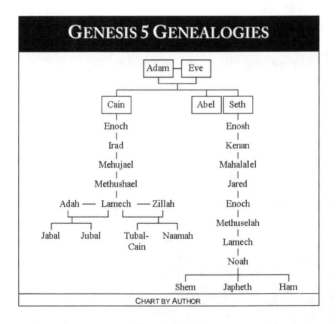

I would like to tell you about some of Seth's descendant's names, beginning with Jared, along with their meaning and a brief comment on how the name tells the story. Jared means "descent."[9] The ancient Jewish book called 1 Enoch—a book quoted by Jude as containing the real words of Enoch—comments on this saying that it was in the days of *Jared* that the sons of heaven *descended* upon Mt. Hermon (1 Enoch 6:6). Enoch is using a word play in his retelling of the story.

Jared's son Enoch has a possible meaning of "initiated or teacher." This possibly has reference to the story told in 1 Enoch, that these heavenly beings began to teach mankind all sorts of hidden knowledge—"the eternal secrets preserved in heaven"—from astronomy and astrology, to aborting a fetus, to warfare (1 Enoch 8:1-3; 9:6; 69:1-13). Whether any of that happened or not, an informed opinion must take into consideration that the same story is told around the world.

Enoch's son Methuselah, usually known for being the oldest named person in the Bible, living an incredible 969 years, has a name that can mean "man of the dart," as in an arrow, a javelin, or even a missile of some kind. In other words, from his name we can gather that warfare is being learned. It is also becoming common place. Of course, this is part of the violence that later brings God to destroy the earth in the Flood, so this isn't speculation.

Methuselah's descendant is named Lamech which means "powerful/destroyer." The impression is that things have gone from bad to terrible. Lamech then has a son and names him Noah. Noah means "rest," because through him the vanity of life, the violence, wickedness and corruption of the earth will come to an end.

For good measure, I should throw in the last few names of the line of Cain, who we get the impression were probably contemporaries with those mentioned here in the line of Seth. Methusael means "asking God for death." His son Lamech, again, means "destroyer/powerful." This is the Lamech who marries two women, murders a man, and arrogantly defies God to come and kill him. Lamech has three sons all known for their cultural achievements: Jabal (father of tent dwellers and livestock), Jubal (father of those who play the lyre and pipe), and Tubal-Cain (forger of metal, perhaps implying weapons). Curiously, much of this is also said in the book of Enoch to have been taught by a group called the Watchers, who in Enoch and other ancient books are just another name for the sons of God. In the Bible, a Watcher is a heavenly angelic being that looks over the affairs of mankind (cf. Dan 4:13, 23). In the Dead Sea Scrolls they were described as tall and serpentine in appearance.[10]

There is a progression in the names moving from innocence to corruption to violence to death to hope. This is the story of our early history. Reading Genesis 6:4 in conjunction with these names (if that is legitimate) shows that the giants had no special regard for one group of humans over another, but waged war against any of us whom they chose. This idea of violence was also part of the traditions handed down by the Jews in their ancient books.[11]

What else can we learn about the giants before the Flood? Moses did not give us a lot of information, but if we read other passages in the Bible together with the Jewish literature circulating in Israel during the time of Jesus, we may be able to discern a few more things. I'm not suggesting that these books necessarily depict history with 100% accuracy, but knowing what they say does tell us how those in Bible times understood it. (If you have a problem using ancient Jewish literature to determine facts about giants, I would challenge you to read the Appendix: Extra-Biblical Literature at this time).

Time and Place of the Giant's "Arrival"

Targum Pseudo-Jonathan has this for Genesis 6:4, "Schamchazai and Uzziel [*Aza'el*], who fell from heaven, were on the earth in those days; and also, after the sons of the Great had gone in with the daughters of men, they bare to them: and these are they who are called men who are of the world, men of names." If you read the Introduction, you will remember that targums are Jewish paraphrases of the Scripture that sometimes elaborate to provide further explanation. Some of this was ancient oral tradition. Who are Schamchazai and Uzziel? According to the even earlier writings, these were the names of two of two hundred sons of God who fell from heaven. 1 Enoch says,

> It came to pass that when the sons of men multiplied, in those days beautiful and fair daughters were born. And the angels, the sons of heaven, saw them and desired them, and said to one another: 'Come! Let us choose for ourselves wives from people, and we will beget for ourselves children.' And Semiaza [also written as Shemhazai] who was their ruler, said to them: 'I fear that you will not desire to do this deed, and I alone will be a debtor of a great sin.' Therefore they all answered him: 'Let us swear an oath and let us all anathematize one another, not to turn away from this plan, until we should complete it and do this deed.' Then they all swore together and anathematized one another by it. And these were the two hundred who descended in the days of Jared to the summit of Mount Hermon, and they called the mountain Hermon, because they swore and anathematized one another by it.
>
> (1 Enoch 6:1-6)

If Jude is correct and this part of the book of Enoch really does remember historical events,[12] then it tells us when the Nephilim first arose on the earth. It says it happened in the day of Jared. There is a word play going on here with "Jared," which as we have seen means "descend." The idea is that his father named him after the incredible events that took place in those days: the descent of the sons of God (also called sons of heaven, angels, and Watchers). Jared was born a minimum of 1,000 years before the flood. This gives plenty of time for the entire earth to become corrupt by the time Noah is called to build the ark.

The location of the descent of these sons of God is Mt. Hermon. Mt. Hermon stands as the highest point in Israel, at 9,320 ft. above sea level. Mt. Hermon is also used in a word play in this passage. Hermon (spelled *kh-r-m-n* without the vowels in Hebrew) is almost identical to *kh-r-m*, the word "anathema." On Mt. Hermon the Watchers cursed themselves. Later on in the days of Moses and Joshua, the *kherem* was called "the ban." This is where Israel was to "devote to destruction" all of the men, women, children, animals, and belongings of the inhabitants of Canaan. We will return to Mt. Hermon again in this book, for in the Bible it is the Grand Central Station of the giants of old.

Giants of Great Height

After this Enoch reports,

> The women became pregnant and bore great giants of three thousand cubits, who devoured the labors of people. And when the people were not able to sustain them, the giants dared (to attack) them, and they devoured the people. And they began to sin with birds and wild animals and reptiles and fish, and to devour one another's flesh, and drink blood. Then the earth appealed against the lawless ones.
>
> (1 Enoch 7:2-6)

The text is obviously corrupt when it says "three thousand cubits," but there are other manuscripts that simply read, "They grew in accordance with their greatness."[13] No one knows how tall the original copy of the book says they were. Clearly, they soared above other men. One passage in Jubilees ("the little Genesis") says that the Rephaim giants who lived after the flood in the land of Gilead were "ten, nine, eight, down to seven cubits tall" (Jub 29:9). That puts them anywhere from 10½ - 15 ft. tall, which is within the range of known height of two of the giants in the Bible who lived after the flood. Amos 2:9 provides partial biblical verification of this saying of the giants after the Flood that their "height was like the height of cedars."

Cannibalism

What Enoch then describes is an unthinkable horror, also reported by the spies who entered the land of Canaan who returned so frightened that they did not care that they would be punished to wander in the wilderness for 40 years because of their unbelief in God's ability to save them. It tells us that these giants were cannibals. "They devoured the people." There is a parallel in the book of Jubilees which reads, "They begat sons the Naphidim, and they were all unlike, and they devoured one another" (Jub 7:22).[14] This is not made-up, but is again verified by the biblical text, for this is exactly what the spies report in Numbers 13:32-33, "The land, through which we have gone to spy it out, is *a land that devours its inhabitants*, and all the people that we saw in it are of great height. And there we saw the Nephilim." According to the Enochian tradition, they became so full of blood-lust that they began to eat one another, even drinking the blood. 1 Enoch 7:5 says, "They began to sin with birds and wild animals and reptiles and fish, and to devour one another's flesh, and drink blood."

Vampires and Giants

There is a curious side-note to this blood-drinking by the giants. Some scholars have suggested that this is the origin of vampire myths that go back to ancient Babylon.[15] Most people think that Bram Stoker made up the legend, but nothing could be further from the truth. In China it is called *giang shi*, a demon who drinks blood. In Peru it is the *pumapmicuc* who sucked blood from sleeping victims. In Greece they were the *empusa*, winged demon-women who lured handsome youths to their deaths to drink their blood and eat their flesh. In India they speak of a vampire who hangs upside down from a tree like a bat. The Maya worshiped a giant blood-sucking creature named *Camazotz*—half man, half bat. The Apache and Comanche Indians speak of the giant cannibal owl. Jews called one version the *Lilith*, the female night-roaming monster that drank the blood of babies[16] (in Chapter 13 I will show you that the Lilith comes up in the OT in some very interesting contexts). An ancient Babylonian spell reads,

> Spirits that *minish* heaven and earth, that minish the land, of giant strength, of giant strength and giant tread, demons like raging bulls, great ghosts, ghosts that break through all houses, demons that have no shame, seven are they! They rage against mankind; they spill their blood like rain, devouring their flesh and sucking their veins."
>
> (Utakki Limnuti Tablet V.Col.IV.10-18, 25-27)[17]

What does each story have in common, besides blood drinking? These vampires are all viewed as *demonic* entities. Vampires are spirits who wander the earth seeking those upon whom they might feed. This is a far cry from the American pop-culture romanticism of the vampire. If you wonder how spirits and demons are related to the giants, keep reading. We will have more to say about this.

Bestiality / Cross-Breeding

Finally, as we saw a moment ago, the ancient text tells us that some kind of sin was committed between the giants and animals. While Enoch probably refers to the *eating* of animal flesh, it cannot be ruled out that this refers to bestiality or even to genetic experiments done upon the brute beasts of the earth. The bestiality idea is definitely connected to the giants in the *Torah* (Law). Leviticus 18:23-24 and 20:15-16 both command Israel not to engage in bestiality.[18] The first begins, "You shall not have intercourse with any animal to be defiled with it, nor shall any woman stand before an animal to mate with it; it is a perversion." The word "perversion" is *tebel*, literally "confusion, violation of nature, or of the divine order,"[19] or an "abominable confusion, contamination."[20] The verse then gives the giant reference (which will be explained more in a coming chapter), "Do not make yourselves unclean by any of these things, for by all these the nations I am driving out before you have become unclean [or "defiled]."

Jubilees seems to confirm that this was one ancient view in its expansion of the Genesis story. "Lawlessness increased on the earth and all flesh corrupted its way, alike men and cattle and beasts and birds and everything that walks on the earth--all of them corrupted their ways and their orders, and they began to devour each other, and lawlessness increased on the earth and every imagination of the thoughts of all men (was) thus evil continually. And God looked upon the earth, and behold it was corrupt, and all flesh had corrupted its orders, and all that were upon the earth had wrought all manner of evil before His eyes" (Jub 5:2-3). Bestiality between the inhabitants and the animals of the land of Canaan is frighteningly similar to the cross-breeding of heavenly men and human women that produced these ogres in the first place.

Here we also find room to run with speculations derived from other ancient stories and depictions that seem to indicate that the ancients understood something about DNA. If you have never come across this idea before, it is stunning. Keep in mind, this is speculation. There is a hint that something strange was going on in the land by the size of the grape cluster carried back to Moses by the 12 spies from the land of Canaan.[21] There is also the strange law referred to in the Introduction about not wearing mixed clothing. The whole verse reads, "You shall keep my statutes. You shall not let your cattle breed with a different kind. You shall not sow your field with two kinds of seed, nor shall you wear a garment of cloth made of two kinds of material" (Lev 19:19). The idea is similar to that of bestiality in that it was an unlawful mixing. The mixing of kinds was obviously a real problem. It was a problem that went against the very core of creation, where God made each after its *own* kind. This law, it should be noted, is found in the middle of the context of the previous laws on bestiality. Therefore, it too is associated with the abominable inhabitants of Canaan.

Confirming that this idea of genetic manipulation is not recent, the Jewish *midrash* *The Book of Jasher*, which claims to be from antiquity, but was first published into English in 1625 (but well before the advent of modern genetic manipulation) says, "And every man [...] corrupted the earth, and the earth was filled with violence. And [...] the sons of men in those days took from the cattle of the earth, the beasts of the field and the fowls of the air, and taught the mixture of animals of one species with the other, in order therewith to provoke the Lord; and God saw the whole earth and it was corrupt, for all flesh had corrupted its ways upon earth, all men and all animals"

(*Jasher* 4:17-18). Along these kinds of highly scientific lines, scholars have noted that the ancient texts even include stories of the taking of an embryo from one womb to another in a kind of ancient alchemy.[22] In modern times, abduction claims made by hundreds of thousands of people say they have been experimented upon and probed. While bizarre, if there is some basis of truth, it could very well be Satanic (probably not alien in the sense we normally think of it) in nature. This would offer rather frightening parallels to more ancient tales.

I'm not going to press this point. Nevertheless, I have found it most curious that many people, both Christian and non-Christian, have seen a relationship between the ancient symbol of the entwining serpents and the modern DNA strand. The old U.S. Army Medical Core logo is familiar.

FIG. 1.1. CADUCEUS

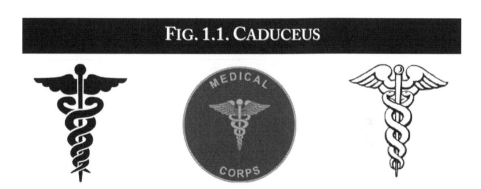

The image is called the caduceus. It depicts two serpents entwined around a sacred pole (tree) which has wings like a bird (seraphim?). Its earliest use goes back over 4,000 years to Babylon where a staff surmounted by two serpentine heads represented the supreme sexual powers of the serpent.[23] We have seen a similar depiction already with regard to the half-serpent, half-human first rulers of China, but you find similar ideas in Egypt, Assyria, Scandinavia and other places as well.

FIG. 1.2. CADUCEUS IN WORLD MYTHOLOGY

FUXI AND NÜWA   **(TOP)**: *"THE SERPENT LORD ENTHRONED" (MESOPOTAMIA, C. 2200 BC).* **(BOTTOM)**: *PERUVIAN TEXTILE (LATE PARACAS, 300-200 BC).*   **(TOP)**: *"LIBATION VASE OF GUDEA"* (NINGISHZIDA C. 2100 BC. **(BOTTOM)**: *QUETZAL-COATL FIGURINE* (PRE-SPANISH CONQUEST).

Curiously, the modern depiction of the caduceus became the rod or "Wand of Hermes" (Mercury) and was said to depict his "patronage of peace, trade, commerce, and communication."[24] However, two things should be noted. First, Hermes is also the god of healing. Though not a demi-god (e.g., a giant like Hercules; Hermes is the son of an adulterous affair between Zeus and Maia the Nymph, who is technically descended from the gods, although nymphs have a lot in common with demons as well), Hermes is etymologically related to Mt. Hermon and in fact his son Pan had a cult at the foot of Mt. Hermon for untold centuries.[25] Along these lines, one of the main names for the giants in the Bible is a word that can mean "healing."[26] The word is *rapha*. The giants are the Rephaim. Also remember, Mt.

Hermon is where the sons of God were said to have descended in the days of Jared. Second, at least as early as the 3rd cent. A.D., oculists (eye physicians) were using the caduceus as a seal, thus connecting it to medicine,[27] taking us full circle back to Hermes.

When given this kind of a history, it is extremely interesting to compare these figures with the DNA double-helix. In fact, the two depictions are easily found side by side in a search on Google Images. Given the uncanny resemblances and the incredibly bizarre history that is spoken of in Genesis 6 and around the world, it is not difficult to see why some people make such speculations.

FIG. 1.3. DNA: DOUBLE HELIX

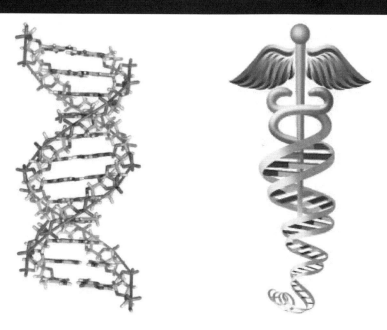

Chapter 2: The Giant of Babel

And Chus [Cush] begot Nebrod [Nimrod]:
He began to be a giant upon the earth.

Gen 10:8 (LXX)

The Curse of Canaan

Genesis 6:1-4 is the gateway to the story of the Great Flood. Like the tale of the giants, this epic is widely known. In fact, it has been told by at least 270 cultures on every continent and every major Island group on the planet.[1] This isn't a recounting of the Biblical story from Christianized peoples; it is their own primordial memories of the same epic event as remembered by their own cultures.

FIG. 2.1. WORLD FLOOD TRADITIONS

□ : 1

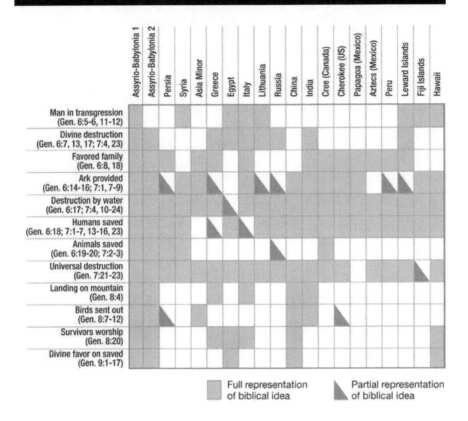

FIG. 2.2. COMPARISON OF EVENTS IN FLOOD TRADITIONS

The Flood was sent to wipe out "all flesh" from the face of the earth. It succeeded. Everything on land and in the air was obliterated, save that which was safe inside the ark where Noah and his family were hidden by God. After the Flood, when Noah leaves the ark behind, we learn very quickly that the Flood did not succeed in eliminating sin. Of course, it was never sent for that purpose. The point I'm about to make is that Noah was most definitely not a perfect man.

The claim is sometimes made that Noah was sinless because, "Noah was perfect in his generations" (Gen 6:9).[2] As we saw in the Introduction, perfection does not refer to Noah's moral quality—God never chooses a person and shows grace to them because they "earned" it. Rather, it refers to his physical purity in the same way that a sacrificial lamb had to be physically perfect. Noah was unblemished. That is, he was fully human, the untainted seed of the woman. Noah walked with God because he had first found grace in God's eyes (Gen 6:8).

Noah was still a sinner. The first (and last) thing we learn about him after leaving the ark and sacrificing to the LORD, is that he builds a vineyard, gets drunk, and this allows his son Ham to slip into his tent and have sex with his mother. This last part is often debated, because the passage doesn't say this is so many words. But when we let Scripture interpret itself, we come to see that this is what it has to mean, because the language to "see a father's nakedness" always means to have sex with another man's wife.[3]

The reason I bring this story up is because a strange thing occurs when Noah comes to his senses. It relates directly to the giants. He curses his "son," but it is not Ham. Instead, he curses his grandson ... Canaan. The reason why, in my opinion, is because Canaan was the incestuous child of a union between Noah's wife and Noah's son. Stop right here and notice that there is a similarity to the events of Genesis 6:1-4. Both contain unholy unions and unholy children are born from them. The difference here is that we have little reason to believe that Ham was anything less than fully human. Noah's curse on Canaan becomes the foundation of the hostility that will ensue over the next 2,000 plus years between Israel and the Canaanites who live in the Promised Land. In one form or another, it is still going on to this day.

Noah does something else. He blesses his other two sons: Japheth and Shem. In fact, the promised Seed of Eve is narrowed through the line of Shem in Noah's blessing to him. Eventually, Abraham will be the chosen descendant of Shem. He will be blessed by God and become a blessing to all the nations of the earth. Noah's blessing brings a convergence of Shem's descendants and those of Canaan. "Blessed be the LORD, the God of Shem; and let Canaan be his servant" (Gen 9:26). To put this all another way, the hostilities foretold to Eve are being narrowed down to those who come from the line of Canaan and those who come from the line of Shem. By the time of the great exodus out of Egypt, this will become crucial to the overall story of the Bible.

Nimrod the Giant Hunter

Let's go back to Ham for a moment. Ham has several descendants. His sons are named Cush, Egypt, Put, and Canaan (Gen 10:6). We've talked about Canaan; now let's follow the line of Cush. The sons of Cush were Seba, Havilah, Sabtah, Raamah, Sabteca, and a fellow named Nimrod. The information on Nimrod in the Bible is scant. It is found in Genesis 10:8-12.

> [8] Cush fathered Nimrod; he was the first on earth to be a mighty man. [9] He was a mighty hunter before the LORD. Therefore it is said, "Like Nimrod a mighty hunter before the LORD." [10] The beginning of his kingdom was Babel, Erech, Accad, and Calneh, in the land of Shinar. [11] From that land he went into Assyria and built Nineveh, Rehoboth-Ir, Calah, and [12] Resen between Nineveh and Calah; that is the great city.

From this passage we learn that Nimrod is situated in Mesopotamia.[4] His sphere of influence was based in the south (Babylonia), and later extended to the north (Assyria) at least as far as Nineveh, the famous city in the book of Jonah.

One important clue about Nimrod's identity is found in the phrase "a mighty hunter." We have seen the word "mighty" before; it is the word *gibbor* (*gibborim* refers to a group, as "-*im*" is the plural ending of Hebrew words). The ESV translates it "mighty" in both passages. The LXX reads "giant" (*gigas,* the singular form of *gigantes*), saying that Nimrod "began to be a giant upon the earth." Just like the ESV, the Greek is consistently translating the word in Genesis 6:4 and Genesis 10:9. Since the LXX translated both *gibborim* and *nephilim* as *gigantes* in Genesis 6:4, this is strong evidence that very early on it was thought that Nimrod was a giant. Before we can say any more about this, I would like to see more evidence than just this word.

In Gen 10:9 Nimrod has some kind of a relationship to Yahweh. The question is of what kind? Most translations say something like Nimrod was "a mighty hunter *before* the LORD." What would it mean to be a mighty hunter before the LORD? Many think of it as a positive attribute, that Nimrod was a hero of the chase who hunted wild game and that this was a gift of God's grace.[5]

There are several problems with this interpretation. For one, it does not seem to make a lot of sense. Why would being a good hunter be a gift of God's grace, and why would this trait be something to be singled out in a mere mortal? This is, after all, the only trait of any of the 70 people(s) mentioned in the entire chapter. He could shoot a deer with a bow and arrow? So what?

Next, *gibborim* and "men of renown" seem to be viewed as evil beings in Genesis 6:4. They are one of the reasons God brought the Flood. If that is true, what justification in the text allows us to see Nimrod as a *good* hero? Certainly it is not his lineage, which comes from Ham. Nor is it his association with Babel, the great anti-city of the Bible. Nor is it the fact that he is a city builder, for though cities are not always viewed negatively in the Bible, up to this point the only city builder has been Enoch the son of Cain (Gen 4:17). Nor is one of the popular etymologies of his name helpful. Many people think that Nimrod comes from the word *m-r-d* which means "rebel."

It may be possible to identify Nimrod in the pagan cultures, and this might demonstrate a positive relationship to Yahweh. After all, Moses says that this character was very well known in ancient times, still having a proverbial saying attached to him many centuries later. Because of this, scholars have gone looking to the stories of the Middle East for the identification of this person. The problem is, outside of Israel, the name Nimrod is not known as such. That doesn't stop people from trying.

Throughout the ages, Nimrod has been identified as some pretty remarkable figures: *Zoroaster*, *Marduk* the main god of the Babylonian creation story, Hercules, Orion, and an Assyrian god named Ninurta. The last three heroes are often said to depict the same historic person. Osiris in Egypt, Thor in Scandinavia, and the Hopi Indian god of the underworld Masau'u are also sometimes linked to Orion, which, if also identified with Nimrod, would make him truly world-renown (remembering, of course, that the nations were dispersed after Babel).

There is one character in Assyrian mythology that many scholars see as most resembling the little we know about Nimrod: Ninurta—Lord of Earth. Some have suggested that Ninurta is derived through this transformation: $*nwrt > *nmrt > nmrd$.[6] If not his name, it is his extracurricular activities that really fuel the speculation. Like Nimrod, Ninurta was a mighty hunter. His exploits were famous in ancient times. He is said to have gained eleven trophies including a seven-headed serpent, a terrible lion, a buck or stag, the mythological Anzu bird, a large crab, and a bull-man. These stories are so similar to the 12 labors of Hercules, that many scholars think the two figures are the same person. Among his quests, Hercules killed the *Hydra*, the *Nemean Lion*, the *Cerynean Hind*, the *Stymphalian Birds*, a crab that assisted the Hydra, and the *Cretan Bull*.[7] (It is curious that Osiris, mentioned above, is son of heaven: Nut, and earth: Geb. He is said to be the god of the heavens and the underworld. When viewed from the 12 constellations, which proceed around the earth night and day, there is a bull: Taurus; a crab: Cancer; a lion: Leo; and other figures that correspond to the labors of Hercules). The thing about these two heroes is that they had positive relationships with their divine fathers (Ninurta to Enil and Hercules to Zeus). Both fathers are the head gods of their respective pantheons. Thus, if Nimrod is related to them, the argument goes, we should see Nimrod in a positive light.

FIG. 2.3. ORION AND OSIRIS

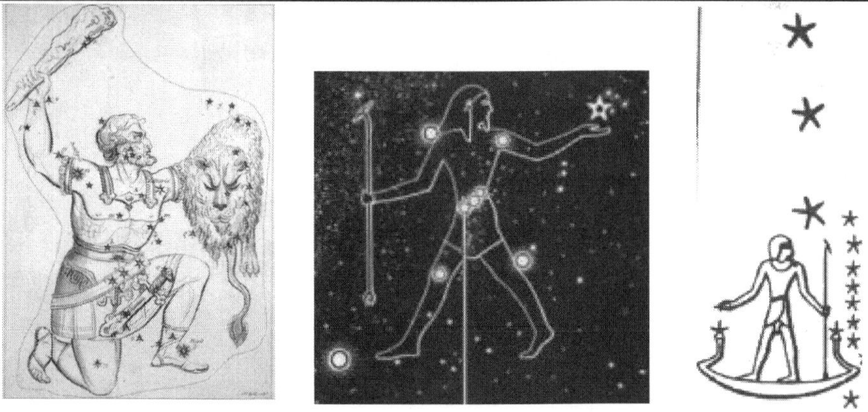

Greco-Roman Orion, depicted with club   Osiris with spear-like object and Orion's Belt

FIG. 2.4. HERCULES AND NINURTA

Hercules wearing the lion skin
Boston 99.538, Attic bilingual amphora,
ca. 525-500
Photograph, Museum of Fine Arts, Boston.

Ninurta pursues Anzu B.C.
Stone sculpture of Ninurta, Nimrud, Iraq
Drawing: Austen Henry Layard (1853)

The problem with this "son of a god" interpretation is that Nimrod is said to descend from Cush, not Yahweh. Cush does not appear in any way in the Bible to be a heavenly figure like a god. He is just the son of Ham who was the son of Noah. So why think that Nimrod was a god worshiped by the pagans? Many have taken this argument and run with it the other way, concluding that Nimrod was nothing but a mortal, which of course is possible.

But let us think about this for a moment. As we come to later passages in the Bible, we see that giants are indeed on the earth after the Flood. This is an indisputable fact. They had to get here somehow. Furthermore, these post-Flood giants are not just tall people. They are said to have come from two groups of ancestors, both of which are viewed as semi-divine *in the Bible*. One of these is the Nephilim of Genesis 6:4. The other group are the Rephaim.

Given these basic facts, there are all kinds of possibilities as to how they could have gotten there in ways that do not contradict the Bible. To speculate a bit, we could imagine, as many Jews did, that some of the Nephilim before the Flood actually made it through the Deluge alive. For instance, they say that Og, a famous giant of the Bible, made it through by holding onto Noah's Ark. To my mind, this solution does not do justice to the fact that the Flood destroyed "all flesh" upon the earth. So I personally rule this out as implausible.

Perhaps a better solution is that genetic manipulation was going on after the Flood. This could also help explain how the gigantic cluster of grapes brought back to Moses by the 12 spies (Num 13:23) came into being.[8] If such business occurred prior to the Flood, this information could have been known by someone like Ham who then transmitted it to his descendants, especially if he was godless and longed for an earth like it was before God destroyed it. Curiously, some have speculated that this is exactly what happened to Nimrod. The grammar allows for this translation, "Nimrod began to become a giant."[9] In other words, he was a willing participant in a grotesque genetic experiment. This kind of conjecture is pretty far out there, but given what we can do today, it might be plausible. In fact, the more you learn about the subject of genetic manipulation, the less you realize you want to know about it. Only if we have a presupposed bias against this kind of a thing from the start (because of a worldview like Darwinism for instance), will we be prevented from at least entertaining its possibility.

Still another solution is that another group of the sons of God fell after the Flood and began doing similar kinds of things that their brothers did prior to it. It could be that it was taking place in Nimrod's day. This could have been sexual and/or genetic in nature.

At any rate, if Nimrod's father is human, how could we account for nephilimism (for lack of a better word) in Nimrod? One could suggest that Nimrod's line is incomplete. In Hebrew there is no word for "grandpa" or "great grandfather." So there could be gaps that would allow for a fall of angelic beings to come to Nimrod's mother, while his ancestor Cush was entirely human. Again, this is highly speculative, but the ancients who were wrestling with the very same questions didn't seem too troubled by the speculation. The point is that there are ways to conceive of Nimrod's gigantism and demi-god status without contradicting the text.

We move to firmer ground by returning to the Bible. There is quite possibly more information that points to Nimrod being a *demigod*. The first is 2 Kings 19:37. The passage refers to Sennacherib king of Assyria returning to Nineveh (the city built by Nimrod). It says, "It came about as he was worshiping in the house of Nisroch his god ..." Nisroch has been identified as another name for Ninurta[10] (like many rulers in history, perhaps Nimrod had several names), and/or as a corruption of the word Nimrod.[11] If this is the case, then it is probable that Nimrod was at least semi-divine, because ancient peoples did not worship mere mortals.

The second place of interest is Job 38:31, "Can you bind the chains of the Pleiades or loose the cords of Orion"? This verse, which seems so innocuous when you just read it like this, is actually pretty fascinating. The word translated into "Orion" is the Hebrew word *kesil*. *Kesil* was translated by the Jews at the Dead Sea with the Aramaic word *naphil* which, as we saw in the Introduction, is a word that means "giant," and itself possibly derives from the Hebrew *nephilim*. This same verse was also translated by the Syriac church to the word *gabbara*, which is that languages equivalent of *gibborim*. There is an

Akkadian word equivalent to both of these which means "the broad man, giant."[12] So you could translate the verse, "Can you bind the chains of the Pleiades or loose the cords of the giant"?

The Orion/Nimrod association is curious. In Greek culture, Orion was the "hunter ever famed" (Homer, *Odyssey* 11.397) and "The huge Orion" (*Odyssey* 11.721). Odysseus sees him hunting in the underworld with a bronze club, as a great slayer of animals. In other words, he was known as a giant hunter just like Nimrod. Thus, there are traditions that have equated the two throughout the centuries.[13] The idea, according to some is that Job's reference to Orion is one of "a giant who, confiding foolishly in his strength, and defying the Almighty, was, as a punishment for his arrogance, bound for ever in the sky."[14] Is this a cryptic reference to Nimrod, the hero of old?

One more possibility of the meaning of the name Nimrod has associations with Canaanite religion and giants. Though the Bible does not say that Nimrod extended his reign any further west than Nineveh, there are legends aplenty that he came all the way to Lebanon (ancient Phoenicia) where he is said to have built a most remarkable structure called Baalbek and was finally buried in Damascus (in western Syria).

Baalbek is in the heart of Philistine country, about 25 miles east of modern Beirut. Its origins are very old. The complex there has been built and rebuilt by various civilizations. It boasts some of the largest cut stones on earth. Three (known as the trilithon), were set into place midway up a retaining wall which acts to level the entire compound. They weigh around 800 tons each. The two largest stones still sit at the quarry a mile or so away. One weighs an estimated 1,000 tons; the is estimated at an unbelievable 1,200 tons (that's 2.4 million lbs., see Figure 16) making it the largest hewn stone on earth.

Giants of the Bible

There was an Arabic manuscript found at Baalbek that reads, "After the flood, when Nimrod reigned over Lebanon, he sent giants to rebuild the fortress of Baalbek, which was so named in honour of Baal, the god of the Moabites and worshipers of the sun."[15] In the legends, Nimrod himself was said to be a giant.[16] These legends surrounding Baalbek and Nimrod probably confuse the earlier pre-Roman and Canaanite site with the later Roman reconstruction which was most likely responsible for building and placing the megalithic stones.[17] It is his association with giants and Baal that is our purpose here.

As the name suggests, Baal was a chief god worshiped here. The meaning of Nimrod associated with Baal has been proposed: "Panther of Hadd" (Hadd = Baal).[18] Since we do not have solid evidence that Nimrod's kingdom extended this far, the stories of him in these places have to remain in the realm of fiction. The point of mentioning them is to give you a flavor for the many stories of him in history which say he was a giant.[19]

FIG. 2.5. MEGALITHS OF BAALBEK, LEBANON

Trilithon	"Stone of the Pregnant Woman"	Great Stone
(est. 800 tons each)	(est. 1,000 tons)	(est. 1,200 tons)

For these many reasons, it is better to see Nimrod as being a mighty hunter "against" the LORD. Both the Hebrew word and the Greek translation can be interpreted "against."[20] If the *gibborim* of

Genesis 6:4 were violent (and it clearly seems that they were), then for Nimrod to be both a *gibbor* and a hunter would almost certainly associate him with violence, at least against animals, but possibly also against human beings.

The Tower of Babel

From the passage on Nimrod, we see two important things about his kingdom. First, "The beginning of his kingdom was Babel." Second, this was "in the land of Shinar." This foreshadowing is the reason so many people think that the person behind the building of the Tower of Babel was Nimrod. Babel was *his* city.

The story of Babel occurs immediately after the genealogies of the sons of Noah end (Gen 11:1-9). It tells us that the whole earth had one language. Then as the people migrated from the east, they found a plain in the land of Shinar and settled there. Immediately they sought to build for themselves both "a city" and "a tower" (Gen 11:4). Note, they did not only build a tower, but also the city. Because of the famous arrogance of this episode where they said, "Let us build a tower with its top in the heavens, and let us make a name for ourselves, lest we be dispersed over the face of the whole earth," God came down and confused their language. Therefore the name of "the city" was Babel (Gen 11:8-9). This means that Nimrod has to have been the architect behind the whole sordid affair.

Take notice of the motive for the Tower. "Let us make a name for ourselves." Now compare this to the Nephilim of Genesis 6:4. They were the famous "men of renown." "Renown" is literally "the name." It (*shem*) is the same word in both passages, thus linking the Nephilim, Nimrod, and the Tower of Babel together. Did Nimrod seek to align himself with the Nephilim of old?

The Giants and Babel

Let's look at the legends that exist regarding the building of this fabled tower. Consider the work of Pseudo-Eupolemus (150 BC) whom Eusebius (the first great Church historian, c. 263-339 AD) quoted.

> The Assyrian city of Babylon was first founded by those who escaped the Flood. They were giants, and they built the tower well known in history. When the tower was destroyed by God's power, these giants were scattered over the whole earth."[21]

The Sibylline Oracle to which Josephus refers[22] has something similar. First it equates Noah's three sons to the three Titans (giants):[23] Cronos, Titan and Japetus, where Japetus is the Greek equivalent of Japheth. It says they ended up fighting a great war after the Tower fell. The languages were confused. The three sons were given equal realms to rule on the condition that they would not fight one another. But due to the treachery of Cronus (Shem?) against Titan (Ham?)—who had bound him not to have any sons so that he could reign when Cronus died—a war arose between the seventy sons[24] of Titan (who used to kill any male born to Cronus but let the females live) and the sons of Cronus. According to the *Sybil*, parties were completely destroyed, and soon thereafter the great kingdoms of men rose up (Egypt, Persia, Babylon, etc.).[25]

These stories clearly link giants with the Tower of Babel. Pretty strange, right? How about this one found in ... *Central America*:

> A Flood tradition of the Toltecs mentioned by Ixtlihochitl states that after the Deluge [giants] built a *zacuali* of great height to preserve them in the

event of future deluges. After this their tongue became confused, and not understanding each other, they went to different parts of the world."[26]

In fact, the natives of this part of the world have several stories, where giants survived the Flood and build their impressive pyramids only to bring down the gods' anger, disperse them, and confuse their languages.[27]

We move across the world to India for the next story. The Hindus remember the Asuras, evil beings variously translated as demons or giants.[28] They seek to imitate the great fire altar of heaven and "ascend to the sky." This altar is said to rise from the earth to Heaven. These enemies of the heavenly gods, tried to imitate it, but their undertaking came to nothing, as the gods overthrew it by taking away the foundation of bricks.[29] As you can see, not only is the Tower of Babel story told around the world, so is the association of it *with giants*.

Let us stop for a moment and catch our breath. I want you to think about something. I have long been intrigued how many Christians are quick to use the plethora of Flood stories throughout the world as arguments against *uniformitarian* science to demonstrate that there really was a Great Deluge. Yet, many of these same people scoff at any idea that the equally wide spread stories of the giants could ever be taken seriously. This is even more ironic when we consider that these stories of the Flood and/or Tower include stories of the giants, and still more ironic since there is significant reason from the Bible itself to see that this is in fact quite plausible in a biblical worldview.

Why did they build this thing? Was it simply because they wanted to see how high they could get? Are modern sky-scrappers the equivalent of the Tower of Babel? Maybe they were so close to Neanderthals that they actually thought if they could go high enough they could somehow build their way into heaven? I know a lot of children have this idea in mind when they are told about this story. In fact, neither one of these is the truth. What was taking place at the tower was deeply religious. It was based upon an age-old idea that through this tower, they would be able to interact with heavenly beings.

The Ziggurat of Babel

To understand this, you have to know what the Tower of Babel was. It was not a sky-scrapper like the Empire State Building. The Tower of Babel was an ancient *ziggurat*. Ziggurats are ancient temples made to look like mountains. They are found all over the world. When you understand what is going on here, it will blow your mind.

"Ziggurat" can be defined very simply as "a staged tower for which the stages were consciously constructed."[30] To reach the top, you would walk up the *simmiltu* or "stairway." Recall the language of the Tower of Babel, the most famous ziggurat of history. "Let us build ourselves a ... tower with its top in the heavens" (Gen 11:4). Not coincidentally, the *Akkadian* word *ziqqurat* means "to be high."[31] Here are a few examples of ziggurats from around the world.

FIG. 2.6. STAGED ZIGGURATS

Artistic Rendition: Tower of Babel

FIG. 2.7. ZIGGURATS OF THE MIDDLE EAST

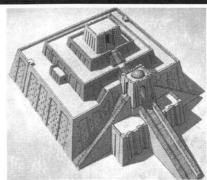

Top: Ur-Nammu (2,100 B.C.?) in Ur, Iraq Oldest Reconstructed Ziggurat in the World;
Bottom: Ziggurat of Chogha-Zanbil (1,250 B.C.?). Model: Rijksmuseum van Oudheden, Leiden (Holland).

FIG. 2.8. ZIGGURAT OF NORTH AMERICA

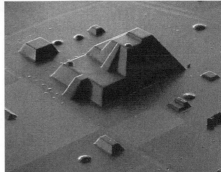

Monks Mound (Cahokia Mounds State Historic Site), Collinsville, Illinois

FIG. 2.9. ZIGGURATS OF AFRICA AND ASIA

Pyramid of Djoser (Step Pyramid) 2630-2611 B.C
Photo by hiro008

Goguryeo's Pyramid Korea, 500 A.D.
Photo by Auws

FIG. 2.10A. ZIGGURATS OF SOUTH AMERICA

Above: Pyramid of the Sun Teotihuacán, Mexico;
Below: Pyramid of the Moon, Teotihuacán, Mexico
Models: Wolfgang Sauber

FIG. 2.10B. ZIGGURATS OF SOUTH AMERICA (CONT.)

Above: Temple of Kukulkan, Summer Solstice Note: shadow of the serpent (left) only occurs on the solstice. Chichen Itza, Yucatan.
Upper Right: Temple from Google Earth; Serpent Head at the base of the Temple;
Lower Left: Pyramid of the Niches (66ft. high), El Tajin.
Lower Right:Tikal (Temple of the Jaguar), Chichen Itza.

FIG. 2.11. ZIGGURATS OF THE FUTURE

Plans of the Modern Day "Ziggurat Project," Dubai, UAE.

Giants of the Bible

What did the *ziggurat* signify? The only truly objective way to know is to study the names given to them. The oldest ziggurats of Syria and Iraq still have the names recorded on tablets.[32]

ZIGGURATS OF BABYLON

Ziggurat Name	Ziggurat Location
Temple of the Foundation of Heaven and Earth	Babylon
Temple of the Wielder of the 7 Decrees of Heaven and Earth	Borsippa
Temple of the Mountain Breeze	Nippur
Temple of the Stairway to Pure Heaven	Sippar
Temple of the Exalted Mountain	Ehursagkalamma
Temple of the Foundation of Heaven and Earth	Dilbat
Temple which Links Heaven and Earth	Larsa
Temple of the Ziggurat, Exalted Dwelling Place	Kish
Temple of Exalted Splendor	Enlil
Temple of the god Nanna	Kutha
Temple of the god Dadia	Akkad

In these names we can clearly identify the idea of a mountain, a mirror, a stairway between heaven and earth, and the home of the god(s).

Think for a moment about where the gods were said to live in pagan mythology. It was upon Mt. Olympus that Zeus would hold council with the twelve Olympian gods. The Titans, the adversaries of the Olympians, lived on Mt. Othrys until Zeus overthrew them.

Like the Flood, the Tower story, and the giants, this theme is also replicated around the world. In China, two gods (Holy Shu and Yü Lü) live upon a beautiful mountain called *Tu-shuo*.[33] Another mountain called Kun-Lun is the "mountain abode of the celestial lords."[34] In Egypt, upon *Ta-tenen* the Ennead (the nine) gods meet and hold court.[35] In India it was upon Mount Meru that Lord Brahma and the Devas[36] (these are not attention starved American pop stars, but *demigods* or angels) would hold council. In Scandinavia, Heimdall would regularly gather with the gods in his hall called *Himinbjörg* ("Sky Mountain")[37] where they would drink delicious honey-mead. Day after day he would sit there guarding the bridge from Hill-Giants. Even in North America you find *Nunne Chaha*, the Great Hill upon which the god Esaugetuh Emissee ("Master of Breath") resided.[38]

We find a similar idea in the Bible. Zion and Sinai are both referred to as the mountain or abode of God, his temple and his house (cf. Ex 3:1; Ps 68:15-17; Isa 2:2-3; Joel 3:17; Micah 3:12; Heb 12:22). It was from Mt. Sinai that God met with Moses and gave him his law. Curiously, the Bible also says that there were angels there too (Deut 33:2-4; Acts 7:53; Gal 3:19). These angels are referred to as the *divine council* (Ps 82:1).

The idea of the *ziggurat* as a mirror is also significant. What is it a mirror of? Heaven. Jesus himself taught us to pray "on earth as it is in heaven" (Matt 6:10). Jesus has the correct take on a very old, but often twisted, idea. It is not up to man to replicate heaven in an attempt to reach up to it. It is up to God to bring heaven down to you. Nevertheless, you can get an idea of how the ancients also understood the basic premise by looking at the layout of some ancient complexes and how they seem to mimic the constellations.

FIG. 2.12. EARTHLY MIRRORS OF THE HEAVENS

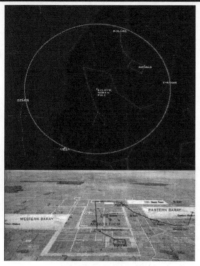

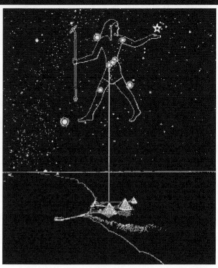

Ankor Thom, Cambodia
Jim Alison

Pyramids of Egypt Reflecting Orion the Hunter
(The Nile is the Milky Way)

The picture (above right) of the pyramid complex at Giza is particularly of interest, since the complex seems to be a mirror of Orion (Osiris) the Hunter.[39] Along the same lines, there are other interesting hypotheses that on the other side of the world, the ancestors of the Hopi Indians and Mexican builders did the same thing.[40]

Speculation about ancient complexes is one thing, but we know that ancient peoples tried to replicate heaven in their earthly temples from their own words. The *Enuma Elish* (6.113) describes *Marduk's* temple, "He shall make on earth the counterpart of what he has brought to pass in heaven." Similarly, Pharaoh Ramses III (1195-1164) wrote about his god, "I made for thee an august house in Nubia… the likeness of the heavens." He also said, "I made for thee an august palace… like the great house of [the god] Atum which is in heaven."[41]

The idea of a *ziggurat*, that it is a holy residence for God, has some similarities with the design of Solomon's Temple, which has several corresponding architectural traits in common with Ziggurats, including the tiered levels and stairways.

FIG. 2.13. REPRESENTATION OF SOLOMON'S TEMPLE

Solomon's Temple and Altar

The idea of a stairway is important. The Hebrew word for a stairway is *sullam*. It is related to the word *simmiltu*.[42] It occurs only one time in the Bible, in Genesis 28:12. Unfortunately, it often gets translated as "ladder." It refers to something that Jacob saw in a dream. He says, "The top of it reached to heaven. And behold, the angels of God were ascending and descending on it! And behold, the LORD stood above it. . . This is none other than the house of God, and this is the gate of heaven" (Gen 28:12-13, 17). Notice in the following pictures of a famous *ziggurat* in Iraq and how it appears to be a stairway to heaven (Led Zeppelin didn't invent the idea).

FIG. 2.14. STAIRWAY TO HEAVEN

Central Stairway at Ur-Nammu

Like Mt. Sinai, angels are here also ascending and descending upon this stairway that Jacob saw in his dream. Like Sinai, this too is the "house of God." This was none other than a gateway, a place where the visible and invisible worlds meet. Thus, all of the signs point to this idea—what Jacob saw was a kind of *ziggurat*.[43]

The purpose of the Tower of Babel thus seems to have been to make some kind of forbidden contact with the invisible world, with the sons of God who had previously descended upon another mountain, Mt. Hermon. Here, then, is our link between Nimrod and the sons of God, which seems to be necessary to relate him to the Nephilim. Through sacred astronomy and ancient astrology, through the architecture and the principle of the mirror of heaven, we can now see the Tower story in a much more dubious light. This was not about seeing how tall they could make a skyscraper. Neither were these people metaphorically trying to "work" their way to heaven. They were trying to bring heaven down through powerful magic. They knew well about the ancient Genesis 6 story. They wanted to make contact with the gods of old.

Curiously, God comes down,[44] and sees what they are doing (Gen 11:7). In an ironic way, their attempt worked. But they did not bargain for what they received, which was not power or fame, but a curse, a dispersion, and the end of their unified attempts at trying to breach the heavenly domain, to force an intersection between heaven and earth on their terms. What we will find after Babel, are scattered, fragmented, incomplete attempts to contact the other world (to reach up to heaven), and while those attempts still rest upon ancient knowledge, nothing like the concerted power of all people together takes place again, at least not until the very end of time.

Returning to the beginning of our chapter, long prior to this end of time, something foreshadowing its culmination occurs in God's statement to Shem. Shem, as we have seen, is the word "name," but it is also the name of a son of Noah. God tells Shem in the story immediately preceding the Tower of Babel that Canaan will be his servant and that he would be the one through whom the promises to Eve would come (Gen 9:26-27). Indeed, it will not be the people of Babel who will make a name for themselves, but God who will make a name for himself through Shem—the Name.

Chapter 3: Abram and the Giant Wars

They made war.

Gen 14:2

The Line of Canaan

Babel does not stop the spread of the giants or their desire for world domination. Very quickly we see them spread from one person (Nimrod) to entire clans that are waging wars throughout the Middle East. In fact, it only takes three chapters for them to come back into view. Genesis 14 preserves for us an ancient story of the wars of the giants. The groundwork for these wars is laid in the chapter before Babel, in Genesis 10.

Genesis 10 is the famous "Table of Nations." When you don't know what's going on here, it makes for a long boring list. It gives seventy names,[1] many of which are not individuals but people groups.[2] We spent an entire chapter on just one of these names: Nimrod. Now we need to take note of a few more. If you spend the time to look into this, you will be rewarded with great understanding of coming events.

Like Nimrod, all the names I want to look at here come from the lineage of Ham. Ham is one of three children of Noah. The genealogy gives us four children of Ham: Cush (from whom Nimrod sprang), Mizraim (that is the Egyptians), Put, and Canaan. Canaan, of course, was the son cursed by Noah after the incident in the tent. It is Canaan's line to which we want to pay particular attention.

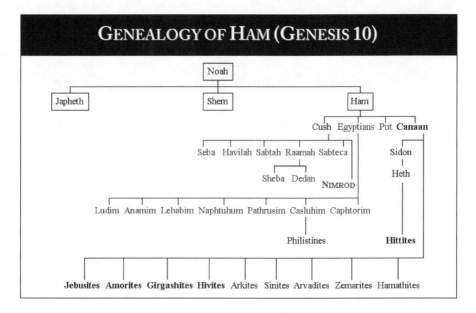

Canaan is the father of the infamous Canaanites. These are very important people in the Bible. According to Herodotus and other early historians, the Canaanites first lived near the Cushites (from whom Nimrod is descended), their brother race, on the western banks of the Erythraean Sea (Persian Gulf), south of Iraq on the eastern side of Saudi Arabia.[3] Only after long years of war did they flee this land, move west, and settle in *the already inhabited* land of Canaan. These Canaanites seem to have mixed with the indigenous "peoples" of the land and the place became known as the land of Canaan.

The name "Canaan" tells us something important. It can mean "to be brought low."[4] In a nutshell, this *is* the story of the giants. The name is *apropos*, for Canaan is the ancestor of most of the giants mentioned in Scripture. Another option is a "trafficker" (a harsher term than the possible "trader"). Often we speak of human trafficking as in illegal trading for the purposes of slavery or sexual exploitation. Does this tell us anything about what kind of people these were?

Though there are many descendants of Canaan mentioned in the Table of Nations, only one son is mentioned by name. This is Sidon. The city of Sidon was famous throughout biblical history and continues with this name to this day. It is actually located in the same nation as Baalbek (see pp. 72-73). Sidon had a son named Heth. Heth was the father of the Hittites. Both Heth and Hittite mean "dread" or "fear." The Hittite Empire ranged all the way from modern Turkey (the NT Galatia) around and down the Mediterranean Sea to Canaan and the city of Hebron (Gen 23:1-20).

The Table mentions nine more descendants of Canaan, all are groups named after famous sons. Five we know very little about (Arkites, Sinites, Arvadites, Zemarites, Hamathites). Some of their names, however, are illustrative. Arkite can mean "to gnaw" (cannibals?). Arvadite can mean "I shall break loose." Hamathite can mean "fortress" or "furious" or putting them together "enclosure of wrath."

The other four peoples are infamous throughout the Old Testament. These are the Jebusites, Amorites, Girgashites, and Hivites. Along with the Canaanites, Hittites, and a group called the Perizzites, these four are listed together in three different passages (Deut 7:1; Josh 3:10; Josh 24:11). Together they make up seven nations "greater and stronger" than Israel. (You can find at least three of the four listed with the Canaanites and Hittites another 15 times).[5]

Again, let's look at the names. An Amorite is a "talker" or "slayer," and it seems to be a term that can stand in for many of the other tribes.[6] Jebusite means "treading down" (because they were tall?) or "polluted" (an idea we looked at regarding the mixing of species in the Introduction).[7] Girgashite means "driven out." Hivite has the same consonants as a Hebrew word for snake (*chivvi*) and thus may be referred to as the serpent clan,[8] reminding us of the serpentine Gigantes of Greek stories. If the names tell us anything, these peoples were ruthless fierce warriors who brought dread with them and trampled down everything in their paths. Undoubtedly, many of these people were of normal size and stature, until they began mixing with the giants of the land. Then, due to breeding with giants, at least a few of them likewise began to exhibit gigantic traits.

After listing these tribes, the Table of Nations subsumes them all under the name Canaanite (Gen 10:18) and then tells us the extent of their territory. It extends to the north into modern Lebanon and moves south, taking up the upper two thirds of ancient Israel. Thus, the Land of Milk and Honey—otherwise known as the Promised Land—was in earlier days called Canaan (cf. Gen 11:31), because this is where the Canaanites settled.

ANCIENT LAND OF CANAAN

Abraham and the Giants

The Call of Abram

Obviously, if these people settled in Canaan, this is the primary reason why they are singled out in the Table of Nations. They will end up playing a large role in the history of Israel. We first begin to see this in the life of Abraham.

Born "Abram," the most famous Patriarch came from the land of Babylon (called Chaldea, in the middle of southern Iraq), in the city of Ur (which today is a vast wasteland in the middle of the Iraqi desert). When his brother Haran died, his father Terah packed up and headed northwest to the modern day border or Syria and Turkey where they settled and appear to have named a city after the dead boy. Abram was called from this place by the LORD in a vision. He too packed up, and at the age of 75 headed southwest to the land of Canaan and the valley of the giants. A more frightening prospect for a faithful servant of God is difficult to imagine.

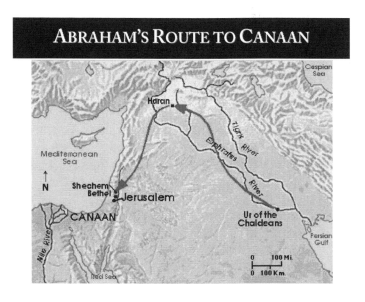

ABRAHAM'S ROUTE TO CANAAN

Four Great Kings

We pick up the story in Genesis 14.

> [1] In the days of Amraphel king of Shinar, Arioch king of Ellasar,
> Chedorlaomer king of Elam, and Tidal king of Goiim, [2] these kings
> made war with Bera king of Sodom, Birsha king of Gomorrah, Shinab
> king of Admah, Shemeber king of Zeboiim, and the king of Bela (that
> is, Zoar). [3] And all these joined forces in the Valley of Siddim (that is,
> the Salt Sea). [4] Twelve years they had served Chedorlaomer, but in the
> thirteenth year they rebelled. [5] In the fourteenth year Chedorlaomer and
> the kings who were with him came and defeated the Rephaim in
> Ashteroth-karnaim, the Zuzim in Ham, the Emim in Shaveh-
> kiriathaim, [6] and the Horites in their hill country of Seir as far as El-
> paran on the border of the wilderness. [7] Then they turned back and
> came to En-mishpat (that is, Kadesh) and defeated all the country of the
> Amalekites, and also the Amorites who were dwelling in Hazazon-
> tamar.

This chapter of the Bible is mostly known for what happens later,
when Abram meets the king of Salem, a mysterious individual named
Melchizedek. What precipitates that joyous encounter is this very
strange, very ancient war. Before moving forward, check out how the
Targum of Genesis 14:1-7 reads,

> [1] And it was in the days of Amraphel,--he is Nimrod, who commanded
> Abram to be cast into the furnace; he was then king of Pontos; Ariok, (so
> called) because he was (*arik*) tall among the giants, king of Thalasar,
> Kedarlaomer, (so called) because he had bound himself (or gone over)
> among the bondmen of the king of Elam, and Thidal, crafty as a fox, king
> of the peoples subjected to him, [2] – made war with Bera, whose deeds were
> evil, king of Sedom, and with Birsha, whose deeds were with the wicked,
> king of Amora: Shinab, who had hated his father, king of Admah, and

Shemebar, who had corrupted himself with fornication, king of Zeboim; and the king of the city which consumed (Bela) the dwellers thereof, which is Zoar. [3] All these were joined in the vale of the gardens (paredesaia), the place that produced the streamlets of waters that empty themselves into the sea of salt. [4] Twelve years they had served Kedarlaomer; and in the thirteenth year they had rebelled. [5] And in the fourteenth year came Kedarlaomer and the kings who were with him, and smote the Giants (*gibboraia*) which were in Ashtaroth-Karniam, and the Strong who were in Hametha, and the Terrible who were in the plain of Kiriathaim, [6] and the Choraee (dwellers in caverns) who were in the high mountains of Begala, unto the valley of Pharan, which was nigh upon the edge of the desert. [7] And they returned, and came to the place where was rendered the judgment of Mosheh the prophet, to the fountain of the waters of Strife, which is Requam. And they smote all the fields of the Amalkaee, and also the Emoraee, who dwelt in En-gedi.

(Gen 14:1-7 PJE)

Note the strange meeting between Nimrod and Abram. This is clearly a later legend, but it was the attempt of Pseudo-Jonathan to give an ancient interpretation for the events of this passage.[9]

What exactly is going on in this war? We have four powerful kings (suzerains) of the east fighting five petty kings (vassals) of Canaan. These eastern kings appear to have ruled territory from modern day Iran, Iraq, Syria, and Turkey. Let's look at each briefly.

We'll look at the eastern kings in the order of their territory, moving from east to west. The first is Chedorlaomer king of Elam. Elam is Persia (Iran). Chedorlaomer appears to be the most powerful of the four, as he has the major role in the story. The five petty kings had served under him for twelve years, but in the thirteenth year, they rebelled. Chedorlaomer's name has an uncertain meaning. It may be related to the Assyrian underworld god Lagamar so that his name means something like "Protector-No Mercy."[10] It is also probable that the ancient Arabian people knew of him, calling him Codar el Ahmar meaning "the Red."[11] In this light, it is very interesting that throughout the world, the giants are always described as having either blonde or red hair. Could there be a relationship?

The second king is Amraphel of Shinar. It is the association with Shinar and a legend of him throwing Abraham into the fire[12] that caused the Jews to associate him with Nimrod. Nimrod was either long gone or long dead, and this king arose after him in the city Nimrod built. Nevertheless, the ancient association between the two is interesting to say the least.[13]

The third king is Arioch, king of Ellasar. Ellasar is farther north and west in Syria, probably near the source of the Tigris River.[14] The name can be derived from a word (*'rwk*) meaning "tall." Thus, the *Targum* rendered it "tall among the giants."[15]

The fourth king is Tidal, king of Goiim. There are four Hittite kings who bear this name between the 18th and 13th centuries, making it pretty certain that Goiim (literally "the nations") is located in Hittite country in Turkey. Tidal can mean "knowledge of elevation,"[16] or another possibility is "You shall be cast out from heaven," a name reminiscent of the fall of Satan or the descent of the sons of God on Mt.

Hermon. To summarize, each of the names has some connection to the other-world, be it to a god of the underworld, to Nimrod and the land of Babel, to great height, or to heaven itself. That does not mean any of these kings *were* giants (plenty of later kings had the same names and were not giants), but it does give us reason for pause, especially when we learn about their ferocity in battle and the people whom they killed in these wars.

Five Lesser Kings

It was because of a rebellion in Canaan that the four mighty kings went to war. The rebellion was localized around the area of the Dead Sea. Five city-lords were responsible for the mutiny. These are Bera, Birsha, Shinab, Admah, and (possibly) Zoar. Let's look at these five kings.

The first two are famous only for the places where they ruled. Bera was king of the city of Sodom, which is where Abram's nephew Lot settled. Sodom was later destroyed by God with fire after a particularly horrific incident involving the men of Sodom and the two "strangers" who came to get Lot out of the city. These two strangers are called both "men" and "angels" in Genesis 19.

First, it says, "Two angels came to Sodom in the evening" (Gen 19:1). These are two of the three "men" who came to Abram earlier (Gen 18:2), whom Abram instantly recognized by their mere appearance as extraordinary individuals, so much so that he threw a huge feast for them. One of these men ends up being the Angel of the LORD. The other two are his emissaries sent to Sodom. Lot apparently notices the same physical characteristics, for as soon as he sees them, without a word spoken, he "bowed himself with his face to the earth."

Later, when the men of Sodom see these two individuals, they call out to Lot, "Where are the men who came to you tonight"? (Gen 19:5). "Bring them out to us so that we can have sex with them" (NET). What many people fail to recognize about this story is that there is more going on here than homosexuality. It is that, but it is also more. These men want to have sex ... with angels. Have you ever noticed this before? This is a clear reference back to Genesis 6:1-4, but is an even more wicked perversion of the heavenly/earthly mixing that went on prior to the Flood. Even Calvin, who called our interpretation of Genesis 6:1-4 "absurd" is forced to note that the same kind of "absurd" crime is sought after here.[17]

This story of Sodom is an indication of the kind of evil that was taking place in this city. Not coincidentally, Bera's name foreshadows that evil. His name means "son of evil." Birsha--king of the sister city of Gomorrah—does not fair much better. Birsha means "son of wickedness." If the sickening story of Genesis 19 was not an isolated incident, and if these men were aware of the Genesis 6 story, then it is logical to presume that Sodom was at least connected to giants, if not also a city with some of them living there.

Two of the three other kings are also associated with Sodom and Gomorrah. Shinab was king of Admah, and Shemeber was king of Zeboiim. Both of these cities were also overthrown with fire and sulphur from heaven by God in his great wrath against Sodom (Deut 29:23). Shinab translates to "sin is my father,"[18] but can also mean "tooth of the father" or "hostile." When I first read this definition, I was amazed. It is probably just a coincidence, but one of the strange physical characteristics of giant remains reported in the Americas are that some have been found with double rows of teeth.[19]

Shemeber has that son of Noah as its root word: *shem*. We have seen it before in the Nephilim, the men of renown, and in Nimrod's towering boast, "Let us make a name for ourselves." Shemeber means "powerful name."[20] But it can also mean "a winged name of great celebrity" or "soaring on high" or "a winged hero." Does this have anything to do with fallen angels and their offspring of old (not that he is one, but that the name remembers events of ancient days), a name taken in order to incite fear in his enemies?

The fifth name is not known with certainty. The text may not even give us a name, though it is possible that Zoar is the name of the king of Bela. Zoar comes from a word meaning "small," but means "bringing low." The common theme of these names is great evil and wickedness. But just as we saw with the four kings, these five hint at something gigantic behind the scenes.

The Giants Defeated

When these five kings of the Levant rebelled, it says that Chedorlaomer gathered his confederation, and within the year was marching upon the peoples immediately to the north and east of the Dead Sea. Here is where things get truly bizarre. First, they defeated a group called the Rephaim. As we will see in much more detail later, "Rephaim" becomes the most unsettling generic term for giants. Then they made the Zuzim in Ham kneel before them. "Zuzim" means "high standing" or "to buzz." After this they came against the Emim ("terrible ones"), the Horites ("troglodytes" or "cave-dwellers"), the Amalekites ("vexation" or "to lick up"), and finally the Amorites ("mountain people" or "renowned"). Only after this did the five kings finally engage the battle.

The rebellious kings had figured that they were safe as long as these six clans stood between them and the powerful rulers of the east. They figured this because those six clans were giants. Though we cannot be certain that any of the kings—the four or the five—were giants (although from their names and the stories associated with them there are certainly hints that some of them either were giants, or felt themselves greater than giants, or enlisted giants in their armies), one thing is *absolutely certain*. The clans dispelled by Chedorlaomer in Genesis 14 were giants. They were not just tall warriors. They were ancient tribes, the original inhabitants of the land, peoples associated with dark magic, the underworld, insatiable appetites for human flesh and blood, unthinkable immoral behavior, otherworldly size and proportions, and preternatural lineage. Beginning in the next chapter, we will look at these giant clans individually. Their history and run-ins with Abraham's descendants are fascinating.

For now, there are two passages that prove each of these clans were giants. The first is Numbers 13:21-33. At the end of the text it says, "All the people that we saw are of great height" (13:32). Two of the nations listed in Genesis 14 are listed in Numbers 13. These are the Amalekites and the Amorites (13:29). The other passage is Deuteronomy 2-3. This passage lists the Emim, Zamzummim (Zuzim), Horites, and Amorites which also appear in Genesis 14. It says of each that they were "tall" and were part of the Rephaim. Therefore, there is no question that the six tribes defeated by Chedorlaomer before turning to the rebel vassals of Sodom and Gomorrah were giants.

GIANT CLANS (TEXTUAL COMPARISON)

Gen 6	Gen 14	Gen 15	Num 13	Deut 1-3
Nephilim			Nephilim	
	Rephaim	Rephaim		Rephaim
	Zuzim			Zamzummim (Zumim)
	Emim			Emim
	Horites			Horites
	Amalekites		Amalekites	
	Amorites	Amorites	Amorites	Amorites
		Kenites		
		Kenizzites		
		Kadmonites		
		Hittites	Hittites	
		Perizzites		
		Canaanites	Canaanites	
		Girgashites		
		Jebusites	Jebusites	
			Anakim	Anakim
				Hivites/Avvim

FAMILY TREE OF THE NEPHILIM

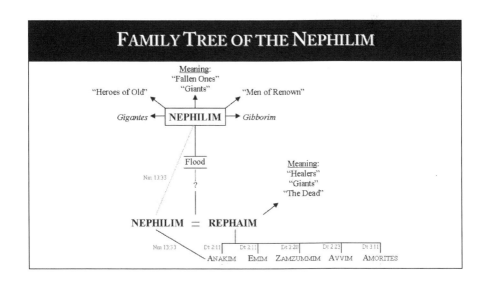

Chapter 4: Patriarchal Giants

*And when Shechem the son of Hamor the Hivite,
the prince of the land, saw her, he seized her and
lay with her and humiliated her.*

Genesis 34:2

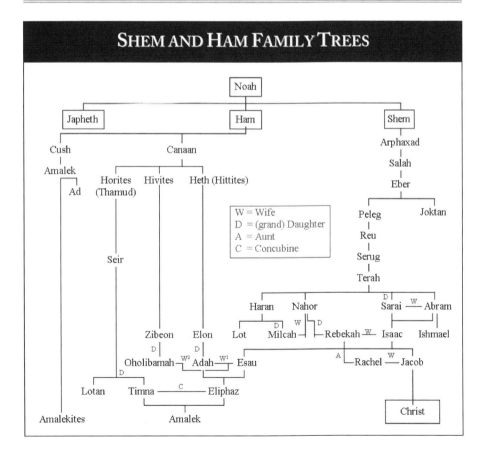

SHEM AND HAM FAMILY TREES

Abraham and the Seed

The story of Abram really begins with Shem. Shem was given the promise: "Blessed be the LORD, the God of Shem, and let Canaan be his servant" (Gen 9:26). Before the Table of Nations, this verse foresees a conflict between Shem and Canaan. This conflict continues the promise given to Eve that there would be a war between two seeds, but that her Seed could win.

Beginning at this curse, the Canaanites become the arch enemies of God. Thus, important clans from the stock of Canaan are traced out, as we saw in the previous chapter. Meanwhile, the genealogy of Shem is the critical lineage for redemptive history, because it traces out the origins of Abram. It is through Abram that Israel, and eventually the Messiah—the Christ—will come. The Giant Wars of Genesis 14 are the first in a seemingly never ending series of battles between the two seeds. Both seeds are spiritual. Both seeds are physical.

Mamre, Eschol, and Aner

Let's take note of what is happening at this point in the story with the seed of the woman. It is a most intriguing thing. Abram is living near the city of Hebron and has allied himself with three of the Amorites(!) from that area: A man named Mamre (after whom the famous Oaks of Mamre were named), and his two brothers Eschol and Aner. Of these three, Eschol's name is the most interesting. It means "a cluster of grapes," a curious idea that will return in Numbers 13 when the spies return from Eschol's ancient home with a cluster of grapes so large that two men had to carry it on a pole (Num 13:23).

At this point there were peaceful relations between the Amorites and Abram. Soon that would change. God gives Abraham a prophecy.

It concerns the coming Exodus and the return to the land of Canaan in the days of Moses/Joshua. God said,

> Know for certain that your offspring will be sojourners in a land that is not theirs and will be servants there, and they will be afflicted for four hundred years ... They shall come back here in the fourth generation, for *the iniquity of the Amorites* is not yet complete ... To your offspring I give this land, from the river of Egypt to the great river, the river Euphrates, the land of the Kenites, the Kenizzites, the Kadmonites, the Hittites, the Perizzites, the Rephaim, the Amorites, the Canaanites, the Girgashites, and the Jebusites.
>
> Genesis 15:13, 16, 18-21

Why is Abram hanging out with Amorites? Well, if the land is filled with giants, perhaps he is trying his best just to stay alive. He has to befriend someone, because he is not powerful enough to fight them all by himself (even with his modest army). Also, we can suppose that not every person in a tribe was a giant. Perhaps the tribes were ruled by a small group of giants, a giant family as we will see later with the Anakim. Or perhaps, even if all of the Amorites were tall (which is what the spies told Moses, perhaps exaggerating, perhaps not[1]), their corruption was not as bad as it would become a couple hundred years later. In fact, the text says this outright.

Sodom and Gomorrah

As we would expect, if Canaan was filled with giant tribes, the patriarchs (Abraham, Isaac, and Jacob) would have come into contact with them regularly. There are some really strange stories in Genesis that seem to confirm this. For instance, we have already looked at the Sodom and Gomorrah story with two angels coming as men to the city and the men desiring to have intimate relations with them. This is straight out of the Genesis 6 worldview and it offers a glimpse, not only into the immorality of those places, but to the supernatural worldview they held as well.

Abimelech

Another interesting character is a king named Abimelech (Genesis 20, 26). Abimelech is said to be "king of the Philistines" (Gen 26:1), who are descended from the Egyptians (and Ham). Later in the days of David, we run into both giant Egyptians (1 Chron 11:23) as well as giant Philistines (1 Sam 17:23). It is probable in my mind that the Egyptians and Philistines enlisted outsider Rephaim giants into their armies, and so we should not make claims that these *peoples* were giants. There is little question, however, that they were in league with giants.

At any rate, Abimelech was said to rule in a place called Gerar. In those days, the whole region was known as "Negeb of the Cretans" (Crete being an island in the Mediterranean Sea), and was under the political patronage of Gaza, and later Gath.[2] We have no evidence of Abimelech's size. Yet it is curious that in the Greek stories, Olympus was a *Cretan* giant who mentored Zeus, and Mylinus was a *Cretan* giant slain by Zeus. Also, Gaza and Gath were two of three cities where the giant Anakim lived, and they remained unconquered in the days of Joshua (Josh 11:22). In other words, circumstantial evidence allows for the possibility that Abimelech was a giant.

Consider further the stories told of this great king. Following in the tradition of Pharaoh (Gen 12:10-20), he sees the "beautiful" sister of Abraham (he was told she was his sister) and takes her to be his wife (Gen 20:2). Apparently, taking whichever women sojourning in your land that you liked was perfectly acceptable to this king. The beauty for the "taking" is certainly not put into a positive light, and thus harkens back to the story of Genesis 6:2.[3]

What happens to Abimelech? The first time this happens, God comes to him in a dream and tells him that he is a dead man, because he took another man's wife. Abimelech pleads innocence and God lets him off with a warning, but only after making sure that he knows it was God who kept Abimelech from touching Sarah. Later, Abimelech sees Isaac and Rebekah together, warns his men not to touch her, and eventually tells Isaac to flee because God has made him more powerful than Abimelech. The key point here is that in both stories (as well as the story with Pharaoh), God does not let anyone touch his chosen women. He will not allow the line to be contaminated. I'm not dogmatic that Abimelech was a giant, but the story and the setting have too many coincidences to be completely unrelated to events prior to the Flood.

Shechem and Hamor

Another strange story in Genesis involves two of the sons of Jacob: Levi and Simeon, and a city they destroyed called Shechem (Genesis 34). Shechem was the son of Hamor the Hivite. As we have seen, the Hivites are among the giants listed in the land of Canaan. The story goes that Shechem, the prince of the land, saw Dinah the daughter of Jacob and Leah. So, he "took" her and lay with her by force. Again, a woman in the line of the promise is involved. Again intercourse is in view. Again, echoes of Genesis 6:2 sound off the pages of this story, except this time we are certain that the union was forced. Where this story takes a new spin is in the response of Levi and Simeon to this outrage.

They conceive a plot to utterly destroy every man in Shechem. Shechem decides that he loves Dinah and wants to marry her. He goes to his powerful father Hamor and instructs him to ask Jacob for Dinah's hand in marriage. He proposes mutual "intermarriage" between his people and Jacob's. When the brothers hear it, they demand that all the men of the city be circumcised. Amazingly, Shechem obliges. At the moment all of the men in the city undergo the procedure, the two sons of Jacob swoop in and murder them all, thus defending the honor of their sister. This is the first full scale genocide in the Old Testament, and it is committed against a family which is known to be related to (if not to be) giants.

Jacob was not at all pleased with what his sons had done. At the end of his life, he curses the two boys for it (Gen 49:5-7). In the story he gives his reason. "You have brought trouble on me by making me stink to the inhabitants of the land, the Canaanites and the Perizzites. My numbers are few, and if they gather themselves against me and attack me, I shall be destroyed, both I and my household" (Gen 34:30).

As an addendum to these stories in the latter parts of Genesis, it should be noted that Jewish traditions say that the sons of Israel were fighting with giants on a regular basis. In the *Testament of Judah*, for instance, we read about how Judah killed a king named Achor, "a giant of a man" (TJud 3:5) and how Jacob killed Belisath, "King of all kings" and a giant "twelve cubits tall" (TJud 3:7). Obviously, the Jews a long time ago thought that this was a land full of amazing people.

Chapter 5: Moses Meets Amalek

Then Amalek came and fought
with Israel at Rephidim.

Exodus 17:8

Esau and the Hivites

However you view the story of Shechem and Hamor, one thing is certain. The actions of Levi and Simeon should be contrasted with those of their uncle, Jacob's twin brother, Esau. One chapter later, the Hivites return again, this time in the genealogy of Esau.

Unlike his brother who retrieved a wife from his own kind, Esau took his wives from the Canaanites. One was named Oholibamah the granddaughter of Zibeon the Hivite; the other was called Adah the daughter of Elon the Hittite (Gen 36:2). "Elon" means "magnificent oak" and is related to the word "God Almighty" (*Elyon*). Given the lineage, the name reminds me of the words of Amos about the Amorites who were "tall like cedars" (Amos 2:9). Esau was wicked because he mixed his line with that of the wicked Canaanites.

What happens to Esau? He moves into the strange land of Seir the Horite who appears to have been a giant (Gen 36:20; Deut 2:12, 22). His mixing with those people makes a lot of sense politically, though it was a godless act. If you live in a land of giants, then do all you can to make alliances with them and to become like them. That is what reason would dictate. There is no better way to do those things than through marriages and children. At any rate, Esau becomes Edom and disappears from the land of Canaan.

The same thing goes for Jacob, though in his case, not by choice. Soon after the story of Shechem, a famine comes to the land, driving him to seek refuge in Egypt. Because God had providentially sent Joseph (his son) before him, Jacob ended up staying in Egypt where he died. Thus, there is no significant interaction between Israel and the giants between the days of Joseph and Moses. This is where we find things at the beginning of the book of Exodus, only now Israel is not a free people living in Egypt. They are slaves that need deliverance and a return to the land of promise, the land of Canaan.

Moses Meets Amalek

Having been in captivity for over 400 years,[1] God was now going to redeem his people out of slavery in Egypt. To put it another way, the sins of the Amorites is nearing completion. Thus, God told Moses, "I have come down to deliver them [the Israelites] out of the land of the Egyptians and to bring them up out of that land to a good and broad land, a land flowing with milk and honey, to the place of the Canaanites, the Hittites, the Amorites, the Perizzites, the Hivites, and the Jebusites" (Ex 3:8). Why does God mention the names of these tribes so often? Because this deliverance will truly be miraculous, for these tribes are made up of giants.

The story goes that Moses comes to Pharaoh with terms of surrender. "Let my people go." Pharaoh is hardened and will not comply. Thus, God sends ten mighty plagues to Egypt to humble Pharaoh and mock his gods. Finally Pharaoh lets the people go, only to follow them into the wilderness where he surrounds them at a dead end at the coast of the Red Sea. God performs another mighty miracle, opens the sea so that his people can cross on dry land, and then shuts the sea over the Egyptian army that is closing in hot pursuit. Safely on the other side, God leads his people towards the Holy Mountain: Mt. Sinai. Along the way, they are attacked by a fierce tribe of warriors and heroes. They are called Amalekites. This story is the first instance of a tribe of giants attacking God's people in hopes of utterly destroying them. Here is what we read,

> [8] Then Amalek came and fought with Israel at Rephidim. [9] So Moses said to Joshua, "Choose for us men, and go out and fight with Amalek. Tomorrow I will stand on the top of the hill with the staff of God in my hand." [10] So Joshua did as Moses told him, and fought with Amalek, while Moses, Aaron, and Hur went up to the top of the hill. [11] Whenever Moses held up his hand, Israel prevailed, and whenever he lowered his hand, Amalek prevailed. [12] But Moses' hands grew weary, so they took a stone and put it under him, and he sat on it, while Aaron and Hur held up his hands, one on one side, and the other on the other side. So his hands were steady until the going down of the sun. [13] And Joshua overwhelmed Amalek and his people with the sword. [14] Then the LORD said to Moses, "Write this as a memorial in a book and recite it in the ears of Joshua, that I will utterly blot out the memory of Amalek from under heaven." [15] And Moses built an altar and called the name of it, The LORD Is My Banner, [16] saying, "A hand upon the throne of the LORD! The LORD will have war with Amalek from generation to generation."
>
> Exodus 17:8-16

When discussing the identity of this Amalek, most dictionaries and commentaries assume it is the grandson of Esau (Gen 36:12). This is one of the reasons I wanted to tell you about him at the beginning of this chapter. This idea is highly improbable and has several problems.

Most basically, it assumes that there is only one Amalek in Scripture. This is not true, since Amalekites were there in the Genesis 14 wars with Abram. Obviously, if the Amalekites are there in Abraham's day, then there is more than one group of Amalekites. Also, Moses is told that they are not to despise the descendants of Esau (Deut 23:7) and yet the prophecy says that God will utterly blot out the name of Amalek through his chosen people. If they are the same people, how do these two statements jive? Amalek keeps returning, again and again, to fight against Israel. Israel is told to totally destroy everything associated with these Amalekites. This is what God always commands Israel do to the inhabitants of the land of Canaan, but they are not allowed to do this to the descendants of Esau, because they are his brothers (Deut 2:5-8). Finally, Numbers 14:45 refers to a second encounter with the Amalekites, who came this time with the Canaanites, and this time won. But Deuteronomy 1:44, referring to this same incident, calls those who fought against Moses "Amorites" who "chased you as bees do and beat you down in Seir as far as Hormah." Nowhere in the Bible are Edomites referred to as Amorites.

For the sake of argument, let's assume for the moment that Moses did fight the sons of Esau. Even if this were true, these people would still be mixed with two giant races. Recall that Esau's wife Adah was a Hittite. It was Adah who bore Esau a child named Eliphaz, and Eliphaz was Amalek's father. His mother was taken by Eliphaz as a concubine *from the Horites*. This woman, a girl named Timna, bore Eliphaz a son named Amalek. Thus, even Esau's grandson Amalek is potentially one half giant.

Yet, even if Moses did fight these people against every argument I gave above, it still does not explain who the Amalekites were that lost in the Giant Wars to Chedorlaomer. According to the LXX of Genesis 14:7, this Amalek fought in the giant wars. He may have been closely related to Nimrod.[2]

The Bible says some strange things about the Amalekites. Balaam was the infamous pagan prophet who was involved in the favorite Sunday school story of the talking donkey. In Numbers 24, the prophet takes up an oracle where he curses the enemies of God. One of the peoples he cursed was the Amalekites, whom he called "the first among the nations" (Num 24:20). This can hardly refer to the grandson of Esau. Instead, it speaks of a most ancient race of people, the same race smitten (but not exterminated) by the kings of Persia in the days of Abram.[3]

The Arabians speak of an ancient hero they call *Imlāq*, which is their name for Amalek.[4] It should not surprise you to discover that this word means "giant."[5] The form of the word *Imlāq* is clearly related to Amalek. Amalek can mean "vexation," or possibly "to lick up" (more cannibalism or perhaps violence or both?). Here is the true origin of the Amalekites that came out to fight Moses in the wilderness.

These same Arabs also tell of one of Imlāq's famous sons, a behemoth named Ad,[6] who some say made his way down to Egypt, which would certainly fit Israel fighting them so close to Egypt in the wilderness. A tradition told in the famous *Al-Khitat*, a history of Egyptian lore compiled by al-Maqrizi (1364-1442 AD), recounts the teaching of one master Ibrahim bin Wasif Shah (d. 1203 AD) who said that King Adim (Ad) was,

A violent and proud prince, tall in stature. He was he who ordered the rocks cut to make the pyramids, as had been done by the ancients. In his time there lived two angels cast out of heaven, and who lived in the Aftarah well; these two angels taught magic to the Egyptians, and it is said that 'Adim, the son of El-Budchir, learned most of their sciences, after which the two angels went to Babel. Egyptians, especially the Copts, assure us that these were actually two demons named Mahla and Bahala, not two angels, and that the two are at Babel in a well, where witches meet, and they will remain there until the Day of Judgment. Since that time they worshiped idols. It is Satan, they say, who made them known to men and raised them for men. According to others, it was Badoura who raised the first idol, and the first idol erected was the Sun, yet others claim that Nimrod ordered the first idols raised and the worship of them.[7]

The Coptic reference is a giveaway that the book of Enoch had at least some influence on this tradition (for it was the Ethiopian Coptic Christians who preserved the book during the Dark Ages); however it does seem from this citation that this was a common belief held by other Egyptians as well, including Muslims. Of course, this is not to say that Ad actually built the pyramids, for the same book says that there is no agreement on the time or architect(s) of their construction, and it recounts many conflicting legends about them. Nevertheless, a giant named Ad is one of those legends.

The Adites and the Thamudites (Horites) were contemporaries who early on dwelt in the same region of western Saudi Arabia, after the Thamudites were forced to flee their home on the eastern shores of the Persian Gulf. Like the Thamudites, the Adites are remembered as "very powerful, that they were giants, and that their king, *Sheddad Ben Ad* (the son of Ad), reigned over the whole world."[8] The mystical Jewish Zohar remembers the same tradition of Amalekites being giants. *Beresheet* A, 20.224, "There are five races of mixed multitude. These are the Nefilim (fallen), the Giborim (mighty), the Anakim (giants), the Refaim (shades) and the Amalekim." Some traditions trace the origin of Ad and Amalek to Shem,[9] but others trace them to Ham.[10] The later probably makes the best sense, because of the close proximity of these giants to those that were certainly spawned from Hamites.

THAMUDITES AND ADITES FLEE WEST

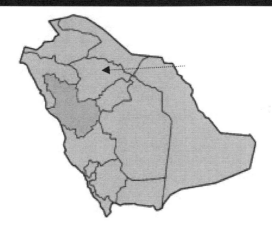

The Amalekites will return in the days of king Saul, and also again in the days of queen Esther. Before we move on, I want you to consider the other side of this story with Amalek. Joshua—the Hebrew form of "Jesus"—is told to listen to the prophecy that God will utterly blot out the memory of Amalek. Given what comes next, this must be viewed as prophetically of the coming work of Christ, as it was seen in the early church.[11]

After the victory over Amalek, it says that Moses built an altar and called it "The LORD Is My Banner" (Ex 17:15). This is a title or name of God: *Jehovah Nissi*. "Banner" reflects the positions of Moses' hands during the battle—outstretched, like Jesus on the cross. Banner is a word (*nes*) used two other times by Moses. One is of the bronze serpent pole (Num 21:8-9), which Jesus says typifies his death (John 3:14). The other is of the earth swallowing up Korah (Num 26:10), which is more language used of Jesus' death (compare Jonah 1:17-2:6 with Matt 12:39-40, 1 Cor 15:54). In this case the banner of Moses is taken up by the prophet Isaiah when he says, "In that day there shall be a root of Jesse, who shall stand as a banner to the people" (Isa 11:10; cf. Gal 3:1). In other words, the story of Moses slaying the giants prefigures the work of Jesus on the cross.

Earlier fights in Genesis between people and giants involved either unbelieving kings or localized warfare with the children of Abraham. This war now takes the prophecy given so long ago to Eve of warfare between two seeds up a notch. It is the first blood bath between a whole army of God's chosen people vs. an entire clan of giants. As such, it is a foreshadowing of the Great Battle to come.

Chapter 6: Spying Out the Land

There we saw the giants.

Numbers 13:33 LXX

---

10 Faithless Spies

It has been difficult to keep relatively silent about the passages we are looking at in this Chapter. They explain so much about what we have already learned that I have had to allude to them at least a little. Most people do not realize that the stories we have looked at in the previous Chapters are about giants, because we are too far removed historically and culturally from the air that Israel breathed to taste and smell what those ancient people all took for granted. The stories we will look at beginning in this chapter put any doubt about the giants of earlier times to rest.

In Numbers 13, God commands Moses to send twelve spies into the land of Canaan. Everything about this story is strange. The first thing we learn is that they enter the land in the far north, probably near Mt. Hermon.[1] They then travel south through the heart of the land to Hebron. Hebron is 19 miles south of Jerusalem in the hill country.

Hebron is where the oaks of Mamre the Amorite were located. It is where Abraham and Isaac sojourned. Abraham and Sarah, Isaac and Rebekah, and Jacob's wife Leah were all buried there. It is also just south of the very fertile Valley of Eshcol (remember, Eshcol was the brother of Mamre and his name means "grape cluster"). Moses had asked the spies to bring back some of the produce of the land. All of these facts make Hebron a natural destination to spy.

Hebron was a cyclopean city with walls 10-13 feet thick. One archaeologist wrote that the houses, doors, gates, walls, and other things appear to be "just such dwellings as a race of giants would build."[2] Hebron was also called Kiriath-Arba (cf. Gen 23:2 etc.) after the name of its founder: Arba "the greatest of the Anakim" (Josh 14:15). Arba can mean "perfect stature" (physical size?).[3] I've mentioned these Anakim several times, but this is the first time you run into them in the Bible. Who are they?

A person named Anak is the progenitor of the Anakim. His ancestor was Arba (Josh 15:13, 21:11). Anak originally meant "neck," but came to mean "long-necked," as in a giant.[4]

The very end of the passage gives us one of the most important links to understanding the proliferation of giants after the Flood. "There we saw the Nephilim (the sons of Anak, who come from the Nephilim), and we seemed to ourselves like grasshoppers, and so we seemed to them" (Num 13:33). The verse specifically links the Anakim to the pre-Flood Nephilim, saying that these Anakim *are* Nephilim. In fact, the older versions (LXX) do not have the parenthetical: ("the sons of Anak, who come from the Nephilim").[5] This means that the spies thought everyone in the land was a Nephilim, not just the Anakim. You can gather as much from the previous verse which says that everyone in the entire land was very tall.

Nevertheless, the Anakim are said to be tall in other Scriptures too. "Hear, O Israel: you are to cross over the Jordan today, to go in to dispossess nations [note the plural] greater and mightier than yourselves, cities great and fortified up to heaven [note the size], a people great and tall [note the height], *the sons of the Anakim*, whom you know, and of whom you have heard it said, 'Who can stand before the sons of Anak?'" (Deut 9:1-2; also Deut 1:26). The Egyptians also knew of the Anakim. They called them *Iy'anaq*[6] and *Shasu*.[7] One particular text, a letter viewed as the model for training royal Egyptian scribes, refers to their tremendous height. "The face of the pass is dangerous with Shasu, hidden under the bushes. Some of them are 4 or 5 cubits, nose to foot, with wild faces.[8] This puts them at a range between 7 – 9 feet tall.[9]

Recent archaeological discoveries of skeletons between seven[10] feet and ten feet six inches[11] have been discovered in Palestine. For the record, my present view of the size of these giants in Palestine and also around the world[12] is that they were almost all between 8 feet and probably less than 12 feet tall, for the overwhelming range of giants reported across the world and in Palestine fall in this range. Obviously, these people brought dread and fear to peoples far and wide. In Deut 2:11 they are called Rephaim, and other nations like the Emim, Zamzummim, and Amorites are compared to them.

The first thing we are told about the spies' visit to Hebron is that they see "Ahiman, Sheshai, and Talmai, the descendants of Anak" (Num 13:22). Rabbinical tradition said that Ahiman was the most feared.[13] Josephus tells us about these "boys" saying that they were a "race of giants, who had bodies so large and countenances so entirely different from humans, that they were amazing to the sight and terrible to the hearing. These bones are still shown to this very day, unlike to any creditable relations of other men" (Josephus, *Antiquities*, 5.2.3). It is possible they were buried in graves which were still around in the days of Micah. The 1st Century record "The Lives of the Prophets" records that Micah was buried "in his own district by himself, near the burial ground of the Anakim" (LivesProph 6:3). Archaeologist J. Jeremias, who wrote a detailed treatment of holy graves in Palestine, said that in 1932, he and a colleague personally discovered the "cemetery of the giants" in a Seleucid graveyard (the eastern Macedonian portion of Alexander's empire), 1.25 miles north of Beit Jibrin (which is 13 miles northwest of Hebron).[14] Quite a story, isn't it? It gets better.

After seeing these three behemoths, the spies travel north to the valley of Eschol where the cut down a single cluster of grapes. The thing is, they have to carry it on a pole between two of them (Num 13:23).[15] Ten of the twelve spies brought the grapes back *in order to discourage the people from going into the land*. The grapes were gigantic and the people who grew them were even larger. Is it any wonder that I speculated about the size of Mamre and Eschol in an earlier chapter?

People often do not realize why the ten spies were so frightened. It is so easy to dismiss the fear we read about them having in the Bible and smugly begin to think, "I would never have acted like that!" Now you are beginning to see that by the looks of things, there is no natural reason to believe anyone could have defeated these people. Only the eyes of faith and the trust in the promise of God to Eve could have safely seen them through. It gets better still.

The spies report to Moses that not only are Anakim in the land, so are Hittites, Jebusites, Amorites, and Canaanites. Caleb quieted the people who were obviously frightened saying, "Let us go up at once and occupy it, for we are well able to overcome it." Caleb remembered God's past miraculous deliverances, not the least of which was their victory over the Amalekites. For his faith, Caleb will eventually be given Hebron as his own settlement.

The rest of the spies were not so well inclined. "They brought to the people of Israel a bad report" (Num 13:32). They said the land "devours its inhabitants." Following the ancient tradition, I have suggested that this refers not to the harshness of the land (which produces such great fruit, milk, and honey), but to the inhabitants themselves. The giants killed people and then ate them.

They also said "all the people that we saw in it are of great height." <u>All</u> of the people. It is possible that the spies were exaggerating of course, but the words of Moses (not the spies mind you, but Moses) seem to suggest minimal exaggeration. For instance he says, "Hear, O Israel: you are to cross over the Jordan today, to go in to dispossess nations greater and mightier than yourselves, cities great and fortified up to heaven, a people great and tall, the sons of the Anakim, whom you know, and of whom you have heard it said, 'Who can stand before the sons of Anak?'" (Deut 9:1-2; also Deut 2-3). Apparently, the spies were not completely lying. That was not their problem.

Instead, they were not *trusting*. It really did seem to them like they were grasshoppers. To the giants, they were little edible insects. God had promised to make Israel like hornets (Ex 23:28), not grasshoppers, stinging bees that make much larger men flee in agony and terror. But they would not believe. The whole point of going into the land was to see whether or not the people would trust God to deliver them from the giants.

The people heard the report and took the side of the ten. Joshua and Caleb were in the clear minority. Moses pleaded with the majority to have faith, but they would not trust God. Instead, they grumbled. For their unbelief, God punished that generation with forty years of wandering in the desert, a year for every day the spies were in the land.

Chapter 7: The "Law" of Canaan

Defile not ye yourselves in any of these
things: for in all these the nations are defiled
which I cast out before you.

Lev 18:24 KJV

Perversion

I want to take a short break from the history of the giants to look at their lifestyle. Most people never stop to consider the fact that the abominable practices going on in the land of Canaan were directly related to the giants, or that their wickedness becomes the background of God's giving Israel her own laws. Recall how God told Abraham that the sins of the Amorites (giants) had not come to their full fruition in his day (Gen 15:16). Part of the reason for not giving Abraham the land right then and there was that these inhabitants of the Promised Land, no matter who—*or what*—they were, rightly possessed it. God does not just throw people out of a land—much less utterly destroy them—unless there is compelling moral justification for doing so. God is holy, not capricious. It is not until a people reach a point of no return that the "land will vomit" out its inhabitants (Lev 18:28). Until that time, wherever that line is drawn in God's mind, the people have a right to be stewards in the land, apparently, even if they are giants.

Torah: Be Separate

During the forty years of wandering, God gave Moses the *Torah*. *Torah* means "law." Sometimes Torah refers to the first five books of the OT. In this case, I'm thinking of it as those portions of those books that specify law. God gave his laws to this chosen people so that they would be "separate," and unlike the nations they were going to dispossess (Deut 7:8). They had to be righteous people, people that knew and understood what their God was like. As it says, "You shall be holy, for I the LORD your God am holy" (Lev 19:2).

This law, made so famous by Jesus (Matt 5:48), comes at the end of a series of laws wherein Israel is instructed, "You shall not do as they do in the land of Canaan, to which I am bringing you" (Lev 18:3), and "Do not make yourselves unclean by any of these things, for by all these the nations I am driving out before you have become unclean ... and the land vomited out its inhabitants ... for the people of the land, who were before you, did all of these abominations, so that the land became unclean" (Lev 18:24, 25, 27). This same idea is repeated in Deuteronomy as well. "When you come into the land that the LORD your God is giving you, you shall not learn to follow the abominable practices of those nations ... whoever does these things is an abomination to the LORD. And because of these abominations the LORD your God is driving them out before you" (Deut 18:9, 12). Not every law in the Torah has the nations of Canaan as its explicit backdrop, but there are certainly many of them that do.

Before we get to those and for the sake of recollection, in case we forget too quickly, these people are specified time and again in the Torah as, "The Hittites and the Amorites, the Canaanites and the Perizzites, the Hivites and the Jebusites" (cf. Ex 3:8; 23:23; Deut 7:1; 20:17, etc.). Israel was to "utterly destroy" to "devote to complete destruction" these people so that they would not learn their detestable practices" or follow their gods (Deut 20:18; cf. 12:30; Ex 23:33; Josh 23:13, etc.).

The wicked practices were done "for their gods" and in order to "serve" them (Deut 12:30-31; 20:18). This is important, because it says that their customs (especially religious) were not ends to themselves. There was greater depravity here than you may think. Their gods loved and desired these things. In the case of any people who were actually giants, remember that their gods were actually their progenitors, fallen created heavenly beings that desired to be worshiped.

This is more easily seen when you understand the kinds of sins that are mentioned when these inhabitants of Canaan are specifically called out like this. As I said before, there are categories of laws that are sandwiched between these calls not to be like those nations. You can divide these sins into four basic groups:

ABOMINATIONS OF THE GIANTS			
FALSE WORSHIP	SEXUAL IMMORALITY	CROSSING OVER	OPPRESSION
Altars, pillars/poles, carved images	Incest/fornication: mother, mother-in-law, sister, granddaughter, step-sister, aunt, uncle, daughter-in-law, sister-in-law	Necromancy of ghosts or familiar spirits	Neglecting, discriminating against, or otherwise harming the poor
Burn children in fire (to Molech)	Bestiality or other mixing of kinds	Fortune telling	Unfair wages
Groves	Homosexuality	Interpreting omens	Robbery
Sacrifices	Adultery	Sorcery	Slander/gossip
Cutting the body	Prostitution	Charmer	Hate
Tattooing		Medium	Disrespecting the old
Religious prostitution		Eating blood	Unjust weights and measures
		Divination	

Of course, other nations, *including the Hittites and Canaanites* had legal codes dealing with injustice and sexual practices,[1] though both kinds of laws are different in some important respects from those in the Bible. Sexual practices considered deviant (such as adultery) were not as varied as those delineated in the Bible, nor were they judged as harshly or as fairly. For instance, in the Code of Ur Nammu and the Code of Eshnanna, only the woman was put to death. In the Bible, both parties get the death penalty. Perhaps more striking is a Hittite law against bestiality. The Code of the Nesilim[2] 199 (cf. 1650-1500) says that anyone having intercourse with a pig or a dog shall die, but "if a man has intercourse with a horse or a mule, there is no punishment. But he shall not approach the king, and shall not become a priest."

Laws of social justice (which often overlap those of the Bible) were not divvied out equally either. This is because not all men (let alone women) were created equal in these cultures. For instance, the Sumerians had three distinct social classes: the *amelu* (senior class—government officials, priests, soldiers), the *mushkinu* (citizen class—merchants, shopkeepers, farmers, etc.), and the slave class.[3] A person's tooth was considered more valuable if he was of the senior class (*Hammurabi Code* 200-201). Similarly, the penalty of striking someone on the cheek was more severe if committed by a lower class (*Hammurabi Code* 203-204). Of course, without some basic working of civility and law you can have no society. Anarchy does not build dynasty.

Curiously, these nations have almost no laws regarding contacting the dead, and the few examples we have are themselves littered with superstition. For instance, The Code of Hammurabi 2[4] and the Code of Ur-Nammu 13[5] both refer to a person accused of sorcery. But to find out if they really were a sorcerer, you have to throw them into the river to see if they would float (no, the practice did not begin in the Middle Ages as you might think, if you are familiar with the famous skit by Monty Python).

As far as religious restrictions on temple prostitution (both male and female), idols, groves, sacrifices (including human) etc., well, *there are no laws forbidding any of it.* Combined with the previous set (contacting the dead), this is most revealing. It is religious lawlessness that is especially in mind when God says these things were done "for their gods." To a lesser but related degree, the sexual perversion of these peoples was tied to their religious practices. For example, it is not difficult to get from legal temple prostitution to general prostitution. In the Bible, having other gods and committing idolatry *is* adultery (Ex 34:15-16; Deut 31:16; Ezek 23:37; 1 Cor 6:9, etc.).[6]

The thing to keep in mind about all of this is the origin of the giants. They come from some kind of immoral union between heavenly beings and earthly women. They owe their very existence to sexual rebellion and religious pluralism. Even though these peoples had some sexual, civil, and religious order (even demons have this; cf. Col 2:18; 1 Tim 4:1-3), it was deeply perverted, an affront to God's sovereignty, holiness, and righteousness.

When God gave Moses the Torah, he was making a sharp distinction between himself and the gods of the giants. Because they followed the wickedness of their fathers, and perhaps multiplied it a thousand-fold, God would not let them live in the land any longer. Not only would he not let them live in Canaan, but he gave them over to the other tribes surrounding Canaan, as they too devoted them to complete destruction. It is exactly the same thing we saw prior to the Flood, only this time God's wrath will be carried out through his people. Perhaps this ancient interpretation of Genesis 6:1-4 discovered in the Dead Sea Scrolls serves to illustrate the point best:

> And now, sons, listen to me and I shall open your eyes so that you can see and understand the deeds of God, so that you can choose what he is pleased with and repudiate what he hates, so that you can walk perfectly on all his paths and not allow yourselves to be attracted by the thoughts of a guilty inclination and lascivious eyes. For many have gone astray due to these; brave heroes stumbled on account of them, from ancient times until now. For having walked in the stubbornness of their hearts the Watchers of the heavens fell; on account of it they were caught, for they did not heed the precepts of God. And their sons, whose height was like that of cedars and whose bodies were like mountains, fell. All flesh which there was on the dry earth expired and they became as if they had never been, because they had realized their desires and had failed to keep their creator's precepts, until his wrath flared up against them.
>
> CD 2.14-21

In light of this, the biblical warning should be read anew,

> Take care that you be not ensnared to follow them, after they have been destroyed before you, and that you do not inquire about their gods, saying, 'How did these nations serve their gods?--that I also may do the same.' You shall not worship the LORD your God in that way, for every abominable thing that the LORD hates they have done for their gods, for they even burn their sons and their daughters in the fire to their gods.
>
> Deuteronomy 12:30-31

Chapter 8: On the Way to Canaan

King Og of Bashan was the last survivor of the giant Rephaites. His bed was made of iron and was more than thirteen feet long and six feet wide. It can still be seen in the Ammonite city of Rabbah.

Deut 3:11 NLT

Dispossession of the Giants by the Nations

Near the end of their wanderings in the wilderness, as Israel was preparing to conquer the land, God recapped, at the beginning of Deuteronomy, the history of their wanderings, culminating in two battles east of Canaan. Along the south-eastern corner, in the land of Edom, the descendants of Esau had already destroyed the giant Horites of Seir (Deut 2:12). To the north of them, in the land of Moab, the descendants of Lot had destroyed the Emim (Deut 2:9-10). Farther north yet, their brothers the Ammonites (not to be confused with the Amorites), also descended from Lot, destroyed the Zamzummim (Deut 2:20-21). Even the Avvim who lived along the Mediterranean in villages as far as Gaza were displaced by the Caphtorim, that is the Philistines (Deut 2:23). These people were "as tall as the Anakim" (Deut 2:10, 21), and they were all counted among the Rephaim (Deut 2:11; 20).

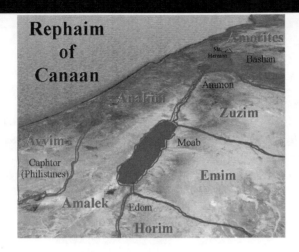

GIANTS IN THE PROMISED LAND

Each of these shorter tribes dispossessed the giants because God was punishing the wicked inhabitants of the entire region. God fought for these distant relatives of Israel and descendants of Abraham (Deut 2:21, 22). Notice that all of the tribes destroyed, even by other nations, were giants. In fact, in the same story, Israel is told in unconditional terms, that they were to leave the descendants of Esau, Moab, and Ammon alone. They could only buy food and water from them (Deut 2:5-6). Why would God be so choosy? This speaks to something about the nature of God that biblical critics completely misunderstand.

The claim is often made that the God of the OT is a capricious, vindictive tyrant. Has anyone ever put it more bluntly than Richard Dawkins when he said, "The [fictional] God of the Old Testament is ... jealous and proud of it; a petty, unjust, unforgiving control-freak; a vindictive, bloodthirsty ethnic cleanser; a misogynistic, homophobic, racist, infanticidal, genocidal, filicidal, pestilential, megalomaniacal, sadomasochistic, capriciously malevolent bully."[1] We can't deal with all of these charges here, but one part we will discuss.

God would not let Israel *touch* many different peoples, let alone utterly destroy them. He promised he would not fight for Israel in a battle like that. But the giants were a different breed (literally). They had become utterly wicked over the centuries, and this is on top of the fact that they were preternatural creatures. Besides this, if the giants were in the land and the people mixed with them, then the promise of the Seed of Eve would be stopped cold. Satan may have greatly desired this, but God would not let anything hinder his prophecy.

Sihon the Amorite

This dispossession of the giants *by other nations* becomes a moral justification for Israel doing likewise. It is also a motivation for them not to fear (which they should not have anyway, since God already fought for them against the Amalekites 40 years earlier). At this point, God recalls for Israel how he commanded them to go and take possession of the Valley of Arnon held by Sihon the Amorite, king of Heshbon (Deut 2:24). Arnon is a river and valley that divides Moab and Ammon, splitting the Dead Sea in half on its eastern shore.

Very little is known from the Bible about Sihon except that God hardened his heart so that he would not let Israel pass through his land (Deut 2:30). The Jews recorded stories about him—exaggerated or historical, it is not always possible to tell. They said that Sihon was born after the Flood to the wife of Ham who committed adultery with Ahiah[2] (the son of Shemhazai the angel[3]) after the deluge. Sihon was a giant "of enormous stature, taller than any tower in all the world."[4] They also said that he was actually the infamous Canaan, Ham's son.[5] This demonstrates that the tradition of Sihon as a giant is ancient.

FIG. 8.1. OG AND SIHON AND THE CONQUEST OF CANAAN

We also know that Sihon was an Amorite—like Mamre, Eschol, and Aner. It is curious to discover that the Amorites were reported to be, not Semitic peoples, but more like Caucasians, having blonde and red hair and blue eyes, but with elongated heads[6], a practice actually copied in the Egyptian Pharaoh's headdress and by the very painful practice of head-binding. Were they trying to emulate the giants?

More curious still is that Giants in the Americas are depicted with these same features. The graves of these North American giants, anywhere from 7 to over 12 feet tall,[7] included blondes in Mexico[8] and red-heads in Nevada.[9] The Indians tell stories that make the blood run cold (see Appendix – Giants in the Americas). These people were cruel, man-eating monsters. Like their Middle-Eastern counterparts, they were dispossessed from the land.[10] Perhaps these were the same peoples who fled after they were dispossessed in the old world?

FIG. 8.2. HEAD BINDING AND ELONGATION

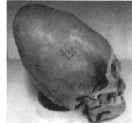

Pharaoh's "White Crown of Upper Egypt."

Above left: Queen Nefertiti – 18ᵗʰ Dynasty (note the head and neck (Anak = 'long necked'). **Above right**: African head-binding. **Lower left**: One of Pharaoh Akhenaten's daughters. **Lower right**: elongated head, Museo De National, Lima Peru.

Og the Mighty Giant

The Jews also said that Sihon was the younger brother of Og, king of Bashan, whom they believed was born *before* the Flood to the same father.[11] Of all the giants in the Bible, Og is by far the most colorful and embellished. The *Targum* tells us, for instance, that Og hitched a ride on Noah's Ark (in other stories he rides on the back of a *Reëm*[12] that was too big to fit into the ark), sustained by food that Noah fed him through a hole, all after promising Noah that he would serve his descendants as a slave forever. God did not spare Og because he was righteous, they said, but so that the world "might see the power of the Lord, and say, 'Were there not giants who in the first times rebelled against the Lord of the world, and perished from the Earth?'"[13]

Only two of the dozens of giants in the Bible have their height recorded. Og is the first. The Bible says that Og had a bed,[14] or perhaps a sarcophagus (coffin made of stone),[15] over 13 ft. long and 6 feet wide (Deut 3:11). This was not a result of Og's penchant for narcissism. He needed this coffin. To put that in perspective, Robert Earl Hughes (1926 – 1958) became the heaviest person in history, weighing in at an astonishing 1,070 lbs (that's almost as difficult to believe as giants existing). They say that Hughes was buried in a coffin the size of a piano case. I don't know if that was an upright or a grand piano. Let's assume it is medium grand piano called a Parlor Grand, because this piano has the right length dimensions at 6'3". This piano is also 4'10" wide. Og's coffin is twice as long as this and half again as wide, meaning that Og was one seriously large fellow.[16]

In the same verse where we learn about his size, the Bible also tells us that Og was all that was left of the remnant of the Rephaim (on the east side of the Jordan River, since the Anakim-Rephaim were still in Canaan). According to the *Ugaritic* tablets which parallel the Biblical record, the Rephaim were considered to be the original inhabitants of their country north of Bashan, specifically in northern Syria, at Mt. Saphon, going all the way down to Mt. Hermon and beyond into Bashan where Og ruled. In our story, now that Sihon was dead, all that stood between Israel and the Promised Land was Og. But like Sihon, God hardened Og's heart too (and God hardened it), and thus Og turned against Israel and fought them at a place called Edrei.

Home Sweet Home

Og was the king of the land of Bashan. Joshua tells us that Og ruled "over Mt. Hermon and Salecah and all Bashan" (Josh 12:5). Somewhere between Og and Sihon is the land of Gilead, which was also part of their territory. Bashan is the region of today's Golan Heights in the upper northwest portion of Israel. At its northern end is Mt. Hermon. Both Bashan and Hermon have absolutely fascinating histories.

Recall that Mt. Hermon is where the Jews believed the fallen heavenly beings (Watchers) first descended upon the earth. The Babylonians tell a very similar story. For them, Hermon was the home of the *Anunnaki*[17] ("the princely blood; royal offspring") gods who lived with men a long time ago. Remember also that Hermon and "anathema" or "devote to destruction" are the same root word. What is God doing to the giants? He is having Israel devote them to complete destruction, just as God himself did in the Flood. Remember also that at the base of Hermon sits Caesaera Philippi or Banias (from the god Pan whose father was Hermes). Pan was a satyr, a half-goat, half-human hybrid in the Greek stories. Jubilees records a bit more detail,

> But formerly the land of Gilcad was called "the land of Raphaim" because it was the land of the Raphaim. And the Raphaim were born as giants whose height was ten cubits, nine cubits, eight cubits, or down to seven cubits. And their dwelling was from the land of the Ammonites to Mount Hermon and their royal palaces were in Qarnaim, and Ashtaroth, and Edrei, and Misur, and Beon. (Jub 29:9-10).

This puts the height of the Amorites between 10 ½ and 15 feet. This mountain oozes Genesis 6, as does the whole of Bashan.

Bashan has an interesting meaning. It is related to other Semitic words for ... *serpent*.[18] Why is this significant? This deserves a short detour. In the Bible, Satan is called the serpent (Gen 3:1; Isa 27:1; Rev 20:2). The particular Hebrew word used in Genesis 3:1 is *nachash*. Nachash is a synonym for a more familiar word: *Seraph* (from whence we get Seraphim or the famous flying angels of Isaiah 6). In Numbers

21:6-9 and Isaiah 14:29, both words are used to describe the same thing. In Numbers, for instance, God sends "fiery serpents" (*seraph*, vs. 6), and the people beg to Moses to have God remove these serpents (*nachash*, vs. 7). God told Moses to make a "fiery serpent" (*seraph*, vs. 8) and set it on a pole. So Moses made a bronze serpent (*nechosheth nachash*, vs. 9). Both words can mean "serpent" and both words can mean "shining" (just like the bronze metal which is from the same root word above). It is also very interesting that *nachash*, when used as a verb, is translated as "divination."[19] The point is, certain angelic beings are identified as having some kind of serpentine shining form, though they are actually angelic beings and not reptiles.[20] The reason there is so much of a relationship between things pertaining to giants and serpents is because these angelic beings were their progenitors.

Bashan is "the settlement of the serpent." In this regard, one of the groups that lived in the region of Bashan, in fact at the very foot of Mt. Hermon (Josh 11:3), and are always associated with giant tribes, are the Hivites. "Hivites" (*chivvi*) has the same consonants as another Hebrew word for snake, and thus some have referred to them as the snake-clan.[21] They have a curious history in the legends of the Greeks. Samuel Bochart (1599-1667), a French Huguenot divine who knew 18 languages, reported in his book *Geographia Sacra* that the Hivites fled to the Islands of Asian Minor (Cyprus, Rhodes, Samos, Chios, Icaria, etc.) after their defeat at the hands of Joshua.

The Greek Historian Pliny (23 -79 AD) states that Cyprus was originally called Ophiusa, "The place of serpents" (from the word *ophis*). Rhodes was also called Ophiusa. Perhaps the most fascinating is the tiny island of Chios. According to Bochart, "Chios" is derived from *chivia*, the same root of Hivite and serpent. At Chios was a mountain called Pelineus or "The Stupendous Serpent." Under this mountain, according to the Greek historian Claudius Aelianus (175-235 AD), there lived a huge dragon, whose voice was terrible and no one could approach his cave. The people killed him by setting fire to the mouth of the cavern. Here, on this mountain, the Hivites erected a temple called "AN IMMENSE DRAGON."[22] Satan is also called "the dragon" (Isa 27:1; Rev 20:2). Certainly the worship of the serpent among the giants was not an accident.

Think again about Bashan ("place of the serpent"). Smack dab in the middle of Bashan, there is a tantalizingly mysterious serpentinesque ravine 1.1 miles in length (Fig. 8.7). Visible from over 60 miles above on Google Earth, the figure begins at the head and dissipates near the tail. The rest of the creek, which goes on for miles in both directions from the "snake," looks nothing like this segment. The head is 21.5 miles south of Mt. Hermon.

FIG. 8.3. SERPENTINE RAVINE, BASHAN

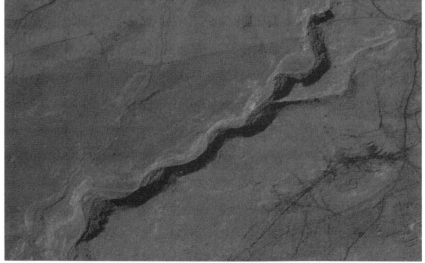

7.2 miles to the Southwest sits another strange serpentine formation, this time arising out of the earth rather than cut from it. Are these natural contours of streams and hills, or has one or both been intentionally manipulated by someone? There are, in fact, serpent mounds to be found in Britain, Ohio (U.S.A), and other places around the world, so such an idea has precedent. Archaeological study is needed to see if these serpentine figures in Bashan are artificial. But if they are, they could be well over 4,000 years old.

FIG. 8.4. SERPENT MOUNDS

Serpent Mound(?) next to Gilgal Refaim, Bashan, Israel

Above: Serpent Mound, Loch Nell, Scotland. Taken from Constance Cumming's *In the Hebrides*, 1883. **Below**: Serpent Mound, Ohio.

The Serpent Mound of Bashan has ruins on its "head" and "tail." These ruins are square (altars?) on top of small circular mounds. It's location is also fascinating. The formation is situated a mere .2 of a mile at its closest point to one of the most ancient structures in all of

Israel. It is called Gilgal Refaim, which translates as "The Wheel of the Giants." Is it a coincidence that Og's name can mean "a circle"?[23]

The "Wheel" is located a mere 25 miles northwest of Edrei. It contains some 42,000 tons of partly worked stone, built into a circle 156 meters in diameter and 8 ft. high on the outer wall. It is aligned to the summer solstice. The area is littered with dolmans (burial chambers made up of vertical slabs weighing several tons), including one in the middle of the structure which was found to contain objects associating it with a grave. The objects were dated to before the time of Abraham.[24] If you go exactly due north of the Wheel, through the strange serpentine mound for 28 miles, you will run straight into the summit of Mt. Hermon.

FIG. 8.5. WHEEL OF GIANTS, SERPENT MOUND & MT. HERMON

It is curious that at this place, the land of the giants, which is so heavily charged with angelic (Watcher) history, they would build a "wheel." The prophet Ezekiel once had a vision. In his vision he saw shining heavenly beings. "I looked at the living creatures, I saw a wheel on the earth beside the living creatures, one for each of the four of them" (Ezek 1:15). The wheels appeared as "gleaming beryl" (1:16). The wheels ("their bodies") had spokes and rims (Ezek 10:12). Ezekiel also notes that they were "whirring wheels" (Ezek 10:2).

The word for a "whirring wheel" is related to Gilgal. It is the Hebrew: *galgal*. These wheels were not space ships, but rather Ezekiel is giving a classic description of a Middle Eastern throne platform. Could the giant-wheel be a representation of the house of the god?

FIG. 8.6. WHEEL-THRONE PLATFORM

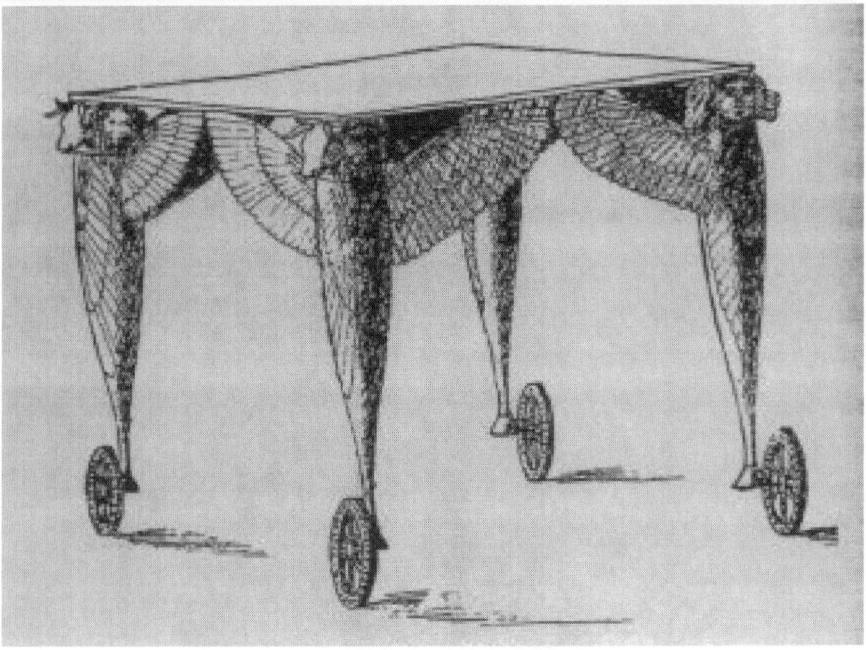

Note: Four seraphim with four hooved legs ending in wheels
Syrio-Palestine[25]

FIG. 8.7. GILGAL REFAIM & OTHER ROUND SITES IN BASHAN

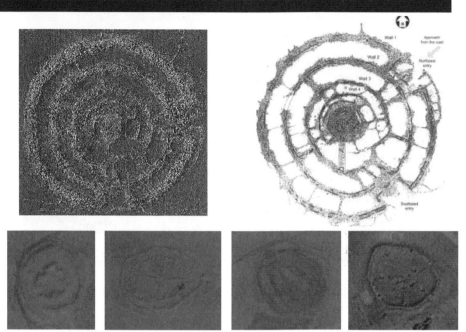

It is not known for sure where the idea of circular ceremonial centers originates. However, it is without question that such sites are found all over the world, whether in stone or dirt. Many of these ancient circles are associated in old world stories with builders who were thought to be giants.

In the Bible, before Joshua begins his conquest of the land, God performs a duplicate miracle of the Red Sea. He opens the waters of the Jordan and all the people pass through on dry land. To commemorate the event, Joshua commands the men to take twelve giants stones from the Jordan and set them up in Gilgal as a memorial. Gilgal, as we have seen, means "wheel" or "circle." Did Joshua set up a stone circle? We may never know with certainty.

FIG. 8.8. CIRCULAR CEREMONIAL SITES OF THE WORLD

STONE CIRCLES

ABOVE (LEFT AND RIGHT): Göbekli Tepe, Turkey – The Oldest Temple in the World (computer generation: DAI/German Archaeological Institute). **Below (left):** Qoy Qirlig' an qala, Uzbekistan. **(Middle):** Stone Circle, Saharan Desert, Africa. **(Right):** Arakaim ("Russian Stonehenge"), Southern Urals, Russia.

CIRCULAR CEREMONIAL CENTERS

(**Above**): Hill of Tara, Ireland

(**Above**): Stonehenge, England

(**Above**): Avebury Stone Circles, England

(**Left** and **Right**)
Great Kiva, Chayco Canyon, New Mexico; Moundbuilders State Park, Newark, Ohio

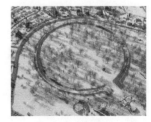

Chapter 9: Giant Wars, the Sequel

The fear of you has fallen upon us, and that all the inhabitants of the land melt away before you.

Joshua 2:9

Preparation for Battle

With Sihon and Og out of the way, the Transjordan (all the land east of the Jordan River) is now cleared of the giant threat. Israel may safely pursue war without fear of being attacked from behind. Now it is the giants' turn to fear. Whether or not Og survived the Flood, the *Targum* certainly got one thing correct: Giants were allowed to be in the land of Canaan so that all people "might see the power of the Lord" and fall to their knees in terror. If the giants serve any purpose in the Bible, it is to die by God's omnipotent hand.[1] They also show God's steadfast love for his chosen people. As the giants are exterminated from the land, it is because the LORD fights for his people and goes before them, causing the inhabitants to melt away in fear.

The nations began melting with fear when God drowned the Egyptian army in the middle of the Red Sea. Moses sang, "Now are the chiefs of Edom dismayed; trembling seizes the leaders of Moab; all the inhabitants of Canaan have melted away. Terror and dread fall upon them; because of the greatness of your arm" (Ex 15:15-16). This theme is predicted to continue (Ex 23:27; Deut 2:25; 11:25; 28:10).

Some forty years later, the prostitute Rahab (who alone was saved in the destruction of Jericho) acknowledged that the prophecy had come true. She told the two spies, "I know that the LORD has given you the land, and that the fear of you has fallen upon us, and that all the inhabitants of the land melt away [in fear] before you" (Josh 2:9).

The opposite of fear is courage. The book of Joshua begins with a saying: "Be strong and courageous." It is easy to find this saying in Evangelical bookstores or to find someone quoting it as their "life verse." But the saying has a context. The first time I read this chapter, not realizing what was going on, I wondered why in the world Joshua would need to be told to be courageous so many times. Yes, he was going into war, but plenty of people have gone into war, including Joshua, during the past forty years.

This is a rare saying, repeated in only three other places in the entire Bible. Yet it is applied *four* times to Joshua in one chapter (Josh 1:6, 7, 9, 18). So what gives? Why does Joshua need to be so courageous? The context is the destruction of the giants from the land of Canaan. Joshua 1 picks up where Deuteronomy 31:3-7, 23 left off.

[3] The LORD your God himself will go over before you. He will destroy these nations before you, so that you shall dispossess them, and Joshua will go over at your head, as the LORD has spoken. [4] And the LORD will do to them as he did to Sihon and Og, the kings of the Amorites, and to their land, when he destroyed them. [5] And the LORD will give them over to you, and you shall do to them according to the whole commandment that I have commanded you. [6] <u>Be strong and courageous.</u> Do not fear or be in dread of them, for it is the LORD your God who goes with you. He will not leave you or forsake you." [7] Then Moses summoned Joshua and said to him in the sight of all Israel, "<u>Be strong and courageous</u> ... [23] and the LORD

commissioned Joshua the son of Nun and said, "Be strong and courageous."

This passage now makes a total of seven times that the saying is applied to Joshua. "Seven" (the number of completion) makes the perfect
repetition for the ultimate fight about to ensue, the battle over the
Promised Land, and the outworking of the battle of the two seeds.

The preparation for battle begins in Joshua 1:14 where Joshua
commands all the "men of valor" among the tribes of Reuben, Gad, and
the half-tribe of Manasseh that they must cross the Jordan and fight
with their brothers before they may possess the now empty lands of
Og and Sihon. "Men of valor" is the phrase *chayil gibborim*. We have
mentioned this phrase previously. It often comes in the context of Israel fighting literal *gibborim*: Giants. It is an ironic turn of a phrase—
the little guys will become giants by defeating the giants of Canaan. It
is sort of like when Jesus said, "the last will be first" (Matt 20:16).

After assembling all Israel together, Joshua gives them a little
pep-talk before something extraordinary happens. "Come here, and
hear the words of the LORD your God. By this you shall know that
the living God is among you, and that He will assuredly dispossess
from before you the Canaanite, the Hittite, the Hivite, the Perizzite,
the Girgashite, the Amorite, and the Jebusite" (Josh 3:9-10). At that
moment, the Levites are summoned. They bring the Ark of the Covenant to the shores of the Jordan River and when they step into it, the
waters stand and rise up in a heap some miles upstream.

Before devoting the peoples to destruction, we learn two more
facts. First, "When all the kings of the Amorites who were beyond the
Jordan to the west, and all the kings of the Canaanites who were by the
sea, heard how the LORD had dried up the waters of the Jordan be-

fore the sons of Israel until they had crossed, their hearts melted, and there was no spirit in them any longer" (Josh 5:1). Again, God's prediction had come true. Second, after circumcising the new generation of Israelites at Gilgal(!) on the day of Passover, the people ate for the first time from the food of Canaan. The manna stopped that same hour. Then, as Joshua was surveying the land he lifted up his eyes and, "Behold, a man was standing before him with his drawn sword in his hand. And Joshua went to him and said to him, 'Are you for us, or for our adversaries?' And he said, 'No; but I am the commander of the army of the LORD. Now I have come.' And Joshua fell on his face to the earth and worshiped." The captain of the LORD's host said to Joshua, "Take off your sandals from your feet, for the place where you are standing is holy." And Joshua did so (Josh 5:13-15).

This extraordinary story gives Joshua a glimpse of the supernatural battle that will be fought *for* him. This Captain (or prince) is none other than the LORD himself, the LORD in visible form, otherwise known as the Angel of the LORD. This is confirmed by the repetition of the "holy ground" story that Moses hears some 40 years earlier on the side of Mt. Sinai at the burning bush, when the Angel of the LORD appeared to him there (Ex 3:2-5). Also, Joshua worships this person and he accepts Joshua's worship (unfallen created angels never accept worship in the Bible). God will fight for Israel because he promised he would. But he will also fight for Israel because his promise to Eve is on the line. The time of the extermination of the giants from Canaan will now begin.

Jericho

The beginning of the conquest takes place because the inhabitants of Jericho had shut themselves inside the city. God said to

Joshua, "I have given Jericho into your hand, with its king and mighty men of valor" (Josh 6:2). The inhabitants of Jericho, including the *gibborim* giants among them, are very afraid.

Like Hebron, Jericho is a city showing, in places, gigantic proportions. For instance,

> An approaching enemy first encountered a stone abutment, eleven feet high, back and up from which sloped a thirty-five degree plastered scarp reaching to the main wall some thirty-five vertical feet above. The steep smooth slope prohibited battering the wall by any effective device or building fires to break it. An army trying to storm the wall found difficulty in climbing the slope, and ladders to scale it could find no satisfactory footing. The normal tactic used by an enemy to take a city so protected was siege, but Israel did not have time for this, if she was to occupy all the land in any reasonable number of months.[2]

Because the walls were unbreachable, because the city was full of giants, and in order to bring great glory to himself and even more fear upon the wicked inhabitants of Canaan, God performed an astounding miracle. After marching around the city walls, silently, for seven days, suddenly and without notice, the trumpets blew and walls a dozen feet thick instantly explode *outwards*. The Commander of the heavenly army had struck. Israel rushed in and put everyone who did not flee to the sword, except for Rahab. The Arabs, who have legends that some of the inhabitants of Jericho fled to Africa and became the Berbers, call Jericho "The City of Giants."[3]

Taking Other Cities

The next city taken (though not without difficulty because a man from Israel [Achan] had taken some of the things devoted to destruction) was Ai. Ai was next door to Jericho, to the west, a step closer to Jerusalem (which Joshua would not conquer). It, too, was a strong fortress, though nothing could surpass the glory of Jericho. Was Ai a city of giants? The Bible does not say, but the Jews certainly thought that it was. When Joshua took Ai they report that he said, "Enter into this town; for God has taken it from the giants, and has given it to you to be your inheritance. But when you pass through the gates, prostrate yourselves, with your heads in the dust, and adore God, saying, Hittaton, hittaton, which is by interpretation, Pardon our sins."[4]

After this, the people of the city of Gibeon, the next city in line of the march, become so frightened that they trick Israel into making a covenant of peace with them. The Bible calls these people Hivites and Amorites, and the LXX calls them Horites (who presumably fled here when Esau took over their lands; Josh 9:7). It was a grave mistake to make peace with these people, but because they made a covenant with them, Israel could not go back on its word. Joshua destroyed many cities in the northern part of Israel after this.

From here Joshua set his sights to the south, and the lands filled with Anakim. They conquer Bethel, the ancient home of Jacob. They take Makkedah, Libnah, Lachish and Gezer. Excavations at Gezer and other sites produced skeletons over nine feet tall which, "bear out the unusually tall stature of individuals in ancient Palestine."[5] One city in the vicinity known as Beit Jibrim or "House of the Gibborim" contains "one of the most amazing cave-cities in the world" where you can find labyrinths of caves upwards of eighty feet tall hewn with picks.[6] Guess who the stories say built them? No wonder they call it the House of the Giants.

Some Giants Remained in Gaza, Gath, and Ashdod

Greatly emboldened by victory after victory, Joshua set his sights on the crown jewel of Canaan—Hebron. Hebron is the headquarters of the giant Anakim and, especially, the three terrifying sons of Anak. They destroy all the Anakim from the hill country, from Hebron, Debir, and Anab (Josh 11:21). "Only in Gaza, Gath, and Ashdod did some remain" (vs. 22).

Ashdod is another city referred to as the "city of giants," this time it is the Egyptians who gave it this name.[7] Gath was said to be the home of an early Christian saint known as St. Christopher. This saint became fabled more than most, his history steeped in the mists of legend. "The legends say that St. Christopher was from the city of Gath; and that this day men who are born there are said to be stronger and more warlike than other men."[8]

As the story goes, Christopher was born Reprobus ("wicked"). They say he was a third century Christian martyred during the reign of Emperor Decius (249-51). A thirteenth century Italian historian wrote, "Christopher was a Canaanite[9] by birth, a man of prodigious size—he was twelve feet tall—and fearsome of a visage."[10] By the time the story got to the British Isles, he belonged to a tribe of dog-headed, cannibalistic giants. The tale is told in the Beowulf manuscript.[11]

This accounting of Christopher bears a remarkable resemblance to one Abominable—a cannibal "with a face like unto that of a dog, four cubits in height with eyes like lamps of fire, teeth like the tusks of a wild boar or of a lion, nails like curved reaping hooks, both awful and terrifying"—who met the disciples Andrew and Alexander, was baptized, and renamed Christianus in the ancient legendary *Contendings of the Apostles.*[12] Christopher is even depicted as dog-faced in early Byzantine art.

FIG. 9.1. ST. CHRISTOPHER

St. Christopher as depicted in the Eastern Church

Although the legends of Christopher grew into tall-tales, they do tell us one thing. A very long time ago, people made the same kinds of connections of giants coming from Canaan that we are seeing here.[13] The mention of Gaza, Gath, and Ashdod as the remnant of the giants in Canaan is important for what it foreshadows. As we will soon see, Christopher is not the only giant that is said to come from Gath. There is a citizen of Gath much more famous than Christopher. He is found in the Bible. Giants were still in the land. They put up a good fight. But they would have to be destroyed sooner or later.

Chapter 10: Goliath and His Brothers

There was again war at Gath, where there was a
man of great stature, who had six fingers on each
hand and six toes on each foot, twenty-four in num-
ber, and he also was descended from the giants.

1 Chronicles 20:6

He Really Did Slay the Giant in His Life

He is undoubtedly the best known giant in the Bible. His story is said by some to be pure fantasy, the invention of Jewish sages who needed new bedtime tales to tell their tots. Others think his place in the Bible is that of a fable—a fictional story with a moral at the end. "Have you slain the giants in your life"? I'm talking, of course, about Goliath.

Many Christians have this idea that Goliath is the *only* giant in the Bible. The story of his demise at the hands of a tiny shepherd boy named David is universally known. People are often shocked, however, to discover that there are other giants in the Bible. That is why I waited until now to speak of him. I wanted to talk about Goliath in his own context and moment in history. His story makes so much more sense that way. If you see Goliath in his ancestral milieu as you are now able to do, you can actually process his story and understand why he is in the Bible in the first place. As I mentioned previously,

God did not give us the story of Goliath in order to help us slay the "Goliath's in our lives." It is so very much more important than that.

FIG. 10.1. "THE GOLIATH SHARD"

The "Goliath Shard"
Discovered in 2005 at Tel es-Safi
9th cent. B.C. destruction Level. Gath, Israel[1]

They Did Not Drive Them Out

Before we get to Goliath himself, let's see how it is that David came to fight this monster in the first place. Continuing with the story, we pick it up at the end of the book of Joshua. On the whole, the story of Joshua is positive. Israel obeyed their commander, went from city to city, and destroyed all the giant inhabitants or those who mixed themselves with them. Thus the book concludes, "Not one word has failed of all the good things that the LORD your God promised ... The LORD gave them rest on every side just as he had sworn to their fathers. Not one of all their enemies had withstood them, for the LORD had given all their enemies into their hands" (Josh 23:14-15). This did not mean, however, that Israel had taken all of the land. It means that wherever Joshua went, God routed the giants before him.

Israel was able to settle the land, eat from its produce, and live in its houses, all because God had delivered on his word.

Then Joshua died. The story of the book of Judges picks up immediately after the people swear an oath that they will do everything that the LORD has commanded them (Josh 24). Joshua warned them that they could not serve the LORD, because he was holy and they were not. But they thought themselves to be invincible. A subtle pride had crept in and changed their thinking. Perhaps they were really responsible for the victories they fought and won?

With Joshua gone, the conquest of other cities, not taken earlier, began. Judah took the lead, defeated many cities of the Canaanites and Perizzites, and the LORD was with Judah. "But he could not drive out the inhabitants of the plain because they had chariots of iron" (Jdg 1:19). This is a strange verse, because in Joshua's day the chariots did not seem to hinder them at all (Josh 11:4-9). Furthermore, Joshua's promise to another tribe was that they would not hinder them if they were faithful to God (Josh 17:18). Why did Judah not succeed?

From here it only gets worse. It says, "The people of Benjamin did not drive out the Jebusites who lived in Jerusalem" (Jdg 1:21). Manasseh did not drive out the peoples of Bethshean, Taanach, Dor, Ibleam, Megiddo or any of their villages "for the Canaanites persisted in dwelling in that land" (Jdg 1:27). "They put the Canaanites to forced labor, but did not drive them out completely" (vs. 28). Ephraim did not drive out the Canaanites in Gezer (vs. 29). Zebulon left two cities full of Canaanites, but made them slaves (vs. 30). Asher did not drive out Canaanites in seven cities (vs. 31). Naphtali left Canaanites in two cities and turned them into slaves as well (vs. 33). Perhaps worst of all, the Amorites continued to live in the high country in Dan (by Mt. Hermon), but they too were put into labor camps (vs. 34-35).

Slavery was not what Israel was supposed to do with these people. They were supposed to utterly destroy them. But it was the LORD who left these nations here "to test Israel by them," "to see if Israel would obey the commandments of the LORD," and "to teach war" and to the generations coming up that had not been involved in the previous victories (Jdg 3:1-5).

But Israel did not obey. They "took their daughters for themselves as wives, and gave their own daughters to their sons, and served their gods" (Jdg 3:6). These things they did with Canaanites, Hittites, Amorites, Perizzites, Hivites, and Jebusites (vs. 5). My thought on this is that perhaps most of the giant Rephaim that lived among these peoples had by now been destroyed, and so Israel figured such mixing would not be such a bad thing now. The problem is, God wanted these nations destroyed because they had mixed with the Nephilim of older days and had become utterly corrupted by their vile worship and abominable practices.

The rest of the book of Judges tells the story of a disintegrating cycle. The cycle begins with Israelite apostasy, moves to Israelite captivity at the hands of some group of Canaanites or Philistines etc., then Israel cries out to God for deliverance, and finally the LORD delivers them by giving them a Judge. By the end of the book, the Judge and the people are drifting ships and wandering stars, without morality, without a compass, doing whatever they personally believe is right in their own eyes.

And giants are left in the land.

Give Us a King

This is the context which we find Israel finally crying out to the LORD, "Appoint for us a king to judge us like all the nations." (1 Sam

8:5). This was not a good request, but was in effect a rejection of the LORD as their king (8:7). Because the chosen Seed would eventually become King of Israel, the LORD told Samuel to give into the people's demand. Everyone was sent to his home to await the choosing of the new king.

It tells us that there was a man of Benjamin, an Israelite, whose name was Kish. Kish was a wealthy man who had a son named Saul. Including Saul, we are given a genealogy of seven names (1 Sam 9:1), in other words he was a man of perfect generations (remember Noah?) of Israelites. Saul was handsome and more important, "from his shoulders upward he was taller than any of the people" (9:2). Isn't this a strange detail to add? Not really. Israel wanted a king just like the other nations, and in Saul's stature, it looks like they got the best that could be found.

Now we are able to pick up the story of Goliath. We read about it in 1 Samuel 17. The Philistines gathered their armies for battle and Saul and his men were gathered and encamped in the Valley of Elah to fight them. The valley is an unremarkable place set between two small hills where the two armies could have set up camp, taunted one another from a distance, and prepared for war. But on this day, the Philistines did not want a war. Rather, they found themselves a champion whom they figured could defeat any Israelite in hand-to-hand combat, and in representative fashion, would win the battle with much less bloodshed. These were civilized people after all.

Their champion was "a Philistine" (1 Sam 21:9), Goliath "of Gath" (1 Sam 17:4). "Goliath" is an interesting name. It can mean "soothsayer," which certainly bears affinity to what we know about the giants of Canaan. It can also mean "taken captive." Perhaps Goliath's name was given to him by the Philistines who captured him in their attempt to take the giant fortresses that remained in Gath and Ashdod by the Sea. It needs to be noted again, the Philistines (like many of the other tribes) were probably not, properly speaking, giants. That is, they were not descended from the Rephaim or Nephilim. After all, Goliath is seen here as being much taller than they are too. It is their mixing with the older giants that aroused the wrath of God so that he decided to destroy them from Canaan as well as the giants.

Just how tall was this champion of Gath? There is actually a discrepancy in the Biblical account. The more recent Hebrew Masoretic text says one thing, while the older LXX and Dead Sea Scrolls have a different height. Most English Bibles put his height at 9'9" inches ("six cubits and a span"), following the Hebrew of 1 Sam 17:4.[2] This view has recently been defended, with a slight modification.[3] Others have argued that the oldest LXX readings of "4 cubits and a span," or a height of 6'9" tall, are correct.[4] Which is right?

I'm not a giant. I'm about 5'11." Compared to David, who was probably a typical Israelite a little less than 5'6",[5] I might be considered tall, but definitely not a giant. My roommate in college was a little over 6'5". To me, that's tall and it is also relatively close to the size Goliath is said to be in the older manuscripts. Curiously, no one, not even my friend's wife—who is 5'0" tall if she stands on a telephone book—ever called my roommate a giant. However, Goliath *is called* a giant.[6]

In a non-scientific experiment, I had my wife measure the length of my head with a ruler. Add in about three inches for my neck, and I have about a foot of length above my shoulders. Saul is said to be taller than the other Israelites starting at his shoulders. Given the average known height of an Israelite at that time, this would put Saul only a few inches shorter than 6'9".

Here's the thing. Once Goliath begins to yell out to the Israelites to fight him, we read that Saul was *deeply afraid* and *terrified* of this monster Philistine (1 Sam 17:11). Now, I would not have liked to have fought my roommate in college, because I would have lost, especially after he gained a hundred pounds of weight and tried out for the Minnesota Vikings. But even though I would have been more than twice as short to him as Saul (supposedly) was to Goliath, I certainly wouldn't have fled to the hills (along with all the rest of my floormates) had he challenged me in a fight.

Next, let's compare Goliath to his armor. We discover that Goliath's armor weighed in at a total of 160 lbs, which was three times as heavy as that worn by a fully armoured Greek hoplite soldier who trained their entire lives to fight battles (1 Sam 17:5-6).[7] I'm not saying it is impossible for a man at 6'9" to carry that much armor, but it certainly would have been extremely cumbersome.

Consider also the size of Goliath's spear. The spear would have been thrust at an enemy (as opposed to thrown like his javelin). Its tip alone weighed in excess of 15 lbs. The spear, which was like a weaver's beam (perhaps 2 ½ - 3 inches diameter or the size of the barrel of a baseball bat), must have had a total weight anywhere between 35-65 lbs. Such proportions seem excessive even for a man 6'9" tall, but not for a man almost ten feet tall, especially if he had proper proportions.[8]

The most important thing, however, is Goliath's ancestry. Whereas the Scripture calls Saul a Benjamite, it says of Goliath that he was from Gath (1 Sam 17:4), and descended from the *Rephaim* (2 Sam 21:22). Goliath was obviously not a Jew. His residence (Gath) and his lineage (Rephaim) tell us exactly who (or what) Goliath really was. If we remember that Og's bed/sarcophagus was thirteen feet long, is it really that inconceivable that the Hebrew manuscript got it so wrong?

Heights of Heroes Compared

David at Average Jewish Height	King Saul "A Head Taller"	Goliath (LXX, DSS, Josephus)	Goliath (Symmachus, Vulgate, Masoretic Text)	King Og of Bashan (A Foot shorter than his Bed/Coffin)
5'5"	6'6"	6'9"	9'9"	12'0"

With that said, there is a theory that there is no discrepancy at all between the two variants, and that Goliath was in reality somewhere between eight and nine feet tall in *both* the Hebrew and Greek texts. This argument depends on the LXX using the much longer Egyptian cubit (Egypt is where the LXX was translated), rather than the shorter Hebrew cubit (note the same word for length, but different measurement). The translator would have converted the Hebrew cubit to the correct height in his own unit of measurement.[9] If so, then even the LXX (which itself has a variant reading of 5 cubits), would place Goliath between 7'8" and 9'5". In considering the height of this behemoth man, it should be noted that the historian Josephus said that in his day (1,000 years later), there was a "Jewish" man named Eleazar whom Artabanus III of Parthia sent as a gift to Tiberius Caesar. Eleazar was seven cubits or around eleven feet tall.[10] Josephus does not blink when conveying a height taller than the tallest given for Goliath.

One of the other curious facts about the story of Goliath is that there are several other giants who were his contemporaries. Have you ever wondered why David picked up *five* smooth stones (1 Sam 17:40)? These were not his five weapons for spiritual leadership, for pastoral ministry, or Christian faith (wouldn't David have picked up only one stone if the five stones were signs of his faith?). David needed five stones, because Goliath had four other brothers who were all said to be giants.

Goliath had a brother named Lahmi. From the only physical description given of Lahmi, it appears that he was a virtual twin of Goliath, for it says that both had spears "like a weaver's beam" (1 Chron 20:5; cf. 1 Sam 17:7). This would put the spear around 3" diameter, or approximately three times the width of the average spear. Their spear is similar to that of an unnamed Egyptian giant who was 7 ½ feet tall (1 Chron 11:23). Like Goliath, Lahmi is said to have been descended from the Rephaim.

In the same passage you read about three other giants, all slain by David's mighty *gibborim*. Sippai (2 Sam 21:18; 1 Chron 20:4) and Ishbi-benob (2 Sam 21:16) are mentioned by name. Ishbi-benob had a spear-tip that weighed 7 ½ lbs.[11] There is an unnamed giant who had the incredible physical characteristic of having the 24 fingers and toes (2 Sam 21:20). The same kind of genetic defect can be found today among people of quite ordinary stature. However, here we are lead to believe that the defect came from the ancestry of this giant freak.

This ancestry is the Rephaim, or in the case of six-fingered giant—the Rapha. Rapha may be a proper name, perhaps the first or a prominent person among the Rephaim. The KJV translates it as "the giant." Thus, these three giants were descended from "the giant" on this interpretation. Since Lahmi is Goliath's brother,[12] the idea is that this is all one clan of giants, among which Goliath is the most famous.

I recently discovered yet another giant in this story. You don't read about him in the Hebrew text, but he is in the LXX. His name is Dan son of Joa. He is found in 2 Samuel (2 Kingdoms) 21:11 LXX in a gloss. The context is David giving up seven sons of Saul to the Gibeonites, "the remnant of the Amorites" to be hanged. Saul had dealt treacherously with these people and their heads was a kind of payback. Apparently, this giant named Dan overtook Respha/Rizpah, the mother of some of these sons of Saul, but the wording is confusing. It is difficult to find anyone who even knows about this giant. The story does not say what happened to him.

I do find it curious that his parents would name the giant baby Dan, as Dan is "a serpent in the way, a viper by the path, that bites the horse's heels so that his rider falls backward" (Gen 49:17). Dan is the land of Bashan, Grand Central Station for the Amorites in the OT, and home of the serpent mound just north of the Wheel of Giants.

So why is the story of David vs. Goliath in the Bible? The battle falls within the broader scope of the holy war that began, for Israel, at the fall of Jericho. This is, in a nut-shell, Israel vs. the giants. If you think about it, however, Saul—the tall one—should have been the one to fight Goliath. But Saul was a coward (even though he was supposedly only three inches shorter than the behemoth). Saul was also not God's chosen man, nor was he from the royal line through which Messiah would be born.

Long before, in the days of Jacob, Judah his son was promised, "Judah is a lion ... The sceptre shall not depart from Judah, nor the ruler's staff from between his feet, until tribute (lit: *Shiloh*) comes to him; and to him shall be the obedience of the peoples" (Gen 49:10). "Shiloh" is a Messianic title. The *Targum* has a beautiful paraphrase, "Kings shall not cease form the house of Judah ... until the time that the King Meshiha [Messiah] shall come, whose is the kingdom, and to whom all the kingdoms of the earth shall be obedient. How beauteous is the King Meshiha, who is to arise from the house of Judah."

In the larger picture, this is the story of the seed of the serpent mocking, taunting, and battling the seed of the woman. Notice what David says just prior to lopping off the head of the belligerent ogre,

> You come to me with a sword and with a spear and with a javelin, but I come to you in the name of the LORD of hosts, the God of the armies of Israel, whom you have defied. This day the LORD will deliver you into my hand, and I will strike you down and cut off your head. And I will give the dead bodies of the host of the Philistines this day to the birds of the air and to the wild beasts of the earth, that all the earth may know that there is a God in Israel, and that all this assembly may know that the LORD saves not with sword and spear. For the battle is the LORD's, and he will give you into our hand.
>
> (1Sa 17:45-47)

David defeats Goliath in anticipation of the greater battle to come between the Messiah and Satan.

Chapter 11: Agag the Amalekite

Let a gallows fifty cubits high be made, and in the morning tell the king to have Mordecai hanged upon it.

Esther 5:14

Saul's Failure as King

In this chapter I want to take you to the end of Old Testament history in order to show you that the theme of giants runs all the way through the story. Simply put, the giants are no minor key or dangling thread. They are one of the major storylines of the Bible. To do this I want to focus in on one group of giants that we ran across earlier: The Amalekites.

Recall that we first encounter the Amalekites in the days of Abraham in the giant wars (Gen 14:7). These Amalekites then come out of nowhere and attack Israel as it is making its way to Mt. Sinai (Exodus 17:8-16). For their crime, Moses tells the people "When the LORD your God has given you rest from all your enemies around you, in the land that the LORD your God is giving you for an inheritance to possess, you shall blot out the memory of Amalek from under heaven; you shall not forget" (Deut 25:19). We do not run into the Amalekites again until the book of Judges, but we cannot be certain that the Amalekites here are the descendants of Esau or the more primitive giant tribe.[1]

It is not until a very important incident in the life of King Saul that we unequivocally come across the people that attacked Moses in the wilderness. This episode also happens to be the event in his life that brought about God's removal of Saul as king of Israel. What did Saul do that was deserving of such great punishment as this? It was not some moral failure such as murder or adultery, but rather his blatant disregard for the command of Samuel to eradicate the giants. This is what brought about Saul's dispossession.

God sends Samuel to the king who tells him, "The LORD sent me to anoint you king over his people Israel; now therefore listen to the words of the LORD. Thus says the LORD of hosts, 'I have noted what Amalek did to Israel in opposing them on the way when they came up out of Egypt. Now go and strike Amalek and devote to destruction all that they have" (1 Sam 15:1-3). Here we see the familiar "ban" which God placed upon all the giants of the land of Canaan. At first it appears as if Saul will comply. He gathers an army and lies in wait in the valley outside the city of Amalek (vs. 5). Saul then chases the Amalekites from Havilah (perhaps in western Arabia) to Shur (east of Egypt; vs. 7).

Next, Saul meets Agag the king of the Amalekites. Agag means "flaming; to burn; blaze with fire" or "lofty, I will overtop." As an Amalekite, Agag is clearly related to the giants. Perhaps his name hints at his tall stature, especially in light of tall Saul, who was chosen because he was like the other kings of the surrounding nations. There is also a single reference to Agag in Numbers 24:7. The LXX renders "Agag" as "Gog" (which may mean "shining"[2]) of the famed Gog and Magog of Ezekiel 38-39. Both of these names are steeped in sons of

God and giant mythology. Some scholars have suggested that they may be supernatural princes, much like the princes of Persia, Greece, and Israel in Daniel 10.[3] Gog's army consists of nations that originate in Genesis 10 (Ezek 38:2-6). In the LXX[B], Gog sometimes replaces Og (Deut 3:1, 13: 4:47), and in one Greek manuscript of Ezekiel 38:2,[4] Gog becomes Og. Finally, according to Josephus, Magog is related to Celtic giants. "Gomer founded those whom the Greeks now call Galatians [Galls], but were then called Gomerites. Magog founded those that from him were named Magogites, but who are by the Greeks called Scythians" (*Antiquities of the Jews* 1.123).

After meeting Agag, Saul commits his fatal blunder. "He took Agag the king of the Amalekites <u>alive</u>" (1 Sam 15:8). He spared both Agag and the best of the sheep and oxen, fattened calves and lambs ... "all that was good" (vs. 9) and would not utterly destroy them. God tells Samuel that he regrets making Saul king because he is a worthless fellow who will not obey his commandments. After a long confrontation, Samuel curses Saul and removes the kingship from him (vs. 28). But there is still the messy little detail of what to do with king Agag.

Samuel commands, "Bring here to me Agag the king of the Amalekites." Agag comes cheerfully thinking that death has passed him by (1 Sam 15:32). But when Samuel meets Agag, he curses him and "hacked Agag to pieces before the LORD in Gilgal" (vs. 33). Why such a violent reaction, really, unparalleled in any story in the entire Bible? It is because Agag, whether he was personally of large stature or not, was descended from and king of the Amalekites whom God swore to blot out from the face of the earth. Like David and Goliath, this too is a story of God vs. the giants. It is the story of the seeds battling it out. The promise must be fulfilled. God must win the war.

You would think that the story of Agag stops here, since he is put to death by Samuel. You would be wrong. Many centuries later, near the very end of the chronological history that is preserved for us in the Bible, we run into him again.

Esther is the last book in the history section (Genesis – Esther) of Protestant Bibles.[5] Really, the only major biblical figures to come after Esther in the OT are Nehemiah and Malachi. In this book, there is a villain named Haman; his nemesis is named Mordecai (Mordecai and Esther are the heroes). The author of the book felt it necessary to give us a genealogy of both men. Why?

It has more to do than with the author simply being a good historically minded Jew. Mordecai is the son of Jair, son of Shimei, son of *Kish*, a *Benjaminite* (Est 2:5). To put it more practically, he is a relative of King Saul. Mordecai has a curious name. It means "little man." Why does this matter? Well, let's look at the genealogy of Haman.

Haman is referred to as the son of Hammedatha an *Agagite*. In fact, it mentions this not once, but *five* times (Est 3:1; 10; 8:3; 5; 9:24). To put this in more practical terms, the story of Esther is, in a sense, a replay of the story of Saul and Agag. Haman was the first Hitler. His goal in life was the complete annihilation of every Jew on earth. This is quite the ironic turn of events for the kindness and mercy that Saul showed to Agag. Haman obviously remembered the deed of Samuel.

In the story, it is Esther who saves the day. The theme of divine providence through "accidental" events that keep happening at just the right time shows that God is orchestrating everything in the book, because this is among the last OT battles between God and Satan. Esther is the Babylonian name given to Hadassah. Esther means "star." Curious, isn't it? A star rises to the throne to defeat Haman.

The story of Haman's death comes at this own hands, though he does not realize it, of course. Haman, who is reveling in his apparent victory over the Jews and his nemesis Mordecai, commands, "Let a gallows <u>fifty cubits high</u> be made, and in the morning tell the king to have Mordecai hanged on it" (Est 5:14). That puts the death instrument at 75 ft. These are "giant" gallows. But in the end, just like David and Goliath, the "little man" wins, and Haman the Agagite Amalekite is strung up on his own gibbet and hanged; a fitting finale to the giants in the OT.

Again we might ask why is the story of Mordecai, Esther, and Haman in the Bible? Among the reasons must certainly be included that this book details for us the battle of the two seeds prophesied so long before to our first mother. In conclusion, I want to return to a prophecy I mentioned earlier. Numbers 24:7 tells us, "Water shall flow from his buckets, and his seed shall be in many waters; his king shall be higher than Agag, and his kingdom shall be exalted." The "seed" here is the seed of Jacob/Israel (vs. 5). But just who is he?

In the very same prophecy, just a few verses later, Balaam uses the same language of the sceptre prophesied to Judah. "I see him, but not now; I behold him, but not near: a star shall come out of Jacob, and a sceptre shall rise out of Israel; it shall crush the forehead of Moab and break down all the sons of Sheth [Seth]" (Num 24:17). Just a couple verses later, Amalek is brought up, "Amalek was the first among the nations, but its end is utter destruction" (vs. 20). Agag, Amalek, and the Star who rules over them in Israel are all here in such a short span in a book that has its setting a thousand years before Esther. It truly is amazing. The star here is Messiah, Christ, the Seed of Eve who will ultimately bring about the final demise of Amalek and Agag. He is the Seed that will crush the head of the serpent.

Chapter 12: Demons and the Giants

The Rephaim tremble under the waters.

Job 26:5

What is a Demon?

We are going to take a detour from the storyline now. Or are we? You may be asking, what is a chapter on demons doing in a book on giants? The answer might surprise you.

The common misconception is that demons are fallen angels. This mistake is illustrated by the discussion between Cyril of Alexandria (376-444 A.D.) and a certain deacon named Tiberius, sometime after the Council of Ephesus in 431. Tiberius asks, "[How shall we respond] to those who say, 'How did the demons, being incorporeal, have intercourse with women?'" Cyril's answer basically follows Augustine's interpretation that the sons of God were Sethites, not demons.[1] This completely misses the point, and shows how an important piece of information had by this time been lost to the catacombs that became Christendom and the Dark Age.

The earliest Church Fathers would have answered very differently. While some believed that demons were the disembodied spirits of dead people, the most wide spread and influential position of the early church was that demons are the disembodied spirits of the giants, *not angels.*[2] If this is correct, then demons would be the *children* of the fallen angels. Here are some examples:

- "But the angels transgressed this appointment, and were captivated by love of women, and begat children who are those that are called demons" (Justin Martyr, *2 Apology* 5).
- "In my opinion, however, it is certain wicked demons, and, so to speak, of the race of Titans or Giants, who have been guilty of impiety towards the true God, and towards the angels in heaven, and who have fallen from it, and who haunt the denser parts of bodies, and frequent unclean places upon earth, and who, possessing some power of distinguishing future events, because they are without bodies of earthly material, engage in an employment of this kind, and desiring to lead the human race away from the true God" (Origen, *Against Celsus* 4.92).
- "For one might say that these daemons are those giants [Gen 6:4], and that their spirits have been deified by the subsequent generations of men, and that their battles, and their quarrels among themselves, and their wars are the subjects of these legends that are told as of gods" (Eusebius, *Preparation for the Gospel* 5.4).
- "These angels, then, who fell from heaven busy themselves about the air and the earth and are no longer able to rise to the realms above the heavens. The souls of the giants are the demons (*daimones*) who wander about the world" (Athenagoras, *A Plea to Christians* 24).

The Jews were of the same opinion,

- "The demon answered: 'I am called Ornias. . . I am offspring of the archangel Uriel, the power of God. . . The demon Asmodeus [answered]. . . I was born an angel's seed by a daughter of man. . . I [another enslaved spirit] am a lascivious spirit of a giant who died in the massacre in the age of giants" (Testament of Solomon 9-10, 23).
- "And when the angels of God saw the daughters of men that they were beautiful, they took unto themselves wives of all of them whom they chose." Those beings, whom other philosophers call demons, Moses

usually calls angels; and they are souls hovering in the air" (Philo, *On Giants* 6).

- "And now, the giants, who are produced from the spirits and flesh, shall be called evil spirits upon the earth, and on the earth shall be their dwelling. Evil spirits have proceeded from their bodies; because they are born from men and from the holy Watchers is their beginning and primal origin; they shall be evil spirits on earth, and evil spirits shall they be called. [As for the spirits of heaven, in heaven shall be their dwelling, but as for the spirits of the earth which were born upon the earth, on the earth shall be their dwelling.] And the spirits of the giants afflict, oppress, destroy, attack, do battle, and work destruction on the earth, and cause trouble: they take no food, but nevertheless hunger and thirst, and cause offences. And these spirits shall rise up against the children of men and against the women, because they have proceeded from them. From the days of the slaughter and destruction and death of the giants, from the souls of whose flesh the spirits, having gone forth, shall destroy without incurring judgment—thus shall they destroy until the day of the consummation, the great judgment in which the age shall be consummated, over the Watchers and the godless, yea, shall be wholly consummated" (1 Enoch 15:8-16:1).[3]

I will argue that they were correct. Where would these Jews and Christians get such an idea? Considering the Greeks had the same concept,[4] perhaps it was handed down to them through oral tradition. Since they were Scripture loving people, perhaps they get it from the Old Testament. This is where we will turn in our investigation.

Keep in mind that the original giants were destroyed in Noah's Flood. One of the more fascinating places where this idea might be found is Job 26:5. "The *rephaim* tremble under the waters." The LXX translates the word as *gigantes*: Giants. It puts it in the form of a question, "Shall giants be born from under the water"? Curiously, we find several English translations rendering the word as "ghosts" (CJB) or "shades" (JPS, TNK, RSV, BBE). Ghosts and shades are usually evil spiritual entities. Thus we seem to have at least a shadowy, ethereal connection between the Rephaim and evil spirits.

To what does this "under the waters" refer? The next verse talks about Sheol, the OT place of the dead. Sheol is often associated with a watery abyss. It is sometimes parallel with "the pit" (*bor*), a word that means a cistern or deep well (Ps 30:3; Prov 1:12; Isa 14:15; 38:18; Ezek 31:16). Likewise, it is parallel with "the deep" (*tehom/abussos*), the watery mass present at creation (Ezek 31:15). As one commentary explains, "Sheol was thought to lie under the ocean and to be a murky, watery abode."[5] In other places the Rephaim are said to be somehow residing in Sheol (Ps 88:10-11; Prov 2:18-19; 9:18; 21:6; Isa 14:9).[6]

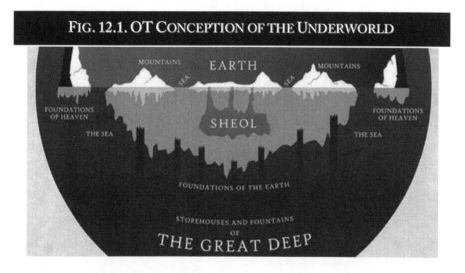

FIG. 12.1. OT CONCEPTION OF THE UNDERWORLD

It is tempting to read this with some commentaries as a reference to the Flood, under which the giants perished in the days of Noah.[7] The broader context seems to fit either the Creation story or the Flood.[8] Verse 12 mentions a being named Rahab (not the woman of Jericho), who appears sparingly in the Bible (Ps 87:4; 89:10; Job 9:13; 26:12; Isa 30:7; 51:9). These texts make it plain that it refers to the mythological sea-monster,[9] the ancient dragon, also called a serpent or leviathan. In fact, words used for Satan are also put in parallelism with Rahab.[10]

The other reference to Rahab in Job mentions "the helpers" of Rahab (Job 9:13). The Babylonian *Enuma Elish*[11] has a monster parallel with Rahab called Tiamat. Tiamat also has helpers. These helpers are called monster serpents, fierce dragons, hairy hero-men, lion monsters, lion men, scorpion men, mighty demons, fish men, and bull men—*chimeras* (half-man half-beast) known in many world mythologies. Similarly, the Canaanites tell of the "Big Ones," monsters who support the sea god Yam (who is eventually destroyed by Baal),[12] and of helper-gods who reside in the netherworld.[13] Curiously, when Tiamat is destroyed by *Marduk*, like the Rephaim under the waters, they "trembled, terrified."[14]

Knowing this background, scholars have argued that these helpers can be translated as "demons." For example, Ps 40:4 could be translated as; "Blessed is the man who makes the LORD his trust, who does not turn to demons (*rehabim*), to those who go astray after a lie."[15] Are the "Rephaim under the waters" similar or even identical to the *rehabim*/demons in the Psalm and other near eastern cultures?[16]

While the OT consistently views the Rephaim as being in Sheol (the point being that they greet wicked men—especially human kings—who go down there, and this is to serve as a kind of deterrent, because you don't want to go to where the Rephaim are), perhaps not all of them were put there,[17] or perhaps they are not bound there (yet).[18] Remember, these are not men we are talking about here, so they may not necessarily be confined to the pit as men would be.[19] Whether this is a consistent theology is a question I'll let someone else figure out, but it may explain something Moses sings about.

In our now famous hymn (recall Deut 32:8-9), Deuteronomy 32:17 says, "They sacrificed to demons (*shedim*), not God (*eloah*), to gods (*elohim*) they had never known, to new gods ("new ones") that had come recently, whom your fathers had never dreaded." Earlier, Moses has said that the older gods (i.e. sons of God) were allotted to the nations and that these nations feared and worshiped them.[20] Who might these demons be? Perhaps they were the spirits of the giants they had been killing in the desert. This conjecture, while uncertain, makes sense of how there could be new gods that were not dreaded by earlier peoples while simultaneously acknowledging that these beings are not mere idols but actual entities (i.e. demons are real). It also makes sense of where the ancient idea that demons are the spirits of the giants might have originated with earlier Christians and Jews.

Shedim

The word "demon" only appears in two places in the OT: Deuteronomy 32:17 and Psalm 106:37 (although the LXX adds Ps 96:5; Isa 13:21; 34:14; and 65:3).[21] The word is *shedim*. It is clearly related to the Babylonian word *shedu*. A shedu is a tutelary spirit—a guardian/protector of a place or a person or a thing. They could be either malevolent or beneficent. They were often depicted as winged-bulls or lions with the head of a human, making them *chimeras* or half-breeds and also pointing to their half-human origin. You can see the resemblance between a shedu and a *minotaur* (which is its reverse) or a sphinx (below).

FIG. 12.2. CHIMERAS

Lamassu (shedu)   Minotaur   Sphinx

Most people do not realize this, but it wasn't until the NT that demons were viewed as exclusively evil (certainly the two OT references do not put them in a good light). For almost all pagan peoples, demons were viewed as morally ambiguous. They could be described as good or evil, and a single demon could bring both good or ill, inflict harm or fulfill your desires when worship and service was rendered to it, depending upon your piety or fate.

The Greek (and hence English) word "demon" is of unknown origin, but suggestions help show you why the ancients did not necessarily view demons as evil. Plato derives it from a Greek word *daémōn* meaning "knowing." Homer derived it from *daimōn* meaning "divinity." Eusebius derived it from *deimainein* meaning "to fear." Modern dictionaries derive it from *daiō* meaning "to divide (destinies)," hence the idea of fate or the ability of the spirit to control your fate.[22] None of these definitions are necessarily evil by nature (Eusebius' comes closest).

Augustine has an extensive discussion on demons and the victory Christ won over them *(City of God,* Books 8-10). In it he explains that demons dwell in the air, the space between heaven and earth (9.8.1), and were therefore considered mediators between the gods and mankind (8.23.1). Perhaps this is where the confusion of them as fallen angels (messengers) arises? Or perhaps it also points at their not quite human, not quite heavenly nature.

Because they protected, were powerful to harm or heal (the root word of *rephaim* is *rapha*: "to heal"), interceded, had great knowledge and the like, these beings were revered and venerated. The first time I studied this topic, I was struck by the similarities between the pagan view of demons and the Roman Catholic view of the veneration of the saints. The similarities are uncanny and unnerving. Both may be viewed as spirits of dead people, be they giant or not. Both are guardians and protectors. Both are intercessors. Both can be healers. Both have idols associated with them. The only real difference is that Rome thinks it has eliminated the problem of troublesome evil demons. Yet, the practice of veneration is identical, because the makeup of those being venerated is ... *identical*. It's something to think about anyway.

You will see the word "demon" appear in one or two other OT passages. Leviticus 17:7 talks about goat-demons (the KJV adds 2 Chron 11:15). The Hebrew word is a *sair* or *sairim*. It is variously defined as a demon or a satyr. Ever heard of a satyr? These are the strange half-human, half-goat *demigods* of antiquity. If you think the idea that demons are the disembodied spirits of the giants is strange, just wait until you get a load of what is to come.

Chapter 13: Chimeras

The Lord bless you and keep you.
The Lord make His face to shine upon you,
  and be gracious to you.
The Lord lift up His countenance upon you,
  and grant you peace.
The Lord bless you in all your deeds, and protect you from
the demons of the night, and things that cause terror,
and from demons of evening and of the morning,
and from evil spirits and phantoms.

Numbers 6:24
(Targum Pseudo-Jonathan)

FIG. 13.1. MORE CHIMERAS

Centaur   Satyr

Sirens

Lilith

Two Strange Passages

I cited the LXX of Isaiah 34:13-14 and 13:21-22 in the last chapter. Now I want to look at them in detail. In light of the helpers of Rahab and Tiamat, these are truly fascinating texts. I will begin this chapter using the ESV's translation as a starting point. The first passage reads, "It shall be the haunt of jackals, an abode for ostriches. And wild animals shall meet with hyenas; the wild goat shall cry to his fellow; indeed, there the night bird settles and finds for herself a resting place." The second is like it, "But wild animals will lie down there, and their houses will be full of howling creatures; there ostriches will dwell, and there wild goats will dance. Hyenas will cry in its towers, and jackals in the pleasant palaces; its time is close at hand and its days will not be prolonged."

You ask, what's so interesting about that? The answer is nothing, particularly, *if* the ESV's translation faithfully captures what is in the prophet's mind. But when we start to look into the Hebrew, the *Septuagint*, and most important, the NT interpretation of this passage, things become very strange, very quickly. The whole thing ends up leading us right back to the giants.

Context

Seir and Babylon

The first pair of verses come in a larger context of God cursing Edom, the land of Esau, which in older days was called the land of Seir (Gen 32:3). Do you recall how we finished the previous chapter? The goat-demon was called a *sair*. Notice any relationship between those words? You will also run into other related words as we continue the study of this chapter. The second pair of verses is God's cursing of Babylon. As we have seen, Babylon was first built by Nimrod the *gibborim* ("giant") hunter. Therefore, in both instances, the lands in view have their most ancient origins with the giants.

Sodom and Gomorrah

Our verses on Babylon are prefaced with these words, "Babylon, the glory of kingdoms, the splendor and pomp of the Chaldeans, will be like Sodom and Gomorrah when God overthrew them. It will never be inhabited or lived in for all generations" (Isa 13:19-20). Curiously, Isaiah refers to the destruction of Edom in the same way. Her streams and land are turned into pitch, and her soil into sulfur (Isa 34:9). "Night and day it shall not be quenched; its smoke shall go up forever, from generation to generation it shall lie waste; none shall pass through it forever and ever." (vs. 10). In Genesis 19 we read, "Then the LORD rained on Sodom and Gomorrah sulfur and fire from the LORD out of heaven ... and, behold, the smoke of the land went up like the smoke of a furnace" (Gen 19:24, 28). Jeremiah reminds us, "When Sodom and Gomorrah and their neighboring cities were overthrown, says the LORD, no man shall dwell there, no man shall sojourn in her" (Jer 49:18).

Sodom and Gomorrah were places of unparalleled bounty (Ezek 16:49), but also unspeakable sins, including homosexuality and rape (Gen 19:5, 8), lack of care for the poor and needy (Ezek 16:49), open shameless flaunting of sin (Isa 3:9) and pride (Ezek 16:50), not dissimilar to what we see happening in our own day. One sin that is not often considered, however, is how the men of the city not only wanted to "know" the men who came to Lot's house, the *men* they desired to know were actually ... *angels* (Gen 19:1, 11). This was deformation of a perversion. The original perversion, of course, is when "sons of God" left their proper abode and married the daughters of men (Gen 6:1-4).

In light of this, remember what we established in the last chapter. The ancient view was that the giant offspring produced by such unions who were destroyed in the flood became "demons." Most of this chapter will be taken up with exploring this idea in our two passages. Sodom and Gomorrah were on the front lines of the "giant wars" of Genesis 14, so their cultural context was smack dab in the middle of this very strange worldview. The intentional comparison between Babylon, Edom, and Sodom and Gomorrah is necessary background to a proper interpretation of at least some of the "animals" that Isaiah has in mind.

NT Inspired Commentary

The most certain proof that Isaiah has something more in mind than desert animals (he has them in mind too, but not exclusively), is John's inspired commentary on the Babylonian passage. He writes, "An angel called out with a mighty voice, 'Fallen, fallen is Babylon the great! She has become a dwelling place for <u>demons</u>, a haunt for every <u>unclean spirit</u>, a haunt for every unclean bird, a haunt for every unclean and detestable beast" (Rev 18:2). The parallels with Isaiah 13:19-21 are uncanny. Thus, commentators recognize that John is drawing his language from Isaiah.[1] Since this is the case, to *not* interpret these passages in light of John's inspired text is to ignore clearer revelation. In these verses then, this makes the ordinarily stellar ESV's translation a travesty of interpretive justice.

Birds

While Sodom and Gomorrah are part of the metaphor used to describe the future judgment of Edom and Babylon, the other metaphor is wild desert creatures. These creatures can be divided into two kinds. The first are birds. The birds described are all "unclean" according to the law (see Lev 11:13-19). John noticed this as well in Revelation 18:2. There is no fundamental problem with the translation of the birds in the ESV. While various translations give different birds, the basic idea is that ravens, owls, and vultures will haunt the new desert wastelands. Here I want you to think back to the beginning of the chapter and take note of the Lilith (see picture above). See how owls are associated with her cult? The thing to note, then, is that from Merlin and his raven, to Lilith and her owls (or owls used in Harry Potter in contemporary use), unclean birds are often associated with *the underworld* and demonic entities.

Mythical Beasts

The second kinds of creatures are desert animals. This is where we begin to run into problems with the ESV's entirely natural translation. We read about jackals, hyenas, wild goats, and the generic "wild animals." Now, it certainly fits the idea of desolation that these kinds of animals would accompany the unclean birds, for they too feed on dead carcasses in wild places. But there are serious objections to this interpretive decision, not the least of which is that it completely ignores Revelation 18:2, especially in light of the LXX.

The problem is that not one of the "animals" here has an uncontested translation *as a pure animal* (see the Table at the end of the chapter). To put that another way, across the board, the birds are all translated as birds (with the exception of the ostrich, see below). But the animals are called anything from dragons, to satyrs and goat-demons, from devils, to night monsters, to monsters, and "howlings" in different English translations.

These are the demons of Revelation. They are the kinds of beings that accompanied Tiamat in the Babylonian epic. These kinds of translations are also consistent with the way the Jews understood the words Isaiah uses. For example, 2 Baruch 10:8 uses many of the same words. It is translated, "I shall call the Sirens from the sea, and you, Lilin, come from the desert, and you, demons and dragons from the woods."[2] It is to these "animals" that I now wish to turn our attention.

Dragons and Sirens

After a list of four birds (Isa 34:12),[3] the first disputed animal is the "jackal." The Hebrew word is a *tan*. *Tan* is the root word for the *tannin*. This is a word sometimes associated with the devil. In Isaiah 51:9, for example, it is parallel with the monster Rahab. The ESV translates it very differently there, "Was it not you who cut Rahab in pieces, who pierced the dragon"? In Isaiah 27:1 it is parallel with the Leviathan and the Nachash (the word used for Satan in Genesis 3:1). The *tannin* is basically a monster who lives in the sea. The Greek usually translates it as *drakon* ("dragon"). It is therefore not a coincidence that modern and ancient translations render the ESV's "jackal" as a dragon, which as we have seen, the ESV itself does in other places.

The LXX gives *tannin* the curious translation of *sieren*. According to the biblical dictionaries, *sieren* are "mythical sisters on the south coast of Italy, who enticed seamen by their songs, and then slew them."[4] We call them sirens. We saw as much in the 2 Baruch passage (above).

Sirens are properly depicted in movies such as *Harry Potter and the Goblet of Fire* and *Pirates of the Caribbean: On Stranger Tides*. Back in ancient literature, in 1 Enoch 19:2, it is the women who were led astray by the sons of God in Genesis 6:1-4 who become the sirens. In the LXX of Micah 1:8 we read, "Therefore shall she lament and wail, she shall go barefooted, and being naked she shall make lamentation as that of serpents, and mourning as of the daughters of sirens [same Greek word as is found in the LXX of Isa 34:13 and 13:21]." That should give you a flavor for how Jewish interpreters understood the word. So, yes, incredibly, the Bible talks about "little mermaids," but that cute happy Disneyland feel is completely absent.

As noted above, the LXX also renders the word *yaanah* in Isaiah 13:21 ("ostrich" in the ESV) as *sieren*. *Yaanah* is also found in Isa 34:13. But here it translates *yaanah* as *strouthion* ("sparrow," or more likely "ostrich") rather than *sieren*. Why the difference? Because in 13:21 the word is prefixed with the strange phrase: "*daughters of* the ostrich." No one knows what a daughter of an ostrich might be, so most leave "daughter" untranslated. Given the context, it must have something to do with monsters (hence, the English translation of the LXX: "monsters"). Seeing it is a female monster that is in mind for the Jewish translators of the LXX, the sirens of mythology seem to fit nicely.

Apparitions and Phantoms

Verse 14 continues the strangeness. The ESV begins with a very tame translation: "wild animals." The Hebrew word is *tsiyiim*. According to one Bible dictionary, "The term is rather a collective designation for demonic desert beings (perhaps 'those that belong to the dry land'').[5] The LXX renders no translation at all, though the same word is found (again) in 13:21 where it calls them *theron* ("wild beasts"). More curious is Jeremiah 50:39 (27:39 LXX), a passage with a similar grouping of animals at Babylon (including the daughters of the ostrich). It translates the same word with the fascinating word *indalma* which means "an appearance, form, or apparition."[6] In other words, it means a ghost or a phantom. Yes, the Bible actually talks about such things, and believes them to be real.

Demons, Devils, and Hairy Beasts

The next word in the ESV is the "hyena." Most English translations offer this or some related kind of an animal. The LXX however, gives the view of Jewish scholars before the coming of Christ. It calls them *daimonion*, "demons."[7] This is where John the Revelator (Rev 18:2) gets it. The Hebrew word is poetically related to the *tsiyyim*. The word is *'iyyim*. The word is derived from "dog" or the Arabic "jackal," or from a word meaning "(ghostly) islander, beach demon, goblin ... The context is demonic."[8] What might they be?

Since the Babylonian Gilgamesh Epic and the story of Enkidu, people have been told tales of wild hairy men (we saw as much in the later tales of St. Christopher in Ch. 9). Created by the goddess Aruru, Enkidu was "shaggy with hair is his whole body" who lives with wild beasts outside the human population.[9] The story is repeated from culture to culture, across seas and oceans.[10] In in keeping with the fabulous flavor of the ancient translation, one specific creature that comes to my mind is the werewolf or lycan.

In the Greek story of Lycaon—the earliest story of the werewolf (popularized in movies like *Underworld*)—Lycaon was the wicked king of Arcadia, who tested Zeus by serving him a dish of a slaughtered and dismembered child in order to see whether Zeus was truly omniscient. In his quest to test Zeus' immortality, Lycaon attempted to murder the god while he slept. In return for these gruesome deeds, Zeus transformed Lycaon into the form of a wolf, and killed Lycaon's fifty sons by lightning bolts. Do you remember what happened to Nebuchadnezzar, king of Babylon? He comes to resemble a lycan during his seven years of punishment by God (Dan 4:23, 33-34). Of course, I'm not saying that Nebuchadnezzar *became* a werewolf. I'm saying that the *idea* of werewolves is ancient, and werewolves were often viewed as demonic. Nebuchadnezzar is likened to a werewolf. Not a very flattering depiction of the king of the world, is it? A similar or perhaps even stranger occurrence of hairy men are the two *ariel* slain by Benaiah in 2 Sam 23:20. Translated "lionlike" by the KJV, some scholars have suggested that they may have been some kind of "mythical figure,"[11] which certainly fits the context of David's valiant warriors killing giants.

Isaiah's demonic context can be seen, not only in noticing the Greek translation and continuing the study of this passage, but by looking at the earlier passage in Isaiah 13 as well. In this text, all three words (*tan*, *tsiyyim*, and *iyyim*) also occur. The LXX translates the "beasts" in Isa 13:21 as "wild beasts," "howling," "monsters," and "devils" (*daimonion* this time translating the Hebrew word *sair*, see below). This all fits the broader context which uses fabulous language as it refers later to the fallen rephaim (variously translated as "shades" and "ghosts" [14:9]), the fall of Lucifer (14:12-15), and strange winged seraphim creatures that roam in the desert (14:29). Each adds to the historic fall predicted of this most ancient and pagan of cities in the world: Babylon, whose builder was Nimrod, a mighty giant of old.

Satyrs and Centaurs

The third word in Isaiah 34:14 (ESV) is "wild goat." Here, the ESV is breaking with most English translations by rendering the word as completely natural. Preternatural translations offer up the translation of "goat-demons" or "satyrs." The LXX gives the translation: *onokentauros*. Look closely at that word and see if you can identify anything from Greek mythology. The definition of this word in the lexicons is a, "Donkey-centaur, mythic creature (a centaur resembling a donkey rather than a horse)."[12] The English translation of the LXX renders this word as "satyr." The Hebrew word is *sairim* (remember Seir and Sair at the beginning of the chapter?). Again the lexicons are clear. They are "wood demons, satyrs, resembling he-goats, inhabiting deserts, Isa 13:21; 34:14."[13]

There is a lot going on with this word. First of all, it is related to the word for a goat associated with the Day of Atonement, where they would place the sins of Israel upon the goat and lead it into the desert to Azazel (see Lev 16). Azazel is the goat-demon. This Azazel has a strange history in Jewish tradition. He is said to have descended upon Mt. Hermon with the 200 Watchers when they viewed the daughters of men as beautiful and wanted to marry them.[14] There has been a shrine to Azazel in Banias, a cave at the foot of Mt. Hermon since time immemorial.[15] For ages it was referred to as Panias (Pan), but in 20 BC Herod Agrippa II built himself a shrine.[16] In Greek mythology, Pan is the demon-god of shepherds and flocks, of mountain wilds, hunting and rustic music. He is associated with the flute. His hind-quarters, legs, and horns are those of a goat in the same manner as a faun or a satyr.

The associations we have already noted with Esau come back into play here in the strange work called the Book of Jasher. Though written sometime long after the close of the NT, and not published until the early 17th century, it purports to tell stories of the ancient bib-lical heroes. In this story we have Zepho the grandson of Esau as the hero. "And Zepho went and he saw and behold there was a large cave at the bottom of the mountain, and there was a great stone there at the entrance of the cave, and Zepho split the stone and he came into the cave and he looked and behold, a large animal was devouring the ox; from the middle upward it resembled a man, and from the middle downward it resembled an animal, and Zepho rose up against the ani-mal and slew it with his sword" (Jasher 61:15).

Next, the word for a goat is translated by the LXX as *chimaros* (male) or *chimaira* (female).[17] A *chimera* is "a fire-spouting-monster, with lion's head, serpent's tail, and goat's body, killed by Bellerophon."[18] The LXX does not seem to use the term *chimaros* in any supernatural terms, but *chimera* is today used as a catch-all for all of these strange half-breed creatures.

Though the term is not used supernaturally, perhaps the idea is. Azazel is said by the Jews to be judged by Messiah[19] and cast into the "abyss of complete condemnation," the "burning furnace."[20] Yet, he is said to also be *bound* in a place called Dudael,[21] which could very well be Mt. Hermon.[22] In other words, this goat-demon's end is similar to that of Satan, the one who also roams around like a roaring lion and who hissed wicked temptations at Eve as a serpent. Satan is depicted as a goat, lion, serpent. This is exactly what *chimera* is depicted as being. The idea of sacrificing a goat in the desert to Azazel is definitely wrapped up in God's world-view with the fall of Lucifer.

FIG. 13.2. CHIMERA (LION, GOAT, SERPENT) IN GREEK ART

Finally, there is a word play going on between the satyr (*sairim*) and Edom (*seir*). Seir is another name for Edom (cf. Num 24:18), but refers more specifically to the (giant) Horite ancestor who populated the region there before Esau (Gen 36:20-21). The root of satyr means "hairy," and they are always depicted as hairy creatures. Esau, was of course a "hairy (*sair*) man" (Gen 27:11), who clothed himself in a hairy (*sear*) garment (Gen 25:25), and whose ancestors eventually dispossessed the giant Horites in the days of the Exodus (Deut 2:12). That's a lot of background for one little word, but it helps you see how the word transcends the natural realm, fitting the supernatural worldview of these verses in Isaiah.

Lilith

The last word in Isaiah 34:14 (ESV) is "night bird." Again, there is discrepancy among the translations. Some refer to it as a "night-monster." The LXX gives the same *onokentauros* as it did for the *sairim* (see above). Apparently they couldn't think of a better word for this unique Hebrew word.

The Hebrew word is *lilith*. The word is similar to the word for "night" (*lilah/layla*). (Yes, I'm sure that's where Eric Clapton got it from). "Lilith" is used only here in the Scripture, but she has a fascinating history in later Jewish tradition like the 2 Baruch passage (above). The *Targum* (Pseudo-Jonathan) refers to Lilith in an addition to the Aaronic blessing, "May the Lord bless you in all your deeds and protect you from the Lilith" ('demons of the night,' Aramaic *lili*).[23] A Jewish *midrash* teaches that Lilith devours her own newborn children if she cannot find other newborn babies to eat.[24] The Talmud says, "It is forbidden to sleep in a room all alone and whoever sleeps in a room all alone—Lilith grabs him."[25]

Lilith was worshiped throughout the ancient near-east. At the beginning of this chapter, you saw a picture of her surrounded by owls. In Babylonian tradition she was associated with Ishtar who plants a tree, later hoping to cut it down and make a bed-throne for herself. But as the tree grows, a snake makes its nest at its roots, the Anzu-bird settles in the top, and in the trunk *lil-la* makes her lair.[26] Also, like the sirens, Lilith is also said to seduce men in order to kill them.

Suggested Translation

As you can see, these two passages are far from the plain, natural world that is envisioned by the translators of the ESV: Isaiah. From the very earliest times, these texts were taken to incorporate both the natural world and the *super*natural world. Isaiah is not only saying that the end result of Babylon and Edom will be a desert waste, good for only unclean animals and birds. He is adding that God will give these places over to the demonic entities that roam around our planet, as Jesus said, looking for someplace to inhabit (Matt 12:43-45).

Therefore, if I were to be so bold as to offer a translation of Isaiah 13:20-22 it would be something like this, "Babylon will never be inhabited or lived in from generation to generation; nor will the Arab pitch his tent there, nor will shepherds make their flocks lie down there. But phantoms will crouch down there, and their houses will be full of howling, monsters will live there, and satyrs will dance there. Lycans will howl in fortified towers, and dragons in their pleasant palaces." Similarly, Isaiah 34:11-15 would read, "Hawks and owls shall possess Edom; Great owls and ravens shall dwell there... It shall be a home of dragons, an abode of monsters. Phantoms shall meet centaurs, satyrs shall greet each other; there also Lilith shall relax and find herself a resting place. The tree snake shall nest and lay eggs, and shall brood and hatch in its shade. There too the buzzards shall gather with one another."

Could It Be More Than Figurative?

If we recall again that much of the ancient world believed that the demons were the disembodied spirits of the giants who were destroyed in the flood, we can stay grounded to the purpose of our book, which is to think about the giants of old. But why might these creatures be depicted in the Bible? We may only speculate at this point.

Isaiah certainly could have just talked only about the generic "demons," and left it at that. But he didn't (and several other prophets like Micah and Jeremiah employ the same terms). It is possible that he is simply utilizing well known mythology to make a scary point about the ruin of Babylon and Edom. Surely, this *is* at least part of what Isaiah has in mind. But might he have thought there was something more to it than this? Could it have been the case that such creatures were literal, that he *really* believed they *really* existed? I think most Christians will at least admit they believe demons exist, even if they have no real understanding of what they are or what they do.

Traditions across the globe recall the same horrible beings as haunting their own cultures. They talk about giants participating in horrible acts relating to animals. As we have seen even in the Bible, bestiality, for instance, was absolutely forbidden to the Jews because this was the practice of the giants whom God was destroying from before them in Canaan (Lev 18:23-24). We have also looked at how Genesis 6:12 gives the cryptic phrase, "*all flesh* had corrupted their way on the earth," and that included the animal kingdom, which is why God not only destroyed human beings, but all other living creatures on the face of the earth. Could this corruption be more than moral (i.e. animals eating other animals or humans)? Then you have the repeated emphasis found almost exclusively in the creation and the flood on animals (and plants) created "according to their kind" (Gen 1:11; 12, 21, 23, 24, 6:19, 20, 7:14). Why so much obvious repetition about this? I've speculated it had to do with the Nephilim, but perhaps it also had to do with the animal kingdom.

I'm certainly not going to die on this hill, but consider the idea that if they were not breeding with the animals (that seems genetically implausible), the sons of God were somehow involved in genetic manipulation of DNA, producing hideous offspring, even as human beings are tinkering with mixing animal DNA with our own for their misguided altruistic or nefarious and dastardly purposes. Perhaps now is the best time of all to mention that the word *gigantes*—the Greek giants of Genesis 6:4—is derived from the word *gēgenēs* (see *DDD*, p. 24). *Gēgenēs* is a combination of *gēs* and *genes* or literally, "born from earth." Where this really becomes strange is when we realize that words like genetics and genes are guilt around the same root word.[27] This has, of course, led some to postulate a linguistic argument for the giants being genetically altered creatures.

Perhaps you are rolling your eyes right now. I wouldn't be completely offended. Yet, consider what is going on today in the real world of modern man and technology. There is a growing scientific movement known as *Transhumanism* which as Wikipedia states, "Affirms the possibility of fundamentally transforming the human condition by developing and making widely available technologies to eliminate aging and to greatly enhance human intellectual, physical, and psychological capacities." Among the ideas are ways of figuring out how, for example, the eyesight of an eagle might be given to a human being through genetic manipulation or crossing of DNA. Is transhumanism merely a platitude, pie-in-the-sky, science fiction?

Consider the following: In 1954, a mad Russian scientist named Vladimir Demikhov performed a successful head transplant, grafting the neck and head of one dog onto the upper torso of another dog?[28] From the 1970's – the 2000's, another scientist named Robert J. White performed Nazi-like experiments, transplanting heads of monkeys onto the bodies of other monkeys? It got to the point where they could live indefinitely, though no one has of yet figured out a way to overcome the paralysis that occurs from such an operation.[29] In 2003 Dr. Hui Zhen Sheng fused human cells with rabbit eggs.[30] In 2004, the Mayo Clinic successfully created pigs with human blood flowing through their bodies.[31]   Then there was the bizarre creature that washed ashore on July 13, 2008 on Surfside Beach near Montauk, NY. The creature appeared to have raccoon claws, the beak of a bird, and the body of a dog. Was it a clever hoax or a genetic experiment gone mad? Even Snopes.com cannot determine the answer. Coincidentally, there happens to be an "animal disease center" just down the road.

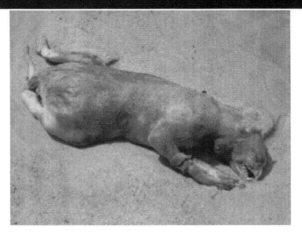

FIG. 13.3. "MONTAUK MONSTER"

It may seem like such an idea as ancient heavenly beings tinkering with human and animal DNA belongs to the world of science fiction, but the Island of Dr. Moreau is real today. These are only the experiments we know about. Ohio, Arizona, Louisiana and other states have all passed laws prohibiting human-animal hybridization,[32] not because state Senates have time to waste or couldn't get their daily fix of Star Trek, but because these are real concerns in the modern world. Given that heavenly beings are much smarter than we are and have been around a *lot* longer than any human living today, why would we think that they were incapable of mixing the human genome with other DNA (be it with their own or some animal) in the past?

Has a Darwinian worldview so shaped the mindset of Evangelicals that they are unable to entertain the thought that our ancestors, given supernatural help, may have actually been capable of such things? Has naturalism so infected us that we can no longer seriously entertain even the possibility that supernatural beings have interacted with humans in the past? We've seen the caduceus and the double helix. We have plenty of evidence from the Bible and other ancient cultures that such creatures could have been real.

As far as I know, little to nothing in the way of bones of centaurs, *minotaurs*, sirens, or satyrs have ever been found (though there have been reports of giant human skulls having horns).[33] The lack of proof is not proof of the lack. What I do know is this. Isaiah employs highly charged mythological language to describe a demon infested ruin of two places with roots deep in the giant legends of antiquity. The idea that the Bible speaks about centaurs, sirens, satyrs, Lilith, and *chimeras* is worth taking the time to ponder.

ISAIAH 34:12-13 AND 13:21-22 COMPARED

Isaiah	Hebrew	LXX	LXX trans.	YLT	NAS	ESV	KJV	JPS	TNK
34:11	qaath	omov	birds	pelican	pelican	hawk	cormorant	pelican	jackdaws
	qippod	echinos	hedgehog	hedge-hog	hedgehog	porcupine	bittern	bittern	owls
	yanshuph	ibis	ibises	owl	owl	owl	owl	owl	great owls
	oreb	korak	ravens	raven	raven	raven	raven	raven	ravens
34:13	Tan	seiren	monsters	dragons	jackals	jackals	dragons	wild-dogs	jackals
	Yaanah	strouthion	ostriches	ostriches	ostriches	ostriches	owls	ostriches	ostriches
34:14	Tsiyyim			ziim	des. creatures	wild animals	wild beasts	wild-cats	wildcats
	'iyyim	daimonion	devils	aiim	wolves	hyenas	wild beasts	jackals	hyenas
	Sair	ovokentauros	satyrs	goat	hairy goat	wild goat	satyr	satyr	goat-demon
	lilith	onokentauros	satyrs	night-owl	night monster	night bird	screech owl	night-monster	lilith
34:15	Qippoz	echinos	hedgehog	bittern	tree snake	owl	great owl	arrowsnake	arrowsnake
	dayyah	elapos	deer	vulture	hawk	hawk	vulture	kite	buzzard
Isaiah	Hebrew	LXX	LXX trans.	YLT	NAS	ESV	KJV	JPS	TNK
13:21		theron	wild beasts	ziim	des. creatures	wild animals	wild beasts	wild-cats	beasts
	Oach	echos	"howling"	howlings	owls	hyenas	doleful creat.	ferrets	owls
	Yaanah	seiren	monsters	daut of ostrich	ostriches	ostriches	owls	ostriches	ostriches
	Sair	daimonion	devils	goats	shaggy goats	wild goats	satyrs	satyrs	goats
13:22	'iyyim	ovokentauros	satyrs	hyenas	hyenas	hyenas	wild beasts	jackals	jackals
	Tan	echos	hedgehogs	jackals	jackals	jackals	dragons	wild-dogs	dragons

Chapter 14: Jesus vs. the Demons

"What do you want with us, Son of God? ... Have you
come here to torture us before the appointed time"?

Matthew 8:29 (NIV)

Common Mistakes

We come now to the climax of our great battle between the two seeds. There are two mistakes that people make when considering what has happened in this war. One is to obsess. The other is to ignore. The giants seem to have been lost in the shuffle of cultural shifts and theological systems. People do not seem to realize that there even were or are giants (in their present form), let alone know what function they serve in the story of redemption.

Meanwhile, most people have almost as little knowledge about what demons are, and how to think properly about them. It is typical in more conservative traditions to never speak of demons (just like the giants). It is almost like a kind of superstition holds us in captivity, so that if we say anything about them, they may come and do mischief or worse. Ironically, superstition is at the heart of those who obsess over demons too. So called "deliverance ministries," seeing devils under every rock, and strange doctrines of tongues (to keep demons from understanding what people are saying), are the kinds of theological systems that develop when superstition and incorrect understanding of demons is at play. Each can get a person into spiritual trouble.

It is important to keep in mind that the giants were powerful, intelligent rulers of earth's remote history. If the early view is in fact correct, their spirits, when departed from the body, seem to continue to display the attributes the giants had while in the flesh. The NT has a lot to say about demons, much more than most people are comfortable acknowledging. We'll discover why in a moment.

Demons in the New Testament

For now, consider just a few things we learn about them in the pages of the NT. 1. Demons love to inhabit or possess. This is not true of angels, because angels are heavenly beings that already have a kind of flesh (cf. 1 Cor 15:40-41), and can take on the appearance of human flesh without possessing a host.[1] This alone ought to tell you that angels and demons are different kinds of beings. If demons were the giants who lost their bodies, it makes sense that they would seek to regain some kind of physical existence, even if it is by proxy.

Jesus talks about this compulsive desire of demons to inhabit. "When the unclean spirit has gone out of a person, it passes through waterless places seeking rest, and finding none it says, 'I will return to my house from which I came.' And when it comes, it finds the house swept and put in order. Then it goes and brings seven other spirits more evil than itself, and they enter and dwell there" (Luke 11:24-26). As we saw with the demons and the desert in Isaiah, notice that Jesus says the demons love "waterless places." Is this because of what happened to them so long ago in the Flood?

This is a theme you find throughout Scripture and it spills over into the surrounding cultures. Think of the time when Jesus commanded an unclean spirit to come out of a man who had been "kept under guard and bound with chains and shackles, but he would break the bonds and be driven by the demon into the desert" (Luke 8:29). This story speaks about a second attribute of demons.

2. Demons are sometimes able to give their host great strength (cf. Mark 5:4). The book of Acts recalls a rather humorous story of seven itinerant Jewish exorcists (exorcism was practiced throughout the ancient world), sons of a Jewish high priest named Sceva, who took it upon themselves to invoke the name of the Lord Jesus over those who had evil spirits. They would say, "I adjure you by the Jesus whom Paul proclaims" (Acts 19:13). Suddenly, an evil spirit answered them and said, "Jesus I know, and Paul I recognize, but who are you"? (vs. 15). These men had never trusted in Christ, but merely used his name like a magic incantation. Then, without warning, "the man in whom was the evil spirit leaped on [the seven men], mastered all of them and overpowered them, so that they fled out of that house naked and wounded" (vs. 16). One might say this man possessed the strength of a giant. Maybe the expression isn't merely figurative.

3. Demons possess great knowledge and the ability to teach that knowledge to human beings, generally through human beings whom they inspire or possess. Paul teaches that in later times men will "devote themselves to deceitful spirits and teachings of demons" (1 Tim 4:1). The repeated warnings of false teachers (1 Cor 10:20-21; Col 2:18, 21; 2 Tim 3:13; 2 Pet 2:12; Jude 8, 12-13, etc.) implies that they are inspired by demons.

4. Demons have a kind of limited power to heal (or make sick). In Revelation 16:14 you have "demonic spirits" performing great signs, and this is in line with a host of verses that tell us about the "signs and wonders" of antichrists, false prophets, and dreamers (Deut 13:1-2,

Matt 24:24; 2 Thess 2:9, etc.). Perhaps a story with Jesus gets at this the best.

Jesus had been teaching the people in the temple at his home in Galilee. His teaching was so astonishing that they began to mutter, "How is it that this man has learning, when he has never studied"? (John 7:15). They began to accuse him of having a demon (vs. 20). Not only do they associate Jesus with a demon because of his knowledge of unknown origin, but because of his *miracles*. Jesus' reply to the accusation is, "I did one work, and you all marvel at it" (John 7:21). He is probably referring to his healing of the invalid at the strange pool of Bethesda in Jerusalem (John 5:2-7).[2] The point being, the people associated Jesus' healing with the work of a demon.

This is curious in light of the fact that the word rephaim comes from the root word *rapha*: "to heal." The LXX even translates two instances of the rephaim in Sheol as "healers" (Isa 26:14; Ps 88:11) and the Samaritan *Targum* translates the living giants of Deut 2:20 and 3:13 the same way. Because of these things, some scholars have argued that "by virtue of their connections with the netherworld, the [Rephaim were] healers *par excellence*."[3] Such is the mindset you enter when you move into the world of NT demonology.

Jesus vs. the Demons

It is strange that demons would be mentioned less than a handful of times in the entire OT, but in the Gospels alone the word *daimonion* occurs 53x. Couple this with dozens of references to "spirits" and "evil spirits" in the Gospels and you get the sense that this is a major theme in the ministry of Jesus. But why? It is because Jesus' encounters with the demons are the climactic final blow to these ancient tormentors of mankind and enemies of God's people. Jesus vs. the demons is the NT equivalent of Israel vs. the giants. It is the beginning of the final battle, as it were, between Eve's Seed and the serpent's seed. In this battle, Jesus shows the demons his power, authority, and ultimate victory.

Jesus' Power over the Demons

The ancient world dealt with demons. Babylonians and Greeks, American Indians and Chinese, Jews and Christians all had their rituals for exorcizing these creatures. You've surely seen some movie where a Roman Catholic priest stands before a demon-possessed person with a book and some holy water. He then carefully and meticulously begins chanting the spells from the book in order to cast the demon out of the person. This often is a long, excruciating ordeal, as it was throughout the ancient world. Sometimes amulets, rings or other talismans are used, such as in the case of the strange Jewish book the *Testament of Solomon* where the archangel Michael comes to Solomon with a magic ring whereby he begins to capture and bind demons to help him build the temple. Oddly, Josephus (*Antiquities* 8.2.5) reports on this same magic ring as having basis in real history. In all, you find spells, formulae, hymns, trinkets, elements (like water), and rituals being used in unison to expel the demons.

Not so with Jesus. Perhaps the most remarkable thing about Jesus' ministry in relation to demons is his power to cast out spirits "with a word" (Matt 8:16). In stark contrast to other exorcists, including even the Disciples (Mark 9:28), it appears as if nothing could be easier for Jesus than to exorcize a demon. And this is exactly what Jesus did. One of the first things we learn about the ministry of Jesus is how he would heal those "oppressed by demons" (Matt 4:24). In fact, it appears that he did this almost everywhere he went.[4]

Jesus' Authority over the Demons

The power that Jesus exercised (and exorcized) over demons was directly related to the authority that he had over them. This was an authority that they instantly recognized and were unable to overcome. The title "Son of God" (there's that idea again ... the son of God; only this son is the Only Begotten Son of the Father, the Creator of all other life in the universe) is often used on the lips ... of demons (Mark 1:24; 3:11; Luke 4:34, etc.). They knew his mission (Mark 5:7) and they knew they had an appointed time to finally perish (Matt 8:31).

One of the more famous episodes is the story of Legion ("many demons") when Jesus came to the country of the Gerasenes (see Mark 5:1-13). As soon as Jesus steps off the boat, a man who lived in the tombs who had an unclean spirit came upon him. He was exceedingly strong so that not even chains could bind him. He was constantly crying out and cutting himself with stones. But as soon as he saw Jesus, he came running over to him, fell down before him, and yelled, "What have you to do with me, Jesus, Son of the Most High God"? He then laid an oath upon Jesus saying, "I adjure you by God, do not torment me," because Jesus had already begun commanding the demon to come out of the man.

The demon pleaded with Jesus, who asked him his name and it replied, "My name is Legion, for we are many" (Mark 5:9). Then it strangely says, "He begged him earnestly not to send them out of the country" (vs. 10). As the demon(s) quickly scanned the landscape, it spotted a herd of pigs and begged the Lord to be cast into them. "Jesus gave them permission" (vs. 13). Instantly, the herd numbering 2,000(!) rushed down the steep bank and were drowned in the sea.[5]

There are a couple of strange "coincidences" here. First, this incident "just so happens" to have the most demons *by far* of any story in the Bible. These demons "just so happen" to be indwelling this man in the home and epicentre of the ancient giants of the OT—the very place where so many were destroyed in the days of Joshua. This was the old stomping ground of Og and the Amorites. With Jesus' exorcism, it's as if they now have to live out the terrors endured by their older brothers in the days of Noah (assuming that these are not those more primeval giants). No more dry places. No more habitation. Only suffering under the waters, down to Sheol, where they joined their brothers of old.

Second, this general area on the east side of the Sea of Galilee is the most probable location for the baptism of Jesus. John 1:28 tells us that John the Baptist was baptizing "in Bethany across the Jordan." Since the times of Origen (184 -254 AD), there has been vigorous debate over this location, because he traveled to the area and could find no such place called Bethany on the east side of the Jordan (the Bethany where Jesus raised Lazarus is right near Jerusalem). Hence the question, where is this place?

Many proposals have been suggested, but the one defended by most scholars today—following old *Targum* spellings of the area, the necessity of a location in the north given the geographical locations in the story and the short time span for these events to occur—is that "Bethany" refers not to a town, but to a region: Bashan (or Bathan).[6] If Jesus was baptized in Bashan on the east side of the Sea of Galilee, then he symbolically came out of the same water in which the demons would later drown. Even earlier symbolism would be apparent, that he came out of the water ordeal *alive*, whereas the original Nephilim *perished* in the Flood. The fact that his baptism could very well have been very near to the place where this Legion of demons was located would also explain how they knew who he was (demons are not all knowing). Perhaps they saw the same thing John saw at Jesus baptism, when the Spirit descended upon him and the Father spoke of his great pleasure in his beloved Son.

Jesus' authority is seen in other instances as well. One time demons came out of a certain man crying, "You are the Son of God!" but he rebuked them "and would not allow them to speak, because they knew that he was the Christ" (Luke 4:41). Often times Jesus would not permit the demons to speak any longer (cf. Mark 1:24-25; 34; 3:11-12, etc.).

You see, what the demons understood was that the Seed of the woman had come down to earth out of heaven and was born now as a man, as the second Adam. This meant he had come to fulfil the promise, and reclaim the authority abdicated so long before by Adam. This, then, would be the beginning of the end for the demons, and so they worked overtime trying to figure out a way to stop him.

But everywhere Jesus went, he proved they were no match—all while the people kept accusing him of having a demon. Perhaps you remember a time when Jesus had cast out a demon that was making a man mute. All the people marvelled, but some of them accused him of casting out the demon by the power of Beelzebub (Luke 11:14-20). Beelzebub is "the prince of demons" and it is probably a title given to Satan himself. Jesus explained that if Satan cast out demons, his kingdom would be divided and could not stand. Such an idea was ludicrous. But instead, Jesus' authority over demons meant that he had ushered in a new kingdom (vs. 20), one over which Satan exercised no authority or dominion.

In this new kingdom, those who had lost authority over Satan and his seed could now reclaim it; not by force, nor by will, but by the grace, power, and authority of Jesus Christ. One of the most important of all the stories regarding demons is when Jesus sends out his seventy[7] disciples and commands them to go before him into every town and place where he was about to go (Luke 10:1). They would be "lambs in the midst of wolves" (vs. 3), a reference, no doubt, to both human and non-human intelligences residing in those places. They could bring "peace" to a house (vv. 5-6) or curses (vv. 11-12), depending upon the reception they received.

What so astonished the disciples is that when they returned to him they said, "Lord, even the demons are subject to us in your name!" (vs. 17). Jesus then tells them, "I saw Satan fall like lightning from heaven" (vs. 18). This is not a reference to the original fall of Satan (what would be the point of mentioning that?), but to his human-earthly battle with the devil in the wilderness temptation. That is, Jesus is talking about a time in the not too distant past when he battled the devil and overcame him, thus securing the fall of Satan's kingdom and the rising up of his own. As he says in another place, I have bound the strongman (who is also called Beelzebub; Matt 12:29). "Now the ruler/prince of this world will be cast out" (John 12:31). "He is judged" (John 16:11).

The next verse mentions a strange group of creatures called scorpions. Jesus explains, "Behold, I have given you authority to tread on serpents and scorpions, and over all the power of the enemy, and nothing shall hurt you" (vs. 19). People have yanked this passage out of context (along with Mark 16:17-18), and all sorts of bizarre serpent cults have sprung up in the exegetical wasteland. It is clear, however, when you understand the cultural background that serpents and scorpions refer to spiritual entities.

Look at the words in the surrounding verses: demons (vs. 17), Satan (vs. 18), spirits (vs. 20). Crawling, slithering animals hardly fits that context. Jesus is not giving the disciples power to be Pied Pipers over rodents and reptiles, except without flutes. The connection of serpents and scorpions probably originates in Deuteronomy 8:15 where God "led you through the great and terrifying wilderness, with its fiery *serpents and scorpions* and thirsty ground where there was no water." In apocalyptic literature, scorpions are given power over the earth (Rev 9:3). In the Babylonian Epic of Gilgamesh, "Scorpion-Beings" act as shedu (demonic guardians) of the Netherworld, and they protect the "assembly of the gods": (*Gilgamesh*, Tablet 9).

FIG. 14.1. SCORPION MAN

Phoenician God: Shadrafa
Palmyra, Syria, 55AD

Then there is the Phoenician god Šadrafa (whose name contains the word *'rafa*) who is likewise a guardian of the underworld.[8] In Jewish literature you have "the guardians of the keys of hell, standing by the very large doors, their faces like those of very large snakes."[9] Serpents and scorpions guarding the doors of hell? Its sounds very much like the Rephaim who "greet" the kings down in Sheol.

In a world filled with snake handling cults, such bizarre practices are not primarily (if even secondarily) what Jesus has in mind. He is speaking about overcoming the devil and his minions ("the helpers of Rahab"). This overcoming is first the authority to cast out demons from the demonized. It is not *our* authority, but Christ's and as the sons of Sceva learned, if you do not have Christ, you do not have the authority of Christ. Also, it is dangerous business to get involved in this kind of a thing. At one point in time, even the disciples came back to Jesus and wondered why they could not cast out a certain demon. Jesus said, "This kind only comes out with prayer" (Mark 9:29).

This authority over demons and the hordes of hell is pronounced in no more powerful way than by Jesus at the foot of Mt. Hermon in that now familiar place called Banias or Caesaera Philippi. Here, where the Watchers of tradition literally came down to earth, Jesus tells Peter (*petros*—The Rock), "On this rock (*petra*) I will build my church, and the gates of hell shall not prevail against it" (Matt 16:18). How much ink has been spilt debating the question of whether or not Jesus is calling Peter the first Pope here? While that question is important, and I take the Protestant position that in one sense "the rock" Jesus refers to is Peter's confession, another rock is almost always overlooked. That rock is Mt. Hermon itself. Jesus is saying in a powerful way that here, at epicentre and origin of the Giant Wars, where fallen Watchers left their positions of authority in heavenly places and came down to earth, here is where Jesus will begin to build his church, and those very same gates will be powerless to stop him.[10] Is it a coincidence that immediately after this, Jesus is transfigured (probably at Mt. Hermon) and then he heals a boy possessed by an evil spirit (Mark 9:17-30)?[11]

Ours is certainly not a book on demonology or a how-to manual for casting out demons. I bring these things up only because they show you the power and authority that Christ displayed over these ancient beings in his ministry on the earth. But as I said, the forces of evil were working double shifts trying to figure out a way to stop Christ from gaining the final victory over them. This is what they thought they had accomplished when they put him to death.

Chapter 15: Victory

[Christ] went and proclaimed to the spirits in prison, because they formerly did not obey, when God's patience waited in the days of Noah.

1 Peter 3:19-20

Common Mistakes

One of the most quoted Psalms in the New Testament is Psalm 22 which begins, "My God, my God, why have you forsaken me"? These words and several more passages from this Psalm are quoted or alluded to throughout Jesus' ordeal at Calvary.[1] This includes Psalm 22:12, "Many bulls encompass me; strong bulls of Bashan surround me." Knowing now that Bashan is Grand Central Station for ancient giants, "bulls of Bashan" takes on a richer meaning.

It is clearly the case, in the prophecy-fulfillment of the Gospels, that the bulls of Bashan are viewed as human beings. I submit that in Matthew's reconstruction of the event, he has in mind "the whole battalion" of Roman soldiers that gathered around Jesus during the mock trial (Matt 27:27). But it is also the case in biblical theology that behind humans there often stand satanic and demonic forces. One thinks, for instance, of David numbering his fighting men (2 Sam 24:1), but also of Satan inciting him to do it (1 Chron 21:1); or of Judas betraying the Lord (Luke 22:48), but Satan entering into him

(Luke 22:3); or of Peter denying Christ (John 13:38), but Satan asking to sift him like wheat (Luke 22:31). In the case of the bulls of Bashan, a few scholars have suggested that these are demonic hordes that aligned themselves against Christ.[2] It is certainly a plausible idea, given the demonic geography of Bashan.

The thing is, at just the point the demons thought they had defeated Christ—surrounding him, mocking him, inspiring men to put him to death—he surprised them and gained the decisive victory. Christ's death was not, ultimately speaking, the doing of men or demons, but God. "It was the will of the LORD to crush him" (Isa 53:10). "Both Herod and Pontius Pilate, along with the Gentiles and the peoples of Israel" did whatever God's hand and plan "had predestined to take place" (Acts 4:27). Apparently, the demons had misread the Scriptures as badly as the Jews and even Jesus' own Disciples who did not understand that Messiah must be put to death in order to win the war. "You will bruise his heel," God had told the serpent (Gen 3:15). Did that really mean he must die in the process?

Satan bruised Christ's heel, but the Seed of the woman "bruised the head" of the seed of the Serpent. Both will die, but one will live again. So, at Christ's death, the Apostle tells us that Christ disarmed the rulers and authorities and put them to open shame, by triumphing over them (Col 2:15). In his resurrection he is seated "far above all rule and authority and power and dominion, and above every name that is named" (Eph 1:20). These rulers and authorities include all natural and *supernatural* rulers. All those on earth *and in heaven*, visible and *invisible* (Col 1:16; cf. Eph 3:10; 6:12; 1 Pet 3:22). At the name of Jesus "every knee should bow, of those who are in heaven, and on earth, and *under* the earth" (Php 2:10).

1 Peter 3:19: Christ's Proclamation of Victory

Questions on 1 Peter 3:19

With that I come to one of the most significant verses in the Bible for understanding Christ's victory over the giants. It is a verse found in 1 Peter 3:19-20, "[Christ] went and proclaimed to the spirits in prison." In one way, this verse brings us full circle. Just like Genesis 6:4, the meaning of this passage is disputed among scholars and laymen alike. If the reasons are anything like those we've seen in the Genesis passage, it may be because some people can't (or won't) believe what it says.

The best short treatment of this passage I have been able to find is in the *Word Biblical Commentary* on 1 Peter.[3] It is fair, exegetically sound, not predisposed to any particular view, thorough, and yet brief enough to be read in a single sitting. To understand our verse properly, we need to read the verse preceding and following.

[18] For Christ also suffered once for sins, the righteous for the unrighteous, that he might bring us to God, being put to death in the flesh but made alive in the spirit, [19] in which he went and proclaimed to the spirits in prison, [20] because they formerly did not obey, when God's patience waited in the days of Noah, while the ark was being prepared, in which a few, that is, eight persons, were brought safely through water."

There are basically four issues that must be addressed in verse 19.

1. To what does the "in which" (at the beginning of vs. 19) refer?
2. Who are these "spirits"?
3. What was the nature of the proclamation?
4. Where was this proclamation made?

Views of 1 Peter 3:19

Before we look at this verse in more detail, I'll give you my view. Following Michaels (see note #3 above), I believe this verse refers to *Christ, proclaiming to demonic spirits, in his new spiritual body, a message of their defeat, wherever they might be.* Adding to what he says, Christ certainly made the initial proclamation all by himself, but it is also possible that an ongoing proclamation, a confirmatory proclamation, is made through his body on earth—the church. That is, every time the gospel goes out, Christ proclaims his victory and authority over these creatures so that they no longer have the right to hold people captive. He began this proclamation himself, made it forcefully and fully, but each time the gospel goes forth, the demons now know that they hold no power over God's elect. This is why demonic strongholds seem to melt away when the gospel comes for the first time to a people group. It is also why it sometimes makes it so hard for these same gospel changed people to understand or remember what things were like for their ancestors before the gospel came to them.

In the history of interpretation on this verse, this position is not among the most popular. The main interpretations have been:

1. Christ preached to the souls of Noah's contemporaries dwelling in the lower world (Sheol) while he was in the grave before his resurrection.
2. Christ preached to Noah's contemporaries who were alive before the flood in his pre-incarnate state through the person of Noah.
3. Christ preached to the fallen angels in Tartarus (see 2 Pet 2:4; Jude 6) that he defeated them at the cross.[4]

I'm presenting a fourth view, though certainly not a novel view. In each case above, the nature of the proclamation is all over the map.

Some think Christ preached salvation in the first two categories. Some think that Christ only preached salvation to those who were converted. Others think there was a sort of second chance in Sheol for those who perished in the Flood. Some think Christ proclaimed condemnation to these people. Certainly, those taking the angelic view think the message was one of judgment not salvation. The point is, this has been a rather messy passage in church history. For that reason, I certainly do not hang my entire argument upon this single verse of the Bible. If one of these interpretations happens to be the correct view, it does little to change anything we've said in this book. Christ still has the victory, whether Peter talks about it or not.

If the interpretation I present here is correct, however, it means that Christ made a definitive proclamation to the spirits of the giants that he now has won the final victory, that the promise given to Eve has been fulfilled, that victory is secure, that he is bringing new citizens into their lands (think about Canaan, the giants, and the conquest), that their time is short, and that they no longer have any authority over anyone that he chooses to bring out of their kingdom and into his own blessed eternal realm. This is a powerful message indeed. It is a reversal of all of redemptive history outside of the nation of Israel, as these beings (along with the sons of God) did have a certain authority to keep the world in darkness, though they did so in rebellion against God. They did have authority over those in their kingdoms. God did not have a legal right to take anyone out of their realm (due to his own legal promise to these entities in ancient times past), unless that person transferred allegiance to the nation of Israel. This becomes the whole impetus for the evangelism of the nations, for Paul's proclamation to Gentiles that "today is the day of salvation" (2 Cor 6:2) or that "now God commands all people everywhere to repent" (Acts 17:30).

Proclamation of Victory to the Lystrian Galatians

A particularly interesting combination of these two ideas is found in the people of Lystra in Galatia (Acts 14:8-19) who believed for some reason that Barnabas was Zeus and that Paul was Hermes (Acts 14:12). Why? I think you will enjoy this little excursion.

Galatia is today's modern Turkey. It has a particularly eerie relationship to the giants. It is home to the oldest ceremonial center known to exist: Göbekli Tepe (p. 150) and is the more ancient home of the peoples known as the Celts, or their less known name the Gauls. (We normally think of the Celts as being Irish, but Gaul is an ancient term that describes France, Luxembourg, Belgium, most of Switzerland, the western part of Northern Italy, and parts of the Netherlands and Germany on the west bank of the Rhine).[5] "Gaul" is thought by some to derive from a word meaning "powerful."[6] Others suggest that "Celt" and "Gaul" have the same meaning, something like "potent" and "valiant men."[7] Why might they have been so powerful?

Many ancient historians tell us that these Gauls, and especially their princes, were giants. The early 18th Century historian Paul Pezron says these Gauls "exceeded all others in bulk and strength of body; and hence it is that they have been looked upon to be terrible people, and as it were Giants."[8] For example, the Roman historian Julias Florus (2nd Century A.D.) describes one Teutobocchus (a blue eyed, yellow haired Gaul king) as "a man of extraordinary stature" who used to "vault over four or six horses at once" but "could scarcely mount one when he fled." When captured he "was seen above all the trophies or spoils of the enemies, which were carried upon the tops of spears."[9] The Greek historian Polybius (200 – 188 B.C.) laments that thanks to the Celts, the Roman legionaries had become super fighting machines.

"Once they had got used to being struck down by Gauls they were incapable of imagining anything worse."[10] This was eventually very bad news for the Greeks. Some of the largest giant remains of the medieval period come from this region.

The Celts across the Rhine were called Germani (*germani* meant "true Celts" according to Strabo [63 B.C. – 24 A.D.; *Geography of Strabo* 7.1.2.]). The Christian historian Hegesippus (110 – 180 A.D.) wrote that the Germans "are superior to other nations by the largeness of their bodies and their contempt of death."[11] The Roman Vegetius (4th – 5th Cent. A.D.) wrote, "What could our undersized men have done against the tall Germans"? Columella (4 – 70 A.D.) says, "Nature has made Germany remarkable for armies of very tall men."[12] Sidonius Apollinaris (430 – 489 A.D.) reports that so many of the people were seven feet tall and up that he could not address them properly.[13] Augustine reports of a German (Goth) woman being paraded around the streets of Rome who "by her gigantic size over-topped all others."[14] As late as the 1500s, a German by the name of Aymon grew to 11 feet tall. The famed Baron Bentenrieder—who was himself eight feet eight inches—"hardly reached up to Arymon's armpits."[15] Still another named Hans Braw was estimated at 12 feet 8 inches tall.[16] So fierce were these Germans that, "The Gauls," reports Julius Caesar (100 – 15 B.C.), "had not been able to endure even the expression on their faces or the glare of their eyes."[17] The Romans called them "Berserkers," and for decades the greatest army on earth was continually slaughtered by these giants in war (and people wonder where Hitler got the idea of a "super-race." He knew the history of these people and he wanted to reclaim it for himself, curiously, through scientific experiments, DNA manipulation, and the like).[18]

Josephus (37 – 100 A.D.), the Jewish historian, relates that Magog, the brother of Gomer and grandson of Noah, was the ancestor of these people.[19] He believed that Gomer settled in Galatia. "Gomer founded those whom the Greeks now call Galatians [Galls], but were then called Gomerites."[20] The name Gomer in *Akkadian* is Gimirru (they called them Gimmerai). Europeans called them Cimmerians or Cimbri. Many of these Cimbri migrated out of Galatia, north and west into Gaul, and became the Celts.

During the centuries long wars with the up and coming Romans (3rd – 1st centuries B.C.), these Celts began to leave Gaul *en masse* (many had undoubtedly continued past Gaul in earlier times). Some went north into Britannia, and there is speculative evidence to suggest some migrated into North America, where they became the tall blonde/red-haired, white-skinned giants sometimes associated with the mysterious Mound-Builders[21] of Ohio (see Appendix: Giants in the Americas). Curiously, Galatia takes its name from the Gauls (Celts). It comes from a Greek word (*gala*) meaning "milk." *Galatea* means "she who is milk-white," as the Celts were the white skinned blonde giants of ancient times, just as we saw was true of the Amorites.

The migration of these ancient peoples seems to have begun in the region of today's Uzbekistan and Kazakhstan around the Jaxartes River which flows into the Aral Sea.[22] Some moved northwest, north of the Black Sea, into Serbia and finally to Germany. Others went southwest, first into Margiana, Hircania, and Bactriana, and then south of the Caspian Sea into Armenia where they continued to migrate south (into Syria and Arabia) and west (into Galatia, Phrygia and beyond).[23] It is curious the southern migrations go right past the ancient region of Babel, where Nimrod built his famous Tower. It also takes you near the regions of the giant-kings mentioned in Genesis 14 (including Shinar, Elasar and Elam, and Goiim which may have been near Galatia).

All of this is to whet your appetite for understanding the references to Hermes and Zeus when Paul went to Lystra. If these people knew their history, they would have been familiar not only with these Greek gods, but also with the giants. They also clearly had had a similar view of spiritual beings that held rule over the people, as Paul makes clear to them when they seek to worship him.

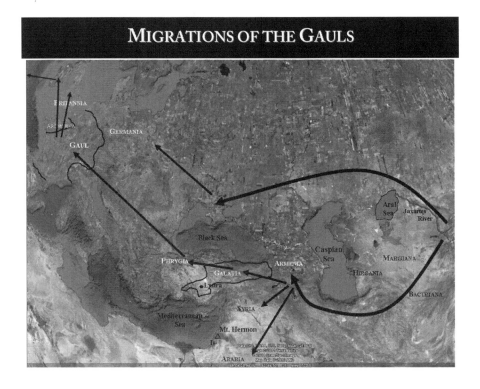

MIGRATIONS OF THE GAULS

But why did they refer to Paul as Hermes? Hermes is the chief messenger of the gods as well as the chief healer (from his name we get *hermeneutic* which deals with interpreting a text and *hermeticism* which deals with magic and healing). In the story, Paul heals a man crippled from birth after he preaches a sermon to them. Thus, he fits the role of Hermes perfectly. When the people seek to worship him and Barnabas, they shout, "Men, why are you doing these things? We also are men, of like nature with you, and we bring you good news, that you should turn from these vain things to a living God, who made the heaven and the earth and the sea and all that is in them. In past generations he allowed all the nations to walk in their own ways" (Acts 14:15-16).

The Apostles do not deny that there are other "men" of a different nature. Nor do they say that Zeus and Hermes are figments of the imagination. Rather, they affirm that they (Paul and Barnabas) are men and not gods. Then they say that the worship of Zeus and Hermes is vanity, a chasing after the wind.

In Galatians, Paul adds that these same people were at one time "enslaved" to something called the *stoicheia* (Gal 4:3, 9). These *stoicheia* are "by nature not gods" (vs. 8). Paul is not denying their existence. He is referring to their demonic origin.[24] Thus, the proclamation of the gospel to these people at Lystra is that they must now repent and turn to Christ, for he has defeated the evil rulers of the spirit world, be they "gods" or demons. This is the drastic reversal of human fortune in the Gentile world outside of Israel. Salvation in Christ apart from national identity can now occur.

Who are the "spirits"?

So let's look at Peter's verse. I'll begin by looking at these "spirits" (*pneumasin,* the plural of *pneuma*—"spirit"). Who are they? First, they definitively have their origin "in the days of Noah." This brings us back to Genesis 6 which begins with the story of the Nephilim.

When we survey the word used here, in the rest of the New Testament the plural is used only one other time for humans (see Heb 12:23).   On the other hand, "spirits" refers to demons at least 34 times.[25]   In some of these verses, "demon" and "spirit" are used as synonyms in the verse (Luke 4:33; 8:2; 9:42; Rev 18:2).   If demons really are not fallen angels, but the children of the sons of God, then spirits never refers to angels in the NT.   The regular usage of the word is a pretty good indication that what we have in this verse is some kind of a proclamation to demonic entities.   In 1 Enoch (which almost all scholars today argue influenced both 1 and 2 Peter and Jude) there is a close parallel.

> The giants who are born from the union of the spirits and the flesh
> shall be called evil spirits upon the earth, because their dwelling shall
> be upon the earth and inside the earth.   Evil spirits have come out of
> their bodies. Because from the day that they were created from the
> holy ones they became the Watchers; their first origin is the spiritual
> foundation. They will become evil upon the earth and shall be called
> evil spirits. The dwelling of the spiritual beings of heaven is heaven;
> but the dwelling of the spirits of the earth, which are born upon the
> earth, is in the earth.
>
> (1 Enoch 15:8-10)

As Ramsey writes, "If this passage is brought to bear on 1 Peter, then the 'spirits in refuge' are neither the souls of those who died in the flood nor precisely the angels whose sin brought the flood on the earth, but rather the 'evil spirits' who came from the angels—probably identified in Peter's mind with the 'evil' or 'unclean' spirits of the Gospel tradition.   If the authors of 1 Enoch saw the 'evil spirits' of their day as offspring of the angelic 'watchers,' there is no reason why Peter may not have viewed the 'unclean spirits' of his own Christian tradition in a similar light."[26] I heartily concur.

Where was the proclamation made?

This identification of the spirits as demons or the evil spirits of the gospels helps to inform the location of the proclamation. As we've seen, the Rephaim are in Sheol, but they do not seem to always reside there, because evil spirits roam the earth (and the air?). It is perhaps better to think of the Rephaim in Sheol as being the guardians of Sheol, creatures free to move back and forth between the realm of the dead and the realm of the living. That would explain how they can be in both places in the Scripture.

Therefore, if Jesus made proclamation to them, it appears that he proclaimed to them wherever they happened to be. Sometimes 2 Peter 2:4 is seen as a parallel to 1 Peter 3:19. This is not appropriate. 2 Peter 2:4 (along with Jude 6) has the sons of God, i.e. the fathers of the evil spirits, in view. That verse calls them "angels" rather than "spirits." "For if God did not spare the angels when they sinned ..."

Just as there are two different groups in mind in these verses, so there are two different places in mind as well. Very few English translations bring this out properly. Most are like the ESV which says, "... but cast them into hell and committed them to chains of gloomy darkness to be kept until the judgment." The normal word for "hell" is *gehenna*. The other word we often associate with hell, but which actually refers to a different (temporary) place is hades. Hades and hell are not identical. But neither word is used here by Peter.

Instead, 2 Peter uses the word *tartarus*. This is the only time the word appears in the NT.[27] This should be a signal. If 2 Peter had meant hell or hades (Sheol), it would have said so. Instead, it uses the word that is steeped in Greek mythology. Here is an example from Hesiod,

> Among the foremost Cottus and Briareos and Gyes[28] insatiate for war raised fierce fighting: three hundred rocks, one upon another, they launched from their strong hands and overshadowed the Titans with their missiles, and buried them beneath the wise-pathed earth, and bound them in bitter chains when they had conquered them by their strength for all their great spirit, as far beneath the earth to Tartarus.
>
> (Hesiod, *Theogony* 313-320)

Hesiod has in mind the story which by now is so very familiar. It is the Greek people's equivalent of Genesis 6:1-4. 2 Peter says that tartarus was where these rebel angels were bound in the days of Noah. But in 1 Peter he does not use hell or hades or tartarus. He says that these spirits are in "prison" (*phulakē*). In light of all we have said about the Rephaim as guardians in the underworld, it is fascinating to learn that this word "refers to the act of guarding or to a place that is guarded."[29] It often refers to a prison, but it does not have to.

As Ramsey points out, guarding can be for the purpose of either confinement or protection. Recall that in the ancient mindset outside of the NT, demons were not viewed as entirely evil. They protected cities. They protected houses. They protected people. The NT tells us, however, that these protectors are not what they appear to be. If these beings protect or guard more than just the gates of hades/sheol, then it becomes apparent that Jesus proclaimed his message to them wherever they might happen to be.

For these spirits, wherever they are happens to be their *phulakē*, their refuge. Think about the demons desiring to indwell people. They seek out their dwellings as homes, refuges. In Revelation 18:2 (a verse which we saw comes directly from Isaiah 34:13), this is quite apparent. Babylon "has become a dwelling place for demons." Some translations say "home" or "lair." Importantly, the word is *phulaké*. In other words, it isn't a prison, but a refuge. Thus, Ramsey prefers the translation, "... to the spirits in refuge" as opposed to "prison."

What was the nature of the proclamation?

Those who insist that Christ somehow preached the gospel to sinners who lived in Noah's time have very little to go on. The word "proclaim" is *kérussō*. But when Peter refers to the gospel in his letter (1 Pet 1:12, 25; 4:6, 17), he uses a form of the more familiar word *euaggelion* (from which we derive evangelism). This is the only time he uses this particular word for a proclamation.

The word is sometimes used to refer to the gospel, but the problem is, if Jesus is preaching to demons (dead giants), what good would it do to preach the gospel to them? Or, if he is actually preaching to humans, why is Jesus so desperately concerned about those who perished in the Flood? Why wouldn't Peter make it more inclusive of everyone who perished prior to Jesus' coming in the flesh?

So what did Christ proclaim? It is tempting to see it as a proclamation of judgment. But it may be better to see it as a proclamation that he has defeated them and that they are no longer able to withstand the intrusion of the kingdom of heaven upon their once safe havens. Their kingdoms can now be raided; their captives, freed. It is a message that the Sovereign Lord of the Universe has fulfilled the promise, and crushed the head of the serpent who now staggers from his mortal wound and very soon will be punished with everlasting punishment in the Judgment to come.

When did Christ proclaim his message?

That leaves us with one final question to answer from this passage. When did Christ proclaim this message? The verb "went" is actually a passive aorist participle. The exact same verb is used in just a couple verses later in 1 Peter 3:22 where it says that Jesus "having gone into heaven" is at the right hand of God, with angels, authorities, and powers having been subjected to him (a verse, by the way, which supports the supernatural interpretation of the "spirits," except that at the ascension it seems that Jesus subjects not the demons, but their fathers and all other angelic beings to his lordship). The verse clearly speaks of something in the past, when Christ ascended into heaven before the eyes of the disciples (Acts 1:9).

It is a good bet that Peter is not using the verb differently in 3:19, and thus it refers to an event of Christ sometime prior to the resurrection. Exactly when that might be, it is impossible to say with certainty. It does seem foreign to the context to think that Jesus did this way back in the days of Noah. Vs. 18 seems to tie it to Christ's death and resurrection. So, it could be in between those two events, or it could be at a time after his resurrection when he was in his new eternal glorified body. Either way, it does not really make that much difference to the interpretation. Christ has proclaimed a message of his absolute authority over the demonic world, and they no longer have the power to keep people in slavery and bondage when Christ is proclaimed.

Conclusion: Why Does It Matter?

I'm not a pragmatist by nature. I don't particularly care about a subject because of what I can get out of it. I seek to know revealed truth because it is an honor to do so. "It is the glory of God to conceal things, but the glory of kings is to search things out" (Prov 25:2). The things we have spoken of here *are* revealed, and they *are* knowable.

I do, however, also believe that the Bible is God's repository of all the truth I need to live eternally and in obedience to him in this world. What does this study of the giants contribute to that end? I hope that you will be able to give your own answer to this question now that we have come to the end of the book. But let me give you my own answer.

Some people are captivated by this entire subject, because for them it serves as proof of some eschatological end-game that they believe will play out very shortly in modern events. That is, this subject is rarely discussed without some kind of end-times speculation that is deduced from the study of the giants. "As it was in the days of Noah ... so will be the coming of the Son of Man" (Matt 24:38; Luke 17:26). This passage is never far behind a book like this.

You have seen none of that kind of speculation here. Whether the giants in a physical form have anything to do with the end of the world, I honestly have no idea. My interest in this subject is not so I can sell you a book that will give you the magic key to knowing when Christ will return and how the whole end-of-the-world scenario will play out. Christ will return. There will be an end of the world. It may be soon, but it may also be long after I'm dead and buried.

For me, the giants are so captivating because they show in a unique way that God has made a prediction, remembered his promise, taken steps to ensure it would be achieved, worked it out in stages in actual redemptive history, always shown himself the master of the seed of Satan through Christ, and then finally delivering the goods, fulfilling the prophecy, conquering the serpents and their wicked spawn, and ruling over them as he is now seated above them. This works on the soul at a profound level. It also works on a more basic level.

I have come to believe that while we still pay lip service to it, many of us really don't take very seriously at all that there is an authentic spiritual war being waged for each of our souls by extremely powerful and intelligent creatures in heavenly places. These creatures not only include Satan, but a host of angelic powers, as well as demonic entities that seek our eternal harm, and want to destroy our joy and delight in God. As with the topic of giants in general, such things are just too weird and bizarre to be taken seriously by educated, intelligent, enlightened, scientific people. Knowledge is power, and you now have the tools to begin appropriating this knowledge into your worldview.

Is anything more practical than knowing the victory is secure, that Christ has won, that such beings hold no power over him or his people, and that no matter what befalls us, God is absolute Sovereign and Lord of this world and the next? If we could ask one of the demonically possessed people freed by Christ himself, I know what they would say. They would tell everyone about the man who set them free with nothing but the power of his word. They would give great glory to God. Then they would live in light of their new freedom by following him and obeying him.

The story of the giants is about glorifying the God of Israel for his holiness, power, foreknowledge, sovereignty, mercy, judgment, truthfulness, faithfulness, love, and grace. Through the story, God has magnanimously displayed these qualities, so that at the name of Jesus every knee *will* bow in heaven and on earth to the glory of God the Father. This is our chief end, to glorify God. Will you do it willingly through faith, or as a one compelled because of his power and wrath? In light of God's sovereignty and victory, how then should you live?

We all come to the Bible with presuppositions, that is, preconceived ideas of what we think it means. As your presuppositions have been challenged, I hope that this "invisible" story of the Bible, the victory and glory of Holy One of Israel will become your sure hope. To this end, I offer up a prayer for you in the form of Psalm 91, retranslated to account for our supernatural worldview (my changes to the usual translation are based upon word studies given in the *Dictionary of Deities and Demons in the Bible*):

Psalm 91

He who dwells in the shelter of the MOST High God will abide in the shadow of Shaddai, "God of the Wilderness."

He will say to the LORD, "My refuge and my fortress, my Elohim in whom I trust."

For he will deliver you from the snare of the fowler and from the deadly pestilence.

He shall overshadow you with his wings, his truth shall cover you with a shield.

You shall not fear the night demon, nor the arrow-shooting Lilith who shoots her arrows in the day.

Nor the diseased ghost that walks in darkness; nor the noon day demon.

A thousand shall fall at your side, ten thousand at your right hand, but it will not come near you.

You will only look with your eyes and see the recompense of the wicked.

Because you have made the LORD your dwelling place—Elyon, who is my refuge.

No evil shall be allowed to befall you, no plague come near your tent.

For he will command his angels concerning you to guard you in all your ways.

Victory

On their hands they will bear you up, lest you strike your foot against a
stone.

You will tread on the lion-headed demons, you shall trample the lion and
the dragon.

Because he holds fast to me in love, I will deliver him; I will protect him,
because he knows my name.

When he calls to me, I will answer him; I will be with him in trouble; I
will rescue him and honor him.

With long life I will satisfy him and show him my salvation.

Appendix: Extra-Biblical Literature

Many Christians do not know how to handle extra-biblical literature, especially Jewish literature, written during the times of the Bible. I've often wondered if maybe this isn't because they are separated into chapter and verse and make people "feel" like they are reading the Bible, and they don't want to be confused. This is understandable, but unfortunate. There are three choices for understanding these books. The first is to ignore them and pretend that they don't exist. Sadly, this is a popular response of many Christians, but it isn't particularly helpful or honest. Ancient peoples from all over the world speak to the issue of giants and heavenly beings.

The second is to deny that they say anything true; "extrabiblical" becomes "fabrication and lies." A softer position is to treat most or everything in them *not quoted in the Bible* as fable and error. This may originate in a strange kind of fundamentalist mistake having its roots in a misunderstanding of what makes Scripture Scripture.

The books in the canon that make up our Bibles are not Scripture because they are true and everything else is false. For example, Einstein could write the formula: $E = MC^2$. The formula is true, but it is not Scripture. I could give you my wife's recipe for the best chilli in the world, which would be a true recipe, but not Scripture. I could have you read a biography of George Washington, which is true history, but not Scripture. While all Scripture is true, is it not the case that everything that is not Scripture is false. It should be obvious as to why the Einstein formula, the recipe for chilli, or the Washington biography should not be considered Holy Wit.

A person can get into some tricky spots when they take this approach that everything said in extrabiblical literature is fabrication. For example, as I said above, Jude quotes the book of Enoch verbatim (see Jude 14 and 1 Enoch 1:9) as being the very words of Enoch, a prophecy that he holds to be quite true. How then do we respond? I've heard more than one person say something like this, "Yes, this particular *verse* of Enoch is true, *but none of the rest of it is.*" This incredible unfalsifiable declaration expects us to shut down all critical thinking, to accept that one verse in Enoch is true because Jude says that it is, and then dump the rest of the book that he quotes and alludes to more than once, *because someone outside of the Bible tells you too.* This is called fideism, the belief that you believe for no good reason. Fideism is opposed to everything taught in the Bible, including the idea of faith. Faith rests on truth, not absurdity.

Enoch is not Scripture for several different reasons.[1] This does not mean, of course, that it relates nothing true about history, or more absurdly, that it gives us only one true verse and Jude happened to discover it. While appealing to Enoch's view of the events of Genesis 6:1-4 cannot, of itself, give us certainty that the view is correct, we can be certain from the material that we presently have available to us that everyone in Jude's day has the same view of the Genesis 6 story that 1 Enoch does. Considering that Jude quotes and alludes positively to 1 Enoch many times (see chart below), it is a good bet that he has the same view as everyone else.[2] Furthermore, neither Jude nor 2 Peter ever says that 1 Enoch is false history. Nor do they hint at it. This is an argument from silence. Rather, Jude says, "The angels who did not stay within their own position of authority, but left their proper dwelling, he has kept in eternal chains under gloomy darkness until the judgment of the great day" (Jude 1:6). 2 Peter is similar. Both clearly have the Enochian tradition of Genesis 6 in view in these verses,[3] as at least Jude does do throughout his little epistle.[4]

SOME OF JUDE'S ALLUSIONS TO 1 ENOCH			
JUDE		**1 ENOCH**	
Jude 6	"The angels that did not keep their own position but left their proper dwelling."	"[The angels] have abandoned the high heaven, the holy eternal place."	1 En 12:4
	"until the judgment of the great day"	"preserved for the day of suffering"	1 En 45:2 (1 En 10:6)
	"angels ... kept in eternal chains under gloomy darkness"	"this is the prison of the angels, and here they will be imprisoned forever"	1 En 21:10 (1 En 10:4)
Jude 12	"waterless clouds"	"every cloud ... rain shall be withheld"	1 En 100:11
	"raging waves"	"ships tossed to and fro by the waves"	1 En 101:2
	"fruitless trees"	"fruit of the trees shall be withheld"	1 En 80:3
Jude 13	"wandering stars"	"stars that transgress the order"	1 En 80:6
	"the gloom of utter darkness has been reserved forever"	"darkness shall be their dwelling"	1 En 46:1
Jude 14	"Enoch the seventh from Adam"	"my grandfather [Enoch] ... seventh from Adam"	1 En 60:8

This gives us the third option for understanding this kind of literature. We can use these extant books and texts wisely and discerningly, without being afraid that we are therefore asking for them to be included in the canon. Christians cite John Calvin and John Wesley, Max Lucado and Chuck Swindoll, and no one ever claims that by quoting them or reading them that they are magically turning them into Scripture. The thought never even crosses our minds. The same grace should be extended to these books as well, especially knowing that they were used by the NT and held up as important by the early church. This kind of an attitude is all the more important for those books written prior to the NT by people in the OT community of

God that very well could have been trusting in the coming Messiah. The fact is, these books were the popular literature of the day and biblical authors read them just as we would read popular commentaries or other Christian writings in our own day. This doesn't make them true or false. It does make them important.

If these books tell us about the sons of God or giants, we should use wisdom, we should compare them with the biblical data, we should inspect them for exaggeration, but we should also realize that this was the view of that day and that the NT writers have the same worldview, as I have repeatedly demonstrated throughout the book.

Appendix: 2 Peter 2:4 and Jude 6

New Testament Commentary

As a Christian who takes biblical inspiration and infallibility seriously, I presuppose that if other parts of the Scripture were to comment upon and explain Genesis 6:1-4, then whatever conclusions they give must be inspired by God and infallibly correct. Most commentators today believe 2 Peter 2:4 and Jude 6 do just that. As all commentators note, these sections of Jude and 2 Peter are interdependent. Either Jude is borrowing from 2 Peter, 2 Peter is borrowing from Jude, and/or one or both are borrowing from a shared tradition.[1] You may want to take the time to read these two chapters now, to see what I'm talking about. I have provided a Table which puts the two passages side by side, and also compares them with an excerpt from Hesiod.

TABLE: ANGELIC SPIRITS IN PRISON		
2 PETER 2:4-5	JUDE 5-6	HESIOD THEOGONY 313-320
(4) For if God did not spare angels when they sinned, but cast them into *Tartarus* and committed them to pits of darkness, reserved for judgment; (5) and did not spare the ancient world, but preserved Noah, a preacher of righteousness. . .	(5) Now I desire to remind you [of] (6) angels who did not keep their own domain, but abandoned their proper abode, He has kept in eternal bonds under darkness for the judgment of the great day. . .	Among the foremost Cottus and Briareos and *Gyes* insatiate for war raised fierce fighting: three hundred rocks, one upon another, they launched from their strong hands and overshadowed the Titans with their missiles, and buried them beneath the wise-pathed earth, and bound them in bitter chains when they had conquered them by their strength for all their great spirit, as far beneath the earth to *Tartarus*."

Since the two letters are parallel, they refer to the same episode, and can therefore shed light on one another. The first thing to notice is that 2 Peter refers to the time when "angels" "sinned." Older Protestant commentators thought this must refer to the original fall of Satan and his angels.[2] But Jude explains the time frame of the sin: when the angels "did not keep their own domain, but abandoned their proper abode" (Jude 6). "Domain" is the Greek word *archēn*, and it refers to the heavenly regions of rule these angels had originally been given. But, they abandoned this realm, their proper sphere, in favor of inhabiting our own realm, the earth. Peter adds that this took place squarely in the days of Noah. This can therefore refer with certainty to only one episode in biblical history: Genesis 6:1-4.[3]

Though this creates enough certainty all on its own, we may add to the force of it in several ways. First, Jude parallels the sin of Sodom with the sin of the angels by the phrases "just as" and "in the same way" in the next verse (Peter likewise discusses Sodom after this event). Jude 7 talks about the sin of Sodom and Gomorrah saying there was "gross immorality" and "going after strange flesh." This is sexual sin, specifically between human males and the "men"[4] from heaven (Gen 18:3, 19:5, 8), who are also called "angels" (Gen 19:1). Therefore, "just as" and "in the same way," the sin of the angels in Jude 6 must have likewise been sexual, and indeed was, as angels were having relations with women in Genesis 6. There is no better way to put either episode than "going after strange flesh."[5] This is the most definitive, explicit link between the "sons of God" being angelic beings in the Scripture. But we may be even more assured than even this.

A second reason for our certainty on this matter is that 2 Peter says that this sin of the angels caused them to be thrown into *Tartarus* at the same time that God "did not spare the ancient world" of Noah's day (2 Peter 2:4-5). Therefore, the sin occurred in the days of Noah. Two more points clarify this. First, the word *tartaroō* is used only here in the NT.[6] It refers to a subterranean region, doleful and dark, which the Greeks viewed as the abode of the wicked dead, where they suffer punishment for their evil deeds.[7] As you can see from the example in Hesiod's *Theogony*, this is where the Titans (i.e. gods or giants) were thrown in a previous age. The fact that Peter did not use the typical word for hades or hell demonstrates he is clearly thinking of this elder time that the poets talk about.

A third reason has to do with the interpretation of Genesis 6:1-4 in Judaism and early Christianity. The idea that this passage refers to angels having relations with women and producing giant offspring was the popular and *universal* interpretation among the Jews[8] at the time these two letters were written, and these sources include the book of 1 Enoch which Jude not only quotes, but alludes to several times.[9]

This is relevant because 1 Enoch 6:1-6 and 7:2-3 are near parallels with Genesis 6:1-4, a fact that was lost to Christianity for over a thousand years until the rediscovery of the book late in the 18th century. You can't blame those who didn't have 1 Enoch, but it is inexcusable when we who do are not willing to interact with the material that we now have. These parallels are explicit in their teaching that the events of Genesis 6:1-4 refer to angels. So, if Jude has been quoting and alluding favourably to Enoch throughout his letter (see Appendix: Extra-Biblical Literature), it is unthinkable that he would radically disagree with its interpretation on this point. It would make no sense that he would continually use other parts of the book to support the rest of his letter, but utterly disagree at this one point. As Thomas Schreiner rightly notes, "If [Jude] does not have the same interpretation in mind as Enoch (and all the other Jewish literature of his day), then he would surely need to make it clear that he is deviating from the tradition, especially since he has Genesis 6 in mind.[10] This is a very powerful argument. Not only does Jude not do this, he and Peter both make it clear that they *accept* the tradition.

Along similar lines, Jude and 2 Peter each have an historical list of events which they are using to make a moral point (that we should not be like those of long gone days who disobeyed). Jude refers to the wilderness, the angels, and Sodom while Peter refers to angels, the flood, and Sodom. The important thing to learn is that lists of this kind, with the *very same events* (and few others), were common place among the Jews of that day to make *the same ethical points*. Table 14 is reproduced from Bauckham's commentary which demonstrates the similarity of the literature.[11]

TABLE: EIGHT HISTORIES COMPARED

Sirach 16:7-10	CD 2:17-3:12	3 Macc 2:4-7	m. Sanh. 10:3	Jub 20:5	T. Naph 3:4-5	Jude 5-7	2 Peter 2:4-8
	Watchers						Watchers
giants	giants	giants		giants	Sodom	Generation of the wilderness	
	generation of the Flood		generation of the Flood	Sodom	Watchers	Wilderness	generation of the Flood
	Flood		Flood			Watchers	Flood
	sons of Noah		generation of the dispersion			Sodom	Sodom
Sodom		Sodom	Sodom				
	sons of Jacob						
Canaanites	Israel in Egypt	Pharaoh and Egyptians	spies				
Generation of the wilderness	Israel at Kadesh		generation of the wilderness				
			Company of Korah				

If Jude has Enoch and other traditions in mind (and it is beyond a reasonable doubt that he does), and if both Peter and Jude are compiling the same lists to make the same points as other literature with which they were obviously familiar (which we know with certainty they are), then there is only one interpretation permissible for the Christian who believes that Jude and Peter were infallibly inspired by God. Genesis 6:1-4 refers to angels who left their proper domains, came to earth, married human women, and had gigantic offspring.[12] Any other opinion blatantly contradicts Jude and Peter and throws the infallibility of Scripture out the window.

Appendix: The Stories of the Greeks

Making Sense of Mythology

Were you one of those people that stayed as far away from mythology as you could in High School, thinking, "What's the use of
learning a bunch of ancient silly sacrilegious stories"? I was. If one
proceeds from the assumption that the ancient stories of the nations—
stories which are called "myths"—but which are usually relegated to
fantasy, fable, and fairy-tale—are based in some kind of real history,
then one naturally begins to wonder how such stories might fit into a
biblical chronology. Sometimes, a single story is pretty easy to identify
and classify. We've seen how there are over 180 different Flood stories
throughout the earth (see pgs. 71-72). Likewise, we have seen widely
spread stories that appear very much to resemble the Tower of Babel
(see pgs. 83-95). These did not spontaneously arise from accident or
coincidence all over the world.

It gets much more difficult very quickly to try and figure out
how multiple stories fit into actual history, especially when these stories often contradict the Bible, let alone themselves. One of the problems with myth is that it is its own unique genre, its own distinctive
way of telling history. Myth is not as concerned with brute facts as
with telling a story. This is why the modern enlightened mind dislikes
it so much (though you would never know it from the Hollywood box
office). It often places history, allegory, and metaphor side by side.
Sometimes, the same story works on all of these levels. Other times,
central figures are often telling one story from two different points of

view, or better, a single figure can be used to tell two different aspects of the same grand narrative.

A good example of this, in my opinion, is a figure like Zeus (Jupiter). Zeus is depicted as the highest god in the Olympian pantheon, the creator of mankind, in some ways a perverted equivalent of the biblical God. Yet, you can also read about very human and mortal events in Zeus' life: his birth where he is hidden from his father Cronus on the Island of Crete, his continual liaisons with mortal women, and even that he has a tomb on the same Island on which he was born.[1] This mortal-immortal lives prior to the Flood, is the cause of the Flood, and continues on long after the Flood. Taken as a composite, the story of Zeus cannot be reconciled to anything in real history, so it is tempting to think of him entirely as a figment of the fertile imagination of the Greeks.

But if we take threads that make up Greek (and Roman) mythology, unwind them from larger tapestry, and look at them in isolation, I think it is possible to make some sense of the convolutions, additions, and perversions of the history.[2] In this Appendix, I want to attempt this very thing for you, to see if we can't see some correspondences in the pagan remembrances of world events.

Chaos

Let's start at the beginning. In the beginning, the Greeks saw only Chaos. Chaos is at the very top of the Greek pantheon. This "god" is really nothing of the sort. He is really an "it." The Greek word has carried over into English in a way that few of the other names of the gods have. Chaos is an impersonal abstract random meaningless way to get everything from nothing. "He" corresponds perfectly to the modern naturalist/atheist god of chance or the Big

Bang. How curious that Greek polytheism would have so much in common with modern atheism. Of course, Chaos is the diametrical opposite of the Biblical God—a personal concrete purposeful God of order, meaning, intelligence, morality, stability, immutability, eternal sovereignty, and power.

For the Greek, Chaos "begot" a pantheon of "children," impersonal things called the Protogenoi (primeval): Tartarus (abyss), Nyx (night), Erebus (darkness), Eros (desire/love), and Gaia (earth). Of these, it is really only Gaia and Eros who have been personified in any meaningful sense today. Since Chaos begat them, they must be generated; but since Chaos is itself impersonal, it is not really correct to say that they were "created," for creation takes intention and intelligence.

These "gods" in turn spawned impersonal forces. For instance, Nyx (night) begat many children: Moros (doom), Oneiroi (dreams), Nemesis (retribution), Momus (blame), Philotes (affection), and Geras (aging), Thanatos (death), Hypnos (sleep), Eris (strife), Apate (deceit), Oizys (distress), Moirae (fate), and Keres. Here it is possible to see some very perverted reflection of the biblical angelic world, except that angels are viewed in the Bible as persons rather impersonal forces of nature. How then does this reflect anything true?

In Revelation, angels are very often *assigned to* the forces of nature (e.g., they bring floods, they speak through dreams, they guard the abyss etc.; for example Rev 16:2-12). Peter and Paul both use the same word (*stoicheia*) to refer to the elements of nature and personal spiritual beings respectively (2 Peter 3:10-12; Galatians 4:3-11). This shows the close relationship in Scripture between heavenly beings and earthly forces. The former have some kind of power over the later.

Gaia and Uranus

Let's focus in on one specific Protogenoi, the goddess Gaia. Gaia has never really gone away. In fact today, she is making a comeback as paganism returns to the west with reckless abandon. She simply personifies earth. But more than the big ball we all live on (in the Roman pantheon, Gaia is Terra), she personifies that which lives upon the earth, especially humanity, we who are made from the dust and return to it. Of course in Gaia worship, as the creation is worshiped rather than the Creator, earth is a living mother, the goddess of all life. Such is the perversion. At any rate, in the myth, Gaia had a son named Uranus. The seventh planet is named after him. Uranus means "heaven" (Gk: *ouranos*). In the Bible, of course, we see that in Genesis 1:1 LXX, "In the beginning God created the *ouranos* and the *ge*."

The Children of Heaven and Earth

In the Greek story, Gaia and Uranus get married and have children. It is at this point that the primeval creation turns into more recognizable history. Think about these children this way—they are the product of a marriage between heaven and earth. When we understand who these children are it is easily understood that they tell the Genesis 6:1-4 story. The sons of God (personified in Uranus) married the daughters of men (personified by Gaia) and begat children called the Nephilim.

At this point, the story gets very interesting. There are several branches of children that are born from this unholy union. These branches take place at two different periods in history, and through two different means of generation. The first group of children all come from the union between Gaia and Uranus. These consist of the

Cyclopes, the Hekatonkheires, and the Titans. One thing unites all of these groups. They are all giants.

There were three great Cyclopes: Brontes, Steropes, and Arges. They were great wielders of metal and weapons. They are often depicted around forges. Though there is no hint that he is a giant, Tubal-Cain, the son of Lamech, is quite similar in terms of what he does and when he does it. There were also three great Hekatonkheires: Briareus, Cottus, and Gyges. The word *hekatonkheire* means "one hundred handed ones." These were hideous monsters, each with fifty heads and a hundred hands. It is possible that they represent a large number of people, or a large number of *large* people.

The third group were the Titans and there were twelve of them. The youngest and most important is Cronus. His name is of unknown origin. The Romans called him Saturn. His is the sixth planet and we also remember him ever *Satur*day. Some have suggested that his name derives from a word meaning "to cut" (Gk: *keirō*). Others, thinking of the Latin equivalent Sadorn, suggest it means "martial" or "warlike." Both are reminiscent of this figure.

What happened to these children? The Cyclopes and Hekatonkheires were an abomination to Uranus because they were so ugly. So he bound them up and placed them in Tartarus, or from Gaia's perspective, he threw them back into her own bowels. Their ugliness has a certain fit with the Nephilim (even if those Nephilim happened to be physically beautiful) in terms of their being an unnatural abomination, violent, and wicked creatures on the earth prior to the flood. The Greek story, however, seems to conflate two different biblical stories.

In 2 Peter and Jude, it is the angels (a NT catch-all term for various heavenly beings), not the giants, who are bound up and thrown into tartarus. If they were retelling the Greek myth, these two would not have made such an obvious mistake. Still, the similarities are difficult to miss. Similarly, 1 Peter tells us that there are spirits who now reside in prison. 1 Peter does not use the word *tartarus* here, but as I have argued (see pgs. 213-225), it does appear that Peter is talking about the giants. The OT equivalent of this is the Rephaim shades who guard the pit. God's question to Job about unbinding Orion (Job 38:31; see pp. 80-81) may be a dim echo of this ancient story. It seems that the Greeks mixed these two stories together in the creation of their own mytho-historical narrative.

At this point in the story, the actions of Uranus make Gaia furious. So she speaks to her Titanic sons and tells them they must to depose their Father. She decides that castration (cutting off heaven?) is the best option. If he hates his sons so much, then perhaps he should not have any more. The only one with nerve enough to do the deed it is Cronus.

The story goes that Gaia set an ambush for Uranus, while Cronus hid with a sickle. At just the right moment, the youngest son of Heaven leapt out of hiding, and with a well aimed swipe, cut his father off in his prime. From here, Cronus becomes the High God of the pantheon, until he becomes paranoid just like his father, and begins to destroy each of his children in the same way as Uranus. Zeus, who was hidden away by his mother, has a similar story as Cronus, and eventually he too deposes his father after being saved by his mother.

This story seems to be the Greek anti-story to the Biblical account of the Flood. In the Bible, it is God who cuts off the inhabitants of the earth by destroying them. In fact the Flood is referred to as a "cutting off" (Gen 9:11), echoing metaphorically the castration of Uranus. The difference, however, is substantial. The Greek story is one of rebellion of earth against heaven, where earth wins. In the Bible, it is one of God's anger against sin against heavenly and earthly beings. But in the end, it is God's grace that overcomes all. If this really was the time when God cast angels and giants into dark places, then I believe the Greeks have remembered a portion of the truth, even though their Flood stories are not connected with the Cronus myth.

The second batch of children between Uranus and Gaia take place *during* the castration. It is through the blood (sometimes semen) of Uranus that is thrown into the sea that the second batch of children are born. These are the Meliae, the Erinyes, and most importantly, the Gigantes. The first two are female. The Meliae are nymph-spirits. The Erinyes are deities that dwell in the underworld to punish whoever has sworn a false oath. Underworld deities and spirits? Hmmm.

The final group, the Gigantes, is where the LXX's translation of *nephilim* originates. Remember, the Nephilim are called *gigantes* in the Greek. Thus, the story of the children of Gaia and Uranus seems to be an interesting, albeit perverted memory of the events of antediluvian and early post-diluvian history where the world, full of giants, perished only to be replaced with wicked spirits and more giants that terrorized humanity all around the globe.

Appendix: Giants in the Americas

"The eyes of that species of extinct giants,
whose bones fill the mounds of America,
have gazed on Niagara [Falls], as ours do now."

Abraham Lincoln¹

In this Appendix, I want to give you a flavor for the myriads of reports of giants, especially in the Americas; then I want to conclude with some thoughts on how to interpret them. Much of this information has been compiled in various non-scientific books on the subject.² I obviously can't vouch for the historicity of every report. Some are also clearly less credible than others. Due to the staggering amount of dubious information concerning giants on the internet (especially the infamous Photoshopped pictures of giant skeletons that make the rounds in e-mail spam and Youtube), we must tread carefully. I *can* give you some specifics reports that I have verified, which have been passed along in encyclopaedias, newspapers (including local and national such as the *New York Times* and *Washington Post*),³ biographical journals, state historical societies, the Smithsonian, and scientific magazines of yesteryear, in a day when people (including Christians) felt they had nothing to fear from such remarkable historical discoveries.

North America, with its "virgin" soil, is especially prone to archaeological reports of giant skeletons. As the Europeans made their way westward, they found undisturbed mounds built by an ancient civilization. Upon excavation, many of these mounds were found to be graves. The settlers told tales of skeletons which they dug up, skeletons ranging from 7 to over 12 feet in such places as Alaska,[4] California,[5] Connecticut,[6] Indiana,[7] Massachusetts,[8] Maine,[9] Nevada,[10] New Hampshire,[11] Ohio,[12] Oklahoma,[13] Pennsylvania,[14] Tennessee,[15] West Virginia,[16] Wisconsin,[17] as well as Arizona, the Dakotas, Florida, Illinois, Michigan, Mississippi, Montana, Texas, Utah, Vermont, Mexico, and others.[18]

Of personal interest for me, this includes Warren, Minnesota. This is the small farming town where my wife was raised. Located within a few feet of the old Pembina trail between Warren and Thief River Falls in Viking Township, they called the mound "Lone mound," presumably because it was the only one around. It is still there and I visited it during the Christmas season of 2011.

Back in the day, it was 12 ft. high x 60 ft. wide. It was examined by the Honorable J. P. Nelson, one of the original founders of Warren. He and those digging discovered bones of more than ten persons of "gigantic stature" but with no specific estimate of height. These human skeletons were mingled with horses, dogs, and badgers. The skeletons almost all disintegrated on exposure to the air with the exception of a single skull, which was obtained by one Theodore Lewis, who helped write the report which was published by the Minnesota Historical Society. A former president of this Historical Society told me he thinks Lewis was hired by the Society to document these ancient places and digs, and that he would have taken the skull for the Society rather than his own collection, though he had not heard of it. Like those in many other mounds around the country, especially out east, the skull appeared to have standard "Caucasian" features.[19] Given other similar finds throughout Minnesota (see below),[20] assuming they were genuine, the skeletons could have been between 7 and 10 feet tall.[21]

Fig. App 1. "LONE MOUND"

Author standing on "Lone Mound," December, 2011
Viking Township, Minnesota
(Thanks to Ryan and Holly Knutson for taking us to the mound)

MINNESOTA SKELETONS WITH HEIGHTS ABOVE 7 FT.

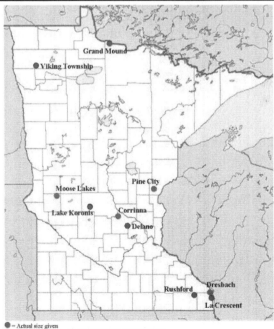

● = Actual size given
● = No estimate of size. Words like "huge" or "enormous" instead.

Other graves of North American giants included blondes in Mexico,[22] and red-heads in Nevada.[23] There are giants with double rows of teeth found throughout the continent.[24] Like the giants of the Bible, as reported by Egyptians, Sumerians, and others, these giants are reported as having Caucasian facial features (which explains the blonde and red hair).

Legends are pervasive. One story is told of no one less than Col. George Washington. During the French and Indian War, Washington was in command of a militia force in Winchester, Virginia. He directed the men to begin digging the foundation of what would become Fort Loudoun. During the dig, the men discovered "Indian" skeletons that Washington reported were seven feet long.[25]

The Indians tell the same kind of history which mostly vanished bone can now only whisper. For example, in her book *Life Among the Paiutes*, Sarah Winnemucca writes,

> Among the traditions of our people is one of a small tribe of barbarians who used to live along the Humboldt River. It was many hundred years ago. They used to waylay my people and kill and eat them. They would dig large holes in our trails at night, and if any of our people travelled at night, which they did, for they were afraid of these barbarous people, they would oftentimes fall into these holes. That tribe would even eat their own dead— yes, they would even come and dig up our dead after they were buried, and would carry them off and eat them.
>
> Now and then they would come and make war on my people. They would fight, and as fast as they killed one another on either side, the women would carry off those who were killed. My people say they were very brave. When they were fighting they would jump up in the air after the arrows that went over their heads, and shoot the same arrows back again. My people took some of them into their families, but they could not make them like themselves. So at last they made war on them.

This war lasted a long time. Their number was about twenty-six hundred (2600). The war lasted some three years. My people killed them in great numbers, and what few were left went into the thick bush. My people set the bush on fire. This was right above Humboldt Lake. Then they went to work and made tuly or bulrush boats, and went into Humboldt Lake.

They could not live there very long without fire. They were nearly starving. My people were watching them all round the lake, and would kill them as fast as they would come on land. At last one night they all landed on the east side of the lake, and went into a cave near the mountains. It was a most horrible place, for my people watched at the mouth of the cave, and would kill them as they came out to get water. My people would ask them if they would be like us, and
not eat people like coyotes or beasts. They talked the same language, but they would not give up.

At last my people were tired, and they went to work and gathered wood, and began to fill up the mouth of the cave. Then the poor fools began to pull the wood inside till the cave was full. At last my people set it on fire; at the same time they cried out to them, "Will you give up and he like men, and not eat people like beasts? Say quick —we will put out the fire." No answer came from them. My people said they thought the cave must be very deep or far into the mountain. They had never seen the cave nor known it was there until then. They called out to them as loud as they could, "Will you give up? Say so, or you will all die." But no answer came.

Then they all left the place. In ten days some went back to see if the fire had gone out. They went back to my third or fifth great-grandfather and told him they must all be dead, there was such a horrible smell. This tribe was called people-eaters, and after my people had killed them all, the people round us called us *Say-do-carah*. It means conqueror; it also means "enemy." I do not know how we came by the name of Piutes. It is not an Indian word. I think it is misinterpreted. Sometimes we are called Pine-nut eaters, for we are the only tribe that lives in the country where Pine-nuts grow. My people say that the tribe we exterminated had reddish hair. I have some of their hair, which has been handed down from father to son.[26]

Incredibly, decades after her book was published and years after she had died, this very cave was excavated in 1911 for its bat guano, a useful fertilizer for the barren desert of Nevada. After digging nearly to the bottom, the men began running across specimens of red hair, human artefacts, and giant bones and skulls. In all, nearly 50 bodies were uncovered.[27] Though many of these have mysteriously vanished, the museum at Winnemucca, NV is still in possession of some of the skulls. The Paiutes claimed that some of these red headed people reached heights up to 12 feet tall. One of the skulls in the museum's possession fit a person over eight feet tall, while skeletons up to ten feet were found in the dried up bottom of the Humbolt Lake.[28]

Another interesting story is told by the legendary Buffalo Bill Cody in his autobiography,

> While we were in the sandhills, scouting the Niobrara country, the Pawnee Indians brought into camp some very large bones, one of which the surgeon of the expedition pronounced to be the thigh bone of a human being. The Indians said the bones were those of a race of people who long ago had lived in that country. They said these people were three times the size of a man of the present day, that they were so swift and strong that they could run by the side of a buffalo, and, taking the animal in one arm, could tear off a leg and eat it as they ran.
>
> These giants, said the Indians, denied the existence of a Great Spirit. When they heard the thunder or saw the lightning, they laughed and declared that they were greater than either. This so displeased the Great Spirit that he caused a deluge. The water rose higher and higher till it drove these proud giants from the low grounds to the hills and thence to the mountains. At last even the mountaintops were submerged and the mammoth men were drowned.
>
> After the flood subsided, the Great Spirit came to the conclusion that he had made men too large and powerful. He therefore corrected his mistake by creating a race of the size and strength of men of the present day. This is

the reason, the Indians told us, that the man of modern times is small and not like the giants of old. The story has been handed down among the Pawnees for generations, but what is its origin no man can say."[29]

Cody's story might be chalked up to a Wild West legend knowing how to *spin a yarn* ... though he did say he was in possession of some of these giant bones. Were they animal bones, dinosaur bones, or human bones? It is reported (I cannot verify it) that the bone(s) were given to a museum, many people saw them, but they have since vanished.

The size of the giant bears a striking resemblance to stories told by the Peruvian natives in the 1500s. Half Spanish, half Peruvian, Pedro de Cieza de Léon was a conquistador and historian of South America. He writes "concerning giants in Peru" who landed on the coast at the point of Santa Elena near the city of Puerto Viejo and were four or five times the height of the native peoples. The entire story is worth citing:

> The natives relate the following tradition, which had been received from their ancestors from very remote times. There arrived on the coast, in boats made of reeds, as big as large ships, a party of men of such size that, *from the knee downwards*, their height was as great as the entire height of an ordinary man, though he might be of good stature. Their limbs were all in proportion to the deformed size of their bodies, and it was a monstrous thing to see their heads, with hair reaching to the shoulders. Their eyes were as large as small plates. They had no beards, and were dressed in the skins of animals, others only in the dress which nature gave them, and they had no women with them.
>
> When they arrived at this point, they made a sort of village, and even now the sites of their houses are pointed out. But as they found no water, in order to remedy the want, they made some very deep wells, works which are truly worthy of remembrance; for such are the magnitude, that they certainly must have been executed by very strong men. They dug these wells in the living rock until they met with water, and then they lined them with mason-

ry from top to bottom in such sort that they will endure for many ages. The water in these wells is very good and wholesome, and always so cold that it is very pleasant to drink it.

Having built their village, and made their wells or cisterns where they could drink, these great men, or giants, consumed all the provisions they could lay their hands upon in the surrounding country; in so much that one of them ate more meat then fifty of the natives of the country could. As all the food they could find was not sufficient to sustain them, they killed many fish in the sea with nets and other gear. They were detested by the natives, because in using their women they killed them, and the men also in another way. But the Indians were not sufficiently numerous to destroy this new people who had come to occupy their lands. They made great leagues against them, but met with no success.

All the natives declare that God our Lord brought upon them a punishment in proportion to the enormity of their offence. While they were all together, engaged in their accursed . . . a fearful and terrible fire came down from heaven with a great noise, out of the midst of which there issued a shining angel with a glittering sword, with which, at one blow, they were all killed, and the fire consumed them. There only remained a few bones and skulls, which God allowed to remain without being consumed by the fire, as a memorial of this punishment. This is what they say concerning these giants, and we believe the account because in this neighbourhood they have found, and still find, enormous bones.

I have heard from Spaniards who have seen part of a double tooth, that they judged the whole tooth would have weighed more than half a butcher's pound. They also had seen another piece of a shin bone, and it was marvelous to relate how large it was. These men are witnesses to the story, and the site of the village may be seen, as well as the wells and cisterns made by the giants [emphasis and paragraph breaks mine].[30]

Curiously, he goes on to note that "at the point of Santa Elena ... there are certain wells, or mines, of such excellent tar, that as many ships as require caulking might be caulked with it." Giants, living near tar-pits, destroyed by fire from heaven, because of immoral behavior that some take as sexual in nature?[31] The whole incredible story sounds like Sodom and Gomorrah.[32] From at least the time of the English translation of de Leon, these stories have been relegated to cases of mistaken identity, confusing human bones with those of giant animals,[33] though they were accepted as true after excavations in 1543 were made of apparently quite ribs, teeth, and other bones.[34]

There are many very famous explorers who report actually seeing *living* giant peoples when Europeans first came to the Americas, though none are close to the height in the two previous stories. Included are Capt. John Smith, Hernando De Soto, Francisco Vázquez de Coronado, Hernando Cortéz, and Ferdinand Magellan.[35] These sightings were all shocking to them because other Indians were so short. In fact, the entire region of Patagonia was named by Magellan for the aborigines who lived there. Patagonia means "Big Feet." As recently as the early 20th century, an encounter in Greenland was related to the *New York Times* by Capt. Christian Jensen who had spent a year living with the Eskimos near Inigtut Bay. He reports how copper colored giants ("seven, eight, and even nine feet tall") who had never been seen by the natives, only rumored to exist, were encountered. Though they could not speak the Eskimo language, they made it clear they had been driven from their homes in the interior by storms and cold weather.[36]

There are also chronicles from around the world (see chart below). In fact, there are so many stories about giants—and I'm not talking about mythology—it staggers the imagination. The most recent story I've heard was told by an American Military Pilot flying a secret mission out of Afghanistan in 2005. He tells how on this mission he personally flew a dead 12 ft. cannibalistic giant out of the Middle East after it destroyed a Special Forces Op. that was hunting Taliban. This giant was white skinned, had 24 digits, red hair, and weighed perhaps as much as 1,500 lbs. You can listen to the testimony of the actual pilot online[37] or read about it for yourself.[38] Take it for whatever it is worth.

Then there is the Georgian (former Soviet Union) news report by Michael Robakidze for the Russian Channel One from August 6, 2008 (also reported by the Rustavi2 tv-channel, Trend N. Kirtskhalia, and other news outlets). They interview Abesalom Vekua (Ph.D.) of the Academy of Sciences of Georgia who, *while holding up the giant bones*, says that this ancient race (he does not refer to them as the kind of giants we are thinking about in this book), "could be from 2.5 to 3 meters tall."[39] Translated, that's 8.2 – 9.8 feet.

Fig. App 2. GIANT BONES FROM BORJOMI GORGE

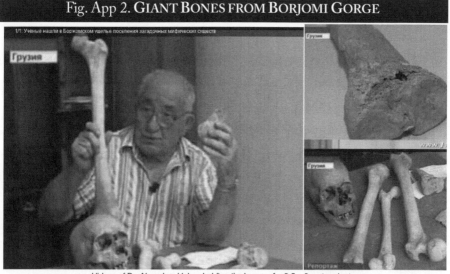

Vidcap of Dr. Abesalom Vekua holding the bones of a 2.5 – 3 meter giant
Lower Right: Normal size femur (middle) next to the giant femur
Borjomi Gorge, Georgia (Russia), courtesy Russian Channel One news

What are we to make of such reports? It is common in present day academia, especially in the west, to scoff. This is partly justifiable, because there is little hard evidence upon which to conduct empirical analysis. There were also known fakes.[40] We should always keep these things in mind, because they are important factors. On the other hand, many of the reports explain why the evidence is missing: The bones were put into private collections, taken to museums (or seized) and never seen again, they disintegrated upon contact with the air, they were reburied, etc.

To some, this only supports their own conspiracy theory ("of course there are not giants, that's impossible") that those who accept such claims are dishonestly engaging in, supporting, or buying the real conspiracy ("the giants are being suppressed"). Others see here non-falsifiable excuses conveniently offered up at a time when sensational journalism, tall-tales, a need to inspire a new wave of immigration, and a Barnum and Bailey circus like atmosphere dominated *all* western expansion. In other words, nothing that any of these people say about anything extraordinary could ever be taken seriously. The bones of seven, not to mention twelve foot giants should be treated to the same level of seriousness as Paul Bunyan and Babe, his giant blue ox. When "Caucasian" hair or skeletal features are included in all this, charges of racism and disdain for the American Indian (institutionalized in things like *Manifest Destiny*) are quickly leveled as certain proof that we *must not* believe all of these lies about giants.

Of course, there was certainly racism and ignorance and hucksters all present in those days, just as there are today. People like Joseph Smith took these and other stories and created entirely new religions out of them. But everyone? Everywhere? Talk about a conspiracy theory. Talk about paranoia. What about the reports by the Indians themselves? Certainly, they are not racist against *themselves*? What possible reason could Miss Winnemucca, the daughter of a prominent Indian Chief, have to lie or trick people about stories and personal belongings, especially seeing that her ancestor's memories were reported as fact after she died? And what about the story being seemingly verified decades after she died?

Also (Buffalo Bill excluded), in many cases we are not talking about an odd-ball bone fragment scattered here or there along the ground which can easily become a case of mistaken identity (something which has been all too prevalent in the history of this subject[41]), but of entire skeletons, intricately dressed and laid out in ceremonial fashion in burial mounds. It is irrational, not to mention prejudiced, to conclude that every person who saw them, including trained palaeontologists and biologists, couldn't tell the difference between a human skeleton and one of, say, a dog or a horse. In fact, as we have seen, in some of the sites dogs and horses were buried along side of the giant human skeletons, *and were reported as such.* Too often, our pioneer ancestors are treated like ignorant, uneducated, superstitious, backwoods hicks who couldn't tell their right hand from their left, or a human skull from that of a wild boar.

What about the missing bones? As I said earlier, this is and should be a factor in making our decision on such stories, but not the *only* factor.[42] Empirical analysis is not the only kind of evidence that is admissible in a court of law. Expert witnesses and eyewitness testimony are a different and significant kind of evidence that should be given its due weight. Often times, doctors were present in the reports. Only if we presuppose that all of these people were *de facto* sinister or out of their minds etc. would we deny their testimony a place as we formulate our own judgments.

In this regard, the similarity and sobriety of the accounts should also be considered. In the reports from North America, not one of them says that 40 foot giants were found, or even 15 foot giants (again Buffalo Bill excluded). None say they had blue hair or one eye socket or other things often associated with giants in mythology.[43] Rather, what we get are mostly the kind of thing we would expect from people digging things up and telling us what they found. It is ordinary, sober, detailed information about some very extraordinary discoveries.

Clearly, some people will take any and every story of a giant that they find and accept it as gospel truth without hesitation or research, even though some of the past discoveries have been discredited. Furthermore, some contemporary writers on this subject do in fact have hidden agendas (e.g. neo-Nazi, new age, or other). Some probably make up or stretch facts and perpetrate them on an unsuspecting public. With this topic, a sucker really may be born every minute (see n. 14). We should be leery of individuals who make incredible claims. Let a matter be heard only on the testimony of "two or three witnesses."

On the other hand, those who take the sceptical position are hardly immune to equally egregious bias such as political correctness, a pre-commitment to naturalism, fear of losing their credibility or even their job, or what have you. Also, it seems to me that the opposite mistake is also often practiced. If some are ultra-gullible, others take none of this seriously, often on the basis that we have no hard evidence. This is patently absurd, predisposed to its own set of biases, and perhaps subject to its own kind of conspiracy theories (i.e. "everyone is lying about this"). As Christians, it is also a double standard. If hard evidence were our only criterion, we could not accept the existence of Goliath, Og, or any giant in the Bible, not to mention *anyone else* in the Bible; for what bones of any of them do we have to do empirical testing (relics found in the crusades not included)?

My own feeling is that somewhere in the middle lies the truth. How close to the edges that truth is, I'm not sure. The majority of credible upper-limit reports seem to taper off at about 12 feet. In the chart below, I offer a sampling of some of these finds, of which as the heights go up, the historical veracity goes down. There are literally hundreds and hundreds of such reports out there on every populated continent and most of the major islands on the planet.

A SMALL SAMPLING OF PAST GIANTS *

GIANT(S)	DESCRIPTION	DATE	PLACE	HEIGHT
Christopher Munster	Tomb has a life size picture,	d. 1676	Yeoman of the guard, Hanover, England	8 ½ ft.**
Chief Thurourangi	Six ft. tall up to his armpits	1600s	Mokoia Island, New Zealand	9 ft.
John Middleton	Painting preserved in the Library of Brasenose College, Oxford.	b. 1578	Manchester, England	9'3"
Secondilla & Pusio			Keepers of the gardens of Sallust	9 ½ ft.
Calbara		Reign of Claudius Caesar	From Arabia to Rome	10 ft.
Mass grave.		Dec. 17, 1615 (as reported by Jacob le Maire)	Port Desire (near the Straits of Magellan)	10-11 ft.
Aymon		Late 1500s	Germany	11 ft.
Funnam		Reign of Eugene II	Scotland	11 ½ ft.
Hans Braw	The 8 ft. plus Baron Bentenrieder came up to his armpits.	1550s	Austria	12'8"
Guanche Giant	80 teeth		Peak of Teneriffe, Canary Islands (Spain)	15ft.
Ricon de Vallemont	Skull held a bushel of corn, shin bone was 4 ft.	Dug up in 1509	Rouen (France)	17-18 ft.
Ferragus		Slain by Orlande, nephew of Charle-magne		18 ft.
Unnamed	Platerus, a famous physi-cian saw these bones.			19 ft.
Isoret	Rioland, a celebrated anatomist saw the bones.	Reported in 1614	St. Germain (France)	20 ft.
Bucart, tyrant of the Vivarais		Found in 1705	Banks of the Morderi, near Mt. Crussol (France)	22 ½ ft.
Theutobochus Rex	Teeth the size of an ox's foot. Shin bone 4 ft. Tomb was 30 ft. long, 12 ft. wide, 8 ft. high. Entire skeleton found in a grave marking the name.	Jan 11, 1613	Discovered in "The giants field" near a castle in Dauphine (France) at a depth of 18 ft.	25 ½ ft.
Unnamed	Two men together could barely put four arms around its head. Legs still (as of the 1800s) kept in the castle of the city.	758	Totu, Bohemia	26 ft.
Unnamed	Head the size of a hogs-head. Teeth: 5 oz.	1516	Mazario, Sicily	30 ft.
Two unnamed skeletons		1548, 1559	Palormo, Sicily in the valley of Mazara	30, 33 ft.
Two unnamed skeletons		Unknown	Athens, Greece	34, 36 ft.

* References are found in Edmund Burke, *The Annual Register: A View of the History, Politicks, and Litera-ture for the Year 1764* (London: J. Dodsley, 1765), 106-07; *Encyclopedia Britannica*, Vol. 9 (Edinburgh: Archibald Constable and Company, 1823), 700; Johann Georg Keyssler, *Travels through Germany, Bohe-mia, Hungary, Switzerland, Italy, and Lorrain* Vol. 1 (London, G. Keith, 1760), 31, 41-42; Georgè Milbry Gould and Walter Lytle Pyle, *Anomalies and Curiosities of Medicine* (Philadelphia: W.B. Saunders, 1901), 325-26; Edward J. Wood, *Giants and Dwarfs* (London: Bentley, 1868). ** Munster's height is put as "4 Flemish ells (27 inches) 6 inches." That would make him 114+ inches or 9 ½ ft., though *Guinness* puts it at 8 ½ feet.

NEWSPAPER CLIPPINGS OF GIANTS

WISCONSIN MOUND OPENED.

Skeleton Found of a Man Over Nine Feet High with an Enormous Skull.

MAPLE CREEK, Wis., Dec. 19,—One of the three recently discovered mounds in this town has been opened. In it was found the skeleton of a man of gigantic size. The bones measured from head to foot over nine feet and were in a fair state of preservation. The skull was as large as a half bushel measure. Some finely tempered rods of copper and other relics were lying near the bones.

The mound from which these relics were taken is ten feet high and thirty feet long, and varies from six to eight feet in width.

The two mounds of lesser size will be excavated soon.

The New York Times
Published: December 20, 1897
Copyright © The New York Times

SKELETON OF A GIANT FOUND.—A day or two since, some workmen engaged in subsoiling the grounds of Sheriff WICKHAM, at his vineyard in East Wheeling, came across a human skeleton. Although much decayed, there was little difficulty in identifying it, by placing the bones, which could not have belonged to others than a human body, in their original position. The impression made by the skeleton in the earth, and the skeleton itself, were measured by the Sheriff and a brother in the craft locale, both of whom were prepared to swear that it was ten feet nine inches in length. Its jaws and teeth were almost as large as those of a horse. The bones are to be seen at the Sheriff's office.—Wheeling Times.

The New York Times
Published: November 21, 1856
Copyright © The New York Times

(above) SKELETON OF GIANT FOUND.--A day or two since, some workmen engaged in subsoiling the grounds of Sheriff WICKHAN, at his vineyard in East Wheeling, came across a human skeleton. Although much decayed, there was little difficulty in identifying it, by placing the bones, which could not have belonged to others than a human body, in their original position. The impression made by the skeleton in the earth and the skeleton itself were measured by the sheriff and a brother of the craft locale, both of whom were ready to swear that it was 10 feet nine inches in length. It's jaws and teeth were almost as large as those of a horse. The bones are to be seen at the Sheriff's office. -- Wheeling Times.

GIANTS' BONES IN MOUND.

Scientists Unearth Relics of Indians Who Lived 700 Years Ago.

Special to The New York Times.

BINGHAMTON, July 13.—Professor A. B. Skinner of the American Indian Museum, Professor W. K. Morehead of Phillips Andover Academy, and Dr. George Donohue, Pennsylvania State Historian, who have been conducting researches along the valley of the Susquehanna, have uncovered an Indian mound at Tioga Point, on the upper portion of Queen Esther's Flats, on what is known as the Murray farm, a short distance from Sayre, Penn., which promises rich additions to Indian lore.

In the mound uncovered were found the bones of sixty-eight men which are believed to have been buried 700 years ago. The average height of these men was seven feet, while many were much taller. Further evidence of their gigantic size was found in large celts or axes hewed from stone and buried in the grave. On some of the skulls, two inches above the perfectly formed forehead, were protuberances of bone. Members of the expedition say that it is the first discovery of its kind on record and a valuable contribution to the history of the early races.

The skull and a few bones found in one grave were sent to the American Indian Museum.

The New York Times
Published: July 14, 1916
Copyright © The New York Times

ST. PAUL, 24.—A skull of heroic size and singular formation has just been discovered among the relics of the mound builders in the Red River Valley. The mound was 60 feet in diameter, and 12 feet high. Near the centre were found the bones of about a dozen males and females, mixed with bones of various animals. The skull in question was the only perfect one, and near it were found some abnormally large body bones. The man who bore it was evidently a giant. A thorough investigation of the mound and contents will be made by the historical society.

These clippings and many more have been posted at one very helpful website:
http://www.sydhav.no/giants/newspapers.htm

Appendix: Giants of Monument & Myth

Monument: Giant Intaglios, Effigies and Statues

Before examining oral traditions, I thought a brief display of some of the enormous human intaglios (incised carvings of figures sunk below the surface) from around the world might be fun. These strange figures were hewn, not only with hands and tools, but with oral traditions of giants.

Southwestern United States

Near Yuma, AZ there is a gigantic glyph depicting Kumastamo, the god who created the Colorado River with his magic rod. This deity then plotted the death of Sky-Rattlesnake, an evil spirit and source of dark powers, by cutting off his head. He then turned himself into a fish-eagle and few off into oblivion.[1] If one is open minded to the possibility, it is not difficult to see echoes of the story of Eden (Genesis 3:15) and Noah's flood with its water and birds. It is curious that all around the desert southwest there are gigantic intaglios of giant people and animals, and no one knows their source.[2]

According to the Hopi Indians, Masau'u (another name for Kumastamo) it to be identified with the constellation Orion, which remarkably, be it in the new world or the old, is often drawn as a giant waving a spear or a club.

FIG. APP 3. INTAGLIOS OF THE AMERICAN SOUTHWEST

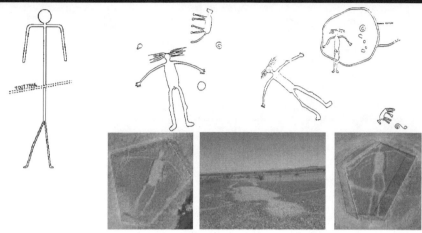

Kumastamo (25 m high and 6 m wide). Near "Solomon's Cross," Yuma, AZ

Above: Part of the Blythe complex. **Below**: "Three Giants" of Blythe, AZ

Britain

Around the world in Britain, located near Dorset, England, there stands the 180 ft. high by 167 ft. wide Cerne-Abbas Giant. Visible in Google Earth, this giant is virtually identical to the depictions of Orion, except that in his left hand there was very probably a decapitated head (it has since been destroyed).[3] Some say the Cerne-Abbas Giant is a representation of the demi-god Hercules. But local folklore says that this was a local giant who terrorized the area of Cerne Abbas. On one occasion he got so greedy that he ate a whole flock of sheep, whereupon he fell asleep on the hillside and was killed by the townspeople. One John Gibbons (1670) wrote that this giant took part in a battle on the famed Salisbury plain between King Divitiacus and the Cerngik Giants. Though it may be as recent as the 17th century, this legend puts the origins of the giant back in the 2nd century.[4]

FIG. APP 4. CERNE ABBAS GIANT AND HERCULES/ORION

Cerne Abbas Giant, Dorset, UK. Greco-Roman Orion/Hercules Osiris (Egyptian "Orion")

Another giant depiction may be found along the southwest coast of England near Wilmington. Also visible from Google Earth, the so-named "Long Man" giant is 227 ft. and appears to be holding two spears in his hands. Originally, he was portrayed wearing a horned helmet which was destroyed in the 19th century. There is no consistent folklore pertaining to this giant, though it has been said that he was killed by the Firle Beacon giant, and that the effigy was made before the flood.[5]

FIG. APP 5. LONG MAN OF WILMINGTON (ENGLAND)

Horned Men

There is some reason to see this figure associated with Celtic and Nordic paganism. Throughout Scandinavia, especially in the 6th and 7th centuries, figures like the Long Man have been preserved in tombs and rock carvings.[6] These horned men straddle two continents.

FIG. APP 6. "HORNED MEN" OF NORTHERN EUROPE

| Sutton Hoo Helmet Figures | 7th Cent. Buckle, Finglesham, Kent (UK) | 7th Cent. Grave Valsgarde, Sweden | 6th Cent. "Dancing Boy" Torslunda, Sweden |

Back in the United States, we travel up to Wisconsin for a most peculiar effigy. It is a 214 ft. long, 48 ft. wide, 3 ft. tall mound called the Man Mound of Baraboo. Actually, there were several "Man Mounds," most of which were destroyed by the early settlers of the area. Some people speculate that these represent the Thunderbird, Waterspirit, or other such creatures.

Frank Joseph suggests that he is Wakt'cexi, the deluge-hero of the Winnebago Indians. In their *Worak* (tribal histories), they speak of the Wolf Clan who came to Turtle Island (North America) after a huge flood destroyed their homeland wearing a horned helmet.[7] A Neolithic rock figure from Rodoy, Norway may depict this same voyage (though my daughter thinks it is a bunny rabbit on skis).

FIG. APP 7. MAN MOUND AND OTHER RELATED EFFIGIES

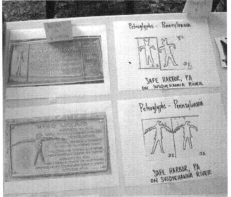

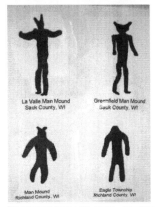

Above: "Man Mound" outlined in chalk. **Below**: Horned & Winged Petroglyphs of the Susquehanna River, PA compared to similar mounds in Wisconsin. Image by Donald Cadzo, Pennsylvania Historical Commission

Above: "Man Mound," Baraboo, WI. **Below**: "Man Mounds" of Wisconsin. Image provided by the Sauk County Historical Society.

Horned Boat-Man. Rodoy, Norway.

This horned man was known across North America. For instance, a Navaho initiation ceremony for children involved a masked man wearing a red wig (i.e. red hair) and horned helmet. His wife's face was painted white (i.e. a white person). This couple represented the family that survived the Great Flood as a reminder of the ancient origins of the people.[8]   A similar ceremony was performed in the Apache Crown Dance.[9]

In the fall of 2009, I had the opportunity to visit some rock carvings in north-western Colorado. These also depict a horned man, sometimes carrying a rod. These were carved by the Fremont Indians who lived in the area from 400-1250 AD. As I began searching out other Fremont rock-art on the internet, it became immediately clear that the figure is almost always depicted with horns, often with a family—which usually has many different animals nearby. Some of these figures are clearly depicted as giants. Among the more interesting of this collection are the serpent hovering over the "Owl Man" and the one I dub "Bigfoot" (see if you can spot him).

FIG. APP 8. FREMONT INDIAN HORNED MEN, COLORADO PLATEAU

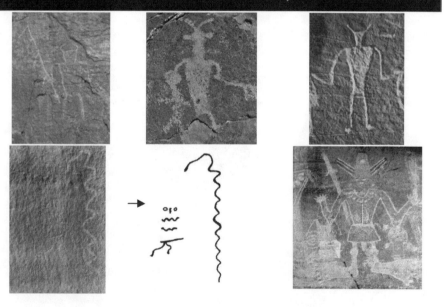

Much earlier glyphs (called "Barrier Canyon" glyphs), made by an unknown race who lived here between 6,000 B.C.(?) and the turn of the turn of the common era are truly bizarre. They are nothing like the art depicted above. They show giant horned men with elongated proportions. At least one of them even seems to have a beard, which Native Americans can't grow. No one knows what they represent.

FIG. APP 9. BARRIER CANYON HORNED MEN, COLORADO PLATEAU

Meanwhile, sites out east near other horned-men glyphs have yielded bones of giants. A grave containing the supposed remains of Susqehannock Indians (whom Capt. John Smith encountered) were found near Spanish Hill, in Athens, PA. These skeletons ranged between 6 to 8 feet in length, shoulders above other Indians and the Europeans of the time.[10] It was actually reported on Wednesday, July 12, 1916 in a local newspaper that sixty-eight skeletons of men living 700 years ago were unearthed. Among the remains was a seven foot skeleton of a man with horns protruding from his skull, which was witnessed by several reputable antiquarians.[11] The story seemed to gain a life of its own. In 1983, the *Reader's Digest* did a story on the find.[12]

Japan

If we travel around the world to Japan, we come across more horned giants called the Oni. Like other horned-giants, he also is depicted as carrying a large club. The term Oni can mean "Ghost" or "invisible spirit," terminology reminiscent of the Rephaim and other giants of the Bible.

Fig. App 10. Japanese Oni-Horned Giants (w/ Horned Samurai)

| Red Oni with his kanabō | Oni Drawing | Oni. Netsuke Carving, 19th Century | Samurai on Horseback, 1878 |

This is all strange, but in accordance with many worldwide stories of giants with horns who terrorized the local inhabitants, such as an African tale of a white horned 24 ft. giant with six fingers and toes (cf. 2 Sam 21:20; 1 Chron 20:6 for giants with six digits) who cannibalized the local people and was carved into a piece of ivory thousands of years ago,[13] or the Celtic horned giant Cernunnos who is often depicted with serpents.

I am not trying to induce belief in such things by mentioning them here. Rather, I am demonstrating that there are common inscriptions, drawings, sightings, and stories around the world that seem to depict a remembrance of the same thing, however distorted it may have become or accurate it may have remained over time.

FIG. APP 11. SIX FINGERS

Six fingered giant African, Ivory Image provided by Klaus Dona to Steve Quayle

Six fingered figurine, Scythian tomb, Altai Mountains, Rusia. Hermitage Museum, St. Petersburg

Six Fingered Hands, Three Rivers, NM

http://fdocc.blogspot.com/2006/01/three-rivers-and-six-fingers-thrice.html

Giants of Mythology

Rome: Titans

While I have an appendix dealing with understanding myth in light of Scripture, this section will go into more detail about particular giant myths (I'll try to keep duplication to a minimum, but it is always nice to have things compiled together). Who were the giants according to the myths? There is no better place to start than with the Greeks. It was the poet Hesiod (ca. 8th cent. B.C.) who gave us the following explanation. This is what he writes,

> And great Sky came, bringing night with him; and spreading himself out around Earth in his desire for love he lay outstretched in all directions. Then his son reached out from his ambush with his left hand, and with his right hand he grasped the monstrous sickle, long and jagged-toothed, and eagerly he reaped the genitals from his dear father and threw them behind him to be borne away. But not in vain did they fall from his hand: for Earth received all the bloody drops that short forth, and when the years had re-

volved she bore the mighty Erinyes and the great Giants, shining in their
armor, holding long spears in their hands, and the Nymphs whom they call
the Melian ones on the boundless earth.

(Hesiod, *Theogony* 176-186)

The Sky spreading himself around Earth is a sexual euphemism,
easily seen in the personification of it in the god Uranus (the sky god),
father of the Titan Kronus (Roman: Saturn, who mutilated him) and
the goddess Gaia (the earth goddess). These giants possessed a peculiar feature that is related to this union between Heaven and Earth.
This feature is the serpentine legs and feet that the giants were often
said to possess.

FIG. APP 12. SERPENTINE GIANTS OF GREEK MYTHOLOGY

Roman Mosaic, 3rd C. A.D. Villa Romana del Casale

Above: Gigantes and Athena, Istanbul Archaeo-
logical Museum, Turkey. **Below**: Wounded
Giants, Villa Romanadel Casale, Piazza Armerina,
Sicily

After the Titans lost their epic battle with the gods of Mt.
Olympus, Gaia roused her other sons, the Giants, against Zeus.
Homer tells us that they tried to storm heaven by building, in effect, a

tower. "They threatened to make war with the gods in Olympus, and tried to set Mount Ossa on the top of Mount Olympus, and Mount Pelion on the top of Ossa, that they might scale heaven itself."[14] Some have suggested that this myth belongs to the Tiamat and Rahab cycles of Babylonian origin, which brings the serpents into sharper focus.[15]

Another generation of giants grew up after the first were destroyed by Heracles (Hercules). According to the Roman poet Ovid (43 BC – 18 AD), these giants were "savage, violent, and eager for slaughter, so that you might know they were born from blood." Then, "When Saturn's son, the father of the gods, saw this from his highest citadel, he groaned, and he called the gods to council." "When the gods had taken their seats in the marble council chamber, their king, sitting high above them, leaning on his ivory sceptre spoke saying, 'I was not more troubled than I am now concerning the world's sovereignty than when each of the snake-footed giants prepared to throw his hundred arms around the imprisoned sky. . . Now I must destroy the human race. I swear it by the infernal streams, that glide below the earth."[16] When he had spoken, some gods encouraged him, others sat silently, but all were saddened at this destruction of the human species. Then, after considering destruction with fire, he rethought and finally "sent down rain from the whole sky and drown humanity beneath the waves."[17]

Scandinavia: Frost Giants, Fire Giants, and Mountain Giants

The Nordic Sagas contain a veritable smörgåsbord of giants. They come in three classes: Frost giants (*hrímþursar*), fire giants (*eldjötnar*), and mountain giants (*bergrisar*); while ogres and trolls (so popular as figurines) make up yet another class. Some giants of interest include Ymir (Brimir?) who had a beer-hall in the land of dwarves (men?), a race which was brought forth from his own flesh and blood.[18] There is a curious feature on this hall, "A hall I saw, | far from the sun, On Nastrond it stands, | and the doors face north, Venom drops | through the smoke-vent down, For around the walls | do serpents wind."[19] Völva, the lady of wisdom who sings the *Völuspá* is herself related to the giants,[20] and furthermore, the giants were related to the gods by marriages. Such giants include *Ægir, Loki, Mimir,* and *Skaði.* At the final battle (*Ragnarök*), the giants will storm Asgard and defeat the gods. Finally, Valhalla (in Asgard) is the place where the spirits of the ancient dead warriors (god-giants) now reside.

North America: Mound Builders

If we recall the Mound Builders in Ohio, we find scholars debating when they were built. There is a peculiar mound near Cincinnati called the Serpent Mound (see below). Some say the Indians built it. However, the Mandan Indians were not in agreement with the professionals of today. For, it was said *by them* to have been built by "powerful, fearsome" beings descended from the "tidal flood."[21] There is evidence that this race may have been quite large.

Many of the mounds built by the Mound Builders were burial mounds. They were excavated in the 19th century, and as we have seen, a good number of them yielded bones of gigantic proportions from 7 ft. – 12ft. in length. A people that archaeologists have dubbed the Adena flourished in this region between 1000 BC – 700 AD. They may or may not have been the builders of the Serpent Mound. But in mounds that they did build, skeletons over 7 ft. were discovered in the 1800s.[22] The legends of the Serpent Mound builders is supported farther south and west in Illinois by the Shawnee Deluge Myth which remember the makers of a now broken 200 mile long stone wall, which they say was built by immigrating giants who survived the Great Flood.[23]

Farther south, along the Mississippi, the Choctaw Indians told of the Nahullo, an ancient race of red and yellow haired, white-skinned giants with tall horns. The folk traditions of the northern Ottawa tell of an alliance with the Ojibwa and Pottawattamic in ancient times to kill "the white giants" called *Yam-Ko-Desh*, and were able to survive *Ron-nong-weto-wanca*, or "Fair-skinned Giant Sorcerers." The Winnebago of Wisconsin have an oral history of their twin heroes, the brothers Red Hair and Yellow Hair, and their crusades with an ancient race of giants.[24] In other words, the stories of the Indians line up with the reports of giant bones dug up during the last three centuries of American expansion to the west.

FIG. APP 13. SERPENT MOUND, OHIO

South America: Bochica

In the farthest southern reaches of South America, in the region of Patagonia, Magellan and his men ran into so many giants that the stories have become legendary, as even the name Patagonia means "big feet." Quetzalcoatl and Viracocha, the bringers of civilization to the Mayan and Aztec peoples, are intimately related to serpent mythology *and giants*. Viracocha was said to be the creator of the giants, but he became furious with them and turned them into stone. It is said that the amazing and impossible megalithic city called Tiahuanaco, which some say is the oldest city on earth, now in a barren wasteland above 13,000 ft, was built by giants called the Huaris. Eventually, Viracocha grew angry with the giants and flooded the earth till all was under water. They say that it rained 60 days and nights, and drown every living thing.[25]

Central America is famous for its fabulous pyramids. Thousands of them dot the jungles. The Cholulu Pyramid is one of the largest structures in the world. Two hundred and ten feet height, it covers forty-five acres. The pre-Conquest Mexican legend about Cholula is very similar to the Biblical account of the Tower of Babel. According to the legend, after the deluge which destroyed the primeval world, seven giants survived, one of whom built the great pyramid of Cholula in order to reach heaven, but the Gods destroyed the pyramid with fire and confounded the language of the builders.[26] "A Flood tradition of the Toltecs mentioned by Ixtlihochitl states that after the Deluge [giants] built a *zacuali* of great height to preserve them in the event of future deluges. After this their tongue became confused, and not understanding each other, they went to different parts of the world."[27]

In South America, throughout coastal Colombia, Venezuela, and Brazil, a white-skinned, long bearded giant named Bochica a once supported the sky on his shoulders, until he dropped it, causing the Great Flood. He later condemns a demon named Chibchacum to hold up the sky after the floods recede, while he takes up residence on the first rainbow. Thus, in *South America*, rainbows are venerated with their association to the Flood.[28]

Middle East: Nimrod

We've discussed Nimrod in detail, but it bears repeating in this Appendix. In legends, giants are said to be the builders of all sorts of cyclopean enigmas throughout the world, from the pyramids in the Americas to Easter Island to Stonehenge to Baalbek in Lebanon. Baalbek has the largest cut stone on earth, weighing in at an unbelievable 1,200 tons (that's 2.4 million pounds, see Figure 16). Michael Alouf writes,

> The Arabs, also, believe that Baalbek is the place where Nimrod built his famous tower... One reads in the Arabic manuscript found at Baalbek that "after the flood, when Nimrod reigned over Lebanon, he sent giants to rebuild the fortress of Baalbek, which was so named in honour of Baal, the god of the Moabites and worshipers of the sun."[29]

Nimrod, according to many legends, was said to be a giant and he used giants to cut the stones and build the temple.[30] While unlikely, as mentioned in an earlier chapter, he was also thought by many to be the builder of the Tower of Babel.

India: Asuras

As for the giants and a tower, variations of the story are recalled throughout the world as well. The Hindus remember the Bakasura, (from *asuras*, meaning "evil" in Sanskrit), red haired, evil beings variously translated as demons or giants,[31] who seek to imitate the great fire altar of heaven and "ascend to the sky." This altar is said to rise from the earth to Heaven. These enemies of the heavenly gods, tried to imitate it, but their undertaking came to nothing, as the gods overthrew it by taking away the foundation of bricks.[32]

New Zealand: Chief Tahourangi

Across the world in New Zealand, many giants appear in Maori legends. One giant is named Ka-whara and was twenty four feet tall. Another, Rau-kawa was over thirty.[33] More plausible (since the Maori also have giants hundreds and thousands of feet tall) are the supposed bones of chief Tahourangi. One person tells his story this way,

> In the Rotorua country, too, there are stories, no doubt based on fact, of huge warriors of the past. There was the chief Tuhourangi, for one; he lived three centuries ago. He was nine feet high, according to tradition, and was about six feet up to his armpits. His bones were buried on the east side of Pukurahi Pa, on Mokoia Island, above the present little settlement on the flat. The old man Tamati Hapimana told me, at Mokoia in 1896, that Tuhourangi's bones were still there, deep in the ground, enclosed in stone slabs. His story was that Sir George Grey, during his first Governorship of New Zealand, visited Mokoia and, hearing about the bones of a man of enormous size, obtained the consent of the chiefs to dig for the skeleton. The men whom he employed purposely dug in the wrong place and so the relics were never brought to light. This long-gone warrior's bones, in olden times, were disinterred at *kumara* planting time and were set up on the edge of the cultivations on Mokoia, while the priest recited the prayers for a

bountiful harvest. The presence of the sacred bones was supposed to promote the fertility of the crop.[34]

Ireland: Fomorians and Grendal

The first inhabitants of Ireland were said to be the demonic Fomorians, said to be giant sea-people.[35] Their first leader, a giant named Cichol Gricenchos was said to have brought them to the Emerald Isle after the deluge, where they became its first inhabitants.[36] One of their later leaders was said to be a giant Cyclops named Balor, whose evil eye would kill anyone (sometimes turning them into stone like the Medusa) in its line of sight, and in the confusion of the mythology, his eye is even said to have caused the flood that brought them to the Island.[37] Since it is so near, I should probably bring up the great Anglo-Saxon giant named Grendal, a cannibalistic monster who lived in a cave, but finally defeated by the hero Beowulf.

Africa: Balor

On the Gold Coast of West Africa, several deluge myths exist among the Yoruba people. They explain how Olokun, the sea god, became angry with sinful human beings and sought to cause their extinction by brining upon them a flood that would drown the whole world. Many nations perished, until a giant hero named Obatala stood in the middle of the waters and through his juju (magical powers) bound Olokun in seven chains.[38] David Livingstone, the famous Scottish missionary, found similar myths in Africa.[39]

So what are we to make of all these stories and sightings and bones and things? My purpose has not been to convince you that any of them are true. Really, I don't care if you believe them or not. As far as giants in particular are concerned, I have no way of knowing if any individual, nor his reported height, is true. The fact is, scant archaeological evidence is available for scientific scrutiny, many of the findings that were present at one time have mysteriously vanished, and so speculation and conspiracy theories abound. This is not *entirely* unjustifiable, since scientific proof of giants would throw the precious sacred theory of evolution into a tailspin. They would also do great damage to the myth that the native Indians were the first peoples to settle these lands. There is a great deal of money, power, and politics at stake here; make no mistake about it. There is no doubt that for some people and some theories, the past is very much better left hidden and buried. But this still does not *prove* anything, so we must remain leery.

My point has been to demonstrate that our ancestors from around the world have, in their most ancient memories (and sometimes not so ancient), stories that ring similar to biblical epics like the Flood, the fall of the sons of God, the Tower of Babel, and that the heroes and villains associated with these stories are regularly identified as gigantic. They lived in caves, made horrible sounds, had too many fingers and toes, had strength of a different order of magnitude, were associated with sorcery and witchcraft, were are extremely violent, and ate the dead. That's the data. What will you make of it?

As a kind of postscript to these last two appendices, I want to bring to bring a word of caution that I hope would be self-evident. On one hand, Israel and the surrounding nations (like Moab, Ammon, and Edom) all fought the Rephaim and won great victories. Many accounts say that the surviving remnant of giants fled, settled, and were dispersed again by newer invaders. There is nothing inherently contradictory to the Bible about saying that these giants spread throughout the world and were destroyed by these other cultures.

On the other hand, just because someone is tall, it does not mean they are necessarily descended from Rapha or a Rephaim. This is a patently absurd and dangerous conclusion. Within a fairly broad range, populations can rise taller or fall shorter from quite ordinary causes such as war, diet, or marriage. As an example, the average height of Americans 100 years ago was significantly shorter than today. The height of the French after the Napoleonic wars went down drastically, as all the big tall men were killed off in the front lines of battle.

FIG. APP 14. ROBERT PERSHING WADLOW (1918-1940).

The tallest man of the 20th century standing next to his father.

Other kinds of gigantism are well documented, such as the pitui-
tary gland gone wild. The most famous giant of this kind was Robert
Wadlow. Wadlow's growth chart is almost incomprehensible. At age 8
he was over six feet tall. He was 7'4" by 13, 8" by 17, and reached the
incredible height of 8'11" at age 22, when he died from complications
of his disease.

Tall populations or improperly functioning organs are *not* what
we are talking about in this book, and perhaps some of the giants in
the appendices fit into those categories. But some people can pervert
just about anything. Hence, the caution. Even if we found incontrovertible proof of living Rephaim today, what should we do about it?
The commands of God towards Israel regarding the slaughter of these
creatures are not commands given to us today. Israel was a temporary
kingdom and her laws in this specific situation no longer obtain. We
have not been given the Promised Land. Furthermore, the whole
point of the book has been to demonstrate that Christ has defeated
these creatures, and it was always and finally his battle to win. Nothing in Scripture gives us reason to commit genocide upon tall people or
even Rephaim (assuming we could even figure out the difference).

However, the more general idea of wicked people overrunning a
peaceful land to institute unthinkable monstrosities such as human
sacrifice, cannibalism, bestiality, and genocide of the native population
(as, for instance, the Indians sometimes speak of the giants in North
America) is a different story. But of course, this kind of activity is not
the sole domain of giants, as all kinds of perfectly human people have
engaged in all of them. It seems to me that a civilization has a right to
protect itself from such things, and, as we saw in the instance of Allied
intervention in the Nazi program, even the obligation to stop its

spread. Until such a time as a mass group of cannibalistic head hunting giants raise their head in the world again, we have no right to or reason to wage war on giants that live among us. Instead, we can go to their basketball games, enjoy the entertainment, collect autographs, and gawk at the amazing physical *human* specimens that stand before our eyes.

Glossary

Akkadian – An extinct Semitic language that was spoken in ancient Mesopotamia.

Anunnaki – Meaning "royal blood" or "princely offspring" (i.e. "sons of God"), in the *Atra-Hasis* flood myth they burden the Igigi (a group sometimes synonymous with the Anunnaki) who rebel after 40 days and there follows the creation of mankind.

Anachronism – A logical fallacy. Inconsistency in a chronological arrangement.

Cerynean Hind – An enormous golden antlered, bronze hoofed deer (hind) that was so fast it could outrun an arrow.

Chimera – A beast possessing the attributes of more than one creature.

Cretan Bull – Zeus in the form of the bull that carried away the goddess Europa (after which Europe gets its name), or the bull Pasiphaë (goddess daughter of Helios, the Sun) fell in love with, giving birth to the *Minotaur*.

Demigod – A half heavenly, half earthly creature.

Demythologization – Ridding the Bible of "mythological" or supernatural events in order to get at the "real" meaning of a text.

Divine Council – "The heavenly host, the pantheon of divine beings who administer the affairs of the cosmos. All ancient Mediterranean cultures had some conception of a divine council. The divine council of Israelite religion, known primarily through the psalms, was distinct in important ways." (From Michael S. Heiser, "The Divine Council," in *Dictionary of the Old Testament: Wisdom, Poetry, & Writings*, ed. Tremper Longman and Peter Enns, InterVarsity Press, 2008).

Eisogesis – Reading "into" (Gk: *eis* = "in") a text whatever you want it to say with little regard as to authorial intent. It is the opposite of *exegesis*.

Equivocation – A logical fallacy. The misleading use of a term with more than one meaning or sense.

Exegesis – Explaining and interpreting "out of" (Gk: *ex* = "out") a text the meaning of the original author. It is the opposite of *eisogesis*, which only wants to explain what a passage means "to me."

Gyes - Giants of incredible strength and ferocity, even superior to that of the Titans. **Hydra** – A guardian of the Underworld, it was a multi-headed sea-serpent so invincible that if one head was cut off, two more would grow in its place.

Manifest Destiny – The 19th century belief that the United States was destined to expand across the continent. It was used to justify the Mexican-American war and, according to the more left-leaning political crowd today, to perpetuate the belief and treatment of native Indians as savages, and that the white man was superior.

Marduk – The patron deity of Babylon; around the time of Hammurabi and Abraham he began to rise to the head position of the Babylonian pantheon. In the Babylonian equivalent of the sons of God, the *Anunnaki* seek a god who can defeat the gods rising against them. Marduk ends up killing Tiamat, the sea dragon, in the Babylonian creation epic: *Enuma Elish.*

Midrash – A form of Jewish interpretation resembling a modern paraphrase translation of the Bible, although midrash also feels free to add ideas not even found in the text, if it is based upon something substantial the Jews felt they could derive from it (such as oral traditions).

Minish – To make or become less; to diminish.

Minotaur – A creature with the head of a bull and the body of a man, he dwelt at the center of the Cretan Labyrinth, built for King Minos on the island of Crete.

Mishnah – The first major written composition of Jewish oral traditions called the "Oral Torah."

Nemean Lion – A vicious golden furred monster at Nemea, impervious to mortal weapons, with claws sharper than mortal swords.

Protoevangelium – Literally "the first gospel." It is a word used to describe Genesis 3:15.

Reëm – Found in Num 23:22; 24:8; Deut 33:17; Job 39:9-10, Ps 22:22; 29:6; 92:11; Isa 34:7; Zech 14:10, it is translated as "unicorn" by the KJV. It is appears to be a mythological creature, but its exact identity is a guess.

Septuagint – (abbreviated: LXX, the Roman numeral "70", for the seventy Jewish scribes who worked on it). The Greek translation of the Hebrew Bible (the

Christian Old Testament) undertaken between the 3rd and 2nd centuries B.C. The LXX is invaluable because 1. It is the Scripture most often quoted by the NT and 2. We have copies of it that date to nearly 1,000 years before our oldest Hebrew manuscripts.

Stymphalian Bird – Man eating, bronze beaked, metallic feathered birds that fled from a pack of wolves loosed by Arabs; they migrated to Lake Stymphalia in Arcadia and quickly overtook the countryside and townspeople.

Sybil – From the Latin *sibylla*, meaning "prophetess;" the sibyls were said to have prophesied at certain holy sites throughout the ancient world.

Targum – An Aramaic paraphrase of the Hebrew Old Testament. Aramaic is a cousin language of Hebrew.

Torah – Hebrew for "Instruction," it is the name given by Jews to the first five books of the Old Testament known as the Books of Moses.

Two Kingdoms – The idea that God has made all things, all things are corrupted by sin, Christians should be active in human culture (Augustine's "city of man") because sin is not only "out there" but also "inside" me (i.e. I can't get away from it), all lawful vocations are honorable, Christians should live out their faith in their daily vocation, *but* human culture is distinct from the culture of heaven (Augustine's "city of God") so that we should view the Christian life in this world as a pilgrim's life, where we are simultaneously citizens of two kingdoms, one temporary and passing away, the other permanent and lasting forever.

Ugarit – An ancient Canaanite city-state in modern Syria along the coast of the Mediterranean Sea. It famously gave up a host of important religious documents used in comparative religion by Hebrew scholars.

Uniformitarianism – A scientific theory that the earth is billions of years old and only sees tiny changes upon its surface through natural processes like erosion.

Ziggurat – Ancient temples made to look like mountains. They were thought to be "stairways to heaven" and replicas of the cosmic mountain—the place where the gods met for deliberation over the affairs of earth.

Zoroaster – From unknown antiquity, the Persian prophet and founder of Zoroastrianism.

Bibliography

Adam, Jean-Pierre. "A propos du trilithon de Baalbek. Le transport et la mise en oeuvre des megaliths." *Syria* 54:1-2 (1977): 31-63.

al-Maqrīzī, Ahmad Ibn 'Ali. *Description Topographique et Historique de l'Egypte* (vol. 1), trans. From the Arabic into French by M. U. Bouriant, ed. Ernest Lerous (Paris: Rue Bonaparte, 1895.

al-Tabarī. *Prophets and Patriarchs: The History of al-Tabarī* (vol. 2). Trans. William M. Brinner. Albany, NY: State University of New York Press, 1987.

Alouf, Michael M. *History of Baalbek.* Escondido, CA: Book Tree, 1999.

The Anchor Yale Bible Dictionary. Ed. David Noel Freedman. New York: Doubleday, 1996.

The Ancient Near East an Anthology of Texts and Pictures. Ed. James Bennett Pritchard. Princeton: Princeton University Press, 1958.

Arnold, Clinton E. *Zondervan Illustrated Bible Backgrounds Commentary Volume 4: Hebrews to Revelation.* Grand Rapids, MI: Zondervan, 2002.

Bancroft, Hubert Howe et al., *The Native Races of the Pacific States of North America,* vol. 5. New York: D Appleton and Co., 1874-76.

Baring-Gould, Sabine. *Legends of Old Testament Characters from the Talmud and Other Sources.* London: Macmillan, 1871.

Barker, Margaret, *The Revelation of Jesus Christ.* Edinburgh: T&T Clark, 2000.

Bauckham, Richard J. *Jude 2 Peter.* Word Biblical Commentary. Waco, TX: Word Books, 1983.

Bautch, Kelley Coblentz. *A Study of the Geography of 1 Enoch 17-19.* Boston: Brill, 2003.

Beale, Gregory K. *The Temple and the Church's Mission: A Biblical Theology of the Dwelling Place of God.* Downers Grove, IL: InterVarsity Press, 2004.

Beckley, Timothy Green. *Giants on the Earth.* New Brunswick, NJ: Global Communications/Conspiracy Journal, 2009.

_____. *The American Goliah and other Fantastic Reports of Unknown Giants and Humongous Creatures.* New Brunswick, NJ: Global Communications, 2010.

Bergsma, John Sietze. "Noah's Nakedness and the Curse of Canaan (Gen 9:20-27)." *Journal of Biblical Literature* 124/1 (2005): 25-40.

Billington, Clyde E. "Goliath and The Exodus Giants: How Tall Were They"? *JETS* 50.3 (2007): 489-508.

Birrell, Anne. *Chinese Mythology: An Introduction*. Baltimore, MD: Johns Hopkins University Press, 1993.

Blum, Edwin A. *Jude*. The Expositors Bible Commentary Vol. 12. Grand Rapids, MI: Zondervan, 1981.

Boice, James M. *Foundations of the Christian Faith*. Downers Grove, IL: InterVarsity, 1986.

_____. *Genesis Vol. 1*. Grand Rapids, MI: Baker Books, 1998.

Brenk, F. E. *Relighting the Souls: Studies in Plutarch, in Greek Literature, Religion, and Philosophy, and in the New Testament Background*. Stuttgart, 1999.

Brenton, Sir Lancelot C. L. *The Septuagint with Apocrypha*. London: Samuel Bagster & Sons, 1851.

Brophy, Thomas G. *The Origin Map*. New York: Writers Club Press, 2002.

Enhanced Brown-Driver-Briggs Hebrew and English Lexicon, electronic edition. Edited by Francis Brown, Samuel Rolles Driver and Charles Augustus Briggs. Oak Harbor, WA: Logos Research Systems, 2000.

Budd, Phillip J. *Numbers*. Word Biblical Commentary. Dallas: Word, Incorporated, 2002.

Budge, E. A. Wallis. *The Contendings of the Apostles*. London: H. Frowde, 1899.

Burke, Edmund. *The Annual Register: A View of the History, Politicks, and Literature for the Year 1764*. London: J. Dodsley, 1765.

Burkert, W. *The Orientalizing Revolution: Near Eastern Influence on Greek Culture in the Early Archaic Age*. Cambridge, 1987.

Burton, Judd H. *Interview With The Giant: Ethnohistorical Notes on the Nephilim*. Burton Beyond Press, 2009.

Calmet, Augustin. *Dictionary of the Holy Bible*. Boston: Crocker and Brewster, 1832.

Calvin John. *Commentary on the First Book of Moses Called Genesis*. Bellingham, WA: Logos Research Systems, Inc., 2010.

Carson, D. A. *The Gospel According to John*. Pillar New Testament Commentary. Leicester, England; Grand Rapids, Mich.: Inter-Varsity Press; W.B. Eerdmans, 1991.

_____. "Jude." In *Commentary on the New Testament Use of the Old Testament*. G. K. Beale and D. A. Carson (eds). Grand Rapids, MI; Nottingham, UK: Baker Academic; Apollos, 2007.

Cassuto, Umberto. *A Commentary on the Book of Genesis: From Noah to Abraham*. Jerusalem: Magnes Press, 1964.

Catholic University of America. *Fathers of the Church: A New Translation*. Washington, D.C.: Catholic University of America Press, 1947.

Catlin, George. *The Okipa Ceremony*. Norman, OK: University of Oklahoma, 1958.

Champion, Betty. *Yes We Can Be Perfect Inn Our Generation*. LaGrange, GA: World Overcomer's Church Int., 2002.

Clark; Ernest G. *Targum and Scripture: Studies in Aramaic Translations and Interpretation*. Boston: Brill, 2002.

Clarke, Adam. *Commentary on the Bible*. Nashville: Abingdon, 1977.

Clines, D. J. A. "The Significance of the 'Sons of God' Episode (Genesis 6:1–4) in the Context of the 'Primeval History' (Genesis 1–11)." *Journal for the Study of the Old Testament* 13 (1979): 33-46.

Cody, William F. *An Autobiography of Buffalo Bill*. Aurora, CO: Bibliographical Center for Research, 2009.

Cole, R. Dennis. *Numbers*. New American Commentary (Nashville: Broadman & Holman Publishers, 2001.

Collins, John Joseph; Cross, Frank Moore; and Collins, Adela Yarbro. *Daniel : A Commentary on the Book of Daniel*. Hermeneia. Minneapolis: Fortress Press, 1993.

Commentary on the New Testament Use of the Old Testament. Ed. G. K. Beale and D. A. Carson. Grand Rapids, MI; Nottingham, UK: Baker Academic; Apollos, 2007.

A Concise Hebrew and Aramaic Lexicon of the Old Testament. Edited by William Lee Holladay, Ludwig Köhler, and Ludwig Köhler. Leiden: Brill, 1971.

Cooper, Lamar Eugene Sr. *Ezekiel*. New American Commentary. Nashville: Broadman and Holman, 1994.

Corcos, Georgette. *The Glory of the Old Testament*. New York: Villard Books, 1984.

Cornwall, Judson. *The Exhaustive Dictionary of Bible Names* (North Brunswick, NJ: Bridge-Logos, 1998.

Craig, Robert D. *Dictionary of Polynesian Mythology.* New York: Greenwood Press, 1989.

Culver, Robert Duncan. *Systematic Theology.* Great Britain: Mentor, 2005.

Curtiss-Wedge, Franklyn. *History of Wright County Minnesota*, vol. 1. Chicago: H. C. Cooper, Jr., & Co., 1915.

Dahood, Mitchell J. "Ebla, Ugarit, and the Bible." In *The Archives of Ebla: An Empire Inscribed in Clay,* ed. G. Pettinato. Garden City, NY: Doubleday, 1981.

_____. *Psalms III (101-150).* Anchor Yale Bible. Garden City, NY: Doubleday, 1970.

_____. "Ebla, Ugarit, and the Old Testament." *Theology Digest* 27 (1979): 127-31.

Dalton, William J. *Christ's Proclamation to the Spirits: A Study of 1 Peter 3:18-4:6.* Rome: Editrice Pontifico Istituto Biblico, 1989.

David, Gary A. *The Orion Zone: Ancient Star Cities of the American Southwest.* Kempton, IL: Adventures Unlimited Press, 2006.

Davids, Peter H. *The Letters of 2 Peter and Jude*, Pillar New Testament Commentary. Grand Rapids, MI: Eerdmans, 2006.

Dawkins, Richard. *The God Delusion.* Boston: Houghton Mifflin Co., 2006.

Day, John. *God's Conflict with the Dragon and the Sea.* London: Cambridge University Press, 1985.

_____. *Yahweh and the Gods and Goddesses of Canaan.* New York: Continuum, 2002.

De Forest, J. W. "The Great Deluge." *Old and New* 6 (July 1872-Jan 1873): 437-48.

de la Vega, Garcilaso. *The Florida of the Inca.* Ed. John and Jeanette Varner. Austin, TX: University of Texas Pres, 1951.

de Léon, Pedro de Cieza. *The Travels of Pedro de Cieza de Leon, A.D. 1532-50.* Translated by Clements R. Markham. London: Hakluyt Society, 1864.

de Perceval, Caussin. *Essays on the History of the Arabs before Islamism, during the Time of Mohammed, and down to the Reduction of all the Tribes under his Dominion.* 1847.

de Voragine, Jacobus. *The Golden Legend: Readings on the Saints.* Trans. William Granger Ryan. Princeton, NJ: Princeton University Press, 1993.

Deane, John Bathurst. *Worship of the Serpent: Traced Throughout the World.* London: J. G. & F. Rivington, 1883, republished by Forgotten Books, 2008.

DeLoach, Charles. *Giants: A Reference Guide from History, the bible, and Recorded Legend.* Metuchen, NJ: Scarecrow Press, 1995.

Diaz, Bernal. *The Conquest of New Spain.* Trans. J. M. Cohen. New York: Penguin, 1963.

Dictionary of Ancient Deities. Eds. Turner, Patricia and Coulter, Charles Russell. New York: Oxford University Press, 2001.

Dictionary of Biblical Imagery. Eds. Ryken, L., Wilhoit, J. C., and Longman III, T. Downers Grove: InterVarsity Press, 1998.

Dictionary of Deities and Demons in the Bible, 2nd extensively revised edition. Eds. van der Toorn, K., Becking, Bob, and van der Horst, Pieter Willem. Boston: Eerdmans, 1999.

A Dictionary of the Ugaritic Language in the Alphabetic Tradition (DULAT). Eds. del Olmo Lete, Gregorio and Sanmartín, Joaquín. Boston: Brill, 2003.

Douglas, Mary. *Implicit Meanings: Essays in Anthropology.* London: Routledge & Kegan Paul, 1975.

_____. *Purity and Danger: An Analysis of the Concepts of Pollution and Taboo/* London: Routledge & Kegan Paul, 1966.

Dragoo, Don W. *Mounds for the Dead: An Analysis of the Adena Culture.* Carnegie Museum, 1963.

Driver, S. R. & Gray, G. B. *The Book of Job.* ICC; Edinburgh 1921.

Drijvers, H. J. W. *Iconography of Religions.* Leiden, Netherlands: Brill, 1976.

Eckenstein, Lina. *A History of Sinai.* New York, Macmillian Co, 1921.

Edwards, Frank. *Stranger Than Science.* New York: Lyle Stuart, 1959.

Eiseman, Robert H. and Wise, Michael Owen. *The Dead Sea Scrolls Uncovered.* New York: Penguin Books, 1993.

Encyclopaedia Biblica. Eds. Cheyne, T. K. And Black, J. Sutherland. London: Adam and Charles Black, 1899-1902.

Encyclopedia Britannica, vol. 9. Edinburgh: Archibald Constable and Company, 1823.

Erickson, Millard. *Christian Theology*. Grand Rapids, MI: Baker, 1998.

Emslie, John Philipps and Burne, C. S. "Scraps of Folklore Collected." *Folklore* 26:2 (June 30, 1915): 153-170.

Fulk, R. D. "The Passion of St. Christopher." In *The Beowulf Manuscript: Complete Texts and the Fight at Finnsburg*. Cambridge, MA: Harvard University Press, 2010.

Feinberg, Charles. *The Prophecy of Ezekiel*. Chicago: Moody Press, 1969.

Findlay, G. G. "St. Paul's First Epistle to the Corinthians." in *The Expositor's Greek Testament*. Ed. W. R. Nicoll. Grand Rapids, Eerdmans, 1961.

Fortson, Dante. *As The Days of Noah Were*. Impact Agenda Media, 2010.

_____. *The Serpent Seed: Debunked*. Impact Agenda Media, 2010.

Fosdick, Harry Emerson. *A Pilgrimage to Palestine*. New York: Macmillan Publishing Co., 1949.

Frothingham, A. L. "Babylonian Origin of Hermes, the Snake-God, and of the Caduceus." *American Journal of Archaeology* 20: 2nd series, (1916).

Gaddis, Vincent H. *Native American Myths and Mysteries*. Garberville, CA: Borderland Sciences, 1991.

Garnier, John. *The Worship of the Dead: The Origin and Nature of Pagan Idolatry*. London: Chapman & Hall, 1904.

Gaster, Theodore H. *Myth, Legend and Custom in the Old Testament*. New York: Harper and Row, 1969.

Gesenius' Hebrew and Chaldee Lexicon to the Old Testament Scriptures. Eds. Wilhelm Gesenius and Samuel Prideaux Tregelles. Bellingham, WA: Logos Research Systems, Inc, 2003.

Gimbutas, Marija. "The Kurgan Culture and the Indo-Europeanization of Europe: Selected Articles from 1952 to 1993." Edited by Miriam Robbins Dexter and Karlene Jones-Bley. *Journal of Indo-European Studies Monograph No. 18*. Washington, D.C.: Institute for the Study of Man, 1997: xix + 404 pages.

Gille, Oliver. "Cerne Abbas Giant May Have Held Severed Head." *The Independent*. London, England, Saturday, May 21, 1994.

Ginzberg, Louis. *Legends of the Jews*. ForgottenBooks, 1909, 2008.

González, Justo L. "Demythologization," in *Essential Theological Terms* (Louisville, KY: Westminster John Knox Press, 2005.

Goodrich, Samuel G. *A History of All Nations, From the Earliest Periods to the Present Time.* New York: Miller, Orton, and Mulligan, 1855.

Gordon, Cyrus. "אלהים (Elohim) in Its Reputed Meaning of *Rulers, Judges.*" *Journal of Biblical Literature* 54 (1935): 139–144.

Gould, George Milbry and Pyle, Walter Lytle. *Anomalies and Curiosities of Medicine.* Philadelphia: W.B. Saunders, 1901.

Gray, Jonathan. *Lost World of the Giants.* Brushton, NY: TEACH Services, Inc. 2006.

Green, Gene L. *Jude & 2 Peter.* Baker Exegetical Commentary on the New Testament. Grand Rapids, MI: Baker Academic, 2008.

Green, Michael. *2 Peter and Jude,* Tyndale New Testament Commentaries. Downers Grove, IL: InterVarsity, 1987.

A Greek-English Lexicon of the Septuagint : Revised Edition. Eds. Johan Lust, Erik Eynikel and Katrin Hauspie. Deutsche Bibelgesellschaft: Stuttgart, 2003.

Gunkel, H. *Genesis.* Göttingen, 1910.

Hallo William W. and Younger, K. Lawson. *Context of Scripture.* Leiden; Boston: Brill, 2003.

Hamilton, Victor P. *The Book of Genesis: Chapters 1-17.* The New International Commentary on the Old Testament. Grand Rapids, MI: Wm. B. Eerdmans Publishing Co., 1990.

Hancock, Graham. *Fingerprints of the Gods.* New York: Three Rivers Press, 1995.

_____. *Heaven's Mirror: Quest for the Lost Civilization.* New York: Crown Publishers, 1998.

Hansen, Taylor L. *The Ancient Atlantic.* Wisconsin, Amherst Press, 1969.

Hart, George. *Egyptian Myths.* Austin, TX: University of Texas Press, 1990.

Hart, Gerald D. "The Earliest Medical Use of the Caduceus." *C.M.A. Journal* 107 (Dec 9, 1972): 1107-1110.

Hartley, John E. *The Book of Job.* The New International Commentary on the Old Testament. Grand Rapids, MI: Wm. B. Eerdmans Publishing Co., 1988.

Hayes, Lyman Simpson. *History of the Town of Rockingham, Vermont.* Bellow Falls, VT: The Town, 1907.

Hayward, Robert. "The Priestly Blessing in Targum Pseudo-Jonathan." *Journal for the Study of the Pseudepigrapha* 10 (April 1999): 81-101.

Haywood, John. *The Natural and Aboriginal History of Tennessee: Up to the First Settlement Therein by the White People in the Year 1768.* Kingsport, TN: F.M. Hill-Books, 1973.

Hays, J. Daniel "Reconsidering The Height Of Goliath." *JETS* 48.4 (2005): 701-714.

_____. "The Height Of Goliath: A Response To Clyde Billington." *JETS* 50.3 (2007): 509-16.

Heiser, Michael S. *The Bible Code Myth.* Acid Test Press, 2001.

_____. "Clash of the Manuscripts: Goliath & the Hebrew Text of the Old Testament." *Bible Study Magazine* 1:4 (May-June, 2009): 33-35: http://www.biblestudymagazine.com/interactive/goliath/

_____. "Deuteronomy 32:8 and the Sons of God." *Bibliotheca Sacra* 158:629 (Jan-Mar, 2001): 52-74.

_____. "The Divine Council in Late Canonical and Non-Canonical Second Temple Jewish Literature." A Dissertation at the University of Wisconsin-Madison, 2004.

_____. "The Divine Council in the New Testament: The Archons." *Behind the Façade* 3:9 (Feb 2005): 32-34.

_____. *The Myth That Is True.* Unpublished. Available to purchase at: http://www.michaelsheiser.com/

_____. "The Nachash and his Seed: Some Explanatory Notes on Why the 'Serpent' in Genesis 3 Wasn't a Serpent." http://www.thedivinecouncil.com/nachashnotes.pdf.

_____. "Serpentine / Reptilian Divine Beings in the Hebrew Bible: A Preliminary Investigation." http://www.scribd.com/doc/63497725/Michael-s-Heiser-Serpentine.

_____. "You've Seen One Elohim, You've Seen Them All? A Critique of Mormonism's Use of Psalm 82," *FARMS Review* 19/1 (2007): 221–266.

Hendel, Ronald S. "Biblical Views: Giants at Jericho." *Biblical Archaeological Research* 35:02 (Mar/Apr 2009).

_____. "Of Demigods and the Deluge: Toward an Interpretation of Genesis 6:1–4." *Journal of Biblical Literature* 106 (1987): 13-26.

Herm, Gerhard. *The Celts*. New York: St. Martin's Press, 1975.

Heron, Patrick. *The Nephilim and the Pyramid of the Apocalypse*. New York, NY: Citadel Press, 2004.

Hesiod. *The Works and Days*. Trans. Richmond Lattimore. Ann Arbor: University of Michigan, 1959.

Hibbert Trust. *The Hibbert Lectures*. Cambridge: Cambridge University Press, 1896-1929.

Hine, Charles Gilbert. *The Story of Martha's Vineyard*. New York: Hine Brothers, 1908.

Hitchcock, Roswell D. *Hitchcock's Complete Analysis of the Holy Bible*. New York: A. J. Johnson, 1874.

Hoehner, H. W. "The Duration of the Egyptian Bondage." *Bibliotheca Sacra Volume* 126:504 (1969): 306-16.

Howe, Henry. *The Historical Collections of Ohio*. Cincinnati, OH: Pub by the state of Ohio, 1902.

Jacobsen, Thorkild. *The Harps That Once ... Sumerian Poetry in Translation*. New Haven/London: Yale University Press, 1987.

Jeremias, J. *Heiligengräber in Jesu Umwelt*. Göttingen, 1958.

Jewish Encyclopedia. Ed. Isidore Singer and Cyrus Adler. New York: Funk and Wagnalls, 1912.

Johnson, Robert Bowie Jr. *Athena and Eden*. Annapolis, MD: Solving Light Books, 2002.

_____. *Athena and Cain*. Annapolis, MD: Solving Light Books, 2003.

_____. *The Parthenon Code*. Annapolis, MD: Solving Light Books, 2004.

_____. *Noah in Ancient Greek Art*. Annapolis, MD: Solving Light Books, 2007.

Joines, Karen. *Serpent Symbolism in the Old Testament: A Linguistic, Archaeological, and Literary Study*. Haddonfield House, New Jersey, 1974.

Joseph, Frank. *Advanced Civilizations of Prehistoric America*. Rochester, VT: Bear & Company, 2010.

_____. *The Atlantis Encyclopedia*. *Franklin Lakes*, NJ: The Career Press, 205.

_____. *Atlantis in Wisconsin: New Revelations About The Lost Sunken City*. St. Paul, MN, Galde Press, 1995.
_____. *The Destruction of Atlantis* (Rochester, VT: Bear & Company, 2002.

Keener, C. S. *The Gospel of John* 2 vols. Peabody, Mass: Hendrickson.

Keil, Carl Friedrich and Delitzsch, Franz. *Commentary on the Old Testament*. Peabody, MA: Hendrickson, 2002.

Keyssler, Johann Georg. *Travels through Germany, Bohemia, Hungary, Switzerland, Italy, and Lorrain*. London, G. Keith, 1760.

Kline, Meredith G. "Divine Kingship and Genesis 6:1-4." *Westminster Theological Journal* 24.2 (1962): 187-204.

_____. *Kingdom Prologue*. Overland Park, KS: Two Age Press, 2000.

Koch, John T. *Celtic Culture: A Historical Encyclopedia*. Santa Barbara, CA, 2006.

Köstenberger, Andreas J. *John*. Baker exegetical commentary on the New Testament. Grand Rapids, Mich.: Baker Academic, 2004.

Kraeling, E. "The Significance and Origin of Gen. 6:1-4." *Journal of Near Eastern Studies* 6 (1947): 193-208.

Landa, Gertrude. *Jewish Fairy Tales and Legends*. New York: Bloch, 1919.

Layton, Scott C. "Remarks on the Canaanite Origin of Eve." *Catholic Biblical Quarterly* 59 (1997): 22-32.

Lenormant, François. *A Manual of the Ancient History of the East to the Commencement of the Median Wars*. Trans. E. Chavallier. Philadelphia: Lippincott & Co., 1870-71.

Lewis, C. S. "Autobiography: The Letters of C.S. Lewis to Arthur Greeves." In *The Essential C.S. Lewis*. Ed. Lyle W. Dorsett. New York: Touchstone, 1996.

A Lexicon : Abridged from Liddell and Scott's Greek-English Lexicon. Ed. H. G. Liddell. Oak Harbor, WA: Logos Research Systems, Inc., 1996.

Lindquist, Maria. "King Og's Iron Bed." *Catholic Biblical Quarterly* 73:3 (July 2011): 477-492.

Livingstone, David. *Missionary Travels*. London: Ward Lock, 1910.

Luther, Martin. *Luther's Works*. Ed. Jaroslav Jan Pelikan, Hilton C. Oswald and Helmut T. Lehmann. Saint Louis: Concordia Publishing House, 1999.

Mac Firbis, Duald. *On the Fomorians and the Norsemen*. Christiania: J.C. Gundersens Bogtrykkeri, 1905.

MacCulloch, John Arnott. *The Religion of the Ancient Celts.* New York: Dover Publications, 2003.

Maeir, A. M., Wimmer, S. J., Zukerman, A., and Demsky, A., "A Late Iron Age I/early Iron Age IIA Old Canaanite Inscription from Tell es-Sâfi/Gath, Israel: Palaeography, Dating, and Historical-Cultural Significance." *Bulletin of the American Schools of Oriental Research* 351 (Aug 2008): 39–71.

Marshall, Richard. *Mysteries of the Unexplained.* Pleasantville, NY: The Reader's Digest Association, 1983.

Mathews, K. A. *Genesis 1-11:26.* The New American Commentary. Nashville: Broadman & Holman Publishers, 2001.

Martínez, Florentino García and Tigchelaar, Eibert J. C. *The Dead Sea Scrolls Study Edition (Transcriptions and Translations).* Leiden; New York: Brill, 1997-1998.

Mayor, Adrienne. *Fossil Legends of the First Americans.* Princeton, NJ: Princeton University Press, 2005.

_____. "Giants in Ancient Warfare." *MHQ: The Quarterly Journal of Military History* 2.2 (Winter 1999): 98-105.

_____. *The First Fossil Hunters: Paleontology in Greek and Roman Times.* Princeton, NJ: Princeton University Press, 2001.

McNally, Raymond T. *In Search of Dracula: The History of Dracula and Vampires Completely Revised.* Boston: Mifflin, 1994.

Meyer, A. W. *Critical and Exegetical Handbook to the Epistles to the Corinthians.* Edinburgh: T. & T. Clark, 1892.

Michaels, Ramsey J. *1 Peter.* Word Biblical Commentary. Dallas: Word, 2002.

Millard, A. R. "A New Babylonian 'Genesis' Story." *Tyndale Bulletin* 18 (1967): 3-18.

_____. "King Og's Bed and Other Ancient Ironmongery." In *Ascribe to the Lord. Biblical and other studies in memory of Peter C. Craigie.* Eds. L. Eslinger & G. Taylor). JSOT Sup 67; Sheffield 1988: 481–492.

Mobley, Gregory. "The Wild Man in the Bible and the Ancient Near East." *Journal of Biblical Literature* 116 (1997): 217-33.

Moo, Douglas J. *2 Peter, Jude.* NIV Application Commentary. Grand Rapids, MI: Zondervan, 1996.

Mounce, Robert H. *The Book of Revelation*. The New International Commentary on the New Testament. Grand Rapids, MI: Wm. B. Eerdmans Publishing Co., 1997.

Muller, Jon. *Archaeology of the Lower Ohio River Valley*. Walnut Creek, CA: Left Coast Press, 2009.

Murray, John. *Principles of Conduct*. Grand Rapids: Wm. B. Eerdmans, 1957.

Newman, Robert C. "The Ancient Exegesis of Genesis 6:2, 4." *Grace Theological Journal* 5.1 (1984): 13-36.

Nickelsburg George W. E., and Baltzer, Klaus. *1 Enoch : A Commentary on the Book of 1 Enoch*. Minneapolis, Minn.: Fortress, 2001.

Norvill, Roy. *Giants: The Vanished Race*. Wellingborough, UK: Aquarian Press, 1979.

Oesterle, Joe and Cridland, Tim. *Weird Las Vegas and Nevada*. New York: Sterling Publishing Co., 2007.

Old Testament Pseudepigrapha (2 vols). Ed. James H. Charlesworth. New York: Yale University Press, 1983.

Olmo, H. P. "Giant-Berry Grapes: Principles of Genetics Employed to Propagate Varieties Producing Berries of Larger Size." *California Agriculture* Vol. 4 No. 6 (1950): 5-13.

Orchard, Andy. *Pride and Prodigies: Studies in the Monsters of the Beowulf-manuscript*. Rochester, NY: D.S. Brewer, 1995.

Osborne, Grant R. *Revelation*. Baker Exegetical Commentary on the New Testament. Grand Rapids, Mich.: Baker Academic, 2002.

Palestine Pilgrims' Text Society. *The Library of the Palestine Pilgrims' Text Society*. London: Committee of the Palestine Exploration Fund, 1885.

Patai, Raphael. *Arab Folktales from Palestine and Israel*. Detroit, MI: Wayne State University Press, 1998.

Peet, Stephen D. (ed). *American Antiquarian and Oriental Journal* 6:2 (March 1884): 133-34.

_____. "The Mound-Builders," in *History of Astabula Co., Ohio*. Ed. William W. Williams. Philadelphia: Williams Bros., 1878): 16-20.

Pezron, Paul. *The Antiquities of Nations; More Particularly of the Celte or Gauls*. Trans. Mr. D. Jones. London: R. Janeway, 1706.

Pink, Arthur W. *Gleanings in Genesis*. Bellingham, WA: Logos Research Systems, Inc., 2005.

Phillips, Douglas. "The Mystery of the Nephilim Presented and Solved: Discovering the True Giants of Paganism." In *Mysteries of the Ancient World*, an audio series. San Antonio, TX: Vision Forum, 2008.

Pigafetta, Antonio *The Voyage of Magellan*. London: Yale University Press, 1969.

Porter, Josias Leslie. *The Giant Cities of Bashan; and Syria's Holy Places*. New York: Thomas Nelson, 1884.

Preisendanz, Karl. "Nimrod." In *Pauly, Wissowa and Kroll, Real-Encyclopädie* 17 (1936): 624-27.

Priest, Josiah. *American Antiquities and Discoveries in the West*. Albany, NY: Hoffman & White, 1833.

Quayle, Stephen. *Genesis 6 Giants*. Bozeman, MT: End Time Thunder Publishers, 2002.

Quayle, Stephen and Long, Duncan. *Longwalkers*. Bozeman, MT: End Times Thunder Publishers, 2008.

Readers Digest Association. *The World's Last Mysteries*. Montreal: Reader's Digest, 1978.

Reeves, John C. *Jewish Lore in Manichaean Cosmogony: Studies in the Book of Giants Traditions*. Cincinnati: Hebrew Union College Press, 1992.

Reymond, Robert L. *A New Systematic Theology of the Christian Faith*. Nashville: Thomas Nelson, 1998.

Riesner, Rainer. "Bethany Beyond The Jordan (John 1:28) Topography, Theology And History In The Fourth Gospel." *Tyndale Bulletin* 38 (1987): 29–63.

Riggs, J. R. "The Length of Israel's Sojourn in Egypt." *Grace Theological Journal* 12 (1971): 18-35

Roberts, A., Donaldson, J., Coxe, A. C., and Menzies, A. *The Ante-Nicene Fathers* in 10 volumes. Buffalo: Christian Literature, 1886.

Rodgers, Adam. "Early Nevada History is Traced in Lovelock, Cave, Tomb of the Forgotten Race." *Ancient American* 13:81 (Dec 2008): 32-35.

Rose, Carol. *Giants, Monsters, and Dragons: An Encyclopedia of Folklore, Legend, and Myth*. New York: W.W. Norton & Company Inc. 2000.

Ross, Allen P. "Studies in the Book of Genesis - Part 2: The Table of Nations in Genesis 10 - its Structure." *BibSac* 137:548 (Oct-Dec 1980): 340-50.

Rutherford, Mac. *Historic Haunts of Winchester*. Charleston, SC: Haunted America, 2007.

Giants of the Bible

Sandison, A. T., and Wells, C. "Endocrine Diseases." In *Diseases in Antiquity*, eds. Don Brothwell and A. T. Sandison, 521-31. Springfield, IL: Charles C. Thomas, 1967.

Sarna, Nahum M. *Genesis*. The JPS Torah Commentary. Philadelphia: Jewish Publication Society, 1989.

Sayce, A. H. "The White Race of Palestine." *Nature* 38:979 (Aug 2, 1888): 321-23.

Schaeffer, Francis. "Genesis in Space and Time." In *The Complete Works of Francis A. Schaeffer: A Christian Worldview*. Westchester, IL: Crossway Books, 1996.

Schaff, Philip *The Nicene and Post-Nicene Fathers Vol. II*. Oak Harbor: Logos Research Systems, 1997).

Schreiner, Thomas R. *1, 2 Peter, Jude*. New American Commentary. Nashville, TN: Broadman & Holman, 2003.

Segal, Alan. *Two Powers in Heaven: Early Rabbinic Reports about Christianity and Gnosticism*. Boston, Brill Academic Pub, 2002.

Setzler, Frank M. and Marshall, George C. "Giant Effigies of the Southwest." *National Geographic* (Sept. 1952): 389-404.

Sheldon, George. *History of Deerfield*, vol. 1. MA: Pioneer Valley Memorial Museum, 1895.

Smith, Evans Lansing and Brown, Nathan Robert. *The Complete Idiot's Guide to World Mythology*. Indianapolis, IN: Alpha Books, 2008.

Smith, J. V. C. (M.D.), Morland, W. W. (M.D.), and Minot, Francis (M.D.). *Boston Medical and Surgical Journal*. Volume LIII. Boston: David Clapp, 1856.

Smith, John. *Captain John Smith's America; selections from his writings*. Ed. John Lankford. New York: Harper & Row, 1967.

Smith, William G. *A Dictionary of the Bible: Comprising Its Antiquities, Biography, and Natural History in 3 Vols*. Boston: Little Brown, 1863.

Spence, Lewis. *The Myths of the North American Indians*. New York: Dover, 1989.

Stigers, Harold G. *A Commentary on Genesis*. Grand Rapids: Zondervan, 1967.

Strelan, Rick. "The Fallen Watchers and the Disciples in Mark." *Journal for the Study of the Pseudepigrapha* 10 (Oct 1999): 73-92.

Terrien, Samuel L. *The Psalms: Strophic Structure and Theological Commentary*. Grand Rapids, MI: Eerdmans, 2003.

Thiselton, Anthony C. *The First Epistle to the Corinthians : A Commentary on the Greek Text*. Grand Rapids, Mich.: W.B. Eerdmans, 2000.

Thompson, R. Campbell. *The Devils and Evil Spirits of Babylonia: Being Babylonian and Assyrian Incantations Against the Demons, Ghouls, Vampires, Hobgoblins, Ghosts, and Kindred Evil Spirits, Which Attach Mankind*. Forgotten Books, originally published 1903.

Thomson, C. J. S. *The Mystery and Lore of Monsters*. New York: Bell, 1968.

Tigay, Jeffrey H. *Deuteronomy*. Philadelphia: Jewish Publication Society, 1996.

Tompkins, Peter. *Mysteries of the Mexican Pyramids*. New York: Harper Collins, 1987.

Tolkien, J. R. R. "A Letter to Milton Waldman." Reprinted in *The Simarillion*. New York: Houghton Mifflin Co, 2001.

_____. *The Tolkien Reader* (New York: Del Rey, 1968)

Unger, Merrill F. "The Old Testament Revelation Concerning Eternity Past." *Bibliotheca Sacra* 114:454 (Apr '57): 135-41.

van Binsbergen, Wim. "The Heroes in Flood Myths Worldwide." Leiden: Erasmus University Rotterdam, 2010. http://www.shikanda.net/topicalities/binsbergen_flood_heroes.pdf

van der Kooij, Arie. "Peshitta Genesis 6: 'Sons of God' – Angels of Judges?'. *Journal of Northwest Semitic Languages* 23/1 (1997): 43-51.

van der Toorn, K. and van der Horst, P. W. "Nimrod Before And After The Bible." *Harvard Theological Review* 83:1 (1990): 1-29.

van Dijk, J. *LUGAL UD ME-LÁM-bi NIR-GÁL Le récit épique et didactique des Travaux de Ninurta, du Déluge et de la Nouvelle Création in 2 vols*. Leiden: Brill, 1983.

van Gemeren, W. A. "The Sons of God in Genesis 6:1–4 (An Example of Evangelical Demythologization?)." *Westminster Theological Journal* 43 (1981): 320-348.

van Hoonacker, A. "Eléments sumériens dans le livre d'Ezéchiel"? *Zeitschrift für Assyriologie* 28 (1914): 333-36.

VanDrunen, David. *Living in God's Two Kingdoms*. Wheaton, IL: Crossway, 2010.

Walton, John. *Covenant: God's Purpose, God's Plan*. Grand Rapids, MI: Zondervan, 1994.

_____. "The Mesopotamian Background of the Tower of Babel Account and Its Implications." *Bulletin for Biblical Research* 5 (1995): 155-75.

Watts, John D. W. *Isaiah 34-66*. Word Biblical Commentary. Dallas: Word, Incorporated, 2002.

Way, Kenneth C. "Giants in the Land: A Textual and Semantic Study of Giants in the Bible and the Ancient Near East." A Thesis. Deerfield, IL: Trinity International University, 2000.

Webb, Robert L. "The Use of 'Story' in the Letter of Jude: Rhetorical Strategies of Jude's Narrative Episodes." *Journal for the Study of the New Testament* 31 (2008): 53-87.

Weston, Thomas. *History of the Town of Middleboro, Massachusetts*. Boston: Houghton, Mifflin and Company, 1906.

Wevers, John William. *Genesis*. Vetus Testamentum Graecum. Auctoritate Academiae Scientiarum Gottingensis Editum. Göttingen: Vandenhoeck & Ruprecht, 1974.

Wenham, Gordon J. *Genesis 1-15*. Word Biblical Commentary. Dallas: Word, Incorporated, 2002.

Wickham, L. R. "The Sons of God and the Daughters of Men: Genesis VI 2 in Early Christian Exegesis." In *Language and Meaning: Studies in Hebrew Language and Biblical Exegesis*. Ed. James Barr, 135-47. Leiden: Brill, 1974.

Wilkins, William Joseph. *Hindu Mythology, Vedic and Purānic*. London: Thacker & Co., 1882.

Winchell, N. H. and Brower, Jacob V. *1906-1911 The Aborigines of Minnesota: A Report based on the Collections of Jacob V. Brower, and on the Field Surveys and Notes of Alfred J. Hill and Theodore H. Lewis*. Minnesota Historical Society, 1911.

Winnemucca Hopkins, Sarah. *Life Among the Paiutes*. Boston: Cupples, Upham & CO., 1883.

Winship, George Parker (translator). *The Coronado Expedition: 1540-1542*. Washington: Government Printing Office, 1896.

Wiseman, Donald J. "Medicine in the Old Testament World." In *Medicine and the Bible*, ed. B. Palmer, 13-42. Exeter: Paternoster Press, 1986.

Wood, Edward J. *Giants and Dwarfs*. London: Bentley, 1868.

Wood, Leon. *A Survey of Israel's History*. Grand Rapids, MI: Zondervan Publishing House, 1970.

Woolley, Leonard. *The Sumerians*. New York: W.W. Norton, 1965.

Worcester, Elwood. *The Book of Genesis in Light of Modern Knowledge*. New York: McClure, Phillips & Co., 1901.

Wright, Archie T. *The Origin of Evil Spirits: The Reception of Genesis 6:1-4 in Early Jewish Literature*. Tübingen: Mohr Siebeck, 2004.

Wright, G. Ernest. "Troglodytes and Giants in Palestine." *Journal of Biblical Literature* 57:3 (Sept 1938): 305-309.

Wyatt, N. *Religious Texts from Ugarit*, 2nd ed., Biblical seminar, 53. New York: Sheffield Academic Press, 2002.

The Wycliffe Bible Encyclopedia. Eds. Charles F. Pfeiffer, Howard Frederic Vos, and John Rea. Chicago: Moody Press, 1972.

Young, Gordon Douglas. *Ugarit in Retrospect*. Winona Lake, IN: Eisenbrauns, 1981.

Zimmerli, Walther. *Ezekiel 2: A Commentary on the Book of Ezekiel, Chapters 25-48*. Hermeneia. Philadelphia: Fortress Press, 1983.

Zondervan Illustrated Bible Backgrounds Commentary (Old Testament) Vol. 1: Genesis-Deuteronomy. Ed. John H. Walton. Grand Rapids, MI: Zondervan, 2009.

Image Bibliography

ALL FILES BELIEVED TO BE IN THE PUBLIC DOMAIN (PD) OR ARE USED BY PERMISSION.

FIG. I.1. File: *Terracotta Army Pit 1*, (Xi'an, China), PD, Wikipedia, last accessed (LA) 8-13-2012, http://en.wikipedia.org/wiki/Terracotta_Army.

FIG. I.2. (Left) File: *Villa del Casale*, (Roman Mosaic 3rd C. A.D.), PD, Wikipedia, LA 8-13-2012, http://commons.wikimedia.org/wiki/File:Villa_del_Casale_34.jpg. (Right) File: *Gigantomachia*, Istanbul Archaeological Museum, Turkey, PD, Wikipedia, LA 8-13-2012, http://en.wikipedia.org/wiki/Giants_(Greek_mythology).

FIG. I.3. (Left): *Serapis* (Egypt), Alexander Murray, *Handbook of Mythology* (c. 1881), Plate XLV. (Middle-left) File: *Fuxi and Nüwa* (8th Cent. Tang Dynasty, China), Xinjiang, China, PD, LA 8-13-2012, http://en.wikipedia.org/wiki/File:Anonymous-Fuxi_and_N%C3%BCwa.jpg. (Middle-right) File: *Kukulcan* (Central and South America), PD, LA 8-20-2012, http://en.wikipedia.org/wiki/File:YaxchilanDivineSerpent.jpg. (Right) File: *Kaliya Daman* (India), PD, LA 8-20-2012, http://commons.wikimedia.org/wiki/File:Kaliya_Daman.png.

FIG. 1.1. (Left/Right) File: *Caduceus*; (Middle) File: US Army Medical Corps Branch Plaque, PD, Wikipedia, last accessed 8-20-2012, http://en.wikipedia.org/wiki/File:US_Army_Medical_Corps_Branch_Plaque.gif; http://en.wikipedia.org/wiki/File:Caduceus.svg.

FIG. 1.2. (Left) File: *Fuxi and Nüwa* (8th Cent. Tang Dynasty, China). PD, LA 8-13-2012, http://en.wikipedia.org/wiki/File:Anonymous-Fuxi_and_N%C3%BCwa.jpg. (Top middle): *"The Serpent Lord Enthroned" (Mesopotamia, c. 2200 BC). Joseph Campbell, The Masks of God (New York: Arkana, 1964), 11, all rights reserved.* (Bottom middle): *Peruvian Textile (Late Paracas, 300-200 BC). Ferdinand Anton, Ancient Peruvian Textiles (New York: Thames and Hudson, 1987), 80, all rights reserved.* (Top right) File: *"Libation Vase of Gudea"* (Ningishzida c. 2100 BC), PD, LA 8-20-2012, http://en.wikipedia.org/wiki/File:Ningizzida.jpg. (Bottom right) File: *Quetzalcoatl Figurine* (pre-Spanish conquest), by permission, LA 8-20-2012: http://www.satorws.com/simbolismo-caduceo.htm.

FIG. 1.3. (Left) File: "DNA," PD, LA 8-20-2012, http://en.wikipedia.org/wiki/File:A-DNA,_B-DNA_and_Z-DNA.png. (Right) File: "science_technology_caduceus_DNA," PD, LA 8-20-2012, http://publicdomainclipart.blogspot.com/2006/10/science-and-technology-caduceus-with.html.

FIG. 2.1. Chart in Wim van Binsbergen, 2010, p. 2. Source: Frazer 1918; Dundes 1988; Isaak 2006.

FIG. 2.2. Chart appeared in *Answers Magazine* 2:2 (Apr-June 2007): 20. http://www.answersingenesis.org/articles/am/v2/n2/flood-legends. Adapted from B.C. Nelson, *The Deluge Story in Stone*, Appendix 11; *Flood Traditions*, Figure 38. Augsburg, Minneapolis, 1931.

FIG. 2.3. (Left) Orion in Urania's Mirror, a set of constellation cards, London (1825). File: Orionurania.jpg, PD, Wikipedia, (LA) 12-2-2012, http://en.wikipedia.org/wiki/File:Orionurania.jpg. (Middle): Osirus and Orion's Belt. LA 12-3-2012, PD, http://www.myspace.com/ashkidmusik/photos/4125866. (Right) Theban Tomb 353 was the second tomb of Senenmut, "Celestial diagram from the tomb of Senenmut (TT353), south section of ceiling," uploaded by Larry Orcutt. LA 12-3-2012, PD, http://www.catchpenny.org/xp/images/senmut-s.gif.

FIG. 2.4. (Left) Hercules wearing a Lion's Skin: Attic Amphora, ca. 525-500 B.C. PD, LA 12-3-2012, http://public.wsu.edu/~hughesc/Hercules_labours.html, (Right) God and Monster (865-860 B.C.), Temple of Ninura, Nimrud (Kalhu). PD, LA 12-3-2012, http://bibarchae.tripod.com/003_god_monster_Ninurta_Nimrud.htm.

FIG. 2.5. (Left) Baalbek foundation stones (aka the trilithon), PD, LA 12-4-20120, http://reinep.wordpress.com/2010/03/10/the-baalbek-mystery/ (Middle) "The Largest Stone in the World," Baalbek, Bekaa Valley, abanon, photo from JohnDan1, (Note: This stone is often confused on the internet with the next stone, but they are two different stones), PD, LA 12-4-2012, http://www.redditmirror.cc/cache/websites/www.hottnez.com_81der/www.hottnez.com/the-mysterious-gigantic-megaliths-of-baalbeck-temples/index.html, (Right) File: Baalbek- largest stone.jpg), PD, Wikipedia, LA 12-4-2012, http://en.wikipedia.org/wiki/File:Baalbek-_largest_stone.jpg.

FIG. 2.6. Ziggurat/Tower of Babel Rendition. Unknown artist. PD, LA 12-04-2012, http://www.ancientworlds.net/aw/Journals/Journal/1051353&caldate=2008-04-12%2016:30:00.

FIG. 2.7. (Upper left and Upper Right) The Ziggurat of Ur (actual and artistic), PD, LA 12-4-2012, http://www.zeably.com/Great_Ziggurat_of_Ur. (Lower Left) Chogha-Zanbil, PD, LA 12-4-2012, http://www.thehistorybluff.com/?p=283. (Lower Right) Model of Chogha-Zanbil; PD, LA 12-4-2012, http://www.livius.org/cg-cm/choga_zanbil/choga_zanbil2.html.

FIG. 2.8. (Left) Cahokia: Monk's Mound, Collinsville Road and I-70, photo by Ira Block, PD, LA 12-4-2012, http://nextstl.com/greater-stl-illinois/cahokia-national-park, (Right) Monk's Mound replica, PD, LA 12-4-2012, http://www.iupui.edu/~mstd/e316/news.html.

FIG. 2.9. (Left) "Step Pyramid of Djoser," PD, LA 12-4-2012, (Right) "Tomb of the General," PD, LA 12-4-2012, http://www.touropia.com/step-pyramids-of-the-world/.

FIG. 2.10a. (Upper Left). File: *PyramidOfTheSun Teotihuacan.jpg*, PD, Wikipedia, LA 12-18-2012, http://commons.wikimedia.org/wiki/File:PyramidOfTheSunTeotihuacan.jpg; (Upper Right). File: *Teotihuacán – Modell Sonnenpyramide.jpg*, Wolfgang Sauber; PD, Wikipedia, LA 12-18-2012. http://en.wikipedia.org/wiki/File:Teotihuac%C3%A1n_-_Modell_Sonnenpyramide.jpg; (Lower Left). File: Pyramid of the Moon.jpg, PD, Wikipedia, LA 12-18-2012, http://commons.wikimedia.org/wiki/File:Pyramid_of_the_Moon.JPG; (Lower Right). Pyramid of the Moon reconstruction. Photo: Wolfgang Sauber.

FIG. 2.10b. (Upper Left). File: ChichenItzaEquinox.jpg. PD, Wikipedia, LA 12-18-2012; http://en.wikipedia.org/wiki/File:ChichenItzaEquinox.jpg; (Upper Right). Chichen Itza, Mexico; Google Earth image; (Lower Left). File: Tajin, Veracruz.jpg; PD; Wikipedia, LA 12-18-2012; http://commons.wikimedia.org/wiki/File:Tajin,_Veracruz.jpg; (Lower Right). File: Tikal Temple I.jpg; PD, Wikipedia, LA 12-18-2012; http://commons.wikimedia.org/wiki/File:Tikal_Temple_I.jpg.

FIG. 2.11. Ziggurat Project, Dubai, UAE. http://flashydubai.com/ziggurat-pyramid-dubai-the-most-funkiest-project-ever-envisioned/.

FIG. 2.12.   (Left). Ankor Thom, Cambodia, Jim Alison; PD, LA, 12-18-2012; http://rabbithole2.com/presentation/ancient/images/; (Right). Orion's Belt and the Milky Way aligned with the Pyramids of Giza and the Nile, PD, LA 12-18-2012; http://www.bibliotecapleyades.net/piramides/esp_piramide_8.htm.

FIG. 2.13.   Solomon's Temple. PD, LA 12-18-2012; http://e-ducation.net/architecture.htm.

FIG. 2.14.   (Left). "Looking up the Steps of the Ziggurat," Operation Iraqi Freedom Pictures, Ray Cheung, used with permission, LA 12-18-2012; http://www.rkcheung.com/Iraq.htm; (Right): Same stairway, wider angle; PD, LA 12=18-2012. http://www.bibliotecapleyades.net/arqueologia/worldwonders/ur.htm.

FIG. 8.1.   Map of Giants in Canaan; PD; LA 12-18-2012; http://www.zeably.com/Conquest_of_Canaan.

FIG. 8.2.   (Left). Temple of Hatshepsut, 1550 BC, Egypt. PD; LA 12-18-2012; http://stres.a.gape.org/nedemokrat_simboli_RS/kritika_simboli_absol_fas_oblasti.htm; (Upper Middle). Nefertiti, 18th Dynasty; PD; LA 12-18-2012; http://www.aquiziam.com/weird-skull.html; (Lower Middle), One of Pharaoh Akhenaten's daughters. Cairo Museum, PD, LA 12-18-2012; http://tpuc.org/forum/viewtopic.php?p=130489; (Upper Right). African head binding, PD; LA 12-18-2012; http://tpuc.org/forum/viewtopic.php?p=130489; (Lower Right). Elongated head (some with red hair), Museo De National, Lima Peru; PD; LA 12-18-2012; http://2012forum.com/forum/viewtopic.php?f=3&p=255041.

FIG. 8.3.   Serpentine ravine, Bashan, Israel. Image from Google Earth.

FIG. 8.4.   (Left Upper and Bottom). Serpent mound formation and Wheel of Giants (Gilgal Refaim), Bashan, Israel; image from Google Earth. (Upper Right). (Upper Right). Constance Cummings, *In the Hebrides* (London: Chatto and Windus, Piccadilly, 1883), 46. (Lower Right) File: serpent_mound_L.jpg, PD, Ohio State University, LA 12-18-2012, http://ocvn.osu.edu/serpentmoundljpg.

FIG. 8.5.   Gilgal Refaim and the Serpent Mound looking north to Mt. Hermon. Image from Google Earth.

FIG. 8.6.   Othmar Keel – *Jahwe-Visionen und Siegelkunst: Eine neue Deutung der Majestatsschilderungen in Jes, Ez 1 und 10 und Sach 4* ("Visions of Yahweh and Seal Art: A New Interpretation of the Majestic Portrayals in Isaiah 6, Ezekiel 1 and 10, and Zechariah 4"), Verlag Katholisches Bibelwerk, Stuttgart, 1984-85); abb. 107. http://www.sitchiniswrong.com/ezekielnotes.htm.

FIG. 8.7.   (Top). Gilgal Refaim, Bashan, Israel, Itamar Greenberg, and overview, PD, LA 12-19-2012, http://www.geobiology.co.il/Articles/Mysteries_RUJM.asp; (Bottom). Four unidentified similar ancient round ceremonial centers, Bashan, Israel, Images from Google Earth.

FIG. 8.8.   (Top Row). Göbekli Tepe, Turkey. PD, LA 12-19-2012; http://humansarefree.com/2011/01/gobekli-tepe-12000-years-old-temple.html, Reconstruction, PD, LA 12-19-2012; (Second Row). Left: Qoy Qirilg'an qala, Uzbekistan. PD, LA 12-19-2012; http://www.karakalpak.com/anckoy.html; Middle: File: Africa 1.jpg, African Stone Circle, Saharan Desert, PD, LA: 12-19-2012; http://wiki.atlantisforschung.de/index.php/Bild:Afrika_1.jpg. Right: Arakaim ("Russian Stonehenge"), Southern Urals, Russia, PD: LA, 12-19-2012, http://tidesofepicness.blogspot.com/2012/02/arkaim-ancient-aryan-city-and-russian.html. (Third Row). Left: Hill of Tara, Ireland; PD, LA 12-19-2012; http://www.mythicalireland.com/ancientsites/tara/; Middle: Stonehenge, England. PD, LA 12-19-2012; http://newspaper.li/stonehenge/; Avebury, England; PD, LA 12-19-2012; http://www.bbc.co.uk/wiltshire/content/image_galleries/avebury_gallery.shtml; (Bottom Row). Left: File: Chaco Canyon Chetro Ketl great kiva plaza NPS.jpg, PD, Wikipedia, LA 12-19-2012, http://en.wikipedia.org/wiki/Chaco_Culture_National_Historical_Park; Moundbuilders State Park, Newark, Ohio, PD, LA 12-19-2012; http://consumer.discoverohio.com/popups/media.aspx?projecttype=3&id=5be9e827-016b-48a5-8db1-27cf07a9e1d0.

FIG. 9.1 (Left). File: Christopher icon.jpg. PD, Wikipedia, LA 12-19-2012, http://en.wikipedia.org/wiki/Saint_Christopher; (Right). Eastern depiction of St. Christopher, Byzantine Museum, Athens, PD, LA 12-19-2012, http://www.ucc.ie/milmart/Christopher.html.

FIG. 10.1 The Goliath Shard, released to the public by Bar Ilan University, Nov 8, 2005; http://www.bibleistrue.com/qna/pqna32.htm.

FIG. 12.1 Partial of "The ancient Hebrew Conception of the Universe to illustrate the account of creation and the flood," Michael Paukner, 2009, http://www.flickr.com/photos/michaelpaukner/4077736695/.

FIG. 12.2 (Left). File: Lamassu.jpg, PD, Wikipedia, LA 12-19-2012, http://en.wikipedia.org/wiki; (Middle). File: Tondo Minotaur London E4 MAN.jpg, PD, Wikipedia, LA 12-19-2012, http://commons.wikimedia.org/wiki/Category:Minotaur_in_Ancient_Greek_pottery; (Right). File: Great Sphinx of Giza – 20080716.jpg, PD, Wikipedia, LA 12-19-2012, http://en.wikipedia.org/wiki/Sphinx.

FIG. 13.1 (Upper Left). Image – Greek Centaur.jpg, PD, Wikia, LA 12-20-2012, http://uncyclopedia.wikia.com/wiki/File:Greek_Centaur.jpg; (Upper Right). File: Satyros Cdm Paris DeRidder509.jpg, PD, Widipedia, LA 12-20-2012, http://en.wikipedia.org/wiki/Satyr; (Bottom Left). "Odysseus and the Sirens," PD, LA 12-20-2012, http://www.utexas.edu/courses/ancientfilmCC304/lecture5/detail.php?linenum=4; (Bottom Right). Sumerian/Assyrian Terra Cotta Relief of Lilith, PD, LA 12-20-2012, http://www.lilithgallery.com/library/lilith/Lilith-Gallery.html.

FIG. 13.2 File: Chimera Apulia Lourvre K362.jpg, PD, Wikipedia, LA 12-20-2012, http://commons.wikimedia.org/wiki/File:Chimera_Apulia_Louvre_K362.jpg.

FIG. 13.3 File: RhodeislandMonster.jpg, PD, Wikipedia, LA 12-20-2012, http://en.wikipedia.org/wiki/File:RhodeislandMonster.jpg.

FIG. 14.1 File: ME 125206, Limestone relief of the god Shadrafa, Palmyra, Syria AD 55, British Museum, used with permission, http://www.britishmuseum.org/explore/highlights/highlight_objects/me/l/limestone_relief,_god_shadrafa.aspx.

FIG. App.1 Author standing on Lone Mound, Warren Minnesota.

FIG. App.2 Vidcaps of a Russian (Georgia) news program with Dr. Abesalom Vekua and giant bones. LA: 12-20-2012, http://www.youtube.com/watch?v=XQqc4entqvg.

FIG. App.3 (Left). Kumastamo, File: yuma1.gif and (Upper Right), File: bly1.gif, (Lower Right). Giants of Blythe (Middle pic taken by author). All files are found here: http://www.hows.org.uk/personal/hillfigs/foreign/colo/colora.htm.

FIG. App.4 (Left). File: Cerne-abbas-giant-2001-cropped.jpg, PD, Wikipedia, LA 12-20-2012, http://en.wikipedia.org/wiki/Cerne_Abbas_Giant; (Midde and Right). See Fig. 3.3.

FIG. App.5 Long Man of Wilmington, England. PD, LA 12-20-2012, http://www.thefriendlyfisherman.co.uk/articles/fly-fishing-venues/arlington_reservoir.asp.

FIG. App.6 Four figures of Northern European horned men. PD; LA 12-20-2012, http://www.millennia.f2s.com/dancing.htm.

FIG. App.7 (Upper Left). "Man Mound," Sauk County Historical Society, Aug 9, 2008, http://www.saukcountyhistory.org/manmoundcentennial.html; Man Mound, circa 1908, Sauck County Historical Society, http://www.saukcountyhistory.org/societyparkssites/manmoundpark.html; (Middle). Other Wisconsin effigies, Susquehanna River Archaeological Center, http://sracenter.blogspot.com/2008_08_01_archive.html. (Bottom). Horned "Skier," see Fig. App. 6 for link.

FIG. App.8-9 Various Rock Art of the Fremont Indians, PD, from left to right: author's pic, Fremont Irish Canyon, Moffat County, CO, Google Earth, File: Petroglyph jqjacobs.jpg, PD, widipedia, LA 12-20-2012, http://en.wikipedia.org/wiki/File:Petroglyph_jqjacobs.jpg; http://www.panoramio.com/photo/27361097, "Owl Man" and drawing LA 12-20-2012, http://rockartblog.blogspot.com/2009/09/birds-in-rock-art-burrowing-owls.html; "Bigfoot," James Q. Jacobs art (with many excellent examples), LA 12-20-2012, http://www.jqjacobs.net/rock_art/ne_utah1.html. Barrier Canyon Glyphs, LA 12-20-2012, http://rosebud.moenkopi.net/trips/barrier/barrier.html; Diagram of horned men, jqjacobs, LA 12-20-2012, http://www.jqjacobs.net/rock_art/barrier2.html.

FIG. App.10 (Left). File: Oni.jpg, PD, Wikipedia, LA 12-20-2012, http://en.wikipedia.org/wiki/Oni; (Middle-Left). Oni, PD, Wikia, LA 12-20-2012, http://touhou.wikia.com/wiki/Oni; (Middle-Right). Oni polishing a sceptor, Ronin Gallery, LA 12-20-2012, http://www.roningallery.com/art/netsuke/unsigned/oni/; (Right). File: Samurai on horseback,png, PD, Wikipedia, LA 12-20-2012, http://en.wikipedia.org/wiki/File:Samurai_on_horseback.png.

FIG. App.11 (Left). African Ivory of six fingered giant, PD, LA 12-28-2011, http://www.6000years.org/giant_pics.html; (Middle-Left). Файл: Anty bljashka.jpg, PD, Wikipedia, LA 12-19-2012, http://uk.wikipedia.org/wiki/%D0%A4%D0%B0%D0%B9%D0%BB:Anty_bljashka.jpg; (Middle-Right and Right). Two different rock art depictions of six fingered hands, "The Sacred Ridge," Three Rivers, NM, PD, LA 12-25-2012, http://fdocc.blogspot.com/2006/01/three-rivers-and-six-fingers-thrice.html.

FIG. App.12 (Left). Z43.1 "Wounded Gigantes," Mosaic, Villa Romana del Casale (ca 320 AD), Italy, PD, LA 12-25-2012, http://www.theoi.com/Gallery/Z43.1.html, (Upper Right). File: DSC04529a Istanbul - Museo archeol. - Gigantomachia - sec. II d.C. - da Afrodisia - Foto G. Dall'Orto 28-5-2006.jpg, 1st century AD frieze, the Agora of Aphrodisias, PD, Wikipedia, LA 12-25-2012, http://en.wikipedia.org/wiki/Giants_(Greek_mythology); (Lower Right). K12.9, "Dionysos & the Giant Eurytos, Antikenmuseen, Berlin, Germany, (ca 510 BC), PD, LA 12-25-2012, http://www.theoi.com/Gallery/K12.9.html.

FIG. App.13 (Left). Serpent Mound, Ohio. Photo by author. (Upper Right). Serpent Mound sign, Ohio. Photo by author. (Lower Right). File: Serpent Mound.jpg, PD, Wikipedia, LA 12-25-2012, http://en.wikipedia.org/wiki/Serpent_mound.

FIG. App.14. File: Robert Wadlow.jpg, PD, Wikipedia, LA 12-25-2012, http://en.wikipedia.org/wiki/Robert_Wadlow.

FIG. FN 1. File: Orion Belt.jpg, PD, Wikipedia, LA 12-25-2012; http://en.wikipedia.org/wiki/File:Orion_Belt.jpg; Tenochititlán, Google Earth, Mexico, Pyramids of Giza, Egypt, Google Earth, Thornborough Henges, England, Google Earth.

FIG. FN 2. Screenshot: "Aliens and the Secret Code," 17:00, courtesy The History Channel, http://www.youtube.com/watch?v=iy2ZApn5nhA.

FIG. FN 3. Egyptian Execration text 1900 BC mentioning Jerusalem, Rusalimum, Z. Radovan, www.BibleLandPictures.com.

FIG. FN 4. Huge double axes, Heraklion Archeological Museum, Greece (1700 BC), PD, LA 12-25-2012, http://www.coasttocoastam.com/photo/view/evidence_for_giants/46141.

FIG. FN 5. "The Kurgan Invasions," T.R. Holme, LA 12-25-2012, http://www.trholme.com/garden-e-danu/GG6.htm.

FIG. FN 6. (Left). Scythian horsemen, 4 cent. BC, Black Sea, The State Hermitage Museum, St. Petersburg, Russia, PD, LA 12-25-2012, http://dream-warrior.bestforumonline.com/t326-origins-of-the-sagittarius-mythos; (Right). File: Naqsh i Rustam. Investiture d'Ardaship 1.jpg, Naqsh-e Rustam, 3rd c. AD, PD, Wikipedia, LA 12-25-2012, http://en.wikipedia.org/wiki/Ardashir_I.

FIG. FN 7. Cardiff Giant, courtesy Farmers Museum via Associated Press, 1869, PD, LA 12-25-2012, http://news.nationalgeographic.com/news/2009/03/photogalleries/april-fools-day-hoaxes/#/cardiff-giant_4589_600x450.jpg.

Endnotes

NOTES FOR PREFACE (Pgs. xv-xviii)

[1] My friend called this the "earliest note I've ever seen in a book." I love footnotes and despise endnotes. Nevertheless, this book has endnotes. I've come to discover that not everyone shares my love of footnotes. Endnotes are put in books deliberately to keep you from reading them! For sake of readability and those of you who want to follow the main argument without all those nasty interruptions, I have endnotes for you. Many are references, not really worth the time unless you want to search something out for yourself. But some notes offer further reflections and insights. Some of these, which I think you may find particularly helpful or interesting, I will alert you to in the book with boldface and underline of the number. For example, instead of [1] it will be **[1]**.

[2] Patrick Heron, *The Nephilim and the Pyramid of the Apocalypse* (New York, NY: Citadel Press, 2004).

[3] The link is found here: http://kimriddlebarger.squarespace.com/just-plain-nutty/.

[4] See for example, Michael S. Heiser, *The Bible Code Myth* (Acid Test Press, 2001). Available in PDF.

[5] Some in my own collection include Timothy Green Beckley, *Giants on the Earth* (New Brunswick, NJ: Global Communications/Conspiracy Journal, 2009); Charles DeLoach, *Giants: A Reference Guide from History, the Bible, and Recorded Legend* (Metuchen, NJ: Scarecrow Press, 1995); Jonathan Gray, *Lost World of the Giants* (Brushton, NY: TEACH Services, Inc. 2006); Stephen Quayle, *Genesis 6 Giants* (Bozeman, MT: End Time Thunder Publishers, 2002).

NOTES FOR INTRODUCTION (Pgs. 1-48)

[1] In 1974 some local farmers discovered this remarkable find of 8,000 life-sized army figures along with hundreds of others figures including warriors, horses, chariots, officials, acrobats, strongmen and musicians near the Mausoleum of Emperor Qin in the Lintong District of Xi'an China, which also just so happens to be home of perhaps the largest concentration of ancient pyramids in the world. The terracotta were made famous in the third *Mummy* movie (The Mummy: Tomb of the Dragon Emperor, 2008; Directed by Rob Cohen).

[2] Words denoted with a *___* can be found in the Glossary at the end of the book.

[3] This is the English translation by Sir Lancelot C. L. Brenton, *The Septuagint with Apocrypha* (London: Samuel Bagster & Sons, 1851).

[4] For more on why Jews changed their earlier supernatural theology after the arrival of Christ, see Alan Segal, *Two Powers in Heaven: Early Rabbinic Reports about Christianity and Gnosticism* (Boston, Brill Academic Pub, 2002).

[5] *Genesis Rabbah* 26:5. http://www.archive.org/stream/midrashrabbahgen027557mbp#page/n259/mode/2up

[6] In fact, Jesus seems to make this very point to the Pharisees and they understood it perfectly (these Rabbis in the NT era had not yet squashed the supernatural view). In John 10:34 Jesus cites Psalm 82:6 in support of his claim that he has come from heaven. In citing the verse that says, "I said 'You are gods, sons of the Most High'", it is best not to see this as a reference to human beings, but to heavenly beings of the heavenly divine council (see Ps 82:1 ESV). It makes no sense that Jesus would be telling the Pharisees that they are gods in some limited judicial earthly sense (see note #49 "A note on the word '*elohim*"), and that he is simply claiming to be like them, as it is often interpreted, because the Pharisees still want to stone Jesus for blasphemy (John 10:36, 39). Instead, it is better to see this as a reference to the heavenly beings, of which Jesus says he is greater even than they, as he is one with the Father. See Michael Heiser, "You've Seen One

Elohim, You've Seen Them All? A Critique of Mormonism's Use of Psalm 82," *FARMS Review* 19/1 (2007): 221–266. http://maxwellinstitute.byu.edu/publications/review/?vol=19&num=1&id=643

[7] A. Roberts, J. Donaldson, A. C. Coxe and A. Menzies, *The Ante-Nicene Fathers* (Buffalo: Christian Literature, 1886), 6.131.

[8] Catholic University of America, *Fathers of the Church: A New Translation*. Washington, D.C.: Catholic University of America Press, 1947, 91:134-35. Ephrem is discussed by Arie van der Kooij in, "Peshitta Genesis 6: 'Sons of God' – Angels of Judges?' in *Journal of Northwest Semitic Languages* 23/1 (1997): 43-51, available in PDF: https://openaccess.leidenuniv.nl/bitstream/1887/10388/1/914-36.pdf. The concluding paragraph of this article states, "The time and circumstances of this anti-angelological revision in Gen 6 are not known to us. One might think here of criticism of the dualistic ideas of Mani and his followers by 'orthodox' circles in Edessa in the second half of the third century. If so, these circles would have done so by drawing on a rendering/interpretation which had a Jewish (Targumic) background."

[9] A more detailed study of the history of the interpretation of this passage can be found in Robert C. Newman, "The Ancient Exegesis of Genesis 6:2, 4," *Grace Theological Journal*, vol. 5.1 (1984): 13-36.

[10] Philip Schaff, *The Nicene and Post-Nicene Fathers Vol. II* (Oak Harbor: Logos Research Systems, 1997), 303.

[11] Martin Luther, vol. 2, *Luther's Works, Vol. 2 : Lectures on Genesis: Chapters 6-14*, ed. Jaroslav Jan Pelikan, Hilton C. Oswald and Helmut T. Lehmann, Luther's Works (Saint Louis: Concordia Publishing House, 1999), Gen 6:2.

[12] John Calvin and John King, *Commentary on the First Book of Moses Called Genesis* (Bellingham, WA: Logos Research Systems, Inc., 2010), Gen 6:1.

[13] Justin, *Apology* 1.5.

[14] Irenaeus, *Demonstration* 18; *Heresies* 4.16.2, 4.36.4.

[15] Athenagoras, *A Plea for the Christians* 24.

[16] Pseudo Clement, *Homily* 8:13.

[17] Clement of Alexandria, *Miscellenaries* 5.1.10.

[18] Tertullian, *The Veiling of Virgins* 7; *Against Marcion* 5.18; *On Idolatry* 9.

[19] Lactantius, *Divine Institutes* 2.15.

[20] Eusebius, *Preparation* 5.4.

[21] Commodian, *Instructions* 1.3.

[22] Ambrose, *Noah and the Ark* 4.8.

[23] Jerome, *Hebrew* 6.4.

[24] Sulpicius Severus, *History 1, 2*.

[25] William van Gemeren concurs and puts the question forcefully, "Why does the theology in which creation, miracles, the miraculous birth and resurrection of Jesus have a place, prefer a rational explanation of Genesis 6:1–4? … What concerns me is a seeming inconsistency. Normally, the goal of interpretation has been the elucidation of the Word of God so the community of faith may know what to believe and what to do. When, however, the object of interpretation becomes the removal of apparent obstacles to which the passage may give rise, reinterpretation is introduced, and one may wonder how this differs from demythologization. It is granted that it is hard to imagine how preternatural (angelic, supernatural, demonic) beings have sexual relations with women of the human race and father offspring. But is the difficulty so great that it *must* be removed as something offensive? Is it possible that theology has taken the place of exegesis?" See W. A. van Gemeren, "The Sons of God in Genesis 6:1–4 (An Example of Evangelical Demythologization?)," *Westminster Theological Journal* 43 (1981): 320.

[26] Besides Luther and Calvin, Theodoret, a contemporary of Augustine, calls anyone who holds the angelic view "mad fools" (Theodoret, *Questions on Genesis: XLVII*). Chrysostom may be the harshest of all, throwing the whole tradition not only out the window, but right into the pit of hell when he says, "There is need

to make a careful study of this passage and confute the fanciful interpretations of those people whose every remark is made rashly ... by demonstrating the absurdity of what is said by them ... so that you will not lend your ears idly to people uttering those blasphemies and presuming to speak in a way that brings their own persons into jeopardy" (Chrysostom, *Homilies on Genesis 22.6*). Incredible!

[27] A few, including commentaries on Genesis that do not deal with 2 Peter 2:4, Jude 6, and other biblical texts, still hold to the Sethite view. Cf. K. A. Mathews, vol. 1A, *Genesis 1-11:26*, The New American Commentary (Nashville: Broadman & Holman Publishers, 2001), 322-32; Harold G. Stigers, *A Commentary on Genesis* (Grand Rapids: Zondervan, 1967).

[28] The most famous is Meredith G. Kline, "Divine Kingship and Genesis 6:1-4," *Westminster Theological Journal* 24.2 (1962): 187-204. See also E. Kraeling, "The Significance and Origin of Gen. 6:1-4," *Journal of Near Eastern Studies* 6 (1947): 193-208; A. R. Millard, "A New Babylonian 'Genesis' Story," *Tyndale Bulletin* 18 (1967): 12 and notes 27-29. A variation of this view combines it with ST1 so that these rulers are also divine like Gilgamesh. See D. J. A. Clines, "The Significance of the 'Sons of God' Episode (Genesis 6:1–4) in the Context of the 'Primeval History' (Genesis 1–11)," *Journal for the Study of the Old Testament* 13 (1979): 34–35. To me, this kind of a merging is plausible and perhaps even correct.

[29] Cf. Clinton E. Arnold, *Zondervan Illustrated Bible Backgrounds Commentary Volume 4: Hebrews to Revelation* (Grand Rapids, MI: Zondervan, 2002), 236; Richard J. Bauckham, *Jude 2 Peter*, Word Biblical Commentary (Waco, TX: Word Books, 1983), 50-53; Edwin A. Blum, *Jude*, The Expositors Bible Commentary Vol. 12 (Grand Rapids, MI: Zondervan, 1981), 390; Peter H. Davids, *The Letters of 2 Peter and Jude*, Pillar New Testament Commentary (Grand Rapids, MI: Eerdmans, 2006), 48-51; Gene L. Green, *Jude & 2 Peter*, Baker Exegetical Commentary on the New Testament (Grand Rapids, MI: Baker Academic, 2008), 66-70; Michael Green, *2 Peter and Jude*, Tyndale New Testament Commentaries (Downers Grove, IL: InterVarsity, 1987), 191-92; Douglas J. Moo, *2 Peter, Jude*, NIV Application Commentary (Grand Rapids, MI: Zondervan, 1996), 241-42; Thomas R. Schreiner, *1, 2 Peter, Jude*, New American Commentary (Nashville, TN: Broadman & Holman, 2003), 447-51; Robert L. Webb, "The Use of 'Story' in the Letter of Jude: Rhetorical Strategies of Jude's Narrative Episodes," *Journal for the Study of the New Testament* 31 (2008): 56-57.

Agreement with this interpretation with or without reference to Jude and Peter include: Lamar Eugene Cooper, Sr., *Ezekiel*, New American Commentary (Nashville: Broadman and Holman, 1994), 267; Nahum M. Sarna, *Genesis*, The JPS Torah Commentary (Philadelphia: Jewish Publication Society, 1989), 45-46; W. A. van Gemeren, "The Sons of God in Genesis 6:1–4 (An Example of Evangelical Demythologization?)," *WTJ* 43 (1981): 320–48; Michael S. Heiser, "The Divine Council in Late Canonical and Non-Canonical Second Temple Jewish Literature," A Dissertation at the University of Wisconsin-Madison, 2004: 217-228; Gordon J. Wenham, vol. 1, *Word Biblical Commentary : Genesis 1-15*, Word Biblical Commentary (Dallas: Word, Incorporated, 2002), 139-43; Archie T. Wright, *The Origin of Evil Spirits: The Reception of Genesis 6.1-4 in Early Jewish Literature* (Tübingen: Mohr Siebeck, 2004), 73. Theologians include: James M. Boice, *Foundations of the Christian Faith* (Downers Grove, IL: InterVarsity, 1986), 173; Robert Duncan Culver, *Systematic Theology* (Great Britain: Mentor, 2005), 178; Millard Erickson, *Christian Theology* (Grand Rapids, MI: Baker, 1998), 659; Charles Feinberg, *The Prophecy of Ezekiel* (Chicago: Moody Press, 1969), Arthur W. Pink, *Gleanings in Genesis* (Bellingham, WA: Logos Research Systems, Inc., 2005), 92-95; 161; Robert L. Reymond, *A New Systematic Theology of the Christian Faith* (Nashville: Thomas Nelson, 1998), 659; Francis Schaeffer, "Genesis in Space and Time," in *The Complete Works of Francis A. Schaeffer: A Christian Worldview* (Westchester, IL: Crossway Books, 1996), p. 89; Merrill F. Unger, "The Old Testament Revelation Concerning Eternity Past," *Bibliotheca Sacra* 114:454 (Apr '57): 135-41; and many others.

[30] John Murray, *Principles of Conduct* (Grand Rapids: Wm. B. Eerdmans, 1957), 246.

[31] The Septuagint does read that Seth "called his name Enosh: he hoped to call on the name of the Lord God." But this translation also has problems, for it seems to imply that he did not think he had much hope in doing so. Why would he think this given the grace that God showed to Adam, Eve, and Cain?

[32] The name Enosh can mean either frailty/mortality or "man" (cf. Deut 32:26; Job 4:17; Ps 8:4 etc). The idea seems to be that there is a word play going on between Enosh (a man's name) and *enosh* (mankind).

[33] It could be argued that not all of these men were godly. Methuselah, for instance, has the possible meaning "man of the dart," as in a kind of weapon. Also, his son is named Lamech, who as we have seen was the archetypal polygamist-murderer in the line of Cain. His name means "powerful/destroyer."

[34] The equivocation continues in vs. 3, "The Lord God said, My Spirit shall certainly not remain among these men forever." Obviously, God is referring to all mankind, for he destroys everyone but Noah and his family. Yet, the previous meaning was Sethites. Then again in vs. 4 the "daughters of men" return and we are back to Sethites. Thus, back and forth we go with our interpretation of the word *'adam.*

[35] The ancient Jewish work *The Life of Adam and Eve* actually says that Adam had 30 sons and 30 daughters. VitaAE 24:3.

[36] G. Mussies, "Giants," in *Dictionary of Deities and Demons in the Bible DDD*, 2nd extensively rev. ed., ed. K. van der Toorn, Bob Becking and Pieter Willem van der Horst (Leiden; Boston; Grand Rapids, Mich.: Brill; Eerdmans, 1999), 343.

[37] Francis Schaeffer, "Genesis in Space and Time," in *The Complete Works of Francis A. Schaeffer: A Christian Worldview* (Westchester, IL: Crossway Books, 1996), p. 89.

[38] C. S. Lewis, "Autobiography: The Letters of C. S. Lewis to Arthur Greeves," in *The Essential C.S. Lewis.* ed. Lyle W. Dorsett (New York: Touchstone, 1996), 56; J. R. R. Tolkien, "A Letter to Milton Waldman," reprinted in *The Simarillion* (New York: Houghton Mifflin Co, 2001), p. xv; J. R. R. Tolkien, *The Tolkien Reader* (New York: Del Rey, 1968), 88-89.

[39] Nephilim does not, however, refer _to_ the heavenly beings, as if they _are_ the heavenly beings, as some want to make them.

[40] This view is proposed by H. Gunkel, *Genesis* (Göttingen, 1910), 58-59, and elaborated on by Michael Heiser, *The Myth That Is True* (unpublished), 79-83. Available to purchase at: http://www.michaelsheiser.com/. Ronald Hendel ("Of Demigods and the Deluge: Toward an Interpretation of Genesis 6:1–4", *Journal of Biblical Literature* 106 [1987]: 22 n. 46) sees the word as being a something like a qaṭil passive adjective of *naphal*, but this does not explain the alternate spelling. See the discussion below.

[41] A good discussion of this is found in John C. Reeves, *Jewish Lore in Manichaean Cosmogony: Studies in the Book of Giants Traditions* (Cincinnati: Hebrew Union College Press, 1992), 69-72.

[42] For example, in the aptly titled "Book of Giants" it appears in 1Q23 Frag. 9; 4Q530 col. ii:13, 15; 4Q530 Frag. 6 col. i:8 and many other places. Remarkably, it is combined with *nephilim/nephylin* in 4Q531 Frag. 5:2; cf. 4Q530 col. ii:20.

[43] Shem, of course, is the name of Noah's youngest son. The Bible takes this word *shem* and begins to make a word-play beginning in Genesis 11 and the Tower of Babel. Nimrod, the giant (*gibborim*; Gen 10:9) who built the tower (Gen 10:10) wanted to make a "name" (*shem*) for himself (Gen 11:4). But by the end of the story, it is God who makes the name for himself, first by dispersing the people and scattering them over the face of the earth, and then by choosing Abraham who would come from the line of Shem, of whom the promise was given of the coming Messiah (Gen 9:26-27; 11:10-30).

[44] "...Zeus, son of Kronos, created yet another fourth generation on the fertile earth, and these were better and nobler, the wonderful generation of hero-men, who are also called half-gods, the generation before our own on this vast earth. But of these too, evil war and the terrible carnage took some ..." Hesiod, *The Works and Days*, trans. Richmond Lattimore (Ann Arbor: University of Michigan, 1959), 37.

[45] P. W. Coxen, "Gibborim," in *Dictionary of Deities and Demons in the Bible DDD*, 2nd extensively rev. ed., ed. K. van der Toorn, Bob Becking and Pieter Willem van der Horst (Leiden; Boston; Grand Rapids, Mich.: Brill; Eerdmans, 1999), p. 345.

[46] Chrysostom, *Homilies on Genesis 22.6.*

[47] Keil and Delitzsch refer to Hosea 1:10 "sons of the living God" as proof of their Sethite view. However, this verse is a prophecy which is fulfilled in the NT (cf. John 1:12; Rom 8:14-23; Gen 3:26 etc). See Carl Friedrich Keil and Franz Delitzsch, *Commentary on the Old Testament* (Peabody, MA: Hendrickson, 2002), Gen 6:1.

[48] That is, when it is in the construct form as this is. The normal plural for ben in *benim*.

[49] A note on the word *'elohim*. Despite arguments to the contrary, it has never been demonstrated that this word *incontrovertibly* means a human being in *any* verse in the Bible. The closest is probably 1 Sam 28:13 where the dead spirit of Samuel is described by this term, but importantly, this refers to the dead Samuel's spirit, not to Samuel when alive. Often Psalm 82:6 is referred to as proof that humans can be gods. A quick search of any good Study Bible's notes here shows that it is far from certain that these *'elohim* refer to human beings. Michael Heiser has done the best work on Psalm 82:6 to date. For a synopsis see Michael Heiser, "You've Seen One Elohim, You've Seen Them All? A Critique of Mormonism's Use of Psalm 82," *FARMS Review* 19/1 (2007): 221–266. Other references sometimes cited in support of the idea that "gods" in this Psalm refer to humans include Ex 21:6; 22:8, 9, 20. This understanding is also far from certain, and has been severely criticized by Cyrus Gordon, "אלהים (Elohim) in Its Reputed Meaning of *Rulers, Judges*," *Journal of Biblical Literature* 54 (1935): 139–144.

[50] John William Wevers, vol. I, *Genesis*, Vetus Testamentum Graecum. Auctoritate Academiae Scientiarum Gottingensis editum (Göttingen: Vandenhoeck & Ruprecht, 1974), 109.

[51] The LXX reading is almost certainly the original. See Michael S. Heiser, "Deuteronomy 32:8 and the Sons of God," *Bibliotheca Sacra: 158:629* (Jan-Mar, 2001): 52-74.

[52] Gordon Douglas Young, *Ugarit in Retrospect* (Winona Lake, IN: Eisenbrauns, 1981), 16.

[53] Some terms found in Ugarit are as follows: *phr 'ilm* -- "the assembly of El / the gods" (*A Dictionary of the Ugaritic Language in the Alphabetic Tradition* [*DULAT*] 2:669; *Keilalphabetische Texte aus Ugarit* [*KTU*] 1.47:29; 1.118:28; 1.148:9); *phr bn'ilm* – "the assembly of the sons of El/the gods" (*DULAT* 2:669; *KTU* 1.4.III:14); *phr kkbm* – "the assembly of the stars" (*DULAT* 2:670; *KTU* 1.10.I:4) (parallel to *bn 'il* in Job 38:7-8); *mphrt bn 'il* – "the assembly of the gods" (*DULAT 2:566; KTU 1.65:3); 'dt 'ilm* – "assembly of El/the gods" (*DULAT* 1:152; *KTU* 1.15.II:7, 11); *dr 'il* – "assembly (circle) of El" (*DULAT 1:279-80; KTU 1.15.II:19; 1.39:7; 1.162:16; 1.87:18); dr bn 'il* – "assembly (circle) of the sons of El" (*DULAT* 1:279-80; *KTU* 1.40:25, 33-34); *dr dt šmm* – "assembly (circle) of those of heaven" (*DULAT* 1:279-80; *KTU* 1.10.I:3, 5); *dr 'il wphr b'l* – "assembly (circle) of El and the assembly of Baal" (*DULAT* 1:279-80; *KTU* 1.39:7; 1.62:16; 1.87:18).

[54] On the "seventy" sons at Ugarit see *KTU* 1.4 VI.46; *CTA* 4.6.38-59.

[55] Most notably in Psalm 82:1 where God takes his seat in the "assembly of El" (NET), which is correctly interpreted as the "divine council" by the ESV. See the important article from Michael Heiser in note 51 (above).

[56] In Exodus 15:27 you have the "seventy palm trees" of Elim (*elim* means "gods"). Targum Pseudo-Jonathan Deut 32:8 reads, "When the Most High made allotment of the world unto the nations which proceeded from the sons of Noah, in the separation of the writings and languages of the children of men at the time of the division, He cast the lot among the seventy angels, the princes of the nations with whom is the revelation to oversee the city, even at that time He established the limits of the nations according to the sum of the number of the seventy souls of Israel who went down into Mizraim [Egypt]." See also 1 Enoch 89:59-77; 90:22-27. See the discussions in Margaret Barker, *The Revelation of Jesus Christ* (Edinburgh: T&T Clark, 2000), 226-31; John Day, *God's Conflict with the Dragon and the Sea* (London: Cambridge

Giants of the Bible

University Press, 1985), 175-75; Day, *Yahweh and the Gods and Goddesses of Canaan* (New York: Continuum, 2002), 23-24; Michael S. Heiser, "Deuteronomy 32:8 and the Sons of God." *Bibliotheca Sacra* 158:629 (Jan-Mar, 2001): 52-74.

[57] For example, "Before the gods I sing your praise" (Ps 138:1); "Worship him, all you gods!" (Ps 97:7); "God has taken his place in the divine council; in the midst of the gods he holds judgment" (Ps 82:1). In each case the word "gods" is the Hebrew "*elohim*." God is not asking cartoon characters or figments of the human imagination or sticks in the mud to worship him. He is commanding the heavenly beings, created by him, to worship him.

[58] Isa 44:24; John 1:3; 1 Cor 8:5-6; Eph 3:9; Col 1:16; Heb 1:2-4. Hence he is the "God of gods" (Deut 10:17; Ps 50:1; 84:7; 136:2).

[59] LXX Job 1:6; 2:1; 38:7; Ps 29:1; 97:7; 138:1, etc.

[60] See note #56 and the "seventy palms of Elim."

[61] It is true that sometimes the ancient kings were referred to in the same way (see Kline, "Divine Kingship," 192). What Kline does not take into account, though he should know better because he talks about it in his writings, is the role of the divine council, the heavenly court of sons of God (Ps 82:1), and how this is often the context of the usage in the Bible. You can find a good primer on the divine council on Michael Heiser's website, but I will not discuss it further here, lest we get utterly bogged down and off track. Even if we run with Kline's argument, the most it shows is that humans can also be called sons of God in pagan cultures. Of course, these gods may very well have been semi-divine themselves (Nephilim). Even if the later kinds were not, their ancestors certainly could have been and the later kinds merely retained the title for themselves. Thus, some have tried to merge the angelic view and the divine kingship view together. Taken this way, there is nothing contradictory about a heavenly being or its offspring ruling over humans as tyrants and kings. I tend to think this is exactly what happened.

[62] Meredith Kline, *Kingdom Prologue* (Overland Park, KS: Two Age Press, 2000), 8.

[63] Cf. Gen 9:12; 15:16; 17:7, etc.

[64] Betty Champion, *Yes We Can Be Perfect In Our Generation* (LaGrange, GA: World Overcomer's Church Int., 2002), 119.

[65] This is the typical meaning of the phrase, "saw his father's nakedness" (Gen 9:22) in the OT. See Lev 18:8; 20:11, 17; Deut 22:30; 27:20. See John Sietze Bergsma, "Noah's Nakedness and the Curse of Canaan (Gen 9:20-27)," in *Journal of Biblical Literature* 124/1 (2005): 25-40. Available online: http://www.sbl-site.org/assets/pdfs/jbl1241.pdf.

[66] John Walton, *Covenant: God's Purpose, God's Plan* (Grand Rapids, MI: Zondervan, 1994), 72-73.

[67] This point seems to have been made in the second century B.C. when the book of Jubilees says, "… [Enoch] bore witness to the Watchers, the ones who sinned with the daughters of men because they began to mingle themselves with the daughters of men so that they might be polluted. And Enoch bore witness against all of them" (Jub 4:22).

[68] This reference is found in the ancient Babylonian Talmud, *Sotah* 34a. The text literally says they carried it "between two." English translations supply the word "men" after "two," "between two men." But the Rabbis thought it was rather between two staffs and was so large that it took almost all of the spies to carry it to Moses. Their purpose was to discourage the people from taking over the land by bringing back this (genetically manipulated?) cluster of grapes.

[69] Mary Douglas writes that these "purity laws" serve to keep "distinct the categories of creation." *Purity and Danger: An Analysis of the Concepts of Pollution and Taboo* (London: Routledge & Kegan Paul, 1966) 41–57; *Implicit Meanings: Essays in Anthropology* (London: Routledge & Kegan Paul, 1975) 261–73, 283–318.

[70] See Dante Fortson, *As The Days of Noah Were*, (self published, 2010), ch. 9, www.MinisterFortson.com.

[71] For more on this idea see Ronald S. Hendel, "Of Demigods and the Deluge: Toward an Interpretation of Genesis 6:1–4", *Journal of Biblical Literature* 106 (1987): 23-25.

[72] See Louisiana's RS 14:89.6 http://www.legis.state.la.us/billdata/streamdocument.asp?did=664992, Arizona's S.B. 1307 – 492R: http://www.azleg.gov/legtext/49leg/2r/summary/s.1307pshs_aspassed.doc.htm; Ohio's SB 243 http://www.legislature.state.oh.us/bills.cfm?ID=128_SB_243. Each of these bills has been passed into law.

[73] It reads, "There were men of great strength and size on the earth in those days; and after that, when the sons of God had connection with the daughters of men, they gave birth to children: these were the great men of old days, the men of great name."

[74] See Douglas Phillips, "The Mystery of the Nephilim Presented and Solved: Discovering the True Giants of Paganism," in *Mysteries of the Ancient World*, an audio series (San Antonio, TX: Vision Forum, 2008).

[75] See Appendix: 2 Peter 2:4 and Jude 6.

[76] See Justo L. González, "Demythologization," in *Essential Theological Terms* (Louisville, KY: Westminster John Knox Press, 2005), 44.

NOTES FOR CHAPTER 1: PRE-FLOOD GIANTS (Pgs. 49-68)

[1] The two kingdoms doctrine was further developed by the two wings of the Protestant Reformation: Lutheran and Reformed. For a good Reformed summary of this topic see David VanDrunen, *Living in God's Two Kingdoms* (Wheaton, IL: Crossway, 2010).

[2] Israel is a type of the heavenly kingdom which is inaugurated in Christ's First Coming and consummated in his Second Coming.

[3] As pointed out in the Introduction, Cain cannot be viewed as the physical descendant of Satan as the so called "Serpent Seed" heresy teaches, because Cain is unequivocally said to be the son of Adam (Gen 4:1). For a good, non-technical introduction to this topic see Dante Fortson, *The Serpent Seed: Debunked* (Impact Agenda Media, 2010).

[4] While the Serpent Seed doctrine teaches that Satan had relations with Eve, the curse is more broadly spoken to "the *nachash*" (the serpent). Satan is a *nachash*, but not all *nachash* are Satan. Nachash is a Hebrew term applied to Satan (Gen 3:1; Isa 27:1) as well as to other heavenly beings called *seraphim* (see Num 21:6-9; Deut 8:15; Isa 14:29; Jer 8:17 and the discussions in *DDD*, "Serpent," 744-747; Karen Joines, *Serpent Symbolism in the Old Testament: A Linguistic, Archaeological, and Literary Study* (Haddonfield House, New Jersey, 1974); and Michael S. Heiser, "Serpentine / Reptilian Divine Beings in the Hebrew Bible: A Preliminary Investigation," http://www.scribd.com/doc/63497725/Michael-s-Heiser-Serpentine.

[5] The same idea is found in Gen 4:19 when the wicked Lamech "took" two women who bore him children and in Gen 11:29 when Abram "took" Sarai for his wife. Might the former refer to some kind of unlawful taking? The text does not elaborate.

[6] One of the most frightening contemporary expressions of women being filled with lust for the sons of God can be seen in the Katie Perry video: E.T. The lyrics and video are *extremely* disturbing in light of the Genesis 6 event and Perry's background from Christian fundamentalism.

[7] For example, in the Testament of Reuben we read, "[The Watchers] were transformed into human males, and while the women were cohabiting with their husbands they appeared to them" (TReu 5:6). 1 Enoch says, "Whenever they want, they appear as men" (1 Enoch 17:1). See Kelley Coblentz Bautch, *A Study of the Geography of 1 Enoch 17-19* (Boston: Brill, 2003), 46-49. On shape shifting in Greek mythology see Homer, *Odyssey* 4.315-462; Ovid, *Metamorphosis* 11.250-263. You can also see this in the recent Hollywood production *Clash of the Titans*, when Zeus comes to the human Queen Danaë in the form of her husband King Acrisius and from this union, the *demigod* Perseus is born.

[8] See Chapter 2.

[9] Unless otherwise noted, the meanings of Bible names throughout this book are found in Stelman Smith and Judson Cornwall, *The Exhaustive Dictionary of Bible Names* (North Brunswick, NJ: Bridge-Logos, 1998). Recently, I began seeing a clever usage of the names of Genesis 5 pop up on Facebook and traced its source.

Chuck Missler has argued that all of the names from Adam to Noah tell the story of the gospel in a sort of cryptic Bible-code: Man (Adam) Appointed (Seth) Mortal (Enosh) Sorrow (Kenan) The Blessed God (Mahalalel) Shall Come Down (Jared) Teaching (Enoch) His Death Shall Bring (Methuselah) The Despairing (Lamech) Rest/Comfort (Noah). See Chuck Missler, "Meanings of the Names in Genesis 5," http://www.khouse.org/articles/2000/284/#notes. While clever, this approach probably goes too far because there are other possible meanings for the names, some of the names he gives are dubious, and God doesn't need secret codes of names to give us the gospel. In my study of the names (below), I am only commenting on how those names may be used to explain the era in which the children were born.

[10] For example, "[I saw Watchers] in my vision, the dream-vision. Two (men) were fighting over me, saying . . . and holding a great contest over me. I asked them, 'Who are you, that you are thus empo[wered over me?' They answered me, 'We] [have been em]powered and rule over all mankind.' They said to me, 'Which of us do yo[u choose to rule (you)?' I raised my eyes and looked.] [One] *of them was terr[i]fying in his appearance, [like a serpent, [his] cl[oa]k many-colored yet very dark. . .* [And I looked again], and . . . *in his appearance, his visage like a viper. . ."* Test Amram, Q543 Frag vi: 9-14 (See Robert H. Eiseman and Michael Owen Wise, *The Dead Sea Scrolls Uncovered* [New York: Penguin Books, 1993], 164. Satan, likewise, is depicted not as a snake, but as something like a seraphim. "Standing (something) like a dragon in form, but having hands and feet like a man's, on his back six wings on the right and six on the left." Apocalypse of Abraham 23:7.

[11] For example, Jubilees 7:22, "And they begot sons, the Naphidim, and all of them were dissimilar. And each one ate his fellow. The giants killed the Naphil, and the Naphil killed the Elyo, and the Elyo mankind, and man his neighbor." 1 Baruch 3:26, "There were the giants famous from the beginning, that were of so great stature, and so expert in war." 3 Maccabees 2:4, "It was thou who didst destroy the former workers of unrighteousness, among whom were the giants, who trusted in their strength and hardihood, by covering them with a measureless flood."

[12] Jude quotes from 1 Enoch 1:9 and tells us that these are the words of Enoch who lived before the Flood. This section on giants is less than 20 verses away from the verse quoted by Jude.

[13] George W. E. Nickelsburg and Klaus Baltzer, *1 Enoch : A Commentary on the Book of 1 Enoch* (Minneapolis, Minn.: Fortress, 2001), 182.

[14] Jubilees and 1 Enoch also refer to a group that were apparently the children of the Nephilim (Naphidim). They are called the Eljo or Elioud. "... and the Giants slew the Naphil, and the Naphil slew the Eljo, and the Eljo mankind, and one man another." The word is extremely corrupt but possible meanings of it could be "against God" or "arrogant ones." Nickelsburg, *1 Enoch*, 185.

[15] For instance, Judd H. Burton, *Interview With The Giant: Ethnohistorical Notes on the Nephilim* (Burton Beyond Press, 2009), 24-33.

[16] See Burton, *Interview*, 27; Raymond T. McNally, *In Search of Dracula: The History of Dracula and Vampires Completely Revised* (Boston: Mifflin, 1994), 117-118. Burton also has a bibliography for these ancient vampiric creatures.

[17] See R. Campbell Thompson, *The Devils and Evil Spirits of Babylonia: Being Babylonian and Assyrian Incantations Against the Demons, Ghouls, Vampires, Hobgoblins, Ghosts, and Kindred Evil Spirits, Which Attack Mankind* (reprinted by Forgotten Books at Google Books, originally published around 1903), p. 71.

[18] See also Exodus 22:19 and Deuteronomy 27:21.

[19] Francis Brown, Samuel Rolles Driver and Charles Augustus Briggs, *Enhanced Brown-Driver-Briggs Hebrew and English Lexicon*, electronic ed. (Oak Harbor, WA: Logos Research Systems, 2000), 117.

[20] William Lee Holladay, Ludwig Köhler and Ludwig Köhler, *A Concise Hebrew and Aramaic Lexicon of the Old Testament.* (Leiden: Brill, 1971), 386.

[21] See note 68 in Introduction.

[22] Charlesworth's commentary on 1 Enoch 8:1 n. d reads, "A [an early manuscript of 1 Enoch] adds *tawaleto* *'alam*, 'transmutation of the world.' I render it as 'alchemy.' ... Ethiopian commentators [those who recopied the book over its forgotten centuries] explain this phrase as 'changing a man into a horse or mule or vice versa, or transferring an embryo from one womb to another.'" See Charlesworth, *OT Pseudepigrapha* vol. 1, p. 16.

[23] A. L. Frothingham, "Babylonian Origin of Hermes, the Snake-God, and of the Caduceus," *American Journal of Archaeology* 20: 2nd series, 1916.

[24] Gerald D. Hart, "The Earliest Medical Use of the Caduceus," *C.M.A. Journal* 107 (Dec 9, 1972): 1107.

[25] See Burton, *Interview*, 78-88.

[26] See Hedwige Rouillard, "Rephaim," in *DDD*, 692-700.

[27] Hart, 1107-08.

NOTES FOR CHAPTER 2: THE GIANT OF BABEL (Pgs. 69-94)

[1] A good summary of this can be found in James M. Boice, *Genesis Vol. 1* (Grand Rapids, MI: Baker Books, 1998), 353-59.

[2] See Introduction note 64 (Betty Champion).

[3] For instance, Leviticus 20:11 speaks directly to this, "If a man lies with his father's wife, he has uncovered his father's nakedness." To "see" the nakedness is akin to uncovering it. Leviticus 20:17, "If a man takes his sister, a daughter of his father or daughter of his mother, and sees her nakedness, and she sees his nakedness, it is a disgrace." "Seeing" and being "uncovered" are both in the Genesis 9 narrative. Also Lev 18:8, 20:11; Deut 22:30; 27:20; Hab 2:15; Ezek 22:10. See John Sietze Bergsma, "Noah's Nakedness and the Curse of Canaan (Gen 9:20-27)," in *Journal of Biblical Literature* 124/1 (2005): 25-40.

[4] Bible scholars are perplexed as to how Nimrod could be in Babylon when his ancestor Cush is identified with Ethiopia. The answer is simple. The Ethiopian Cushites were either a separate group or late arrivals to Africa, having migrated here long after Nimrod because of war or natural disaster. The later is probably the case. Greek historians consistently reported that the Cushites originally settled the coast of the Persian Gulf (south of Mesopotamia) along with their Canaanite brothers. See François Lenormant, *A Manual of the Ancient History of the East to the Commencement of the Median Wars*, trans. E. Chavallier (Philadelphia: Lippincott & Co., 1870-71), 144ff.

[5] Cf. Victor P. Hamilton, *The Book of Genesis: Chapters 1-17*, The New International Commentary on the Old Testament (Grand Rapids, MI: Wm. B. Eerdmans Publishing Co., 1990), 339; or the TNK Bible "Like Nimrod a mighty hunter by the grace of the LORD."

[6] K. van der Toorn and P. W. van der Horst, "Nimrod Before And After The Bible," *Harvard Theological Review* 83:1 (1990), 14.

[7] On these comparisons see van der Toorn, "Nimrod," 10-11. See also J. van Dijk, *LUGAL UD ME-LÁM-bi NIR-GÁL Le récit épique et didactique des Travaux de Ninurta, du Déluge et de la Nouvelle Création* (2 vols.; Leiden: Brill, 1983), 17-18; the translation by Thorkild Jacobsen, *The Harps That Once ... Sumerian Poetry in Translation* (New Haven/London: Yale University Press, 1987), 233-72; W. Burkert, *The Orientalizing Revolution: Near Eastern Influence on Greek Culture in the Early Archaic Age* (Cambridge, 1987), 14-19, and in C. Bonnet and C. Jourdain-Annequin (eds.), *Héraclés. D'une rive á l'autre de la Méditerranée. Bilan et perspectives* (Brussels & Rome, 1992), pp.121-124; F.E. Brenk, *Relighting the Souls: Studies in Plutarch, in Greek Literature, Religion, and Philosophy, and in the New Testament Background* (Stuttgart, 1999), 5-7-26.

[8] Viticulturalists have been doing this to modern grapes for several decades now. It doesn't take a god to make a giant grape, but it does take some specialized knowledge of breeding and genetics. See for example, H. P. Olmo, "Giant-Berry Grapes: Principles of Genetics Employed to Propagate Varieties Producing Berries of Larger Size," *California Agriculture* Vol. 4 No. 6 (1950): 5-13.

[9] Genesis 10:8 actually uses the same troubling word (*chalal*) that we discussed in Genesis 4:26 (see Introduction pgs. 13-14). It literally reads, "Now Cush begat Nimrod; he began (*chalal*) to be (*lihyot*) a *gibbor*."

[10] van der Toorn, "Nimrod," 14.

[11] Christoph Uehlinger, "Nimrod," in *Dictionary of Deities and Demons in the Bible: DDD*, 2nd extensively rev. ed., K. van der Toorn, Bob Becking and Pieter Willem van der Horst (eds) (Leiden; Boston; Grand Rapids, Mich.: Brill; Eerdmans, 1999), 628. The idea is to take the two words without English vowels *Nmrd* (נמרד) and *Nsrk* (נסרך) (Hebrew has no vowels). מ becomes ס, and ד becomes ך. Even if you can't read ancient Hebrew, you can see the similarity in the letters, and how easy it could be to confuse them.

[12] Larry Zalcman, "Orion," *DDD*, 649.

[13] Karl Preisendanz, "Nimrod," *Pauly, Wissowa and Kroll, Real-Encyclopädie* 17 (1936): 624-27.

[14] See S. R. Driver & G. B. Gray, *The Book of Job* (ICC; Edinburgh 1921), 86.

[15] Michael M. Alouf, *History of Baalbek* (Escondido, CA: Book Tree, 1999), 29.

[16] Readers Digest Association, *The World's Last Mysteries* (Montreal: Reader's Digest, 1978), 308.

[17] Jean-Pierre Adam, "A propos du trilithon de Baalbek. Le transport et la mise en oeuvre des megaliths," *Syria* 54:1-2 (1977): 31-63. This paper also proposes a plausible explanation for how the stones were moved and set into place by very common, ordinary, yet ingenious techniques.

[18] It has been noted at both Ebla and Ugarit that some proper names combine an animal and a deity. The Ugaritic *ni-mi-ri-ya* translates "panther of Yah," so the idea is that Nimrod means "panther of Hadd" (i.e. Baal), analogous to *nqmd* ("victory of Hadd"). See M. J. Dahood, "Ebla, Ugarit, and the Old Testament," *TD* 27 (1979): 129; idem, "Ebla, Ugarit, and the Bible," in G. Pettinato, *The Archives of Ebla: An Empire Inscribed in Clay* (Garden City, NY: Doubleday, 1981), p. 277 cited in Victor P. Hamilton, *The Book of Genesis: Chapters 1-17*, The New International Commentary on the Old Testament (Grand Rapids, MI: Wm. B. Eerdmans Publishing Co., 1990), 338.

[19] Van der Toorn and van der Horst give an interesting history of these legends among the Jews in their article (see reference n. 5 this chapter), pp. 16-29.

[20] The Hebrew *lipne* is a compound meaning literally "to the face." In 2 Chron 20:12 and Est 9:2 the ESV translates it "against." The Greek *enantoin* is translated "against" in places like Job 15:13, cf. Augustine, *City of God* 16.4.

[21] Eusebius, *Praeparatio Evangelica* 9.17.2.

[22] Josephus, *Antiquities* 1.4.118.

[23] In the LXX "titan" occurs as a synonym for Rephaim (2 Sam 23:13; 1 Chr 11:15) and as "giant" in the Apocryphal Judith 16:6.

[24] See Introduction notes #56 and Chapter 3 note #1.

[25] Sibylline Oracle 3.105-158 (cf. SibOr 1.283-323). See the discussion in Gerard Mussies, "Titans," *DDD*, 874.

[26] Hubert Howe Bancroft et al., *The Native Races of the Pacific States of North America*, vol. 5: Primitive History (New York: D Appleton and Co., 1874-76), 17-18. Quote is from n. 40.

[27] In one story a giant named Xelhua builds an artificial mountain at Cholula after the Deluge. His building angered the gods and they launched fire on the builders. See Elwood Worcester, *The Book of Genesis in Light of Modern Knowledge* (New York: McClure, Phillips & Co., 1901), 500. In another version of the same story, seven giants survive the Flood, one builds a tower, and the gods disperse the people. See Peter Tompkins, *Mysteries of the Mexican Pyramids* (New York: Harper Collins, 1987), 57.

[28] William Joseph Wilkins, *Hindu Mythology, Vedic and Purānic* (London: Thacker & Co., 1882), 364.

[29] See *Satapatha Brahmana* 2.1, 2, 13-16.

[30] John Walton, "The Mesopotamian Background of the Tower of Babel Account and Its Implications," *Bulletin for Biblical Research* 5 (1995): 157.

[31] Ibid., 156.

³² The Table is a partial list of ziggurats mentioned in Walton, 159-60.

³³ Anne Birrell, *Chinese Mythology: An Introduction* (Baltimore, MD: Johns Hopkins University Press, 1993), 234.

³⁴ Patricia Turner and Charles Russell Coulter, "Kun-Lun," in *Dictionary of Ancient Deities* (New York: Oxford University Press, 2001), 279.

³⁵ Cf. George Hart, "Ptah of Memphis," in *Egyptian Myths* (Austin, TX: University of Texas Press, 1990), 18-19.

³⁶ The word "*deva*" is from an older Proto-Indo-European Sanskrit word *deiwos*, which was an adjective meaning "celestial" or "shining."

³⁷ Cf. Prose Edda: *Gylfaginning*, 27.

³⁸ Lewis Spence, *The Myths of the North American Indians* (New York: Dover, 1989), 108.

³⁹ The scholarly paper which first proposed the Pyramids-Orion connection (Robert Bauval, "A Master Plan for the Three Pyramids of Giza Based on the Configuration of the Three Stars of the Belt of Orion," *Discussions in Egyptology* 13 [1989]: 7-18), was popularized in Bauval, *The Orion Mystery* (New York: Three Rivers Press, 1994); Graham Hancock, *Fingerprints of the Gods* (New York: Three Rivers Press, 1995) and *Heaven's Mirror: Quest for the Lost Civilization* (New York: Crown Publishers, 1998); Thomas G. Brophy, *The Origin*

Fig. FN 1. Cross-Cultural Orion Connection

1. Orion's Belt, 2. Tenochititlan, Mexico, 3. Pyramids of Giza.
4. Thornborough Henges, Northern England

Map (New York: Writers Club Press, 2002); Bauval, *The Egypt Code* (New York: Disinformation Co., Ltd., 2008) and others. The theory is not without its detractors. Since then, suggestions that other ancient cites emulate Orion have also been made (see attending picture).

⁴⁰ On the Hopi hypothesis, see Gary A. David, *The Orion Zone: Ancient Star Cities of the American Southwest* (Kempton, IL: Adventures Unlimited Press, 2006). David's images are copyrighted, but have been reproduced by the History Channel. The Mesoamerican Orion connection maybe related to the complex at Tenochtitlan, Mexico (above). Sadly, many of these speculative researchers are into this stuff because of the New Age implications they believe they have "rediscovered," which only fits with the wickedness God saw in such things in the first place.

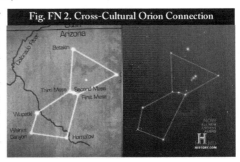

Fig. FN 2. Cross-Cultural Orion Connection

The Orion Complex of Northwest Arizona
Courtesy, the History Channel

⁴¹ Cited in Gregory K. Beale, *The Temple and the Church's Mission: A Biblical Theology of the Dwelling Place of God* (Downers Grove, IL: InterVarsity Press, 2004), 51-52.

⁴² Walton, 161.

⁴³ See John H. Walton, *Zondervan Illustrated Bible Backgrounds Commentary (Old Testament) Vol. 1: Genesis-Deuteronomy* (Grand Rapids, MI: Zondervan, 2009), 106.

⁴⁴ Actually, it says, "Let us go down" (Gen 11:7). As with Genesis 1:26, the plural "us" here refers to the divine council. But just like Gen 1:26, it is God alone who does the action. The council here is powerless to give the people what they want. Instead, the Only Creator curses them and disperses them.

NOTES FOR CHAPTER 3: ABRAHAM AND THE GIANT WARS (Pgs. 95-108)

[1] The number is disputed, but good defenses of a total of "70" are found in Umberto Cassuto, *A Commentary on the Book of Genesis: From Noah to Abraham* (Jerusalem: Magnes Press, 1964), 177–180; Allen P. Ross, "Studies in the Book of Genesis - Part 2: The Table of Nations in Genesis 10 - its Structure," *Bibliotheca Sacra* 137:548 (Oct-Dec 1980): 342.

[2] You can identify most of these groups by the Hebrew plural ending *–im*, such as Ludim, Anamim etc., or by the English plural ending *–ites*, such as Jebusites, Amorites etc.

[3] See François Lenormant, *A Manual of the Ancient History of the East to the Commencement of the Median Wars*, trans. E. Chavallier (Philadelphia: Lippincott & Co., 1870-71), 144ff.

[4] For this and all the names which follow see Note #9, Ch. 1.

[5] Gen 15:20-21 (which substitutes Rephaim for Hivite); Ex 3:8, 17; 13:5, 23:23; 33:2; 34:11; Num 13:29; Deut 20:17; Josh 9:1; 12:8; Jdg 3:5; 1 Kgs 9:20; 2 Chron 8:7; Ezra 9:1 (leave out the Girgashites).

[6] For instance, Genesis 48:23 refers to a "portion" or "mountain slope" that Jacob took from an Amorite. The word for a portion here is *shekem* and the incident probably refers to the events at Shechem with (Gen 33:19) Hamor the Hivite. Thus, a Hivite can be called an Amorite. Another time, the Amorites came and defeated Israel at Hormah (Deut 1:44). But in Num 14:45, we learn that it was the Amalekites and Canaanites who attacked Israel here.

[7] One scholar has suggested that they are a mixture of Hittite and Amorite per the old name for Jerusalem ("Jebus"; Jdg 19:10). A. H. Sayce, "The White Race of Palestine," in *Nature* 38:979 (Aug 2, 1888): 322.

[8] T. K. Cheyne, J. Sutherland Black, *Encyclopaedia Biblica* (London: Adam and Charles Black, 1899-1902), 2:2100.

[9] For a discussion of this see K. van der Toorn and P. W. van der Horst, "Nimrod Before And After The Bible," *Harvard Theological Review* 83:1 (1990): 23-25; also Babylonian Talmud (b.) *'Erubin* 53a.

[10] Bob Becking, "Lagamar," *DDD*, 498-99.

[11] This association was seen by the French orientalist Armand-Pierre Caussin de Perceval (1795-1871) in his *Essays on the History of the Arabs before Islamism, during the Time of Mohammed, and down to the Reduction of all the Tribes under his Dominion* (1847), i.26. It also comports with the Arabian historian Al-Masudi (896 – 956 A.D.) who reported that the ancient prophet Saleh (presumed to be post-diluvian but pre-Abrahamic) came to the rescue of a group called the Thamudites (a group of Canaanites, see J. W. De Forest, "The Great Deluge," in Edward Everett Hale [ed.], *Old and New*, Vol. 6, July 1872-Jan 1873 [Boston: Lee & Shepard, 1872]: 437), who were being threatened by a descendant of Ham (see Masudi, Prairies, c. 38, 3:90 as cited in Lina Eckenstein, *A History of Sinai* (New York, Macmillian Co, 1921), 50.

[12] *'Amar pil* = "He said, 'Throw.'"

[13] Amraphel may also derive from the name of the Amorite storm god Amurru. See van der Toorn, "Amurru," *DDD*, 32-33.

[14] Victor P. Hamilton, *The Book of Genesis: Chapters 1-17*, The New International Commentary on the Old Testament (Grand Rapids, MI: Wm. B. Eerdmans Publishing Co., 1990), 400.

[15] Ernest G. Clark; *Targum and Scripture: Studies in Aramaic Translations and Interpretation* (Boston: Brill, 2002), 26; Roswell D. Hitchcock, "Arioch," "An Interpreting Dictionary of Scripture Proper Names," in *Hitchcock's Complete Analysis of the Holy Bible* (New York: A. J. Johnson, 1874), 1105.

[16] Hitchcock, 1112.

[17] Of course, he does not call this episode "absurd." Here is what he writes, " … so God avenged, with more severe punishment, the shameful lust of the others; who, while endeavoring to do violence to angels, were not only injurious towards men; but, to the utmost of their power, dishonored the celestial glory of God, by their sacrilegious fury." Calvin, *Commentary on Genesis 19:5*.

[18] Hamilton, *Genesis 1-17*, 401.

[19] Here are some examples from New England. In Middleboro, Massachusetts an infamous and mysterious "settler" named "Mr. Richmond" lived prior to 1675 and became an enemy of the native Indians living there. They managed to kill him, but many years later his (supposedly his) skeleton was found and exhumed in the presence of one "Dr. Morrill Robinson" who measured his skeleton as having been "at least seven feet and eight inches." The man also had "a double row of teeth in each jaw." Thomas Weston, *History of the Town of Middleboro, Massachusetts* (Boston: Houghton, Mifflin and Company, 1906), 400. In Deerfield, MA we read, "One of these skeletons was described to me by Henry Mather who saw it as being of monstrous size—'the head as big as a peck basket with double teeth all round.' The skeleton was examined by Dr. Stephen Williams, who said the owner must have been nearly 8 feet high." George Sheldon, *History of Deerfield*, vol. 1 (MA: Pioneer Valley Memorial Museum, 1895), 78. In Rockingham, VT a "remarkable human skeleton" has a jaw bone "of such size that a large man could easily slip it over his face, and the teeth, which were all double, were perfect." Lyman Simpson Hayes, *History of the Town of Rockingham, Vermont* (Bellow Falls, VT: The Town, 1907), 338. At Martha's Vineyard of all places, "a man easily six feet and a half, possibly seven feet, high" had "an unusual feature … a complete double row of teeth on both upper and lower jaws." Charles Gilbert Hine, *The Story of Martha's Vineyard* (New York: Hine Brothers, 1908), 137. One skeleton from Concord, New Hampshire, a 6'3" person with a "very thick" skull and a full head of double teeth was preserved by Dr. William Prescott in his cabinet. This was reported, not in *UFO Magazine* (as one person has quipped), but in the *Boston Medical and Surgical Journal*. See J. V. C. Smith, M.D., W. W. Morland, M.D., and Francis Minot, M.D., *Boston Medical and Surgical Journal*, vol. LIII (Boston: David Clapp, 1856), 456. There are also reports from Lompock Rancho, Santa Rosa Island, and the Catalina Islands, CA; Clearwater, MN (though this one appears to be a conflation of a double-teeth finding from nearby Delano, MN [see Franklyn Curtiss-Wedge, *History of Wright County Minnesota*, vol. 1 (Chicago: H. C. Cooper, Jr., & Co., 1915), 34]; Adams County, Ohio; Jefferson County, New York; Mason County, Virginia, and other places. Compilations from these can be found in Frank Edwards, *Stranger Than Science* (New York: Lyle Stuart, 1959), 129; Henry Howe, *The Historical Collections of Ohio* (Cincinnati, OH: Pub by the state of Ohio, 1902), 350-51. Stephen Quayle, *Genesis 6 Giants: Master Builders of Prehistoric and Ancient Civilizations* (Bozeman, MT: End Time Thunder Publishers, 2002), 260.

[20] Hamilton, Ibid.

NOTES FOR CHAPTER 4: PATRIARCHAL GIANTS (Pgs. 109-114)

[1] It is common for commentaries to say that the spies exaggerated *the height* of the inhabitants of Canaan. In other words, they were not really tall (not more than seven feet). Given that we know that these people were taller than seven feet from other biblical and extra-biblical sources, it is better—if there is exaggeration at all—to think that they exaggerated *how many* of them were tall. It is not necessary to posit exaggeration in the story, however, because the spies were in trouble for their faithlessness, not for exaggeration.

[2] Eliezer D. Orenin, "Gerar," in David Noel Freedman, vol. 2, *The Anchor Yale Bible Dictionary* (New York: Doubleday, 1996), 989.

[3] The verb "to take" (*laqach*) is the same Hebrew word in all three stories.

NOTES FOR CHAPTER 5: MOSES MEETS AMALEK (Pgs. 115-122)

[1] On the time spent in Egypt see H. W. Hoehner, "The Duration of the Egyptian Bondage," *Bibliotheca Sacra Volume* 126:504 (1969): 306-16, (http://faculty.gordon.edu/hu/bi/Ted_Hildebrandt/OTeSources/02-Exodus/Text/Articles/Hoehner-DurationEgypt-BSac.htm) who sees the count beginning in Genesis 35:9-15 and J. R. Riggs, "The Length of Israel's Sojourn in Egypt," *Grace Theological Journal* 12 (1971): 18-35

(http://faculty.gordon.edu/hu/bi/ted_hildebrandt/otesources/02-exodus/Text/Articles/Riggs-EgyptSojourn-GTJ.htm) who sees it beginning in Genesis 46.

[2] John Garnier, *The Worship of the Dead: The Origin and Nature of Pagan Idolatry* (London: Chapman & Hall, 1904), 74ff; Phillip J. Budd, *Numbers*, Word Biblical Commentary (Dallas: Word, Incorporated, 2002), p. 270.

[3] An example of an older dictionary that makes the proper distinction between the two Amaleks is William G. Smith, *A Dictionary of the Bible: Comprising Its Antiquities, Biography, and Natural History* in 3 Vols. (Boston: Little Brown, 1863), 1:56.

[4] "*Imlāq* is an Arabic term derived from the biblical Hebrew "Amaleq," the hereditary enemies of the Israelites (Deut 35:17), whose name appears in Arab tradition as '*Amāliq* or '*Amāliqa*, Amalekites, and also in Arab folklore telling of the evil king 'Amlūq. See *Encyclopaedia of Islam*, new ed. [Leiden: E. J. Brill, 1978], 1:429." See Raphael Patai, *Arab Folktales from Palestine and Israel* (Detroit, MI: Wayne State University Press, 1998), 201, n 5.

[5] "In the Arabic colloquial, '*Imlāq* means both Amalekite and 'giant.'" Ibid.

[6] On the relation of Amalek and Ad see Augustin Calmet, *Dictionary of the Holy Bible* (Boston: Crocker and Brewster, 1832), 50.

[7] Ahmad Ibn 'Ali al-Maqrīzī, *Description Topographique et Historique de l'Egypte* (vol. 1), trans. M. U. Bouriant, ed. Ernest Lerous (Paris: Rue Bonaparte, 1895), 89-90. The English translation is smoothed out by Google Translator.

[8] Garnier, 74.

[9] Samuel G. Goodrich, *A History of All Nations, From the Earliest Periods to the Present Time* (New York: Miller, Orton, and Mulligan, 1855), 315; al-Tabarī, *The History of al-Tabarī* (vol. 2): *Prophets and Patriarchs*, trans. William M. Brinner (Albany, NY: State University of New York Press, 1987), 18.

[10] J. W. De Forest, "The Great Deluge," in Edward Everett Hale (ed.), *Old and New*, Vol. 6, July 1872-Jan 1873 (Boston: Lee & Shepard, 1872), 438ff.

[11] Sibylline Oracle 8:251-53 says, "Moses prefigured him [Christ], stretching out his holy arms, conquering Amalek by faith so that the people might know that he is elect and precious with God his father." Barnabas 12:9 says, "The son of God shall destroy by the roots the whole house of Amalek in the end of days" (taking "end of days" from the Fragment Targum Num 24:20). Also Justin Martyr, *Dialogue* 90; Chrysostom, *Homilies on the Gospel of John* 14; Maximus of Turin, *Sermon* 45.3.

NOTES FOR CHAPTER 6: SPYING OUT THE LAND (Pgs. 123-128)

[1] R. Dennis Cole, vol. 3B, *Numbers*, electronic ed., Logos Library System; The New American Commentary (Nashville: Broadman & Holman Publishers, 2001), 220.

[2] Josias Porter writes of his first-hand experience, "The houses of Bashan are not ordinary houses. Their walls are from five to eight feet thick, built of large squared blocks of basalt; their roofs are formed of slabs of the same material, hewn like planks, and reaching from wall to wall; the very doors and window-shutters are of stone, hung upon pivots projecting above and below. . . The houses of Kerioth and other towns in Bashan appear to be just such dwellings as a race of giants would build. The walls, the roofs, but especially the ponderous gates, doors, and bars, are in every way characteristic of a period when architecture was in its infancy, when giants were masons, and when strength and security were the grand requisites. I measured a door in Kerioth: it was nine feet high, four and a half feet wide, and ten inches thick,--one solid slab of stone. I saw the folding gates of another town in the mountains still larger and heavier. Time produces little effect on such buildings as these. The heavy stone slabs of the roofs resting on the massive walls make the structure as firm as if built of solid masonry; and the black basalt used is almost as hard as iron. There can scarcely be a doubt, therefore, that these are the very cities erected and inhabited by the Rephaim, the abo-

riginal occupants of Bashan." Josias Leslie Porter, *The Giant Cities of Bashan; and Syria's Holy Places* (New York: Thomas Nelson, 1884), 20, 84.

[3] Arba can also mean something like "Foursquare." Kiriath-Arba is literally "city of four" and may have been named after Arba and his three giant sons (see below) or to the four cities of Aner, Eschol, Mamre and Hebron.

[4] "Anak," *Anchor Yale Bible Dictionary* (New York: Doubleday, 1996), 222. A good study of the major giant clan names can be found in Kenneth C. Way, "Giants in the Land: A Textual and Semantic Study of Giants in the Bible and the Ancient Near East," a Master of Arts thesis, Deerfield, IL: Trinity International University, 2000, 33-78.

[5] Nephilim is actually spelled in two different ways in this verse. Scholars suggest that the first spelling is an Aramaic spelling of an Aramaic word for "giant." Aramaic is the language spoken after the captivity in Babylon. The second spelling is the same as that of Genesis 6:4, thus the gloss (the parenthetical in the verse) is an addition (after the writing of the LXX, perhaps as new as the NT era) showing Aramaic readers that the word "giant" and the older world *nephilim* are the one and the same thing. See Introduction, note #40.

[6] For instance, "The Ruler of Iy-'anaq, '*Erum*, and all the *retainers* who are with him; the Ruler of Iy-'anaq, Abi-*yamimu*, and all the *retainers* who are with him; the Ruler of Iy-'anaq, 'Akirum, and all the *retainers* who are with him" (*Execration* Text e1 in *The Ancient Near East an Anthology of Texts and Pictures.*, ed. James Bennett Pritchard [Princeton: Princeton University Press, 1958], 328). This is found on an Egyptian Execration text (ca. 1850) which are broken pottery figurines (see picture to right). The Egyptians would make a clay model of a dreaded enemy and bind its arms behind its back. It is sort of like the practice of voodoo.

Fig. FN 3. Execration Text

[7] Shasu is a general term for the inhabitants of Edom (Horites), Amorites, Amalekites, and the Anakim (*Iy'anaq*). See Clyde E. Billington, "Goliath and The Exodus Giants: How Tall Were They"? *JETS* 50.3 (2007): 500-505.

[8] *Craft of the Scribe* 23.7 (Papyrus Anastasi I); in William W. Hallo and K. Lawson Younger, *Context of Scripture* (Leiden; Boston: Brill, 2003), 3:13.

[9] Pritchard, 477, n. 43.

[10] "Two seven-foot female skeletons were found in a twelfth-century-BC cemetery at Tell *es-Sa 'idiyeh* on the east bank of the Jordan" (Jeffrey H. Tigay, *Deuteronomy* [Philadelphia: Jewish Publication Society, 1996], 17).

[11] Generically, "Skeletons of large size have been excavated in Palestine," and more specifically, "Skeletons 3.2 m. tall [10.5 ft.] have been found elsewhere in Syro-Palestine" (Donald J. Wiseman, "Medicine in the Old Testament World," in *Medicine and the Bible*, ed. B. Palmer [Exeter: Paternoster Press, 1986], 23, 244 n. 58). For other finds consult A. T. Sandison and C. Wells, "Endocrine Diseases," in *Diseases in Antiquity*, eds. D. Brothwell and A. T. Sandison (Springfield, IL: Charles C. Thomas, 1967), 522-25; Theodore H. Gaster, *Myth, Legend and Custom in the Old Testament* (New York: Harper and Row, 1969), 311, 402-3; C. J. S. Thomson, *The Mystery and Lore of Monsters* (New York: Bell, 1968), 133.

[12] See Appendix: Giants in the Americas.

[13] Babylonian Talmud, Sota 34B.

[14] J. Jeremias, *Heiligengräber in Jesu Umwelt* (Göttingen, 1958), 82-86; cited in Charlesworth, OT Pseudepigrapha vol. 2, 391.

[15] See Introduction, note #68.

NOTES FOR CHAPTER 7: THE "LAW" OF CANAAN (Pgs. 129-134)

[1] For instance the Code of Ur-Nammu, king of Ur (ca. 2050 BC, making it contemporary with Abraham); the Laws of Eshunna (ca. 1930 BC); the codex of Lipit-Ishtar of Isin (ca. 1870 BC); and of course the famed Code of Hammurabi (1700 BC).

[2] Nesilim is how the Hittites referred to themselves.

[3] Leonard Woolley, *The Sumerians* (New York: W.W. Norton, 1965), 95.

[4] "If a man charge a man with sorcery, and cannot prove it, he who is charged with sorcery shall go to the river, into the river he shall throw himself and if the river overcome him, his accuser shall take to himself his house. If the river show that man to be innocent and he come forth unharmed, he who charged him with sorcery shall be put to death. He who threw himself into the river shall take to himself the house of his accuser." (HC 2).

[5] "If a man is accused of sorcery he must undergo ordeal by water; if he is proven innocent, his accuser must pay 2 shekels."

[6] Idolatry and having other gods are not the same sin. The former is the second commandment, the later is the first. We will discuss this more in later chapters.

NOTES FOR CHAPTER 8: ON THE WAY TO CANAAN (Pgs. 135-148)

[1] Richard Dawkins, *The God Delusion* (Boston: Houghton Mifflin Co., 2006), 51.

[2] This is found in Louis Ginzberg, *Legends of the Jews Vol 5: Notes to Volumes 1 and 2: From the Creation to the Exodus* (Baltimore: Johns Hopkins University Press, 1998), 53-54.

[3] Shemhazai is mentioned as one of the leaders of the Watchers, the fallen angels who came upon Mt. Hermon in the days of Jared and who was bound up by the archangel Michael afterwards. 1 Enoch 6:3; 9:7; 10:11.

[4] Louis Ginzberg, "Sihon, The King of the Amorites," in *Legends of the Jews* (ForgottenBooks, 1909, 2008), 3:219 and note 668 found in vol. 6 of the same series.

[5] Babylonian Talmud *Rosh ha-Shanah* 3a. See Ginzberg, note 669.

[6] For instance, "The Egyptian monuments inform us that the Amorites of Palestine were white-skinned, blue-eyed, fair-haired, and dolicho-cephalic (long-headed), and that the race was still predominant in Judah in the age of Shishak, while traces of it are still to be met with in Palestine." A. H. Sayce, "The White Race of Ancient Palestine," in *Academy* vol. 34 (1888): 55. "In the sculptures of Ramses II at Abu-Simbel 'the Shasu of Kanana' were depicted with blue eyes, and red hair, eyebrows, and beard, and the Amaur with 'the eyes blue, the eyebrows and beard red.' As 'the Shasu of Kanana' lived a little to the south of Hebron, while the Amaur are the Amorites of the Old Testament, it was clear that a population existed in Palestine in the fourteenth century before our era which had all the characteristics of the white race." A.H. Sayce, "The White Race of Palestine," in *Nature* vol. 38:979 (Aug 2, 1888): 321-22.

[7] An interesting compilation of some of these finds can be found in Josiah Priest, *American Antiquities and Discoveries in the West* (Albany, NY: Hoffman & White, 1833).

[8] Roy Norvill, *Giants: The Vanished Race* (Wellingborough, UK: Aquarian Press, 1979), 84.

[9] Adam Rodgers, "Early Nevada History is Traced in Lovelock, Cave, Tomb of the Forgotten Race," in *Ancient American* 13:81 (Dec 2008): 32-35.

[10] See for example Sarah Winnemucca Hopkins, *Life Among the Paiutes* (Boston: Cupples, Upham & CO., 1883), 26. http://www.yosemite.ca.us/library/life_among_the_piutes/life_among_the_piutes.pdf

[11] On the idea that Og survived the Flood see Targum Pseudo-Jonathan Gen 14:13, Deut 3:11; Babylonian Talmud *Niddah* 61a; *Zebahim* 113b; *Pirke de Rabbi Eliezer* 23.2.

[12] A unicorn? On unicorns (*re'em*) in the Bible see Num 23:22; 24:8; Deut 33:17; Job 39:9-10; Ps 22:21; 29:6; 92:10; Isa 34:7 all KJV). The LXX translates the word as *monokerōs* (lit: one horn) and the Latin translates it as *unicornis*. Modern English translations opt for something like "wild ox." Perhaps this creature is purely fictional. Perhaps we have simply not found its remains. Perhaps it is based upon a now extinct form of rhinoceros, a dinosaur, or something else?

[13] Pseudo-Jonathan Gen 14:13. A lengthy fairy-tale version of Og and Noah for reading to a child on a cold winter night is "The Giant of the Flood," in Gertrude Landa, *Jewish Fairy Tales and Legends* (New York: Bloch, 1919), 9-14. http://www.scribd.com/doc/936703/The-Giant-of-the-Flood.

[14] See Maria Lindquist, "King Og's Iron Bed," *CBQ* 73 no. 3 (July 2011): 477-492. This is an extremely skeptical view of Og and the giants, but presents an interesting case for it being a bed.

[15] Many sources and some translations opt for this idea in light of the large basalt sarcophagi and dolmens found in the area. See A. R. MILLARD, "King Og's Bed and Other Ancient Ironmongery," in *Ascribe to the Lord. Biblical and other studies in memory of Peter C. Craigie* (ed. L. Eslinger & G. Taylor), JSOT Sup 67; Sheffield 1988): 481–492. I like how the *Jewish Encyclopedia* puts it, "The fact that the black basalt bed or sarcophagus of Og was shown at Rabbah, the chief city of the Ammonites (Deut 3:11), confirms rather than confutes the legendary nature of the giant stories." See Emil G. Hirsch, "Giants," in *JE*, http://www.jewishencyclopedia.com/view.jsp?artid=215&letter=G.

[16] This coffin parallels a report recited by the Greek historian Herodotus (484 – 425 B.C.) in Book One (Clio) of his *Histories*. He talks about a certain blacksmith from the city Tegea who had dug up the courtyard there. He relates, "In my digging I hit upon a coffin twelve feet long. I could not believe that there had ever been men taller than now, so I opened it and saw that the corpse was just as long as the coffin. I measured it and then reburied it" (*Histories* 1.68.3). The curious thing about this story is its context. A Spartan named Lichas (no relation to the servant of Hercules) was told by an oracle to look for the bones of Orestes, the son of Agamemnon who famously fought in the mythical battle of Troy. Though the story of Troy is told as "myth," in the nineteenth century it was discovered to be a real city. Herodotus places the battle of Troy around 1,200 B.C. (a possible timeframe for Joshua's conquest of Canaan). After much debate, Lichas persuaded the smith to lease him the land and "he dug up the grave and collected the bones, then hurried off to Sparta with them" (1.68.6). Thus, we have a similar size coffin in a similar timeframe mentioned by two different cultures. Both purport to be telling actual history.

[17] See John Day, *God's Conflict with the Dragon and the Sea* (London: Cambridge University Press, 1985), 117. The *Anunnaki* were made famous by Zechariah Sitchin who believed they were aliens from another planet. Sitchin is simply mistaken. It is much better to see them as identical to the sons of God who came down in the days of Jared.

[18] The Ugaritic word is *bṭn*, the Akkadian is *bašmu*, and the Arabic equivalent is *baṭan*. See G. Del Olmo Lete, "Bashan," *DDD*, 161. For instance, it is paired with the Ugaritic equivalent of Leviathan, "When you killed Litan, the Fleeing Serpent, Annihilated the Twisty Serpent" (KTU 1.5.I.1-2). Heiser has a fascinating discussion of this in *The Myth That Is True* (unpublished), 170-71.

[19] Gen 30:27; 44:5; Lev 19:26; 2 Kgs 21:6. Heiser has an informative article on this as well. Heiser, "The Nachash and his Seed: Some Explanatory Notes on Why the 'Serpent' in Genesis 3 Wasn't a Serpent," available in PDF online: http://www.thedivinecouncil.com/nachashnotes.pdf.

[20] For examples, see Chapter 1, n. 10.

[21] So T. K. Cheyne, J. Sutherland Black, *Encyclopaedia Biblica* (London: Adam and Charles Black, 1899-1902), 2:2101. The word is *chavvah* and is perhaps related to the Aramaic word *ḥewyā*, which means serpent. *Chavvah* also happens to be the name of Eve in Hebrew. Some have tried to connect Eve's name to the serpent, but recent scholarship has deemed this speculative, not to mention it flies in the face of Genesis 3:20 which says that she was called Eve because she was the mother of *all living*. See Scott C. Layton, "Remarks on the Cannanite Origin of Eve," *Catholic Biblical Quarterly* 59 (1997): 29-30.

[22] This summary is found in John Bathurst Deane, *Worship of the Serpent: Traced Throughout the World* (London: J. G. & F. Rivington, 1883, republished by Forgotten Books, 2008), 58-60. This is a fascinating book written by a Christian scholar who taught at Cambridge, a good source for serpent worship throughout the world.

[23] Og's name, like Anak, can also mean "long-necked."

[24] Israel Ministry of Foreign Affairs, "Rogem Hiri – Ancient, Mysterious Construction," Feb 2, 1999: http://www.mfa.gov.il/MFA/History/Early%20History%20-%20Archaeology/Rogem%20Hiri%20-%20Ancient-%20Mysterious%20Construction

[25] This picture depicts the image before Ezekiel in Ezekiel 1, upon which Daniel 7 has many parallels. For more examples of what Ezekiel and Daniel saw in the context of their ancient Persian setting see Michael Heiser's presentation at: http://www.sitchiniswrong.com/ezekielnotes.htm

NOTES FOR CHAPTER 9: GIANT WARS, THE SEQUEL (Pgs. 149-156)

[1] Ronald Hendel writes, "They exist in order to be wiped out: by the flood, by Moses, by David, and others." Their function is "to die" (Ronald S. Hendel, "Of Demigods and the Deluge: Toward an Interpretation of Genesis 6:1–4," *Journal of Biblical Literature* 106 [1987]: 21. Similarly, the *Dictionary of Biblical Imagery* says, "Giants are a negative image in the Bible ... God always instructs his people to destroy them ... It is hardly too much to say that in the Bible giants are towering physical specimens on the verge of being toppled" ("Giants," in *Dictionary of Biblical Imagery*, eds. L. Ryken, J. C. Wilhoit and T. Longman III [Downers Grove: InterVarsity Press, 1998], 328.

[2] Leon Wood, *A Survey of Israel's History* (Grand Rapids, MI: Zondervan Publishing House, 1970), p. 174.

[3] Emil G. Hirsch, "Giants," in *Jewish Encyclopedia* Vol. 5, ed. Isidore Singer, Cyrus Adler (New York: Funk and Wagnalls, 1912), 659. See also Ronald S. Hendel, "Biblical Views: Giants at Jericho," *Biblical Archeological Research* 35:02 (Mar/Apr 2009).

[4] Sabine Baring-Gould, *Legends of Old Testament Characters from the Talmud and Other Sources* (London: Macmillan, 1871), 302.

[5] *The Wycliffe Bible Encyclopedia* vol. 1, ed. Charles F. Pfeiffer, Howard Frederic Vos, and John Rea (Chicago: Moody Press, 1972), 709.

[6] Harry Emerson Fosdick, *A Pilgrimage to Palestine* (New York: Macmillan Publishing Co., 1949), 33.

[7] Georgette Corcos, *The Glory of the Old Testament* (New York: Villard Books, 1984), 108; cited in Charles DeLoach, "Ashdod's Giants," in *Giants*, 18. The term is found in execration texts.

[8] Palestine Pilgrims' Text Society, *The Library of the Palestine Pilgrims' Text Society* (London: Committee of the Palestine Exploration Fund, 1885), 425.

[9] Some, like the German bishop and poet Walter of Speyer (967 – 1027 AD, *The life and the suffering of St. Christopher the Martyr 75)* took "Canaan" and turned it into Chanaenean or the land of dogs where the inhabitants ate human flesh and barked.

[10] Jacobus de Voragine, *The Golden Legend: Readings on the Saints*, trans. William Granger Ryan (Princeton, NJ: Princeton University Press, 1993), 11.

[11] See R. D. Fulk, "The Passion of St. Christopher," in *The Beowulf Manuscript: Complete Texts and the Fight at Finnsburg* (Cambridge, MA: Harvard University Press, 2010), 1-14.

[12] E. A. Wallis Budge, *The Contendings of the Apostles* (London: H. Frowde, 1899), 206-08. Some see Abominable as the predecessor of some Christopher legends. See Andy Orchard, *Pride and Prodigies: Studies in the Monsters of the Beowulf-manuscript* (Rochester, NY: D.S. Brewer, 1995), 14-15.

[13] An interesting, more sober historical survey of the life of St. Christopher can be found in David Woods, "The Origin of the Cult of St. Christopher," 1999. http://www.ucc.ie/milmart/chrsorig.html#Top

NOTES FOR CHAPTER 10: GOLIATH AND HIS BROTHERS (Pgs. 157-168)

[1] This shard depicts two names etymologically similar to Goliath, to which its discoverers say lends support to what we already know: Goliath was a real person. See A. M. Maeir, S. J. Wimmer, A. Zukerman, and A. Demsky, "A Late Iron Age I/early Iron Age IIA Old Canaanite Inscription from Tell es-Sâfi/Gath, Israel: Palaeography, Dating, and Historical-Cultural Significance," *Bulletin of the American Schools of Oriental Research* 351 (Aug 2008): 39–71. It was reported, for example, in "Scientists Find 'Goliath' Inscribed on Pottery," *Associated Press*, 11/10/2005.
http://www.msnbc.msn.com/id/9997587/ns/technology_and_science-science/t/scientists-find-goliath-inscribed-pottery/.

[2] The earliest Hebrew attestation is the second century Greek Symmachus as recorded by Origen.

[3] See Clyde E. Billington, "Goliath And The Exodus Giants: How Tall Were They"? *JETS* 50.3 (2007): 489-508. Billington argues that Goliath was as tall as 8'7".

[4] See J. Daniel Hays, "Reconsidering The Height Of Goliath," *JETS* 48.4 (2005): 701-714; Hays, "The Height Of Goliath: A Response To Clyde Billington," *JETS* 50.3 (2007): 509-16.

[5] For the average height of an Israelite in David's time see G. Ernest Wright, "Troglodytes and Giants in Palestine," *Journal of Biblical Literature* 57:3 (Sept 1938): 305-309. Others suggest a slightly shorter average of between 5'0" and 5'3". See Billington, 493; Hays, "Reconsidering," 708-710.

[6] Hays claims that Goliath is never referred to as a giant (*JETS* 50.3: 516). This is simply not true. 1 Chron 20:8 LXX refers to him and three others as *gigantes*. . . GIANTS! But Saul is never referred to this way. You could argue that the LXX is simply translating *Rephaim*, and since Saul was not one of these, it wouldn't be fitting to call him that. But the word *gigantes* also translates other words that definitely mean "giants." Besides that, it is quite clear that the Rephaim were viewed as giants by people in the Bible.

[7] See Billington, 496.

[8] Gigantic tools and weapons have been discovered reminiscent of Goliath's spear's size. For example, while not weapons *per se*, in Llandudno, Wales, 50 lb. (some reports as high as 64 lb.) stone hammers were discovered in ancient (3,500 year old) copper mines (See John Hicklin, *Llandudno and Its Vicinity* [London: Hamilton, Adams and Co., 1856], 67). For comparison, modern sledge hammers are only between 10-20 lbs. While much less certain that they were literal tools/weapons, on the island of Crete (well known for its relation to giants) in a place called Nirou Háni, several gigantic bronze double ax heads (along with ceremonial tripods) dating between 1700-1300 BC were discovered, and are now on display in the Museum of Herakleion. Similar smaller axes were discovered in what is described

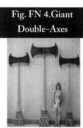

Fig. FN 4.Giant Double-Axes

Museum of Herakleion, Crete

as a "military sanctuary" (D. Rumpel, "The Arkalokhori Axe Inscription in Relation to the Diskos of Phaistos Text," *Anistoriton Journal*, vol. 11 (2008-2009): 1-6).

[9] This is Billington's argument (pgs. 506-07), and I find it persuasive. We do the same thing in translations today, converting a biblical measure to our own, when we say Goliath was 9 "feet" 9 "inches" tall. If, by chance, we happened to call our "foot" a "cubit" as the Egyptians did, then someone, many centuries later, comparing the two texts, might easily assume that we had "changed the height" of Goliath.

[10] Josephus, *Antiquities* 18.103.

[11] The LXX gives the impression that it was the whole spear that weighed this, but that isn't very impressive at all, so why mention it in the first place? A parallel idea in 1 Sam 17:7 has the tip separate from the shaft. If just the tip weighed that much, it would have been quite the spear to throw. Furthermore, this spear-tip is less than half the weight of Goliath's. If Ishbi-benob is said to be a giant, and his spear is so much lighter

than Goliath's, is it really plausible that Goliath was less than seven feet tall? Or, maybe Ishbi-benob was actually a "giant" of around 5-6 ft.

[12] There is a rather glaring discrepancy between 2 Sam 21:19 which says that Elhanan killed Goliath and 1 Sam 17:50 which says that David killed him. Though I disagree with this assessment of Goliath's height, Michael Heiser has an excellent article dealing with the problem. The short answer is, Elhanan killed Lahmi, Goliath's brother. See Michael Heiser, "Clash of the Manuscripts: Goliath & the Hebrew Text of the Old Testament," *Bible Study Magazine* 1:4 (May-June, 2009): 33-35:

http://www.biblestudymagazine.com/interactive/goliath/

NOTES FOR CHAPTER 11: AGAG THE AMALEKITE (Pgs. 169-174)

[1] There are six references to Amalekites in Judges. Three put them near the Midianites (Jdg 6:3; 33; 7:12), another near the Moabites and Ammonites (Jdg 3:13), one near the Sidonians (along the Sea? Jdg 10:12), and the other in the land of Ephraim in the very place where David fought Goliath (Jdg 12:15).

[2] A. van Hoonacker, "Eléments sumériens dans le livre d'Ezéchiel?," *Zeitschrift für Assyriologie* 28 (1914): 336.

[3] Michael Heiser, "The Divine Council in the New Testament: The Archons," in *Behind the Façade* Vol. 3, No. 9 (Feb 2005): 33.

[4] The manuscript is P 967.

[5] The OT is laid out in three sections: history (17 books), poetry (5 books), and prophecy (17 books).

NOTES FOR CHAPTER 12: DEMONS AND THE GIANTS (Pgs. 175-182)

[1] For the discussion see L. R. Wickham, "The Sons of God and the Daughters of Men: Genesis VI 2 in Early Christian Exegesis," in *Language and Meaning: Studies in Hebrew Language and Biblical Exegesis*, ed. James Barr (Leiden: Brill, 1974), 135-36.

[2] See Greg J. Riley, "Demons," *DDD*, 238-39.

[3] See Archie T. Wright, *The Origin of Evil Spirits: The Reception of Genesis 6:1-4 in Early Jewish Literature*, A Dissertation at Durham University (Tübingen: Mohr Siebeck, 2004).

[4] Socrates (Plato, *Apology* 15) suggests that they are the bastard children of gods and nymphs or other women. Hesiod (*Works and Days* 110-27) says they came from the men of the golden age (i.e. prior to the Flood). Josephus makes this connection with the Greeks saying, "Many angels of God accompanied with women, and begat sons that proved unjust, and despisers of all that was good, on account of the confidence they had in their own strength; for the tradition is, That these men did what resembled the acts of those whom the Grecians call giants" (Josephus, *Antiquities* 1.3.1).

[5] John E. Hartley, *The Book of Job*, The New International Commentary on the Old Testament (Grand Rapids, MI: Wm. B. Eerdmans Publishing Co., 1988), 365.

[6] When you read up on the meaning of *rephaim*, you will quickly discover that the word does not always mean "giant," especially in neighboring Ugarit (which has the same word) where it (apparently) never means giant. For this reason, some will argue that *rephaim* in these biblical verses only refers to dead kings of long ago. We should keep in mind, however, that this does not need to be an either/or (the logical fallacy of a false dilemma). Given what we have seen in this book, it is plausible that the Rephaim giants were also the famed heroes and kings of very ancient times.

[7] For example, "There is probably here an allusion to the destruction of the earth by the general deluge. Moses, speaking concerning the state of the earth before the flood, says, Genesis 6:4, 'There were giants (*nephilim*), in the earth in those days.' Now it is likely that Job means the same by rephaim as Moses does by the nephilim; and that both refer to the antediluvians, who were all, for their exceeding great iniquities,

overwhelmed by the waters of the deluge. Can those mighty men and their neighbors, all the sinners who have been gathered to them since, be rejected from under the waters, by which they were judicially overwhelmed"? Adam Clarke, *Commentary on the Bible*, Job 26:5.

[8] CREATION: Job refers to the *tohu* in Job 26:7, "He stretches out the north over the void (*tohu*) and hangs the earth on nothing." *Tohu* was the original condition that we find the earth in Genesis 1:2 ("formless and void"). Binding up the waters in thick clouds (vs. 8) could be viewed against the backdrop of Genesis 1, as the gathering together and separating of water from land as could the boundary between light and darkness in vs. 10. THE FLOOD: He uses a verb first seen in Genesis 7:11 of the "bursting open" of the great deep (Job 26:8). He refers to the "covering of the face of the full moon" (vs. 9) where "moon" can also read "throne." In Psalm 29:10 for instance, God's throne is associated with the flood, "The LORD sits enthroned over the flood; the LORD sits enthroned as king forever."

[9] In some cases Rahab refers to Egypt which is the personification of the sea monster.

[10] Compare the serpent/*nachash*: Gen 3:1 and Job 26:13; dragon/*tannin*: Isa 51:9 and Rev 20:2 Hebrew translation. Isaiah 27:1 also parallels the tannin, nachash, and leviathan.

[11] *Enuma Elish* 1.134-143.

[12] *KTU* 2 1.3 iii:38ff. *Yam* is also the Hebrew word for "sea."

[13] *TUAT* II/3, 317.

[14] *Enuma Elish* 4:105-108.

[15] Klaas Spronk writes, "This last word (lie/*kazab*) is used in Isa 28:15 to describe a 'covenant with death' and in Amos 2:4 it denotes the false gods. All this makes it likely that Ps 40:[4] refers. . . to the forbidden attempt to obtain help from divine forces in the netherworld." See K. Spronk, "Rahab," *DDD*, 685-86.

[16] Further demonstration of this idea may be found in Ezek 32:21 where the *gibborim* (Gen 6:4) greet newcomers in Sheol, and possibly vs. 27 where some have argued that the same gibborim are also called here *nephilim* (usually translated as "fallen"). See Walther Zimmerli, *Ezekiel 2: A Commentary on the Book of Ezekiel, Chapters 25-48*, Hermeneia (Philadelphia: Fortress Press, 1983), 176.

[17] This is Jubilees ("the little Genesis") explanation for the problem of how the giants' spirits could be both in Sheol and wandering the earth. After the Flood, when the spirits began to lead the sons of Noah into sin (Jub 7:26-28; 10:1-2), Noah begs God to imprison them, but Mastema—the chief prince of the spirits—strikes a bargain with God that one-tenth be allowed to stay upon the earth and continue their activity (10:8-11).

[18] As we read in 1 Enoch (above), the spirits of the giants must remain on earth because they were born on earth, and thus they roam about haunting and tormenting the children of men and women.

[19] We will deal with the fascinating verse in 1 Peter 3:19 where Christ preaches "to the spirits in prison" in Chapter 15.

[20] In light of Deut 32:8-9 where the sons of God are allotted to the nations, but Israel is the Lord's "portion" (*chalaq*), see Deut 4:19-20 where the "stars" are allotted (*chalaq*) to all the peoples; Deut 17:2-3 where they are called the "host of heaven;" and Deut 29:26 where they are called "gods" (*elohim*) who were not allotted (*chalaq*) to Israel but to the nations.

[21] Perhaps also Amos 2:1, "Because he burns the bones ... to a demon." Mitchell J. Dahood, *Psalms III (101-150)*, in Anchor Yale Bible (Garden City, NY: Doubleday, 1970), 74.

[22] Riley, "Demons," *DDD*, 235.

NOTES FOR CHAPTER 13: CHIMERAS (Pgs. 183-200)

[1] Cf. G.K. Beale, "Revelation," in *Commentary on the New Testament Use of the Old Testament*, G. K. Beale and D. A. Carson eds., (Grand Rapids, MI; Nottingham, UK: Baker Academic; Apollos, 2007), 1140; Robert H. Mounce, *The Book of Revelation*, The New International Commentary on the New Testament

(Grand Rapids, MI: Wm. B. Eerdmans Publishing Co., 1997), 325-26; Grant R. Osborne, *Revelation*, Baker Exegetical Commentary on the New Testament (Grand Rapids, Mich.: Baker Academic, 2002), 635-36.

[2] This is the translation of the verse as found in Charlesworth's pseudepigrapha. See also the R. H. Charles edition which substitutes "shedim" for "demons." For other Jewish sources see Targum Isaiah 13:21; Midrash Rabbah Lev 5:1; 22:8; Midr Rab Gen 65:15; Sibylline Oracle 8:40-49, Babylonian Talmud Shabbat 151B.

[3] One of these birds is actually translated as an animal by the ESV ("porcupine"). Other translations read anything from a bittern to an owl (see JPS, TNK). This shows how obscure some of these terms are and how we need to be open to alternative ideas of what they might mean.

[4] H. G. Liddell, *A Lexicon : Abridged from Liddell and Scott's Greek-English Lexicon* (Oak Harbor, WA: Logos Research Systems, Inc., 1996), 725.

[5] B. Janowski, "Wild Beasts," *DDD*, 898.

[6] Johan Lust, Erik Eynikel and Katrin Hauspie, *A Greek-English Lexicon of the Septuagint : Revised Edition* (Deutsche Bibelgesellschaft: Stuttgart, 2003).

[7] In Isa 13:22 it renders the term as *onokentauros* (see below).

[8] B. Janowski, "Jackal," *DDD*, 459.

[9] Gilgamesh Epic, Tablet II.36-41.

[10] Though not a world-wide treatment, see Gregory Mobley, "The Wild Man in the Bible and the Ancient Near East," *Journal of Biblical Literature* 116 (1997): 217-33. Mobley is not advocating the reality of such legends, but rather sees them as a motif picked up on in several biblical stories.

[11] Stefan Münger, "Ariel," in *Dictionary of Deities and Demons in the Bible DDD*, 2nd extensively rev. ed., ed. K. van der Toorn, Bob Becking and Pieter Willem van der Horst (Leiden; Boston; Grand Rapids, Mich.: Brill; Eerdmans, 1999), 89.

[12] Lust, *Greek-English Lexicon of the Septuagint*.

[13] Wilhelm Gesenius and Samuel Prideaux Tregelles, *Gesenius' Hebrew and Chaldee Lexicon to the Old Testament Scriptures* (Bellingham, WA: Logos Research Systems, Inc, 2003), 792.

[14] 1 Enoch 6:3-6.

[15] Judd Burton, *Interview With The Giant* (Burton Beyond Press, 2009), 15-23.

[16] See Josephus, *Wars of the Jews* 1.404-406.

[17] LXX Lev 4:28, 29; 5:6.

[18] Liddell, 888.

[19] 1 Enoch 55:4.

[20] 1 Enoch 54:5-6.

[21] 1 Enoch 10:4.

[22] See Burton, *Interview*, 17.

[23] See Robert Hayward, "The Priestly Blessing in Targum Pseudo-Jonathan," *Journal for the Study of the Pseudepigrapha* 10 (April 1999): 85-87.

[24] John D. W. Watts, vol. 25, *Word Biblical Commentary : Isaiah 34-66*, Word Biblical Commentary (Dallas: Word, Incorporated, 2002), 13-14.

[25] Babylonian Talmud Shabbat 151B.

[26] See M. Hutter, "Lilith," *DDD*, 520.

[27] Following the *Online Etymology Dictionary* (http://www.etymonline.com/), we see that "genetics" derives from *genesis* ("origin" or "generation"), from which we get the word for the first book of the Bible. "Genesis" is also said to come from *gignesthai* ("to be born") and *genos* ("race, birth, descent"). Our word "genome" comes from *gen* ("gene"). As you can see, the prefix "-gen" comes from *genes* ("born of, produced by"), so that all of these words are related *gene*alogically in the same linguistic family tree.

English	Greek Root	Translation
-gen	*genes*	"born of, produced by"
Gigantes	*gegenes*	"born from earth"
genetics	*genesis*	"origin, generation"
Genesis	*gignesthai*	"to be born"
	genos	"race, birth"
genome	*genes*	"born of, produced by"
genealogy	*genea*	"generation, descent"

[28] "Transplanted Head," *Time*, Jan 17, 1955: http://www.time.com/time/magazine/article/0,9171,891156,00.html.

[29] "Frankenstein Fears after Head Transplant," BBC News, Friday April 6, 2001: http://news.bbc.co.uk/2/hi/health/1263758.stm.

30 Hui Zhen Sheng, "Embryonic stem cells generated by nuclear transfer of human somatic nuclei into rabbit oocytes", *Cell Research* (2003): 13, 251–26: http://www.nature.com/cr/journal/v13/n4/full/7290170a.html

[31] "Animal-Human Hybrids Spark Controversy," *National Geographic*, Jan 25, 2005: http://news.nationalgeographic.com/news/2005/01/0125_050125_chimeras.html

[32] See Louisiana's "Human-Animal Hybrid Prohibition Act" of 2009: http://thomas.loc.gov/cgi-bin/query/z?c111:S.1435.IS:; Ohio Senate Bill Senate Bill 243 (SB243): http://www.legislature.state.oh.us/bills.cfm?ID=127_SB_243; Arizona's Senate Bill SB 1307: http://www.azleg.gov/legtext/49leg/2r/bills/sb1307s.pdf.

[33] See for instance the burial mound at Sayre, Bradford County, Pennsylvania in the 1880s. An article ("Chemung's Predecessors Huge Giants Were Seven Feet Tall and Had Horns") appeared in the *Moorehead Expedition* on Wed, July 12, 1916 claiming a find of a horned giant human skull. You can read the article here: http://www.spanishhill.com/articles/horned.htm. Another article ("Aboriginal Sites in and Near 'TEAOGA,' now Athens, Pennsylvania") appeared in the *American Anthropologist* (Vol. 23, No. 2, April-June 1921) claiming that the horned skull was mistaken identity. http://www.spanishhill.com/skeletons/pdf/aboriginal_sites_part_I.pdf. I've also been told that you can artificially create "horns" on a skull without any need for hybridization.

NOTES FOR CHAPTER 14: JESUS VS. THE DEMONS (Pgs. 201-212)

[1] Compare 1 Cor 15:40-41 with Dan 8:10; Rev 12:4 etc. On stars as referring to angelic beings see Heinrich A. W. Meyer, *Critical and Exegetical Handbook to the Epistles to the Corinthians* (Edinburgh: T. & T. Clark, 1892): 2:87-88; G. G. Findlay, "St. Paul's First Epistle to the Corinthians," in W. R. Nicoll (ed.), *The Expositor's Greek Testament* (Grand Rapids, Eerdmans, 1961): 2:935-36; Anthony C. Thiselton, *The First Epistle to the Corinthians : A Commentary on the Greek Text* (Grand Rapids, Mich.: W.B. Eerdmans, 2000), 1268-69. For an interesting discussion on the relationship between stars and angelic beings see John Joseph Collins, Frank Moore Cross and Adela Yarbro Collins, *Daniel : A Commentary on the Book of Daniel*, Hermeneia (Minneapolis: Fortress Press, 1993), 331-33. Finally, all angelic *appearances* as men differ qualitatively from Christ—the Angel of the LORD in the OT—who came down out of heaven (John 6:33-58; Rev 20:1), added human flesh to his own nature (John 1:14), was born in the likeness of men (Php 2:7-8), and shares in our flesh and blood (Heb 2:14).

[2] This pool is said in a textual gloss to have healed the first person who came into the waters after a supernatural being would come down from time to time and "stir up the waters." It this light, it makes Jesus' miracle all the more incredible (and suspicious to the people in Galilee).

[3] Rouillard, "Rephaim," *DDD*, 699.

[4] All of Galilee and synagogues (Matt 4:23-24; Mark 1:23-27; 39-41; Luke 4:33-36; 11:14-22; 13:11-17), houses (Matt 8:14-17; Mark 1:32-34; 6:10-15; 7:24-30; 9:33, 39; Luke 4:38-41) the seashore (Matt 28:33;

Mark 3:9-15; 5:2-20; Luke 8:26-39), the coasts (Matt 15:22-28; 16:13-19); the plains (Luke 6:17-19); by mountains (Luke 9:37-42); outside (Matt 9:32-33), everywhere (Matt 10:7-8; Luke 8:1-3), around multitudes (Matt 12:15, 22; 17:14-21; Mark 9:14-27), you get the idea.

[5] Note that the previous three paragraphs have several references to Mark's Gospel. Mark may in fact have the Watcher tradition in mind as he writes. See the fascinating article by Rick Strelan, "The Fallen Watchers and the Disciples in Mark," *Journal for the Study of the Pseudepigrapha* 10 (Oct 1999): 73-92.

[6] Cf. Rainer Riesner, "Bethany Beyond The Jordan (John 1:28): Topography, Theology And History In The Fourth Gospel," *Tyndale Bulletin* 38 (1987): 29–63; also D. A. Carson, *The Gospel According to John* (Leicester, England; Grand Rapids, MI: InterVarsity Press; W.B. Eerdmans, 1991), 146-47; C. S. Keener, *The Gospel of John*. 2 vols. Peabody, Mass: Hendrickson, 450; Andreas J. Köstenberger, *John*, Baker Exegetical Commentary on the New Testament (Grand Rapids, Mich.: Baker Academic, 2004), 65.

[7] Some manuscripts read seventy-two. "Seventy" is significant in light of the seventy sons of God in Jewish and Canaanite tradition as well as the seventy elders of Israel that eventually became the Sanhedrin.

[8] H. J. W. Drijvers, *Iconography of Religions* (Leiden, Netherlands: Brill, 1976), p. 18

[9] 2 Enoch 42:1.

[10] See Burton, *Interview with the Giant*, 57-58, 78-87; Strelan, 83.

[11] Mark does not record Jesus' words to Peter about the church, but he does record the Transfiguration, which occurs immediately after this in Matthew. The story of healing the boy occurs immediately after the Transfiguration in Mark's Gospel.

NOTES FOR CHAPTER 15: VICTORY (Pgs. 213-232)

[1] Ps 22:1 quoted in Matt 27:46; Ps 22:2 in Matt 27:39; Ps 22:7 in Matt 27:39; Ps 22:8 in Matt 27:43; Ps 22:12 in Matt 27:27; Ps 22:14 in Matt 27:26; Ps 22:16 in Matt 27:35; 22:18 in Matt 27:35; Ps 22:19-21 in Matt 28:6.

[2] For instance, Samuel L. Terrien, *The Psalms: Strophic Structure and Theological Commentary* (Grand Rapids, MI: Eerdmans, 2003), 232. This is also Heiser's view. If we are permitted to read into an allegory, it appears to be the idea in C. S. Lewis' *Lion, Witch and the Wardrobe* when Aslan dies on the stone table.

[3] Ramsey J. Michaels, *1 Peter*, Word Biblical Commentary (Dallas: Word, 2002), 205-12.

[4] On this history see William J. Dalton, *Christ's Proclamation to the Spirits: A Study of 1 Peter 3:18–4:6* (Rome: Editrice Pontifico Istituto Biblico, 1989), 27ff.

[5] More technically, it is "a region of northern Europe bounded by the Rhone River on the east, the Alps on the south-east, the Mediterranean on the south, the Pyrenees on the south-west, the Atlantic on the west, and the English Channel on the north-west." John T. Koch, "Gaul," in *Celtic Culture: A Historical Encyclopedia* vol. 1 (Santa Barbara, CA, 2006), 793.

[6] See Helmut Birkhan, *The Celts* (Vienna, 1997), 48.

[7] Paul Pezron, *The Antiquities of Nations; More Particularly of the Celte or Gauls*, trans. Mr. D. Jones (London: R. Janeway, 1706), 276.

[8] Pezron, 48.

[9] Florus, *The Epitome of Roman History*, 1.38.3. http://en.wikisource.org/wiki/Epitome_of_Roman_History/Book_1.

[10] Cited in Gerhard Herm, *The Celts* (New York: St. Martin's Press, 1975), 19. A particularly vivid and short history of the Roman wars with the giants of Gaul and neighboring Germany can be found in Charles DeLoach, *Giants: A Reference Guide from History, the Bible, and Recorded Legend* (Metuchen, N.J.: Scarecrow Press, 1995), see especially the sections "Celtic Giants," "German Giant's Annihilation," and "Giants Who Became Gods." This includes history from the likes of Julius Caesar, Plutarch, and Diodorus among others. http://www.stevequayle.com/Giants/index2.html

[11] Hegesippus, *Histories* 2.9. This book is a compilation of Josephus' *Wars*, and is usually thought to be pseudepigraphal (that is, attributed to Hegesippus, but probably not actually written by him). http://www.ccel.org/ccel/pearse/morefathers/files/hegesippus_02_book2.htm.

[12] These sources are cited in Johann Georg Keyssler, *Travels through Germany, Bohemia, Hungary, Switzerland, Italy, and Lorrain* Vol. 1 (London, G. Keith, 1760), 42 (footnote).

[13] Cited in Cornelius Tacitus (56 – 117 A.D.), "Treatise on the Situations, Manners, and People of Germany," in *Works* 4 (Philadelphia: Thomas Wardle, 1838), note 9.

[14] Augustine, *City of God* 15.23.2.

[15] Keyssler, 31.

[16] Ibid., 52.

[17] Caesar, *Commentary* 1.39.

[18] You can read a good brief account of the history of giants in ancient warfare in, Adrienne Mayor, "Giants in Ancient Warfare," *MHQ: The Quarterly Journal of Military History* 2.2 (Winter 1999): 98-105.

[19] Josephus, *Antiquities* 1:123.

[20] Ibid.

[21] See Frank Joseph, *Advanced Civilizations of Prehistoric America* (Rochester, VT: Bear & Company, 2010), 10-84. 19th century scholarship made this identification of the Mound-Builders with very tall Caucasians. Present scholarship tends to disagree; see Jon Muller, *Archaeology of the Lower Ohio River Valley* (Orlando: Academic Press, 1986; republished by Walnut Creek, CA: Left Coast Press, 2009), 8.

[22] Pezron, 41-42. Pezron's 18th century study of the Gaulish migrations is similar to a recent study of the Kurgan migrations, the proto-European culture (see Marija Gimbutas, "The Kurgan Culture and the Indo-Europeanization of Europe: Selected Articles from 1952 to 1993," ed. Miriam Robbins Dexter and Karlene Jones-Bley. *Journal of Indo-European Studies Monograph No. 18* [Washington, D.C.: Institute for the Study of Man, 1997]: xix + 404 pages). For more on the Kurgan, see note #22.

Fig. FN 5. Migrations of the Kurgan

Map: T. R. Holme, "The Kurgan Invasions."

[23] The Kurgan (note #22) have been connected to the Amorites and to the Adena "Mound Builders" of North America. http://www.mysteriousworld.com/Journal/2003/Summer/Giants/. In fact, "Kurgan" means "Burial Mound." Said to be very tall in legend (see "Kurgan Horsemen" to the right), the Kurgan were popularized in the first *Highlander* movie. At one point, Sean Connery's Ramirez character tells MacLeod, "The Kurgan is the strongest of all immortals. He is the perfect warrior. He cares about nothing or no-one. He is completely evil." Curiously, the Persians depicted their kings as giants, receiving the kingdom from the demigods.

Fig. FN 6. Kurgan Horsemen

Left: 4th century B.C. Scythian horseman. Found at the Kul' Oba kurgan near Kerch (northern Black Sea). Located now in The State Hermitage Museum. Saint Petersburg, Russia. **Right**: Ardashir Coronation from Ahura Mazda, Naqsh-e Rustam, 3rd c. AD. **Note** how the legs of the riders go *all the way to the ground*. These were either very small horses, or very tall men.

[24] L. J. Alderink, "Stoicheia", in *Dictionary of Deities and Demons in the Bible*, ed. Karel van der Toorn, Bob Becking and Pieter W. van der Horst, 2nd extensively rev. ed. (Leiden; Boston; Grand Rapids, Mich.: Brill; Eerdmans, 1999), 815-18.

[25] Michaels, 207.

[26] Ibid., 208.

[27] It is curious that the LXX uses the word three times: Job 40:20; 41:24; Prov 30:16. In the first instance, the behemoth is in view. In the second, it is Leviathan. This means that the term is always used in the Scripture with reference to spiritual-heavenly beings.

[28] Giants of incredible strength and ferocity, even superior to that of the Titans.

[29] Ramsey, 208.

APPENDIX: EXTRA-BIBLICAL LITERATURE (Pgs. 233-236)

[1] Here are just a few. 1. As Augustine reported, the book is too *old* to trust it (*City of God* 15:23). His point is that the actual words of Enoch were preserved only in oral tradition. How do we know where Enoch's words end and some Jewish writers' begin? 2. It has historical anachronisms. We do not find such things in Scripture. A good example is the first chapter which has Enoch—who lived long before the Flood—referring to Mt. Sinai (1 En 1:4). That is obviously historically inappropriate. 3. We have little to no evidence that Jews—even at Qumran who held the book in very high esteem—regarded it as Scripture (See Richard Bauckham, *Jude and the Relatives of Jesus in the Early Church* (London; New York: T&T Clark, 2004), 226-33. 4. 1 Enoch is actually five distinct books: *The Book of Watchers* (1-36); *The Book of Similitudes* (37-71); *The Book of Astronomical Writings* (72-82); *The Book of Dream Visions* (83-90); *The Book of the Epistle of Enoch* (91-107). These in turn include fragments from other books, such as *The Book of Noah* (6-11; 5:7-55:2; 60; 65-69:25; 106-108). (See E. Isaac, "1 Enoch," in *The Old Testament Pseudepigrapha* Vol. 1, ed. James H. Charlesworth [New York: Doubleday, 1983], 7). As such, it cannot be trusted as fully the words of Enoch, though it undoubtedly (as Jude explains) contains many of his actual words.

[2] D. A. Carson reports that he had private correspondence with an important Enochian scholar who suggests that Jude is citing 1 Enoch 1:9 ironically rather than positively. Carson says, "I have not seen that view defended anywhere in print, convincingly or otherwise, so at this juncture the claim still strikes me as odd." D. A. Carson, "Jude," in G. K. Beale and D. A. Carson, *Commentary on the New Testament Use of the Old Testament* (Grand Rapids, MI; Nottingham, UK: Baker Academic; Apollos, 2007), 1078.

[3] Consult any of the Commentaries cited in note 29 in the Introduction.

[4] For more on Jude and other NT allusions to Enoch, see George W. E. Nickelsburg and Klaus Baltzer, *1 Enoch : A Commentary on the Book of 1 Enoch* (Minneapolis, Minn.: Fortress, 2001), 83-86; 123-24.

APPENDIX: 2 PETER 2:4 AND JUDE 6 (Pgs. 237-242)

[1] Cf. Thomas R. Schreiner, *1, 2 Peter, Jude*, New American Commentary (Nashville, TN: Broadman & Holman, 2003), 447-51.

[2] So John Gill, Matthew Henry, even John Milton, *Paradise Lost* I. 48; II. 169, 183 196; III. 82.

[3] For a list of those who agree with this see Introduction note #29.

[4] Not the word *'adam*, which the first human was named, but *'ish*.

[5] That angels have "flesh" and "bodies" and that this differs from humanity see 1 Cor 15:39-41.

[6] It is curious that the LXX uses the word three times: Job 40:20; 41:24; Prov 30:16. In the first instance, the behemoth is in view. In the second, it is Leviathan. This means that the term is always used in the Scripture with reference to spiritual-heavenly beings.

[7] "*Tartaroō*," *A Greek-English Lexicon of the New Testament*, ed. Joseph Henry Thayer (International Bible Translators, 2000).

[8] This includes the following references: LXX Gen 6:1-4; Targum Pseudo-Jonathan Genesis 6:4; Sirach 16:7; 1 Enoch 6-19, 86-88, 106:13, 15, 17; 2 Enoch 7, 18; Jubilees 4:15, 22, 5:1, Testament of Reuben 5:6-7; 2 Baruch 56:10-14; 3 Baruch 4:10; Testament of Naphtali 3:5; Testament of Solomon 5:3; 6:2-3; Wis-

dom 14:6; 3 Maccabees 2:4; Judith 16:6; Damascus Document (4Q266 II: 18-19 and CD 2:16-19); Genesis Apocryphon 2:1; Josephus: *Antiquities* 1.3.1; Philo: *On The Giants* 6-7.

[9] See Appendix - Extra-Biblical Literature.

[10] See Schreiner, *1, 2 Peter, Jude*, 448.

[11] Richard J. Bauckham, *Jude, 2 Peter*, Word Biblical Commentary (Waco, TX: Word Books, 1983), 46.

[12] Notice how the watchers and/or the giants are referred to in *every* list except the most recently written— the Mishnah (*m. Sanh.*)—which dates no earlier than the second century A.D. This is no surprise, since the Jews after the rise of Christianity began to eliminate supernatural ideas from their theology *and Scripture*.

APPENDIX: THE STORIES OF THE GREEKS (Pgs. 243-250)

[1] See Hesiod, *Theogony* 2.453-491. Also Theophilus of Antioch, *Theophilus to Autolycus* 1.10. In Ante-Nicene Fathers, Vol. 2.

[2] One interesting attempt to do this from a Christian perspective is Robert Bowie Johnson Jr., *Athena and Eden* (2002), *Athena and Cain* (2003), *The Parthenon Code* (2004), *and Noah in Ancient Greek Art* (2007), (Annapolis, MD: Solving Light Books).

APPENDIX: GIANTS IN THE AMERICAS (Pgs. 251-266)

[1] "Fragment: Niagara Falls [c. September 25-30, 1848]," in *Collected Works of Abraham Lincoln*, ed. Roy P. Basler (Ann Arbor, NI: University of Michigan Digital Library Production Services, 2001), 2:10.

[2] Timothy Green Beckley, *Giants on the Earth* (New Brunswick, NK: Global Communications, 2009); Charles DeLoach, *Giants: A Reference Guide from History, the bible, and Recorded Legend* (Metuchen, NJ: Scarecrow Press, 1995); Jonathan Gray, *Lost World of the Giants* (Brushton, NY: TEACH Services, Inc. 2006); Stephen Quayle, *Genesis 6 Giants* (Bozeman, MT: End Time Thunder Publishers, 2002). Timothy Green Beckley, *Giants on the Earth* (New Brunswick, NK: Global Communications, 2009), which adds some fresh material.

[3] For the literally scores and scores of newspaper reports, consult the thread on these giant reports: http://ancientlosttreasures.yuku.com/reply/49816/News-Articles#.TviHmtTOyiA or here: http://greaterancestors.com/greater-humans/. One can then go to the *New York Times* and search its archives for the old article here: http://query.nytimes.com/search/sitesearch?query=&submit.x=0&submit.y=0&submit=sub, or the *Washington Post* here: http://pqasb.pqarchiver.com/washingtonpost/search.html. This list has been copy/pasted to many websites, so in case this site goes down in the future, here is a very brief list of some of those articles, so that they can be entered into a search engine and found on another site: (from the *Post*) "An Indian Giants tomb" [Nov 18, 1883], "A Race of Giants" [Mar 16, 1884], "The Bones of a Giant" [Dec 9, 1887], etc; (From the *Times*) "Skeleton of Giant Found" [Nov 21, 1856], Reported Discovery of a Huge Skeleton [Dec 25, 1868], "The Early American Giant" [Feb 8, 1876], etc.

[4] A seven foot tall skeleton found by a miner named James L. Perkinson on his Yellow Jacket claim in the Atlin district. "Skeletons of Giants in Alaska," *San Francisco call* [Nov 18, 1900].

[5] There is a legend from 1833 where a group of Mexican soldiers were digging a pit and struck a 12' tall skeleton with double rows of teeth. Told for example in Jerome Clark and John Clark, *Unnatural Phenomena* (Santa Barbara, CA: ABC-CLIO, 2005), 15. Giants with double rows of teeth were also said to have been discovered on Santa Rosa Island, California, Clearwater, Minnesota and other places (see Chapter 3, n. 19).

[6] In Bridgeport, Connecticut there was an eight foot skeleton near the house of one Daniel Buckingham, Esq. Edward Rodolphus Lambert, The History of the Colony of New Haven (New Haven, CT: Hitchcock & Stafford, 1838), 126.

[7] In 1879, a 9'8" skeleton was retrieved from a stone burial mound in Brewersville, IN. *The Indianapolis News*, November 10, 1975; cited in Richard Marshall, *Mysteries of the Unexplained* (Pleasantville, N.Y.: Reader's Digest Association, 1982), 41.

[8] One example is a 7'8" skeleton with double rows of teeth. Thomas Weston, *History of the Town of Middleboro, Massachusetts* (Boston: Houghton, Mifflin and Company, 1906), 400.

[9] For example, in Monmouth a 7'6" skeleton with the head the size of a common iron tea-kettle was discovered and played with for two or three years by local boys who were "shooting Injuns!" Harry Hayman Cochrane, History of Monmouth and Wales Maine, vol. 1 (East Winthrop: Banner Company, 1894), 9-10.

[10] Among which were a 7'7", 8'0", and nearly 10' skeleton found in the Humbolt Lake bed and nearby Friedman Ranch. Lovelock *Review Miner*, June 19, 1931; September, 29, 1939; cited in Joe Oesterle and Tim Cridland, *Weird Las Vegas and Nevada* (New York: Sterling Publishing Co., 2007), 35.

[11] Around 1820 a seven foot body was discovered in Moultonborough. *Guide to the White Mountains and Lakes of New Hampshire* (Concord, NH: Tripp & Osgood, 1851), 19.

[12] Here is an example of someone clearly within this range, without specific height given (typical of many of these stories). "Mr. Peleg Sweet, who was a man of large size and full features ... in digging, came upon a skull and jaw which were of such size that the skull would cover his head and the jaw could be easily slipped over his face, as though the head of a giant were enveloping his." Stephen D. Peet, "The Mound-Builders," in *History of Astabula Co., Ohio*, ed. William W. Williams (Philadelphia: Williams Bros., 1878), 19.
http://solomonspalding.com/SRP/saga2/1878Ast1.htm#pg017a

[13] Near Braden, OK the femur of a nine foot giant was found among skeletons of average sized people in a "huge" mound. "Oklahoma Indian Relics Unearthed," *The Washington Post* [Aug 26, 1934].

[14] Near Gastersville, PA, scientists from the Smithsonian discovered a 7'2" skeleton with coarse black hair. *American Antiquarian and Oriental Journal*, ed. Stephen D. Peet, 7:1 (January 1885): 52.

[15] A thigh bone "three or four inches longer" than the thigh bone of the seven feet man named James McGlaughlin. John Haywood, *The Natural and Aboriginal History of Tennessee: Up to the First Settlement Therein by the White People in the Year 1768* (Kingsport, TN: F.M. Hill-Books, 1973), 133.

[16] In Kanawha county in a 540 ft x 85 ft mound were at least three skeletons, one of which was 7'6". They were covered in copper jewelry. *American Antiquarian and Oriental Journal*, ed. Stephen D. Peet, 6:2 (March 1884): 133-34. *The New York Times* ran a piece on a 10'9" skeleton, "Its jaws and teeth were almost as large as a horse" found Wheeling, WV [Nov 21, 1856].

[17] Maple Creek, Wisconsin yielded a skeleton over nine feet tall as reported in the local newspaper and then in the *New York Times*, December 20, 1897.

[18] You can read about these and many more finds in many places on the Internet, but my personal warning is to be cautious and meticulous in doing your research. Don't believe everything you read. Check and re-check facts, and by all means seek out original sources. That said, an interesting compilation of some of these finds can be found in the sometimes less than trustworthy Josiah Priest, *American Antiquities and Discoveries in the West* (Albany, NY: Hoffman & White, 1833). At least some of his stories have sources and they fit in both what is reported and how they are reported with the more trustworthy sources. See also the *New York Times* articles posted at the website at the end of the last table in this chapter.

[19] Reported in the St. Paul *Daily Pioneer Press*, May 23, 1882 as summarized in N. H. Winchell and Jacob V. Brower, 1906-1911 *The Aborigines of Minnesota: A Report based on the Collections of Jacob V. Brower, and on the Field Surveys and Notes of Alfred J. Hill and Theodore H. Lewis* (Minnesota Historical Society, 1911), 363. I have found five different newspaper clippings of this excavation. It was a widely publicized story.

[20] The Dresbach mound group (Dresbach, Minnesota) yielded an eight foot skeleton and another of similar length along with strange artifacts like shell beaded necklaces, hematite celts (a stone axe-like instrument with a beveled edge), copper chisels, copper rings, and copper hatchets, all typical finds in Adena burial mounds (Winchell, 89-90). A mound in Corrinna, MN (near Clearwater) gave up seven skeletons from

seven to eight feet high, though a few days later it was reported that the skeletons were "not of unusual size;" yet the "prehistoric" skull did have marked facial differences compared to Indian skulls (Ibid. 217). Mounds near Moose Island lakes gave up <u>seven ft.</u> skeletons (ibid. 301). A very large mound dubbed "Grand Mound" in (old) Itasca county on the <u>US/Canadian</u> border was found to hold at least one skeleton "estimated at over 10 feet." (ibid. 372). Other discoveries included a "<u>huge man</u>" found in a mound near Lake Koronis ("Giants Lived There," *The Saint Paul Globe*, Thursday, August 12, 1897, p. 4), "<u>human remains of men of large stature</u>" in various mounds in La Crescent (Winchell, 80), "<u>large human bones</u>" near Rushford (Ibid. 91), and two skeletons "the size of which indicated the sons of Amalek" with a <u>thigh-bone of 20 inch</u>-<u>es and double rows of teeth</u> (Franklyn Curtiss-Wedge, *History of Wright County Minnesota*, vol. 1 [Chicago: H. C. Cooper, Jr., & Co., 1915]). And that's just Minnesota; and that's just what I've been able to find in Minnesota.

^{21} Some 10 ft. giant reports seem plausible (see note 20); others seem less so. In Oct. 1869, the most famous giant hoax in early U.S. history began. The famous 10 ft. "petrified" Cardiff Giant (New York) was "discovered" when some men were digging a well. However, it was later uncovered that the giant was sculpted and hidden there by George Hull, a rich atheist who had a fight with a Methodist pastor over Genesis 6:4. P.T. Barnum got into the act and later created his own version, decrying the other giant a hoax. From this was born the phrase "a sucker is born every minute." Two months after the Cardiff giant appeared, a story came out of Sauk Rapids (MN) that a 10 ft. petrified giant had been recovered from a quarry near the Mississippi River. This story has hallmarks of a fake. Though no one made any direct

Fig. FN 7.
Fake Cardiff Giant

money from it, it certainly put the little town on the map. For a fascinating recap of this amazing hoax see Timothy Green Beckley (ed.), *The American Goliah and other Fantastic Reports of Unknown Giants and Humongous Creatures* (New Brunswick, NJ: Global Communications, 2010).

^{22} Cf. Roy Norvill, *Giants: The Vanished Race* (Wellingborough, UK: Aquarian Press, 1979), 84.

^{23} Adam Rodgers, "Early Nevada History is Traced in Lovelock, Cave, Tomb of the Forgotten Race," in *Ancient American* Vol. 13, no. 81, 32-35.

^{24} See Chapter 3, n. 19.

^{25} Mac Rutherford, *Historic Haunts of Winchester* (Charleston, SC: Haunted America, 2007), 29.

^{26} Sarah Winnemucca Hopkins, *Life Among the Paiutes* (Boston: Cupples, Upham & CO., 1883), 26. http://www.yosemite.ca.us/library/life_among_the_piutes/life_among_the_piutes.pdf

^{27} Rodgers, ibid.

^{28} *Nevada Review-Miner* newspaper, June 19, 1931.

^{29} William F. Cody, *An Autobiography of Buffalo Bill* (Aurora, CO: Bibliographic Center for Research, 2009), 196-97.

^{30} Pedro de Cieza de Léon; *The Travels of Pedro de Cieza de Leon, A.D. 1532-50*, translated by Clements R. Markham, (London: Hakluyt Society, 1864), 189-91.

^{31} See Adrienne Mayor, *Fossil Legends of the First Americans* (Princeton, NJ: Princeton University Press, 2005), 80.

^{32} Genesis 14:10; 19:1-25.

^{33} See the Markham translation of de Léon, 190-91, note 1; also Mayer, 82.

^{34} Markham, ibid.

^{35} Cf. Garcilaso de la Vega, *The Florida of the Inca*, ed. John and Jeanette Varner (Austin, TX: University of Texas Pres, 1951), 349; See Bernal Diaz, *The Conquest of New Spain*, trans. J. M. Cohen (New York: Penguin, 1963), 181; Antonio Pigafetta, *The Voyage of Magellan* (London: Yale University Press, 1969); John

Smith, *Captain John Smith's America; selections from his writings,* ed. John Lankford (New York: Harper & Row, 1967), 9; George Parker Winship (Trans.), *The Coronado Expedition: 1540-1542* (Washington: Government Printing Office, 1896), 484-85.

[36] "Old Eskimo Legend Proves True – People Nine Feet Tall Visit Coast," *New York Times,* Dec. 19, 1904. Viewable online in PDF, http://query.nytimes.com/gst/abstract.html?res=9402E2D6113DE633A2575AC1A9649D946597D6CF.

[37] *Coast to Coast,* hosted by George Noory (12-3-08).

[38] Stephen Quayle and Duncan Long, *Longwalkers* (Bozeman, MT: End Times Thunder Publishers, 2008), 274-79.

[39] "Scientists have Found a Settlement in the Borjomi Gorge Mysterious Mythical Creature," http://www.1tv.ru/news/world/29635. A video of the original report accompanies the site.

[40] See note 21.

[41] See for example, Adrienne Mayor, *The First Fossil Hunters: Paleontology in Greek and Roman Times* (Princeton, NJ: Princeton University Press, 2001), 104-57.

[42] In fact, there are small museums and castles said to hold such artifacts to this day. There are Indiana Jones like treasure seekers that claim to have bones and have tested the bones. One of the more fascinating is the story of Father Carlos Vaca. In 1964 in Ecuador the locals discovered the bones of a 7.6 meter (nearly 25 ft., the approximate size of the giants of Peru, see note 30) giant after a particularly bad storm exposed them from under an ancient monument. They told Father Carlos who collected them. Two of these bones, a heel-bone and the os occipitale (bone under the skull) were taken by Klaus Dona to Germany where he says it was confirmed that they were both human bones, but no DNA could be recovered because of their extreme antiquity. He shows these bones in his public lectures. A huckster? Truth? Whatever it is, it is an interesting claim.

[43] Strangely, there are reports of giant skeletons with horns. However, this is not an impossible physical trait relegated only to myth. "Cutaneous horns" are well documented conical projections above the surface of the skin that can often grow quite large. See Eray Copcu, Nazan Sivrioglu, and Nil Culhaci, "Cutaneous Horns: Are These Lesions as Innocent as They Seem to Be"?, *World Journal of Surgical Oncology* 2 (2004): 1-18.

APPENDIX: GIANTS OF MONUMENT AND MYTH (Pgs. 267-288)

[1] Cited in Philip Coppens, "America's Nazca Lines," at http://www.philipcoppens.com/intaglios.html.

[2] For instance, the Blythe Intaglios which include several human-like figures, the largest of which is 167 ft. long (see Frank M. Setzler, and George C. Marshall, "Giant Effigies of the Southwest," *National Geographic* [Sept. 1952]: 389-404).

[3] Oliver Gille, "Cerne Abbas Giant May Have Held Severed Head," *The Independent* (London, England, Saturday, May 21, 1994).

[4] Carol Rose, "Cern Abbas Giant," in *Giants, Monsters, and Dragons: An Encyclopedia of Folklore, Legend, and Myth* (New York: W.W. Norton & Company Inc. 2000), 73.

[5] John Philipps Emslie and C. S. Burne, "Scraps of Folklore Collected," *Folklore* 26:2 (June 30, 1915): 153-170.

[6] Pictures and article can be found in Paul Mullis, "The Ravens Warband: The Adventure of the Dancing Men," http://www.millennia.f2s.com/dancing.htm.

[7] Frank Joseph, *Atlantis in Wisconsin: New Revelations About The Lost Sunken City* (St. Paul, MN, Galde Press, 1995), 29.

[8] Vincent H. Gaddis, *Native American Myths and Mysteries* (Garberville, CA: Borderland Sciences, 1991), 48.

[9] Taylor L. Hansen, *The Ancient Atlantic* (Wisconsin, Amherst Press, 1969), 127.

[10] Several newspaper clippings and snippets of books (such as the journal of John Smith) can be found here: http://www.spanishhill.com/skeletons/aboriginal_sites.shtml.

[11] The actual news article can be read online at: http://www.puppstheories.com/forum/index.php?showtopic=40, followed by another article claiming that it was a case of mistaken identity of deer antlers buried with the remains, implying that somehow they had gotten stuck to a human skull. There is a picture of a horned skull circulating on the internet, but I have no way of confirming if it is real or a hoax.

[12] Richard Marshall, *Mysteries of the Unexplained* (Pleasantville, NY: The Reader's Digest Association, 1983), 40.

[13] Steve Quayle reports on this discovery on his website, including a nice picture of the ivory cup: http://www.stevequayle.com/Giants/pics/ivory.African.pot.html.

[14] Homer, *Odyssey* 11:315-316; see also Ovid, *Metamorphoses* 1:151-176.

[15] For instance, Elwood Worchester, *The Book of Genesis in Light of Modern Knowledge* (New York: McClure, Phillips & Co., 1901), 502.

[16] Ovid, *Metamorphoses* 1:177-198.

[17] *Ibid.* 1:244-273.

[18] Poetic Edda: *Vafthruthnismol* 21.

[19] *Völuspá* 38.

[20] *Völuspá* 2.

[21] George Catlin, *The Okipa Ceremony* (Norman, OK: University of Oklahoma, 1958), 39.

[22] Don W. Dragoo, *Mounds for the Dead: An Analysis of the Adena Culture* (Carnegie Museum, 1963), 249.

[23] Frank Joseph, "Shawnee Deluge Story," *The Atlantis Encyclopedia* (Franklin Lakes, NJ: The Career Press, 2005), 248.

[24] Frank Joseph, *Advanced Civilizations of Prehistoric America* (Rochester, VT: Bear & Company, 2010), 73, 78, 80.

[25] Pedro Sarmiento De Gamboa, *History of the Incas*, trans. Clements Markham (Cambridge: The Hakluyt Society, 1907), 28-58.

[26] Peter Tompkins, *Mysteries of the Mexican Pyramids* (New York: Harper Collins, 1987), 57.

[27] Hubert Howe Bancroft et al., *The Native Races of the Pacific States of North America*, vol. 5: Primitive History (New York: D Appleton and Co., 1874-76), 17-18. Quote is from n. 40.

[28] Ibid, "Bochica," 75.

[29] Michael M. Alouf, *History of Baalbek* (Escondido, CA: Book Tree, 1999), 54.

[30] Readers Digest Association, *The World's Last Mysteries* (Montreal: Reader's Digest, 1978), 308.

[31] William Joseph Wilkins, *Hindu Mythology, Vedic and Purānic* (London: Thacker & Co., 1882), 364.

[32] See *Satapatha Brahmana* 2.1, 2, 13-16.

[33] Robert D. Craig, *Dictionary of Polynesian Mythology* (New York: Greenwood Press, 1989), 43.

[34] Hon. Sir Maui Pomare and James Cowan, *Legends of the Maori* (Christchurch, NZ: Kiwi Publishers, 1987), 238-39.

[35] On the Fomorians as giants and/or sea peoples see Duald Mac Firbis, *On the Fomorians and the Norsemen* (Christiania: J.C. Gundersens Bogtrykkeri, 1905), vii; as demons see John Arnott MacCulloch, *The Religion of the Ancient Celts*, (New York: Dover Publications, 2003), 51-52.

[36] Hibbert Trust, *The Hibbert Lectures*, (Cambridge: Cambridge University Press, 1896-1929), 582-83.

[37] Evans Lansing Smith and Nathan Robert Brown, *The Complete Idiot's Guide to World Mythology* (Indianapolis, IN: Alpha Books, 2008), 77.

[38] Frank Joseph, *The Destruction of Atlantis* (Rochester, VT: Bear and Company, 2002), 146-47.

[39] David Livingstone, *Missionary Travels*, cited in Elwood Worcester, *Book of Genesis* (New York: McClure, Phillips & Co., 1901), 498.

Made in the USA
San Bernardino, CA
05 April 2014